the art and
science of •
wine

the art and
science of •
wine

James Halliday and
Hugh Johnson

FIREFLY BOOKS

A FIREFLY BOOK

Published by Firefly Books Ltd. 2007

Copyright © 1992, 2007 Octopus Publishing Group Limited

Text Copyright © 1992, 2007 James Halliday and Hugh Johnson

Illustrations © 1992, 2007 Octopus Publishing Group Limited

First printing

Publisher Cataloging-in-Publication Data (U.S.)

Halliday, James.
    The art and science of wine : James Halliday ; and Hugh Johnson.
[240] p. : col. photos. ; cm.

Includes index.

Summary: An overview of the subtle artistry and sophisticated science of the winemaking process from the vineyard to the bottle. Explores factors affecting the growing and harvesting of grapes, describes the various kinds of wines, and discusses the chemistry and analysis of wine.

ISBN-13: 978-1-55407-247-7
ISBN-10: 1-55407-247-6

1. Wine and wine making. I. Johnson, Hugh. II. Title.
641.22 dc22   TP548.H3555   2007

Library and Archives Canada Cataloguing in Publication

Halliday, James, 1938-
    The art and science of wine / James Halliday and Hugh Johnson.

ISBN-13: 978-1-55407-247-7
ISBN-10: 1-55407-247-6

1. Wine and wine making. I. Johnson, Hugh, 1939- II. Title.

TP548.H24 2007   663'.2   C2006-905917-9

Published in the United States by
Firefly Books (U.S.) Inc.
P.O. Box 1338, Ellicott Station
Buffalo, New York 14205

Published in Canada by
Firefly Books Ltd.
66 Leek Crescent
Richmond Hill, Ontario L4B 1H1

Printed in Hong Kong

This book is dedicated to

the genie in the bottle

Contents

IN THE VINEYARD

IN THE WINERY

IN THE BOTTLE

The vintage scene as idyll, a familiar motif of artists from the ancient world to modern times. Penry Williams painted this idealized scene near Rome in the 1840s. Reality (and certainly the wine itself) was less idyllic. About 90 percent of the advances in winemaking have happened in the last 100 years, and perhaps 60 percent in the last 20.

A Propos

By Hugh Johnson

The rusty cannon gives the Moutardes' yard, divided from the village street by iron railings, its faint air of a comic opera set. It was last fired in 1964, when a cloud the color of a decomposing eggplant and exactly the size of the vineyards of Muligny, hanging poised above the slopes of Chassard, the next-door commune, began to roll ominously toward the Clos du Marquis.

Monsieur Moutarde had towed the weapon into the vineyards behind a borrowed tractor, loaded it with a canister of grapeshot of the vintage of 1815, leveled it at the heart of the threat and plucked up his courage to apply the taper. The explosion was thunderous. Nobody in Chassard was sure whether what clattered down on several roofs was a flurry of hail or straying grapeshot. The cloud rolled on, menacing but still costive, over Muligny and three more communes before suddenly dumping its gumball-size hailstones on the scruffy oak woods on the hill above Beaune.

The oaks were shredded; not a leaf was left. But in Chassard relief for the spared vines was tempered by unneighborly feelings toward Monsieur Moutarde – indeed toward Muligny as a whole. The two villages had never exchanged more than civilities; not in 2,000 years. One must not put too much weight on the cannon incident; it was merely a symbol of the rivalry that had existed since the Romans.

Things were different then, in the early 1960s, in several ways. For a start, nobody had any money – or if there was any cash in the mattress it meant a harvest mortgaged to a merchant in Beaune.

The way the Moutardes made wine had changed very little since the Middle Ages. The most evident progress lay in the vineyards, which since phylloxera had been far more uniform than before: orderly rows of grafted vines that got a good dusting of sulfur and a bright blue spray of *bouillie bordelaise* as often as the weather and Monsieur Moutarde's energy and resources determined.

The vats in the *cuvier* were Napoleonic, the barrels in the mossy cellar dark with indeterminate age. Only the basket press on its iron wheels definitely bore some relation to the Industrial Revolution.

Monsieur Moutarde had a little cache of bottles in a corner of the cellar; no labels, but dates written in chalk that stood up very badly to any handling. In any case he knew the positions of all the bottles, whose vintages stepped back with irregular intervals to before phylloxera and his grandfather's death. To drink one of them was exceptional. The family's daily drinking came in liters from the *cave coopérative*.

In fact the Moutardes had little to do with their own wine at all. They were farmers, on a tiny scale, who picked their grapes, put them through a sort of grinder that tore off most of the stems, then piled them in a vat and waited for the heady, stinging smell of fermentation to fill the barn. Then twice a day the younger male members of the family climbed the ladder to the open top of the *cuve*, wearing only shorts (and sometimes not even these), gripped the edge firmly and lowered themselves in. Their combined weight was sometimes barely enough, even with a fair bit of bouncing, to break the thick raft of skins and still-whole grapes buoyed up on the surface by the fizzing fermentation below. Once you got through into the warm half-wine, the idea was to turn the fragments of raft upside down and tread them back in. This way none of the goodness, the color and flavor of the grapes, would be lost.

Three weeks or so after harvest, with the weather distinctly chilly, the fermentation was finished; it was time to empty the contents of the vat into the barrels below, after washing them out energetically with a length of chain to scour the inside and endless cold water from the well.

That was almost the last the Moutardes saw of their wine. Before Christmas the *négociant* called, tasted each barrel, told them how bad business was, and named a price. In January a truck came over, parked beside the cannon and hoisted the barrels up to take them to Beaune.

Sometimes in good years (meteorologically and financially) Monsieur Moutarde would decide to keep a small barrel in the cellar, taste it from time to time with a neighbor, and at the end of three or four or even five years laboriously round up and wash enough bottles to hold all the dark fragrant liquid. Most of these he would distribute around the family, whose vineyard it was just as much as it was his. His own share would be chalked and squirreled away.

Only he knew the almost celestial satisfaction that lay in the best and oldest bottles: a mingling of plums and earth and game, of heat and cool, of fungus and farmyard, of iron and leather, yet giving off, for all its strength and maleness, a scent as clear-ringing as violets.

This was Burgundy 40 years ago, the most prestigious and sought-after region in the world of wine, but a world where even the rarest and finest of wines from the greatest vineyards went for a song.

Wine-growers dragged along at subsistence level, faintly hoping that some eccentric might come and offer to buy their burdensome inheritance, yet dreading the loss of their ancient bond with the land and its sweetest fruit. Monsieur Moutarde and his generation, like their forebears, were prisoners of their peasant suspicions and superstitions. By regarding even the next commune as a rival, they spurned comparisons, they turned their backs on new ideas, and they rejected progress. But they conserved and intensified the identity of their *cru*. When they planted a new vine it came from their own cuttings. Every move they made at vintage time and in the cellar was ritualized. Muligny could only be made this way.

Frequently the results of such sleepwalking were catastrophic. It was often just as well the *négociant* took away barrels of faulty wine to treat them as far as possible, then blend them with Rhône or Algerian, to produce an approximation the world would accept as Burgundy.

Occasionally ritual was blessed with luck, and the results were sublime. Certainly there was enough of this elusive sublimity to keep the legend of Burgundy alive and waiting for the next generation – and to fire the imaginations of the very few wine-lovers, mostly Americans, who aspired at least to collect, perhaps one day even to emulate, what they considered the loveliest of all wines.

Monsieur Moutarde's children live in a different world. They have been to technical colleges, even to universities with departments of viticulture and oenology. They exchange views, read trade journals – and openly compete with one another. They even see themselves as competing with other countries. Above all, the peasant instinct for secrecy has evaporated.

The years between the 1960s and today have seen the greatest change in the making, the quality and the distribution of wine in its 8,000-year history. This is not something to be surprised at. Which art and which science has not altered almost out of recognition in the era of technology?

Yet wine and our expectations of it are profoundly linked with age and time. Of all the food and drink we consume, only wine can live (and indeed change wonderfully for the better) for decades – even, exceptionally, for a century or more. Yet its lifespan is never certain: its aging process is unpredictable enough to seem to wear a mantle of mystery.

That cars should work better, or microchips have almost magical properties, are things we can accept without surprise, since they are the products of scientific inventiveness. But weren't we always told that the greatest wines are products of evolution, of tradition, of respect for the soil and patience in the cellar? How can technology improve on something that emerges from the womb of time?

Perhaps we need to ask how the standards were set in the first place. Who decided that one wine was "better" than another – or indeed that there were qualities specific to wine that varied from place to place, season to season and time to time?

Wine was apparently discovered (or first exploited) in warm-temperate regions (the Caucasus and the warmer Middle East) before migrating, at first as merchandise, to such temperate zones as central Italy, then progressively to cooler areas in France and (coolest of all) Germany.

While wine growing was limited to Mediterranean regions, its quality was broadly measured in terms of strength and sweetness. As it left the Mediterranean and found niches along the trade routes of central, western and northern Europe, these were presumably still the qualities that exacting drinkers looked for.

What they found, though, in regions where the vine was more and more of a marginal crop, was a drink of a different nature altogether. Sweetness could not be taken for granted. High strength was replaced by relatively high acidity.

This had been (and still occasionally is) the unimproved primitive style of Italian wine, made by growing vines up trees. The "improved" state was achieved by pruning the vines low in what was known as the Greek style; even by drying the grapes to concentrate their sugar.

Using improved viticulture, that is, low-pruned vines, in cooler regions gave rise to flavors more fruity, positive, juicy, aromatic and refreshing than either old or new Mediterranean methods.

How did France become the country where wine was brought to its fullest perfection? Not because it possesses any one physical characteristic that is unique. Nor is "French genius" the answer – although no other country takes its nourishment so seriously. Simply in certain regions intensive cultivation led to the development of local strains and varieties of grape, which in turn led to a wine culture that was closely linked to local prosperity and local pride.

Not coincidentally these regions had either high local populations or strong trading links. Demand encouraged specialization; specialization led to experience, experience to accepted – even stereotyped – local methods, and the stability implied by these to distinctive local styles.

A French author wrote recently, "There are no predestined vineyards; there are only redoubts of stubborn civilization" – called Burgundy, Bordeaux, Champagne, the Moselle, the Rhône ...

This is the theory of natural selection of what were to become the world's model vineyards and their wines. Its most surprising aspect is that it all began nearly 2,000 years ago. Wine culture has had a very long time to develop its local traits; the characteristic style of each French region is the work of 70 or 80 generations.

In modern eyes (French eyes at least) what is most important about the great vineyards is their *terroir* – their combination of soil and climate. It is truer to say that this is what is most distinctive. The major factor in their foundation was not the precise characteristics of their soil. It was their strategic situation. But even where the two combine most luckily and effectively there remains a missing element to explain the ascendancy of France (and, for its white wines, Germany). Perfect *terroir* close to a rich and busy market could equally have been found in Italy or Spain.

The final building block is the pattern of climate; not just as it ripens the grapes, but as it dictates the moment of harvest and influences the progress of fermentation. The farther north you go, the narrower the band of choice of when to pick the grapes. Each vintage is a struggle to achieve full ripeness before cold or wet weather sets in. Perhaps even more important, once the grapes are picked, their fermentation has the benefit (in most years) of perfect natural temperature control: the northern autumn itself.

Without benefit of air-conditioning, of cooling coils or brine circulating in double-walled tanks, in the classic wine regions there is at least an even chance that the must will become wine at the ideal moderate, then gently falling, temperature. At higher temperatures the grape aromas boil off, yeasts become less efficient, and bacteria flourish. If the vat gets too hot the fermentation "sticks" altogether, leaving half-made wine that is fatally prone to becoming vinegar.

These were the problems that almost all winemakers in warmer climates had to contend with until electricity came on the scene. The one chance of avoiding them was a cool, deep-cut cellar. Modern winemaking dates from the introduction of artificial temperature control, first tried tentatively in Algeria a century ago using cold water, then more methodically in Australia, but not generally available or accepted until the 1950s and 1960s.

Until fermentation could be kept in check, there was little purpose in planting the grapes that the north had developed for low-strength table wines. Once cool fermentation was mastered, even at the price of astronomical energy costs, the door was open to making balanced, fruity and light wines in a warm climate. From that moment on the production of sweet fortified wines, the mainstay of Mediterranean-climate vineyards around the world, went into accelerating decline. Technology had claimed its place as the indispensable ally of the winemaker. It was not long before what was seized on as essential in Australia and California had gained an interested following, to say the least, in Europe – even in parts of France. Today the range of controls open to a winemaker (with the money to pay for them) is so great as to be bewildering. European winemakers are at least limited by the conventions and traditions enshrined in their systems of appellations and denominations. European governments want, and now actively encourage, their wine industries to stay within conventional bounds, to exploit their regional traditions – above all to avoid simple varietal labeling. It is their best way of avoiding the head-to-head competition that increasingly threatens from the industries of the New World.

But New World winemakers still start with a clean slate. It is entirely up to them what grape varieties they plant (or buy), in what regions and soils, and how they turn them into wine. The United States is preparing the ground for what may one day become an effective appellation law. Yet its viticultural areas are a very long way from controlling or even influencing winemaking decisions.

South Africa has the most precise wine legislation of the New World. But it is still the farmer, not the government, who decides what to plant and what kind of wine to make.

Australia and New Zealand, meanwhile, flourish in a state of oenological anarchy. Anything goes, so long as the label "tells the truth." It is a cutthroat world, chronically short of cash, but it has proved more fertile in invention, more radical in technology and overall more successful in pleasing its patrons than any other.

This book is about the range of choices open to a winemaker at the beginning of the 21st century. It is the fruit of collaboration between a most unscientific wine-lover and a passionate critic who is also a technocrat. I don't think James Halliday will object to my describing him in this way – so long as I also remind you that, at Coldstream Hills in the Yarra Valley, he has made some of Australia's most technically perfect wines, which just happen to be quite delicious.

It is no coincidence at all that James is Australian. Australia's winemakers and researchers have established themselves over the past decade as the world's most innovative, least reverent, most open-minded, most iconoclastic. And their ideas are taken very seriously indeed.

The vintage season in Europe falling in the least interesting part of an Australian winemaker's year, a number of these iconoclasts are even migrating north in September to supervise the vintage at the invitation of proprietors and cooperative cellars in Europe – and indeed fanning out across the rest of the globe.

I shall never forget the look on the face of a grower in southwest France (this was in the late 1980s) when he tasted the first wine made by an Australian "flying winemaker" from grapes he had delivered to the cooperative. All his life he had been accustomed to a rather hard, perfectly adequate but totally unexciting wine as the outcome of his labors. "*Mais mon dieu!*" he spluttered, "*Ça sent le fruit!*" That was just what it did smell of: grapes. And he was not at all sure that wine was supposed to do anything so obvious.

Australian wine-lovers are hard to restrain from playing a game they call "Options." The rules are simple. An undisclosed wine is served to the company. Only the president of the game (Len Evans is the most infuriatingly skillful protagonist) knows what it is. He names three countries the wine might come from. Anyone who guesses right stays in the game; the rest drop out. Subsequent questions might name three grape varieties, districts, vintages or châteaux until the wine is identified.

"Options" might well have been the title of this book, because at each step in the making of any wine, from the choosing of the vineyard site to the opening of a mature bottle, there are choices to be made; options to be faced.

Many of the decisions are loaded by the economics of the business. Monsieur Moutarde of Muligny was an example of a wine-grower with very few options to give him sleepless nights. But many are not: as the choices and consequences charts show, such factors as timing and temperature can make as much difference to the quality of a wine as the most costly options: stainless-steel tanks, air-conditioning, or all-new barrels.

The most costly option of all, perhaps, is one that is faced at every stage by a winemaker who aspires to quality. It is called selection. Only by constantly downgrading any wine that is not up to the standard you set yourself can you maintain a name and a reputation.

Where, if anywhere, do you draw the line between art and science in producing or designing any product? It is a matter of judgment. Scientific decisions are made on the basis of measurements. Nonscientific decisions are made on the basis of habit or intuition, occasionally of inspiration. Might it be true to say that the first two amount to craftsmanship, only the third to art? "Art" is a grand word to use about the making of a drink. It is justified because exceptional wines can seem to transcend mere sensual enjoyment, to demand to be appreciated on a higher plane of awareness – for which "art" is the *only* appropriate word.

IN THE VINEYARD

The Vine

From the historical perspective to the attitudes and practices of the 21st century

The grape vine in its wild state is a climber. Its natural home is the forest. Hence its botanical name of *Vitis vinifera silvestris*: the woodland wine-bearing vine.

Which woods did it originally inhabit? A vast stretch, in all probability, from western Europe to western Asia. Where was it first used to make wild wine? No one knows. But archaeology can point out the place where it was first cultivated. The scientific evidence (like the Book of Genesis) points to the foothills of the Caucasus. Georgia has produced the earliest evidence of vine selection and hence the emergence of the cultivated variety: *Vitis vinifera sativa*. Carbon dating puts this change to domestication at about 5000 BC. Humanity was therefore still in the Stone Age when people first cultivated the vine – and presumably made wine.

To understand how the grape vine grows, and how it responds to cultivation, one has to remember that it is a climber, and that in its wild state it grows in a tight tangle with other plants and trees, competing with some, supported by others. Competition is for light, soil moisture and nutrients. To reach the light, the vine climbed higher. To survive in soils full of competing roots, it built up a degree of tolerance to drought. The support came from the trees it climbed. These responses to the environment determine how the vine's performance can be manipulated in the vineyard.

European wine-growers have long known (and New World growers more recently) that vines react to sunlight, not only in spring but throughout the growing season – even in winter. Sunlight on the woody parts, especially the new shoots or canes, means a more fruitful vine. At the base of each leaf is a bud – the crop potential of the following year's vintage. The amount of sunlight on the vine when its new buds are forming acts as a signal, determining whether the buds become leafy shoots or embryo flowers for fruit. Thus the yield of each plant is initially dependent on the amount of light reaching the vine up to 15 months earlier – April to June in the northern hemisphere, October to December in the southern

Wine from the woods

What the vine needs

Opposite: "High-vigor" sites, such as this vineyard in Mendocino County, California, demand the use of a high, open trellis to expose the maximum leaf area.

hemisphere. In this knowledge the grower will manipulate the vine to achieve an appropriate balance between the production of leaves and fruit, above all avoiding a dense canopy of leaves that shade the "bud-wood."

Pruning: "vegetable editing"

Unquestionably the annual growth cycle of the vine stirs deep emotions in most wine-growers, and pruning has traditionally been regarded as an art form of fundamental importance to grape and wine quality. Every possible means of vine training has been tried through the centuries. Close planting and hard pruning of vines, almost in the modern manner, to produce small, hedgelike rows was introduced by the Egyptians between 4,000 and 5,000 years ago. When the focus of viticulture and winemaking changed from Egypt to Greece, the practice of pruning to increase the vine's fruitfulness and quality became standard.

The Romans, who learned their wine growing from the Greeks and the Carthaginians, knew and practiced most of the "modern" pruning and training methods: the "goblet"; cane-pruning, now credited to the 19th-century French researcher Professor Guyot; fan pruning; low bush training; high trellising and so on. In the great vineyards of France this task is entrusted only to pruners who have been employed on the estate for decades, and who know every vine as an individual, every nuance of site and *terroir* as a fact of life.

The brutalist school

Is such attention lavished on each vine justifiable? In the 1970s and 1980s Australia engaged in radical experimentation on a large scale, reaching its zenith with so-called minimal pruning. This did away with winter pruning, even mechanized, replacing it with mechanized summer trimming underneath and along the perimeters of the hedgehoglike growth that ensued. What worked in theory did not work in practice; in low-cost, broad-acre viticulture, mechanized winter pruning has taken its place.

The yield– quality equation

The vine in balance

What, though, of crop control? It is an axiom of European wine growing that the grower must choose quality or quantity. Yet there is more to the equation than simply less is better, more means worse. If there is a single truth, it is the concept of a vine in balance: one in which the ratio of roots, canes, leaves and grapes is correct.

Above: *Egyptians, Greeks, then Romans dominated winemaking in the ancient world. A few modern winemakers still prefer treading grapes to extract the maximum color and flavor.*

Right: *Venice, Italy. The undomesticated vine is a climbing plant, here growing through fruit trees. Any shaded bunches will produce grapes that are less sweet.*

There is increasing awareness that this can be achieved in very different ways. The vines may be small, with either no trellis at all or with only the simplest support. For vines grown like this, the density of planting will usually be very high – perhaps 3,200 to 4,000 vines per acre (8,000 to 10,000 per ha). Or the vines may be very large, supported by an elaborate trellis, widely spaced at a density of 600 vines per acre (1,500 per ha). In either system, high-quality grapes or poor ones can result, but that will depend on the skill of the wine-grower.

Planting at a density of 125,000 acres (50,000 ha), which was recommended in Roman times, precluded any form of mechanization. By the mid-19th century, densities of around 8,000 vines per acre (20,000 per ha), (with yields of 3 tons per acre/40 hl per ha or less) meant horse-drawn plows were in widespread use in all but steeply sloping vineyards. The reality of today is mechanization. In modern vineyards densities are often already as low as 600 per acre (1,500 per ha, as opposed to up to 4,000 per acre/10,000 per ha in some old Burgundy vineyards) to accommodate tractors and the increasingly sophisticated array of machinery capable of pruning, picking, summer hedging, lifting and dropping foliage wires, knitting the canopy, plucking leaves around the fruit to enhance exposure, even selectively thinning the crop itself halfway through the growing season. This all sounds distinctly unromantic, and so it is, but it is preferable to the do-nothing, minimal pruning approach. Even with these vastly reduced planting densities, yields have increased and are continuing to do so. The question is whether the quality is dropping at the same rate.

The short history of plant breeding and genetic engineering is a catalog of successes and failures, benefits and disadvantages, opportunities and limitations. And while the French will have none of it, Germany and California, the two principal viticultural stud farms, are forever playing with the genes of the vine. Healthier vines that consistently produce higher yields are the principal goals. Disease resistance and bigger harvests have both been achieved through the breeding of hybrids. Clonal selection is another route to the same goals. What has yet to appear in the commercial

The future

Mechanization

Grape harvesting still means working long, back-breaking hours on many of the Bordeaux estates that do not accept mechanical pickers for their precious crop.

nurseries is a classic grape variety with enhanced disease resistance, or a classic variety with improved flavor, or a new variety that combines the attractions of the existing classics. Should such a vine make its appearance, it will almost certainly be due to genetic engineering.

Sprays and fertilizers   One of wine's great attributes is that it is among the most natural and stable of all food products. It is possible to make wine without any additions whatsoever, and in the vineyard and the winery there is a strong move to minimize human interference with nature. Many think we have been too clever and too profligate in our clonal selection and our use of herbicides, pesticides and fungicides – all in the interest of larger crops of "healthier" grapes. European growers have less flexibility than their New World counterparts in warmer regions, owing to the higher rainfall that threatens the crops in the northern hemisphere, but there is a tendency toward reducing the use of all but the "natural" sprays such as lime and sulfur, elemental sulfur and copper oxychloride or copper sulfate – fungicides that are sanctioned by organic growers – especially in vineyards where quality rather than cost or convenience is at a premium. The same thinking applies to chemical fertilizers. The best vineyard practice is to apply even organic fertilizer very sparingly. A Médoc First Growth uses only cow manure – once every 19 years.

Sustainable viticulture   As the new century dawned, so did a profound realization that sustainable viticulture was the way forward. At its most basic level, it involves the minimization of all sprays, even lime/copper/sulfur fungicides. Herbicides are frowned on; pesticides used only as a last resort; systemic fungicides likewise.

The next level is organic. Once a vineyard is certified organic, herbicides, pesticides and systemic sprays are banned outright. The third level is biodynamic, building on the organic foundations and using a series of soil preparations developed by Rudolf Steiner in 1924. One of the most colorful proponents of biodynamic viticulture is Nicolas Joly of Coulée de Serrant in the Loire Valley, but it is a very serious movement, numbering among its adherents the Domaine de la Romanée-Conti (the horse alone now works Romanée-Conti itself) through to high-profile Californian, Australian and New Zealand wineries. In this area, it replaces science with art, a seminal change in practice and philosophy that we examine in greater detail elsewhere.

These developments necessarily stand alongside viticultural and winemaking practices tailored to produce wines for a society that consumes 95 percent of all the wine it buys within 48 hours of purchase. Here, cost cutting is the sole driving force.

The choice is not a new one. It is between convenience, using the shortcuts offered by mechanization in the vineyard and chemical adjustments in the winery, and the time-consuming alternative of painstaking physical control.

Winemaking that aims for quality, let alone greatness, requires a high level of personal skill and commitment. It minimizes chemical intervention. It focuses on eradicating disease in the vineyard, and depends on hygiene and the control of temperature and oxidation by physical, not chemical, means in the winery. But it would be too simple to see a choice between art and science, between the old ways and the new. The proponents of each method can and should learn from each other: if they do, better wines at all levels will be the result.

Terroir

Do humans matter more than the natural environment?

The French, who have cultivated and studied their vineyards with loving care for centuries, have a word with no precise equivalent in English or any other language. The word is *"terroir."*

The former proprietor of Château Cos d'Estournel in the Médoc, Bruno Prats, explained it thus:

> *The very French notion of* terroir *looks at all the natural conditions that influence the biology of the vinestock and thus the composition of the grape itself. The* terroir *is the coming together of the climate, the soil and the landscape. It is the combination of an infinite number of factors: temperatures by night and by day, rainfall distribution, hours of sunlight, slope and drainage, to name but a few. All these factors react with each other to form, in each part of the vineyard, what French wine growers call a* terroir.

Bruno Prats, former owner of Cos d'Estournel, and Charles Symington in the Douro Valley of Portugal, with a truly unique terroir *as far from that of the Haut-Médoc as one can imagine.*

The identification and the delineation of different *terroirs* go back to the monks of the Middle Ages, and perhaps beyond. First the Benedictines, then from the 11th century the Cistercians, worked and studied the soil, both in France (particularly in Burgundy) and in Germany, so closely that (according to one famous Burgundy grower) they "even tasted it." They were passionately concerned to make, not just the best possible wines, but wines that were as distinctive, as unlike each other, as possible. The patchwork quilt of named vineyards, the *crus* and *clos* of the Côte d'Or, the *Einzellagen* of the Mosel and the Rheingau, derives directly from this pious concentration.

Five hundred years later, this approach was to be imitated in Bordeaux, though on an altogether larger and less precise scale, in keeping with a much broader, flatter and more consistent landscape. From this time (the 17th century) onward, Champagne, Tokay, the port vineyards of the Douro … everywhere that proved capable of producing premium-price wines saw the value of identifying the better and the best sites. Yet for some reason, which can hardly only be jealousy, the notion of *terroir* has stuck in the gorge of the New World.

To quote the American author Matt Kramer:

> *A surprising number of wine-growers and wine-drinkers – at least in the United States – flatly deny the existence of* terroir, *like weekend sailors who reject as preposterous that Polynesians could have crossed the Pacific navigating only by sun, stars, wind, smell and taste.* Terroir *is held to be little more than viticultural voodoo.*

Viticultural voodoo?

Time will tell – and, one suspects, rather quickly. Already, in a mere 40 years, California and Australia have progressed from a fixation with grape varieties (in the 1960s and 1970s "varietal character" was seen as the be-all and end-all) through the cult of the winemaker as romantic hero in the 1970s and 1980s to the increasing emphasis on the vineyard we noted in the previous chapter.

It is now widely accepted that certain "vineyard-designated" wines (Martha's Vineyard in the Napa Valley was the first famous example) are able to fetch premium prices. How long will it be before we hear of the *terroir* of the Rutherford Bench? In

Goût de terroir

South Australia, the bizarre strip of red limestone that defines the district of Coonawarra has exactly the distinctive qualities the Cistercians would have recognized.

Soil and *terroir*, however, are not the same. There is no specific chemical composition, no precise structure that guarantees that wherever a given soil occurs in the world it will produce wine of identical, or even vaguely similar, character and quality. There is, though, growing recognition that structure and drainage may be more important to grapes and wine than specific soil types. The two primary inputs that cause grape vines to grow and produce fruit are sunlight and water: in purely mechanical terms, the function of soil is to provide anchorage (first), water (second) and nutrients (third). All scientific attempts to show a specific translocation of minerals or other substances from the soil, which then impact directly on the flavor of the grape (or the wine), have failed. The French expression *goût de* terroir is precisely that: the taste of *terroir*. So however hard it may be to disabuse yourself of the idea that in drinking, for example, a *grand cru* Chablis you are actually tasting the unique limy clay under the vines, it should always be remembered that soil is just one factor in the *terroir* equation.

Given a *terroir* that has proved its ability to make fine and distinctive wine, the degree of intervention by the winemaker determines how clearly the *terroir* will be expressed.

***Terroir* makes character; people make quality**

A close look at the "character," "quality" and "personality" of a wine will reveal exactly how successful the winemaker's intervention has been. The assessment of these factors culminates in the philosophy developed by the late Peter Sichel. Character, Sichel said, is determined by *terroir*; quality is largely determined by people. Incompetent winemaking can destroy the potential of a given site to produce wine of great character (first) and quality (second) and is precisely the reason why certain châteaus have fallen or risen in reputation – why the 1855 Médoc classification is perpetually under attack. Conversely, the most highly skilled winemaking cannot make a silk purse out of a sow's ear. Above all else, the winemaker cannot invest a wine with character not possessed by the grapes in the first place. He or she can make a good wine, one with commercial appeal, but never a great one.

Above: *The benefits of terroir take many forms, from the slope angle to the positive qualities of underlying rock and soil structure – seen here at Clos de Bèze, Gevrey-Chambertin, comprising a good proportion of light-colored stones in the soil that reflect the sun's heat.*

Gevrey-Chambertin

Burgundy is the best place to relate *terroir* to legal appellations. Gevrey-Chambertin in Côte d'Or (*opposite*) is a graphic example.

Immediately east of the 985-foot (300 m) contour line, soil type and structure closely mirror *appellation contrôlée* (AC) definitions: here, brown calcareous (chalky) soils overlie hard screes, and these, where located on south- and east-facing slopes, are the base for Gevrey-Chambertin's *grand cru* and *premier cru* vineyards.

The aspect and angle of the slope maximize climatic conditions – especially by providing good exposure to sunlight – and the subsoil provides the efficient drainage

essential to a vine's development.

Farther down the AC spectrum, vineyards of the *-villages* appellation, immediately south of Gevrey-Chambertin, are based on the same soil, this time overlying richer marls and alluvium. The difference this makes is that, though fertile and well suited to most types of agriculture, these are too rich for the growth of top-quality vines.

Farther west on the flat river flood plain, vineyards under regional AC status predominate, reflecting the increase in rich river-deposited alluvium, more fertile still, and too poorly drained to grow vines that yield top-quality fruit.

The cross-section (*opposite*) of Gevrey-Chambertin's underlying rock structure shows the slope

from the Côte in the east down to the river plain in the west. AC status similarly declines from *grand cru* in the east to regional status in the west.

East of the fault line, *grand cru* and *premier cru* regions are situated on base rocks of calcareous, mineral-rich marls overlying clay. The better-quality vineyards are on the higher slopes, which provide better drainage and exposure to the sun. Marl conglomerates, alluvium and colluvial rock fragments occur as the slope declines: the base for vineyards of *-villages* AC status. As the harder layer of solifluction rock fragments at the foot of the Côte gives way to pure marls and clays on the flood plain, we are down to plain Bourgogne status.

Gevrey-Chambertin – The Relationship between AC Classification, Soil Type, and Geological Structure

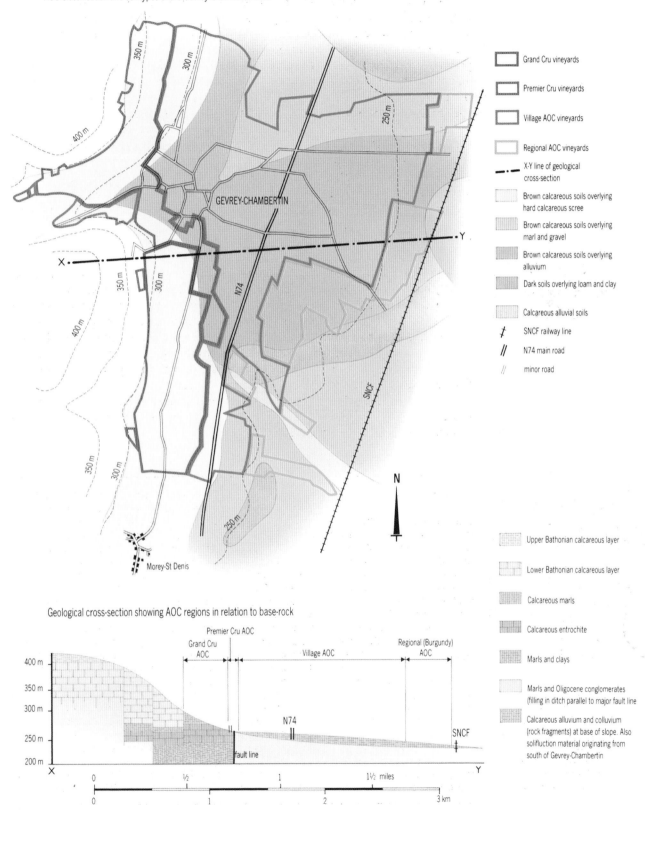

AOC Classification and soil types of the Gevrey Chambertin area

Geological cross-section showing AOC regions in relation to base-rock

... and weather makes personality

The third leg in the tripod in Sichel's analysis, "personality," is – or was – largely determined by the weather. Thus in the first edition we said, "It is the difference between, for example, almost all the Bordeaux reds of 1982 – wines almost thick with ripeness – and the same wines in 1984, when the season produced barely ripe, often meager wines. The 1984s can have the character of their site, the quality of well-made wines (though under difficult conditions), but their personality will never be extrovert or generous."

Today it is easy enough to substitute 2000 for 1982, but how far can 1984 be equated with, say, 1999? Science, supported by money, has intruded to complicate matters with such devices as sophisticated sorting tables (some with electronic eyes to pursue errant or moldy berries), concentration machines and microbullage. Art, in turn, has contributed the strict control of yields, opening canopies, leaf plucking and countless other ploys.

The question is, when is enough enough? How far should vignerons seek to outwit nature? How much should the gap between the best and least vintages be narrowed? The rational mind says that whatever can be done to circumvent the shortcomings of a particular vintage should be done. The same mind, however, says making all vintages nigh on the same would be a disaster. Happily, the latter scenario is a purely theoretical one; weather and *terroir* will always have the last say, even if their dominance is less powerful than it once was.

Character, then, can only come from a particular *terroir* or environment, a belief that substantiates a point of agreement between the New World and the Old – that the role of the winemaker, although critical, is nevertheless limited.

Illustrating this, it is interesting to quote two winemakers' views. Australian Brian Croser of Petaluma, near Adelaide, puts his position clearly:

Reproducible uniqueness

> *I have a minimalist approach. It relies on an innate faith in the choice of an area, in the choice of a variety and in the choice of a management technique in the vineyard to get the maximum expression of quality. That faith then carries through to the processing of the grapes. From my viewpoint, if you put all the ingredients, all the building blocks, in place, the resultant wine will share the quality parameters that all good wines of the world share. The personalities will be different, but they will share the fundamentals of quality, which are vitality, strength and intensity of flavor, length of flavor, subtlety and reproducible uniqueness.*

Great winemakers tend to be modest men. Jacques Seysses of the Domaine Dujac in Morey-St-Denis, Burgundy, casts himself as little more than a quality-control officer:

The lazy way

> *I believe we have been given the opportunity to have Pinot Noir vineyards at precisely the right place to make great wine. So it is my conviction that we should let nature do the work. I am happy to take advantage of modern oenology and to act if something goes wrong, but in fact I prefer to make wine the lazy way and let nature take its course wherever possible.*

And the New World?

If there is this measure of agreement on the importance of *terroir* between the New World and the Old, why has the New World not attempted to emulate the Old World more closely? There are two principal reasons. First, the scale of most New World viticulture makes precise delineation of *terroir* either difficult or of doubtful relevance. Second – and the two factors are inextricably linked – there is not enough evidence that it could pay.

The French classification system has ensured premium prices for the favored vineyards. This in turn means that estates can afford to invest more in maximizing the potential of their grapes: for example, by buying new equipment, new barrels and above all by the luxury of selection: downgrading second-best vats to a second

Pinot Noir on northern slopes: the windmill at Verzenay on the "mountain" of Reims in Champagne.

or third label. The system is thus self-perpetuating, once given the accepted superiority of the site. How long will the lucky and successful among New World wineries be able to resist the attraction of some kind of classification?

The inevitable linking of *terroir* and classification in France has led to exalted land values and wine prices because it has created a finite resource in an ever-growing world market. A seller's market is comfortable in the short term, but in the longer term it creates real risks. It places the wines beyond the reach of those with more taste than money, who in all probability would most appreciate them; it limits or eliminates the possibility of organic business growth from within; and it progressively opens up opportunities for competitors from without.

Nowhere is this more obvious than in Champagne. The Champenois have marketed their products brilliantly, and for the past 50 years have been vigilant in protecting their appellation and the use of the word "Champagne." They argue this word should be used only for wine made within Champagne from the classic varieties and using the *méthode champenoise*; that, in a word, Champagne is unique, and that all other sparkling wine – whatever and however made – is not only different but (by price implication) inferior.

But what is the public to think when the Champagne houses themselves move to other countries and start making and marketing sparkling wines there? Moët & Chandon led the charge a surprisingly long time ago when it established a subsidiary in Argentina, and compounded the problem by using the word "Champagne" on its label (a practice believed to be required by Argentinian law, but discontinued).

More recently a dozen Champagne houses have followed Moët's lead – some into the most improbable places. But there is no doubt many of the Champenois have found the decision difficult. Some have refused altogether to make the move, others have done so reluctantly, as, for better or worse, directly or indirectly, it carries with it the seeds of an attack on the special *terroir*-derived character of the wines made in Champagne itself. This is not to say the attack will succeed, or that the decision to begin production overseas was wrong. On the positive side, it has not only increased their production and sales, it has allowed them to demonstrate

Do the French waver?

Champagne from Argentina?

that the word "Champagne" is not essential (as the world had supposed) to sell an expensive sparkling wine. So far, it appears they can have their cake and eat it too.

It is clear, in other words, that even the French are attracted by the tremendous freedom from the restrictions of *terroir* the New World enjoys. The free-spirited Italians have followed suit without even leaving home. They have managed to turn their DOC/DOCG system upside down in less than 30 years, generally engaging in good-humored anarchy until 1992, when the entire wine law had to be revised, most conspicuously with the introduction of *indicazione geografica tipica* (IGT) for wines selling outside the DOC/DOCG system. After an initial pause, the non-conforming but high-quality wines previously sold as *vino da tavola* switched to the IGT system. Meanwhile, bogged down in an archaic set of laws (both too liberal and too rigid), the great German wine-growers contemplate revolution.

The New World contemplates its *terroirs*

Australian geographic indications

In the New World (South Africa apart) full-scale classification is still many years away. In some countries, though, primitive appellation systems are beginning to take shape. The United States has its approved viticultural areas (AVAs): regions that are supposed to have special viticultural and oenological characteristics. However, this demarcation does not carry with it the constraints of *appellations contrôlées*; most importantly, there is no stipulation as to which varieties may be planted. Nor are pruning methods or yields prescribed.

Australia has followed suit with its geographic indications legislation. This divides Australia into states (the preexisting ones, of course), zones, regions and subregions. The primary purpose has been to define (with great precision) the boundaries and to ensure (unlike the AVA system) there is no overlapping.

Zones are areas with no climatic or physical imperatives; they are simply lines drawn on each state map, breaking it into pieces. A region must be a single tract of land, having at least five independently owned vineyards of at least 12 acres (5 ha) each, and usually producing at least 550 tons (500 tonnes) of grapes a year. It is required "to be measurably discrete from adjoining regions and have measurable homogeneity in grape growing attributes over its area."

A subregion has the same production volume indicia, but has to be *substantially* discrete within the region and have *substantial* homogeneity in grape-growing attributes over the area. Those seeking registration as a region or subregion must supply detailed climate statistics and a description of the soil types – which are usually diverse. There is, however, no requirement, nor any attempt, to link this information with wine style, let alone quality. As with the AVAs, there are no restrictions on varieties chosen for planting, viticultural methods, minimum alcohol levels or yield.

As the new century arrived, Australia became increasingly focused on regionality in its domestic and export marketing. In doing so, it "discovered" what some observers had known for a long time: that there are strong regional links to certain varieties. Thus there is the Hunter Valley with Semillon; Clare and Eden Valleys with Riesling; Yarra Valley, Adelaide Hills and Margaret River with Sauvignon Blanc and Chardonnay; Tasmania and Yarra Valley with Pinot Noir; Coonawarra with Cabernet Sauvignon; and northeast Victoria with fortified Frontignac and Muscadelle. (Limiting Chardonnay to three regions is inherently cheeky; trying to put Shiraz in a regional box or two is impossible.)

Moreover, Australasia has increasingly recognized the importance of *terroir* in increasingly small pieces of vineyard. Brian Croser has eloquently and repetitively preached the importance of distinguished sites, which may be only 1.2 acres (0.5 ha) in size, and singled out from, say, a 12-acre (5 ha) vineyard. Airborne remote imaging (from satellites to small planes) can identify variations in vine vigor (weak or strong) in very small units. Matching them on the ground can give precise correlations with grape quality.

If one Yarra estate could emulate Heitz's Martha's Vineyard and attract the following that leads to a hefty premium, who knows how interested the world might become in Yarra Valley geography? All New Zealand felt the benefit when one winery called "Cloudy Bay" established its delicious Sauvignon Blanc on the world stage.

Individual vineyard names (such as Martha's Vineyard in the Napa Valley) have been joined by a plethora of gimmicky varietal and brand names, increasingly favoring animals (Lucky Lizard, Laughing Magpie, Hermit Crab, Blue Penguin,

The message on the bottle

The red soil of Coonawarra in South Australia is a geological freak that produces Australia's best Cabernet Sauvignon. Only one small area, about 1 mile by 9 miles (1.5 by 14.5 km), remote in the outback, is blessed with this eccentric pedology: 1.6 feet (0.5 m) of mineral-rich, perfect drainage, then 5 feet (1.5 m) of pure limestone, then the water table. Could there be a more perfect argument for appellation laws?

[yellow tail] (*sic*), etc., ad nauseam). One senses that many will have a short life span, but the rest of the New World and even some French wines are for the time being offering them the sincerest form of flattery. Perhaps a more intelligent approach is that adopted by such lateral thinkers (and great winemakers) as Miguel Torres in Catalonia and – most conspicuously – Piero Antinori in Tuscany. They have simultaneously established new styles of wine by employing new varieties and new winemaking techniques and strong brand identity. The varietal and vineyard sources of Torres' Black Label Gran Coronas (now Mas La Plana), of Antinori's Tignanello, Sassicaia and Solaia are no secret, but the bold front labels make no mention of them. This approach allows for flexibility in shaping each wine according to the needs of the vintage, but, more importantly, it builds up goodwill in a proprietary name.

Australia's one acknowledged First Growth, Penfolds Grange, comes from an unidentified swag of small vineyards spread across much of South Australia and that change (albeit not dramatically) from one vintage to the next. The criterion for production is simply highly colored, rich, concentrated fruit, from old, low-yielding Shiraz vines.

The varietal honeymoon

Most New World winemakers have fallen into the trap of using simple varietal names for their wines, focusing attention on Chardonnay, Cabernet Sauvignon, Sauvignon Blanc or Pinot Noir. Yet there is no proprietary goodwill attached to those varieties. There is a delirious honeymoon as they make their debut in markets previously unused to them, but the risk is boredom. Not *another* Chardonnay?

To quote the late Peter Sichel of Bordeaux again:

> *The wine culture based on appellations and soils has been phenomenally successful and one simply must not put it in danger. If you can produce wines with character, you should not emphasize their varietal composition. Sooner or later varieties will cease to mean very much because of the infinite variety of wines that can be made from, say, Chardonnay or Cabernet Sauvignon, depending on soil, weather, viticultural practices, yields, winery techniques, and so on. If you simply call your wine Cabernet Sauvignon, the consumer is going to have difficulty in relating it to other wines; if you are producing a wine that really has to be upmarket, people say, "Why should we pay four times as much for this Cabernet Sauvignon when there are Cabernets that are so much cheaper?"*

Not only is the proportion of the different grapes of Latour or Lafite nowhere mentioned on the label of the wine, but it is considered largely irrelevant. Until Edmund Penning-Rowsell wrote his *Wines of Bordeaux* in 1969, there was little or no published information on the subject, and few people realized just how widely the relative proportions of Cabernet Sauvignon, Merlot, Cabernet Franc and Petit Verdot varied from château to château. Not until even more recently has the extent of the annual variation in proportion (largely owing to flowering conditions) been understood; an abundant year for Cabernet Sauvignon may well be a poor one for Merlot, and vice versa. How far a château succeeds in stamping its character on a wine made from an abnormal mix of grapes is one of the measures of its quality.

... and the fruit of experience

Burgundy's great vineyards grow only a single white variety (Chardonnay) and a single red (Pinot Noir). But just as in Bordeaux, the variety is subsumed into the vineyard: we make Latour, not a Cabernet Sauvignon–dominant blend; we make Vosne-Romanée Les Malconsorts, not Pinot Noir; Puligny-Montrachet Les Pucelles, not Chardonnay. What is unique is the vineyard, the *terroir* – not the grape variety that happens to grow there so perfectly. You can make Cabernet Sauvignon almost anywhere in the wine world; you can make Latour only at Latour.

Climate

And, for that matter, weather

Grape vines will grow in any temperate climate. Whether they will produce healthy grapes or make good wine is another matter altogether. Europe has been living with this question for so long that its vineyards have become fully adapted to local climatic conditions. Its preoccupation now is not with climate, but with weather – and of course *terroir*, and the way the two interact.

The New World sees things from the opposite perspective. While weather can be a considerable irritant, and *terroir* is something for long-term observation and definition, climate is the determining factor in deciding where to plant vineyards, and which grapes to plant in them.

One should be clear, first, about the difference between climate and weather. Climate is measured or described in long-term averages; weather is the day-to-day variation of those averages. Weather may make or break a vintage, and may explain the particular characteristics of a given wine, but it is climate that determines which grapes (if any) will grow and ripen well in any given locality.

The Japanese have been making wine for over a century in a climate where almost everything militates against the vine. Their answer to hot and humid summers and the diseases they bring is a high canopy allowing air to circulate. Traditionally, most of the grapes were for the table; perfect bunches were the priority.

Any discussion of climate should differentiate three levels of dimension. Macroclimate is the climate of a region, mesoclimate is the climate of a site and microclimate is the climate within a single grapevine canopy.

Climate and mesoclimate: a question of scale

If you look at the Médoc, you have an area of gently undulating land, 6 miles (10 km) wide and 30 miles (50 km) long, with a marked maritime influence. In a given season, the weather may vary significantly from one commune to the next, but the macroclimate will be roughly the same. The same applies to Burgundy, although that critical (and ever so narrow) gently rising slope to the west of the 74°N does cause significant variations in what is correctly referred to as the macroclimate (often incorrectly called the "microclimate").

If, however, you turn to Tuscany, Piedmont, Alto Adige, Penedès, the Rhine and Mosel Valleys, the Barossa Valley (and attendant ranges) or the Napa Valley (and its adjacent hillsides), to name but a few well-known regions, you are dealing with areas that are far greater in size and with infinitely more variable topography. Both mesoclimate and microclimate will almost certainly vary significantly according to altitude, aspect and degree of slope. Spring frosts, for example, are such a common problem on the floor of the Napa Valley that it is hard to say they are merely a manifestation of weather; they are a climatic factor, but one absent a few miles away on the first slopes and on the hillsides, because the cold air drains down the hillsides and collects on the valley floor. Most critical, in California, is the climatic effect of the coastal hills in either excluding or admitting the famous clammy coastal fogs.

Perfect growing weather

Given an adequate supply of nutrients and moisture, the optimum temperature for photosynthesis and vine growth is between 73°F and 77°F (23°C and 25°C). At this temperature the growth mechanism should be in perfect balance, with canopy and leaf development using the full sugar production. Whether these are the perfect conditions for ripening grapes is another question. For one thing, a too-leafy canopy deprives the grapes of sunlight and therefore sugar.

If the temperature rises much above this level, the vine does not gain additional nutrition through increased photosynthesis, but instead begins to use sugar for increased respiration, leaving progressively less available for the grapes, and leading to the characteristic light color and soft, flabby flavor of wines from excessively warm areas.

In winter a mantle of snow and temperatures as low as –0°F (–18°C) will not damage a dormant vine.

If the temperature falls below it (as far below as 59°F/15°C), photosynthesis continues perfectly happily. Other factors, though, slow the growth of the vine.

The consequence is that a mean average temperature of around 70°F (21°C) is ideal for the ripening of red grapes, and around 66°F (19°C) for the ripening of white grapes. At these temperatures the vine will produce the maximum amount of sugar surplus to its requirements for growth. This surplus is then used up by the grapes – at first it is accumulated, then it is used for ripening as enzymes come into play to produce coloring and flavoring substances.

The slower the better?

There is a myth that slow ripening produces the greatest flavor in all types of fruits and vegetables, and hence the slower the ripening, the better. In reality, given certain basic temperature limitations, the faster the rate of ripening of grapes between the moment they turn color (or *véraison*) and harvest, the better will be color, flavor, sugar and acidity. It is one of the reasons why, in cool climates, the warm years are the best.

Growers have sharply differing ideas about the significance of seasonal temperature variation, about the effects of short periods of heat and about day-to-day and day-to-night temperature swings. Those who grow grapes in warm climates often argue that cold nighttime temperatures are very beneficial for keeping the acid levels in the grapes relatively (and desirably) high. This may well be true, for virtually all metabolic changes will come to a halt at temperatures below 48°F (9°C), and

cold nights will delay all aspects of ripening. If this means that harvest is delayed until the onset of cooler late summer or autumn weather, so much the better. An equally valid point of view is that the more even the month-by-month growing-season temperatures are, and the less the daily temperature range, the more certain and predictable will be the quality. How high this quality will be then finally depends on the average temperatures (and whether it is Riesling or port you are trying to produce).

The benefits of even ripening temperatures are most frequently met with in strongly maritime climates (such as that of Bordeaux) or in warmer continental

In the vast vineyards of central Spain, the most basic of pruning methods, the bush, gives the vine the best chance of surviving constant intense sunshine and desiccating winds.

climates (as in the Rhône Valley). Less reliable conditions occur in Germany, where the climate is cool and continental, marked by cool to cold springs and rapidly falling autumn temperatures, which mean that a hot, sunny summer is essential for a good vintage. Germany, however, has the perfect grape for such conditions. The Riesling can attain full physiological ripeness, and hence intense flavor, at very low sugar levels – in other words, when it is (in chemical terms) barely ripe at all.

Less fluctuation: more flavor

It can certainly be shown that a marked and consistent change between winter and spring temperatures is beneficial. The grower wants buds to burst in unison, and not too early. Vacillating spring temperatures (all too common in maritime northern Europe) mean ragged bud-burst, longer periods of risk from spring frost, and probably uneven flowering, too. The continental temperature pattern is clearly a benefit here. At the other extreme, in strongly maritime areas (such as the Margaret River in Western Australia) the vine can scarcely differentiate between winter and spring. Its winter dormancy is disrupted, leading to the bizarre sight of Chardonnay enjoying (if that is the right word) bud-burst in midwinter, then barely changing for the next two to three months. In summary, it seems that the more even the growing and ripening temperatures (both in terms of month-to-month ranges and daily fluctuation), the greater will be the progressive accumulation of color, aroma and flavor at any given sugar level.

Riesling wines, the glory of Piesport on the Mosel, have the unique property of achieving intense flavors in cool ripening conditions and at very modest levels of alcohol.

The reasons are both negative and positive. Negative because sporadic, very low temperatures at the start or finish of the season can cause severe frost damage, while extreme heat can cause leaf-burn, defoliation and berry-scorching. Positive because research indicates that at nighttime temperatures of between 59°F and 68°F (15°C and 20°C), photosynthetic ripening continues, and, with it, accumulation of coloring and flavoring substances.

This phenomenon occurs across a range of temperatures. In the coolest quality regions, full flavor ripeness can be achieved at relatively low average temperatures. In warm but not hot climates, maximum flavor is achieved before acidity drops and sugar and pH levels rise too far.

Sunshine hours

Temperature and hours of sunshine are by no means the same thing, however interrelated they may be. The paradox is that in warmer climates the vine needs more sunshine hours than it does in cooler climates; conversely, it is temperature, rather than sunshine hours, that determines growth rates in those cooler climates. The farther one moves from the equator, the longer are the summer days, and the greater the potential sunshine hours. It is a complex equation, made more so by cloud and rain (which are generally both more frequent and more sporadic in the cooler regions).

Rainfall: when and how much?

How much the vine drinks depends on how much it transpires – and, of course, how much water is available. In most of the northern European wine regions nature supplies adequate (at times more than adequate) rainfall throughout the year, while in the southern regions a Mediterranean climate provides a strong winter-spring rainfall (the most critical) and a dry, sunny summer. In much of the New World the patterns of rainfall and humidity are very different, and so-called water stress (the old word is "drought") is much more common. The question of rainfall, stress and irrigation is discussed in later chapters.

Wind: less is better

It is probably the Germans, whose vineyards need all the heat they can get, who have studied the effects of wind most closely. They conclude that less is better, and align their vine rows at right angles to the prevailing wind accordingly. But, as growers in districts such as Carneros in California or Marlborough in New Zealand will attest, wind has a threefold effect. Blowing hard, it will interrupt flowering and reduce the crop. Gales break the tender parts of the vine, removing growing tips, breaking canes and bruising leaves. Even stiff breezes can be damaging; the "windchill factor" to the vine means leaf pores close and photosynthesis is reduced, so the plant is working below its full efficiency. At the other extreme, air stagnation can just as easily inhibit the vine's growth – a slight breeze, however, will refresh the microclimate around the vine and allow healthy respiration.

Climate: how varieties react
Chardonnay

Chardonnay is the most forgiving and the most flexible of all varieties. It will make satisfying wine in any climate from cool to very warm – but the personalities of these wines will be vastly different. Its specialized use in sparkling wine apart, its most restrained manifestation is arguably that of Chablis. Chablis is traditionally described in terms of gun flint and sucking river pebbles – images for the totally dry, only just ripe aspect of cool-grown Chardonnay. Primitive production methods and uninhibited use of sulfur dioxide in the past may have contributed to this image. But Chablis of a fine vintage today (the vintages of 1997, 2000 and 2002, for example), made in the traditional way without new oak, is Chardonnay at its purest and most refined – colored only by the elusive, elemental *goût de terroir* of its pale clay.

As Chardonnay moves from cool to warmer regions, its flavor develops from suggestions of apple, fig and melon to grapefruit, peach and finally to honey. Overlaid on these flavors is (in most cases) a greater or lesser influence of oak (toast, butter, tar), but the increasingly ripe, round and dense personality of the same grape grown in a warmer climate is clear. It is true that these changes are in part structural, associated with increasing natural levels of alcohol, although chaptalization can be a wild card that upsets this neat pattern. Very ripe, warm-grown Chardonnay has precocious appeal, but quickly cloys: one glass is enough. That was the California Chardonnay of the early 1970s, Australian of the 1980s.

Cabernet Sauvignon

Cabernet Sauvignon grown in excessively cool conditions has a weedy, thin, herbaceous flavor, and a bitter, "green" finish. Under perfect ripening conditions it develops its central aroma and flavor of blackcurrant, given tension by echoes of the green pepper character lent by less ripe (or more heavily shaded) fruit, and by the variety's typically astringent tannins. In warmer regions it acquires a more lush aspect, sometimes showing eucalyptus or mint flavors, sometimes a distinctive taste of dark chocolate. Hot-grown Cabernet Sauvignon has a jammy, stewed, mulberry-and-prunes character, and is usually flabby on the finish. If the acidity is as low (or pH is as high) as one might expect, the hue will have an unhealthy, dull, blackish edge right from the outset, which will rapidly degenerate into a dispirited brown.

Pinot Noir

Since the first edition of this book there have been profound changes affecting the growing and making of Pinot Noir in Burgundy. Having falsely succumbed to the allure of high-yielding rootstocks and clones in the 1960s through to the mid-1980s, the wheel has now turned firmly in the opposite direction, clones with small berries and bunches being favored. Much stricter care is taken in the vineyard throughout the growing season; August is no longer the mandatory holiday it once was; bunch-and shoot-thinning are common practices; if hail hits, badly affected bunches will be removed so as not to act as carriers of rot; and all serious producers have sorting tables, some with tables before and after destemmers and vibrating sections.

In the 1970s there were three good red Burgundy vintages (1971, 1972 and 1978) and in the 1980s another three (1985, 1988 and 1990). Since 1990 the only lesser vintages have been 1992, 1994, 2000 and 2004; in between, there have been a procession of good-to-great vintages. Climate change may be having an effect (particularly if 2003 is laid at its door), but attitudes to and practices in viticulture are also playing an important role.

Pinot Noir flavors in ideal conditions range from slightly simple red-cherry or raspberry fruit (as in Volnay) to more textured and voluptuous plum (as in Vosne-Romanée). Dotted around the world are a few areas where Pinot Noir gives glimpses of its inherent greatness: the central coast of California (Santa Barbara

*The climate of the French Alps,
with a short but sunny summer
and low temperatures at night,
stamps its personality on the
low-key, all-refreshment wines
of grapes traditionally grown in
Savoie: the Altesse and the
Roussette. Here the variety
and the* terroir *produce wines
that precisely express the
uniqueness of their origin.*

in particular), the Willamette Valley of Oregon; Carneros, California; the Yarra Valley and other regions grouped around Melbourne, Australia; Martinborough and Central Otago, New Zealand; and perhaps the high Penedès, in Catalonia. Pinot Noir will simply not tolerate excessive warmth – it ripens well enough, and the bunches look perfect, but it produces an utterly nondescript red wine (briefly red before it turns brown) that is devoid of any varietal character. If the climate is too cool, as in Germany, one ends up with the anemic character of Spätburgunder or with wine as thin, herbal and weedy as the most unripe Cabernet Sauvignon.

Riesling

Riesling is a conundrum. On the basis of its distribution in Europe, one would say it needs the coolest of climates, yet if one looks at dry Riesling, its performance in other countries points in another direction. Australia (with 10,685 acres/4,325 ha) has some of the largest plantings outside Germany; there Riesling reaches its stylistic peak in the strongly continental (warm days, cold nights) climate of the Clare Valley and the marginally cooler Eden Valley, both in South Australia. With between 11 and 12 degrees of natural alcohol, the wines are very reserved in their youth, with overtones of passion fruit (Eden Valley examples always smell a little more floral, with a definite suggestion of lime juice). But with over 10 to 20 years in the bottle they develop a fine tension between their limelike acidity and a broader flavor often likened to gently browned toast.

Rieslings from the inland subregions of the Great Southern region of Western Australia are acquiring a reputation not far, if at all, behind the Clare and Eden Valleys. Tasmania, too, has joined the party with steely, crisp wines, one or two in convincing Mosel Kabinett style.

After decades in the wilderness, and many false dawns, Riesling is enjoying a modest worldwide renaissance in popularity. There are still sugary, sickly versions, and thin, flavorless dry (trocken) wines being made in Germany, but serious makers have grasped the nettle of reduced yield to make fine wines from dry to lusciously sweet. For makers in Germany, in particular, and Alsace to a lesser degree, salvation has come from New World markets that value the unique and very different styles of the Mosel-Saar-Ruwer, Rheingau, Rheinpfalz and Rheinhessen.

Syrah/Shiraz

Syrah – or as it is known in Australia and South Africa, Shiraz – is another grape that responds positively and enthusiastically to a range of climatic conditions, taking warmth in its stride. France (the Rhône and the south) and Australia are its two strongholds, but there has been nothing modest about its worldwide surge in popularity since 1991. In that year, Australia crushed 60,400 tons (54,800 tonnes) from 13,500 acres (5,450 ha); by 2004 it reached 482,000 tons (437,000 tonnes) from 96,800 acres (39,200 ha), representing over 40 percent of all red grapes and 22 percent of the total crush. Moreover, the increase has been spread across the entire continent (even Tasmania has a splash), from the coolest to the warmest regions. This has encouraged growers in California, Washington State, British Columbia, South Africa and New Zealand (conspicuously in Hawke's Bay) to hop on board this midnight express.

In the cooler regions of Australia, in Hawke's Bay and in Washington State, black pepper, spice, licorice and black fruits are the focal aromas and flavors, increasingly helped along the way with around 5 percent cofermented Viognier (flattering Côte Rôtie with highly successful imitation). As cool-climate experience has accumulated in Australasia, winemakers have become aware of the necessity for true phenolic ripeness, and no longer fall into the trap of equating pepper alone with desirable varietal character – it may (as the late Gerard Jaboulet pointed out) simply indicate unripe grapes.

As the climate warms, pepperiness diminishes and (while the wine is young) sweet, warm berry-fruit flavors take over, but with a range of secondary aromas and flavors more akin to the ephemeral Pinot Noir than to the imperious Cabernet Sauvignon. The greatest Syrah wines are Jaboulet's Hermitage La Chapelle, the super-cuvées of Guigal

(La Mouline, La Landonne, La Turque) and Penfolds Grange – wines made in roughly similar climates, albeit from very different *terroirs*, the last showing none of the pepper and spice flavors of the Rhône wines. Then there are the Syrahs of the very hot Hunter Valley in Australia, in which secondary characteristics of tar, leather and a certain smokiness are immediately apparent, and pepper and spice are notably absent.

Sauvignon Blanc

Whether one regards Sauvignon Blanc as flexible or limited in its climatic range depends on whether one is an aficionado of Sancerre and Pouilly-Fumé – and indeed whether one accepts it as one of the great grape varieties in the first place (other than in its role in contributing to the great Sauternes). The U.S. palate, consciously or unconsciously, seems to reject its pristine varietal character as expressed in the Loire Valley: tart, crisp gooseberry with a vegetal-tobacco bite, less charitably described as canned peas or cat's pee. Californian winemakers go to considerable lengths to mute these characteristics, making sure the grape is very ripe before it is harvested, blending in a percentage of Semillon, and surrounding it with a coating of oak. Against all expectations, Sauvignon Blanc has flourished in Australia, unabashed by the competition from New Zealand. Older vines, better matching of variety and climate, and a clear choice between Loire Valley style (stainless-steel fermented, early bottled) and white Bordeaux (careful barrel fermentation, Semillon as an equal partner) has driven Sauvignon Blanc into third place after Chardonnay and Semillon.

On the other hand, New Zealand (with an ease tantamount to promiscuity) and South Africa (surprisingly) produce Sauvignon Blanc wines with pungent and precise varietal character. New Zealand does it best of all in Marlborough, with a climate that must be very similar to that of the upper Loire Valley and with the type of meager, stony soil that would bring a smile to the face of the most chauvinistic and hard-to-please French grape-grower. Quite why South Africa does so well is not easy to understand: its climate is much warmer – warmer than that of the Barossa Valley around Stellenbosch, and warmer still at Paarl (though cooler on the Simonsberg hills) – but even Sauvignon Blanc made in the modest cooperatives toward Paarl retains distinctive character. The added-essence scandal of 2004–2005 that greatly affected the industry giant KWV could (retrospectively) provide a partial explanation.

Semillon (Sémillon)

Semillon, like Syrah, finds its greatest expression in France and Australia, producing, when made dry, wines of almost unrecognizably different style in climates that, viticulturally speaking, are as far apart as the Sahara Desert and the South Pole. Given that it is a ubiquitous variety, found in almost all the wine-growing regions of the world, it is strange that it should manifest its greatest character at these extremes – Bordeaux on the one hand, and the Hunter Valley on the other. All the two areas have in common is humidity. Paradoxically, Bordeaux is still only in the process of investigating Semillon. While it is the foundation stone of Sauternes, its role in dry wines in the past has been merely to round out the edginess of Sauvignon Blanc. Its affinity with new oak, with Sauvignon as the junior partner, is a discovery with an exciting future.

Overall, it must be seen as a flexible variety. In the relatively warm, strongly maritime climate of Margaret River in Western Australia, the intermediate climate of the Adelaide Hills and all of New Zealand, it produces wine that is hard to distinguish from a slightly thin Sauvignon Blanc, with pronounced herbal and tobacco overtones. Yet there are a few good examples from South Africa (where the grape is widely planted) and there is potential to produce good wines in South America (there are vast plantings in Chile) with the rapid improvement in fermentation technology and oak handling in that country. Washington State also grows it very well. But to date it is the voluptuous, nutty, honeyed 20-year-old Australian Hunter Valley Semillons – tasting for all the world as if they were fermented in new oak, or at least matured in it, which they are not – that show the Semillon grape to its greatest advantage.

Chenin Blanc has not yet had a fair trial. Even in its home in the Loire Valley it demands exceptional conditions to produce great wine. Yet no one who has tasted a 30- or even 50-year-old sweet Vouvray or Coteaux du Layon can forget its potential. For acidity braced against richness, it is France's only answer to the masterpieces of the Mosel.

This aptitude to maintain its high acidity stands it in good stead in much warmer climates than the Loire, where it is understood. South Africa has long relied on it for everyday wine that stays lively and fruity even in primitive conditions. One or two Californian winemakers regularly make an excellently structured dry wine from it. Its Achilles' heel is its desire to produce huge crops, its pleasant fruit-salad flavors adding to its usefulness as a "filler" in generic blends at low price points.

Chenin Blanc

As each day passes in 2006, the subject of climate change gains ever more headlines around the world, and the existing nexus between given regions and given varieties is more likely than not to be broken. When the first edition of this book was written, there was far less agreement than there is today on the extent of change and the outlook for the next 50 years. Since there has been so much written and said, and since the dramatic and continuing increase in carbon dioxide levels is beyond question, we shall continue our attention to the impact on grape growing and winemaking around the world.

First, there is a broad consensus among the climatologists that the southern hemisphere will be less affected than the northern, simply because of the smaller land mass and greater ocean expanses stretching south to the Antarctic. South Africa has the lowest projected increase in temperature, but the southern parts of Australia, New Zealand and South America are all likely to be (relatively speaking) less affected than northern hemisphere producers

Somewhat controversially, perhaps, the highly respected Australian researcher and viticulturalist Dr. John Gladstones suggests that an increase of 1 percent in average temperature by the middle of the century would favor a shift for any given grape variety toward, not away from, warmer regions in the southern hemisphere. He says increased carbon dioxide supply will raise the upper limit of optimum temperature to produce optimum fruit quality, and may lead to increased color (for red wines) and intensity of fruit flavor. He acknowledges the scenario will change radically if forecasts of 3.2°F to 8.1°F (1.8°C to 4.5°C) prove correct. In these circumstances there will be a marked shift to cooler regions for southern as well as northern hemisphere winemakers wishing to continue to produce their existing wine styles.

If, indeed, the higher temperature levels materialize, the outlook for France (most particularly) is grim. By the end of the 21st century – perhaps earlier – average harvest dates are likely to be three weeks earlier than at present. The climate of Bordeaux will be similar to present-day south of France, Burgundy will be close to present-day Bordeaux and so forth. That is bad enough, but how quickly will the laws regarding permitted varieties, the use of irrigation and the addition of acid change? On present indications, far too late. And when you consider the consequences of Burgundy switching to Cabernet Sauvignon, Syrah (Shiraz), Semillon and Sauvignon Blanc, the cure may seem worse than the illness.

For the United States, Canada and the southern hemisphere producers, changes in varietal plantings are of no concern. They are, and have been, happening for decades quite independently of climate change. Moreover, Australia, Chile, Argentina and North America have areas that, either by virtue of altitude or latitude, are presently too cool for commercial viticulture. A move to these is easy, but you cannot "move" Burgundy, Bordeaux or Champagne without seriously damaging the special value they presently have.

Climate change

Which Variety of Vine?

The flavor starts with the grape

Varietalism

Each long-established wine region has a story to tell about its own grape varieties. Perhaps the Greeks introduced them, perhaps the Romans, perhaps the Cistercians; perhaps they evolved by selection and mutation from some such introduction – or even from wild woodland vines.

In most cases they are so important to the identity of the local product that, ever since there have been appellation laws or their equivalents, the grape variety or varieties have been specified as clearly and definitively as the region itself.

Grape preferences: a new concern

What is perhaps surprising is that very little of this history is particularly old. With the unique exception of Pinot Noir, which was made mandatory (with only mixed success) for the region of Beaune in the 14th century, the designation of varieties comes very late in wine's long history. Not until the late 18th century was Riesling heavily planted along the Rhine and Mosel, or Cabernet Sauvignon recognized as the best of all grapes for the Médoc. Only a hundred years later growers in the Napa Valley came to the same conclusion.

We should not think, then, of two totally separate developments, one Old World and one New World. In terms of modern winemaking, in many ways both worlds have been working out most of their grape preferences over the same short period of time.

Old practices, old plantings

The great difference between the two is that the vineyards of Europe – whatever was planted in them – were a long-established going concern. Changes in old

Cabernet Sauvignon, the classic "claret grape," has shown itself to be surprisingly adaptable in climates quite different from that of Bordeaux: in California's Napa Valley, in Australia, Chile, the Penedès region of Spain and in Italy. It is proving in every sense to be an international variety.

practice (and old planting) were made reluctantly, circumspectly and probably only by those who could afford to make mistakes without risking starvation. Besides, who would pull up an old vineyard and lose several years' harvests? Better to patch a plot where vines had died and see a gradual transformation.

The case of New World growers has always been totally different. The land is bare; there are decisions to be made. Do I want red wine or white? What vines are available from the nurseries? What do the neighbors say, think and do? What do the scientists advise?

True, in the first century of Californian and Australian winemaking most of the wines went to market as "Burgundy," "Chablis," "claret," "Rhine" or "Sauternes" – or, more strictly speaking, most as "port" or "sherry"; table wines were very much in the minority. But the growers had planted their vineyards with Cabernet Sauvignon, Riesling, Syrah (Shiraz) or Zinfandel. It was inevitable that they saw them as blocks of certain grapes, rather than peculiar parcels of land with an immemorial, usually only vaguely identified, vine population.

Peculiar parcels

"Varietalism," to coin a word, was therefore built into the structure of New World viticulture from the start. Then, from the 1930s, the journalist Frank Schoonmaker, advising Almaden Vineyards (California), hit on the idea of making the grape variety the sales pitch. It was harmless, it looked like truth in labeling, and Europe had reason to be pleased that its geographic designations were no longer to be plundered wholesale.

The idea that, half a century later, a French wine might sell not because it was Burgundy, but because it was Chardonnay, would have seemed absurd. No longer, though. Varietalism has come to Europe, and given legitimacy to regions with little or no history. A few classic regions apart, it has already all but destroyed the fragile traditions of Italy, while even in France growers in regions without strong traditions now effectively get their vine-manipulating and vineyard-managing ideas, their marketing strategies and even their winemaking techniques straight from Australia or California.

"White Burgundy" or "Chardonnay"?

Above: *Riesling, Chardonnay's rival for the title of the world's greatest white grape.*

Left: *Chenin Blanc, cultivated in the Loire since the ninth century, has happily traveled the wine world, producing a variety of wines: luscious sweet, off-dry, sparkling … it even makes an appearance in fortified wines.*

Blending

Parallel to varietalism, and by no means at odds with it, lie the tradition and practice of blending. In most old wine regions, blending (of varieties in the vineyard) was taken for granted. The "purity" of Pinot Noir was very much an exception – and very probably a chimera, too: Pinots Blanc, Gris and Meunier, some Chardonnay, a certain amount of the outlawed Gamay and a little Aligoté might all have been found in a red wine Côte d'Or vineyard. At Château Margaux in the 18th century it was the practice to make the white wine (Sauvignon Blanc) separately from the red and blend them together to make the *grand vin*, according to the owner's taste. At Lafite it was more likely to be Hermitage from the Rhône that was blended into the château wine to give it the weight it often lacked.

Dom Pérignon: kid-glove care

Dom Pérignon was celebrated in his day not, as the legend goes, for inventing sparkling Champagne, but as a blender of genius who conjured luxurious white wine almost exclusively from Pinot Noir by using grapes from different *terroirs* and handling them with kid-glove care. He was no fan of Chardonnay; he found it too prone to refermentation, producing the bubbles he tried so hard to avoid.

Chardonnay and Riesling, it is true, are grapes that have nothing to gain and much to lose from blending, but port has always been a blend of grapes, and Châteauneuf-du-Pape has 13 permitted varieties in its appellation; similarly the formulas for Rioja and Chianti both call for a balancing of darker and lighter, more aromatic and more weighty wines. The New World, though, has generally been hesitant about sullying the purity of its varietals. The assumption has been that if Cabernet Sauvignon is good, 100 percent Cabernet Sauvignon must be best. For better or worse "varietal character" has been, and still is, pursued as a goal in itself.

It is true that well-selected New World sites should not need the insurance policy element of a mixed planting. For them, the reason for blending (apart from stretching the supply of an expensive grape as Australia has been known to do by adding Semillon to Chardonnay) must be found in the flavor.

The "donut effect"

Of all the "classic" varieties, Cabernet Sauvignon is the only one that regularly benefits from having a partner in the vat. Memorable as its flavor is, with a structure that demands long aging, anything less than ideal ripening conditions can lead to a "donut effect" on the palate: the wine starts and finishes powerfully in the mouth, its finish in particular boosted by astringent tannins, with the result that the midpalate seems to lack something.

A feeling for orthodoxy?

Bordeaux has its answer, arrived at by centuries of trial and error. It blends in the rounder, fleshier Merlot and more aromatic Cabernet Franc – but still in proportions very much dependent on the vintage. Australia has attempted an answer of its own, whose logic appears impeccable. Syrah (Shiraz) rises in flavor in the mouth just where Cabernet seems to fall. Structurally the two are ideally matched. For all that, though, Cabernet/Syrah blends are going out of fashion. Whether due to a feeling for orthodoxy (which does not sound very Australian) or due to disillusionment with the local formula, winemakers are switching over to the classic "Bordeaux blend." The current argument against Syrah as a companion for Cabernet Sauvignon is that, while structurally compatible, rather than producing a whole greater than the sum of its parts, each blurs the varietal flavor of the other. A plausible explanation may be that Merlot and Cabernet Franc are genetically part of the Cabernet family: Syrah is not.

Petit Verdot is the dark horse. Having wobbled on the brink of extinction in Bordeaux, better clones (and global warming?) have stayed its execution: Château Latour, for example, has increased its plantings, as have other First Growths. In an almost obscene, off-the-planet performance, it is flourishing in the Australian Riverland, where hot sun, abundant irrigation and consequent high yields cannot weaken its color or rob its flavor and structure.

Talk of "varietal character," in other words, is simply an acknowledgment that a few outstanding grapes have flavors we appreciate for themselves. Others need a supporting cast.

Left: *Pinot Noir at* véraison, *when the grapes turn from green to purple. Uneven flowering caused by bad weather (below) can lead to the berries ripening unevenly – a serious problem when it comes to harvest.*

Clones

The Stone Age selection

A clone is a population of plants, all members of which are the descendants by vegetative propagation of a single individual and are therefore, in theory at least, genetically identical.

The selection of clones has been carried out for just as long as the selection of varieties; indeed, in a sense it preceded it. It has also had a single purpose for almost all of the thousands of years for which it has been practiced: to increase or to ensure a healthy yield. The first selections were made in Neolithic times. Wild vines are predominantly female, depending on a lesser population of male vines for fertilization. If properly fertilized, the female vines would bear good crops, but the process was far from certain. The male vines bore no crops at all. There were then a few vines that had a percentage of hermaphrodite flowers: flowers that could self-pollinate. It seems reasonable to assume that the early viticulturists would have been anxious to rid their vineyards of any barren male vines, but the result of rooting out the males would have been to leave the females barren. The hermaphrodite vines, therefore, were seen as the most reliable. Attempts to propagate them by seed would have been both slow and risky. But propagation by transferring cuttings enabled quick and reliable selection, resulting in vineyards of the modern-day composition of totally hermaphrodite vines.

Health and consistency

Today clonal selection has two overt aims: to achieve a defined and consistent level of quality and to eliminate viruses and other diseases. Its effect, whether or not recognized as an aim, has been almost invariably to increase the size of the crop. For its first aim it depends on genetic mutation, however slight. In any given field of vines, some will stand out as having all or most of the desired qualities – above all a good, healthy crop of grapes in bunches that are not too tightly packed together, or too loosely spaced on the stem.

Some varieties offer far more mutants than others. Pinot Noir is famously genetically unstable. All the other Pinots (Meunier, Gris and Blanc) are apparently mutations of this promiscuous parent, while there are said to be some 1,000 clones of Pinot Noir in Burgundy, ranging from the ubiquitous, easy-to-prune and

The German model

If the French have been backward in using crosses, the Germans have more than compensated, with Müller-Thurgau as their flagship. A century after its discovery, the parentage claimed (or supposed) by Dr. Müller is in doubt. Rather than being of Riesling x Silvaner, it may be a cross between two clones of Riesling.

Müller-Thurgau did not in reality combine only the advantages of each parent: its soft wood makes it particularly susceptible to winter frosts, it is more prone to a range of diseases than either parent and it is not particularly easy to grow. If this were not enough, no one disagrees that the wine it produces is exceedingly ordinary.

heavy-cropping "Pinot Droit" (easily recognizable by the peculiar upright and straight growth of its canes) to the tiny population of the shy-bearing "Pinot Fin," which the Domaine de la Romanée-Conti claims as its own.

DNA has enabled research biologists to ascertain the parentage of grape varieties. One of the more recent, and certainly the most interesting, was the research done by Professor Carol Meredith of the University of California at Davis, which demonstrated that Syrah (Shiraz) is the offspring of two exceedingly obscure varieties, Dureza and Mondeuse Blanche, and that its birth occurred in the northern end of the Rhône Valley around the first century AD. The grape does not come from Iran, as is so commonly stated. However, DNA research is not yet able to positively identify clones (either to establish that two vines are of the same clone, or that they are of different clones), although researchers are tantalizingly close.

Hybrids and crosses

A distinction should be drawn between a hybrid (the union between a *Vitis vinifera* vine and another species of *Vitis – Vitis amurensis*, for example) and a cross, involving two varieties of *Vitis vinifera* (such as the crossing of Riesling and Sylvaner to produce Müller-Thurgau).

To breed grapevine hybrids is no less painstaking and costly than are the mechanics of clonal selection, although plant geneticists argue it is more certain and focused in aim (it does not rely on chance mutations for its source). Its purpose is quite different: rather than seek improved versions of existing varieties, it creates new varieties. The process may take place in stages and be repeated many times. Step one involves the selection of two parents. Since the female might self-pollinate, it must be emasculated by removal of the stamens from the flowers. Pollen is then taken from the flower of the male, applied to the female, and a bag placed over the pollinated flower to keep out strange pollen from other flowers. Step two involves removal of the ripened berries from the vines and planting the seeds. Not all will germinate, but those that do will all be different from each other. Several years later, step three involves the selection of the most promising vines, and step four, propagation of multiples of these by cuttings (not seeds). Most will be discarded, perhaps all. If one is selected, it may be both propagated commercially in its own right and/or used for yet further crossings (step five).

Intractable French opposition to hybrids and crosses – and some would say the conservatism of wine producers and wine consumers everywhere – has played some role in slowing the development of the next phase: genetic manipulation. Biotechnology was one of the buzzwords of the 1980s, but its application to woody plants has been slow compared to cereal crops and vegetables. Nonetheless, there is great potential in taking the best features of both plant breeding and clonal selection, and in particular in making directed and deliberate improvements in existing grape varieties. The method used is the in vitro growth of grapevine cells, which are manipulated and subsequently nurtured into an entire plant. The advantages of this approach are numerous, and its perfection will undoubtedly preoccupy viticultural research scientists over the next few decades.

Genetic engineering

As the German experience graphically demonstrates, technique (and technology) must never be allowed to become an end in itself. Clonal selection and vine breeding have to be seen as tools to be used sensitively and with discretion. In the early decades of experimentation, the viticulturists made all the management decisions. The winemaker was scarcely consulted, nor the consumer. The indices of success were vine health, yield and ability to ripen the crop within a stipulated time.

Breeding and selection

The next phase of experimentation was marked by more thorough chemical analysis designed to give a better idea of quality; research was often substantiated by the making of small quantities of wine from trial plots. The problems with these winemaking trials were, first, their very small scale: they seldom provided any close correlation with the results of commercial winemaking. Second, the caliber, experience and expectations of the judges called upon to judge the wines were developed in laboratories, and not in the broader world of wine and, in particular, great wine.

Plant health and yields, however, continued to improve. In some instances quality improved. But the problem in many areas was (and is) the divergence in interest between the grape-grower, who sells the grapes, and the winemaker, who makes and sells the wine. In areas such as Bordeaux, where estates are the rule, this conflict scarcely arises, but in most of the grape-growing regions of the world, much of the production comes from small contract growers.

Quis custodiet?

Having peered into the abyss in the 1960s to 1980s, when viticultural practices were concerned almost solely with yield (selection of high-vigor rootstocks and highly productive clones) and included often slipshod winemaking with outdated equipment, there was an about-face in the last two decades of the 20th century.

Which was the chicken, which the egg, is immaterial. A series of kind vintages, a rash of acquisition and investment, and soaring export prices for the greatest wines of Europe (true, mainly France, but with Italy having a strong domestic market as well, and Spain sharing some of the spoils) led to a complete change of attitude. Clonal selection was no longer driven by quantity; quality (typically via smaller berries and bunches) was the criterion.

Changes such as this are not made overnight. Until better clones are matched with vine maturity (at least 10 years, preferably 20), then remedial treatment by bunch-thinning, sorting tables, concentration machines and so forth must bridge the gap. But the future looks promising for those able to afford the finest wines.

Since the phylloxera vine louse attacked the world's vineyards in the 19th century, prudent growers have grafted their chosen variety onto a rootstock of American parentage. Phylloxera originally came from North America and had coexisted over the millennia with the native vine species, which gradually became largely resistant to it. It soon became apparent, though, that the balance between the American rootstock, the scion (chosen vine variety) and the soil was almost infinitely variable. Some rootstocks are so vigorous that uncontrolled vegetative growth (and hence sharply reduced crop levels) result. Others are too weak. Some, such as hybrid rootstocks ARG1, AXR and 1202 used in California, are not

American roots

Above: *A bunch of newly grafted vines. The pale wood at the top is the "scion" – the chosen variety – with one bud, dovetailed onto the darker wood of the selected rootstock.*

Right: *The grafts are planted in dense rows in a nursery bed with a plastic mulch covering to form roots before going into the vineyard.*

sufficiently resistant to phylloxera. Vulnerability to nematodes is another problem; these tiny, wormlike creatures are not as devastating as phylloxera, but they also attack the roots and debilitate the plant, compelling growers in several phylloxera-free New World regions to use grafted vines.

In the outcome, much the same pattern emerged as with clones: those rootstocks that (however insidiously) gave increased yield came to be preferred. Worse, much of the evaluation work was carried out in France, on infertile, "low-potential" soils; to this day, insufficient work has been done on sufficiently devigorating rootstocks for the fertile "high-potential" sites of the New World.

Selection and breeding vs. the flat-earther

Only a flat-earther could deny the potential benefits of clonal selection, hybrid crossings, genetics and rootstock selection. Many parts of the world have indifferent clones that are neither high-quality nor high-yielding. They need to be able to start again with "clean," well-adapted vines. As we shall see in later chapters, phylloxera has had devastating effects on plant health and the spread of viruses, and no one would argue that low yields from sick vines are desirable. Genetic engineering offers all sorts of possibilities for the natural control of diseases, a subject of increasing significance in a world increasingly wary of the use of chemicals of any kind. And the use of rootstocks – quite apart from saving the European wine industry from oblivion – offers real scope for improvement in wine quality at all levels. In other words, these are tools: if used skillfully and intelligently, they will help make better wine; used clumsily and without sufficient thought, they will make garbage.

Sculpting the Vine

Too much vigor is as bad as too little

The vine is the most adaptable of plants, accepting with equanimity the transition from its forest origins to the ground-hugging, stumpy little bushes of Beaujolais or the Rhône Valley or Rioja, the form it also traditionally took in the Barossa Valley of Australia, the Napa Valley and many other New World vineyards. This severe "bush-pruning" – taking the vine back to only a few buds on each branch – seems orderly and natural, while the ancient Italian (and Portuguese) method of growing the vine up poplars, across high, latticed pergolas, interplanted with every type of crop or fruit tree imaginable, seems chaotic and unnatural. In truth, the Italian approach far more closely resembles the vine's natural habit, even though today it is a fast-disappearing anachronism.

All the great wine regions of Europe have one thing in common: very moderate soil fertility, leading to low natural vigor in their vines. French wine lore is full of aphorisms about vines growing where nothing else is worth planting and, conversely, where grain will grow well, the wine will not be worth drinking.

In the bizarre jargon of today the term for such ideal vineyards is "low-potential sites." Over the centuries a priceless bank of experience has been built up and passed down from generation to generation: the formulas for growing vines in perfect balance on such low-potential sites to make the highest quality of wine.

In Europe, whatever the traditional, regional or local system of vineyard management (pruning, training and trellising), its common features are very close vine-spacing, low yield per vine, small individual bunches and shoots and grapes well exposed to light – these achieved by repeated and meticulous hedging or trimming of the vines through the growing season. In European vineyards the low vigor means that by midsummer the vine's growth has slowed, and it reacts mildly to trimming. This is where the fertile, "high-potential" vineyards of the New World have a peculiar problem: trimming provokes a burst of lateral growth (laterals are shoots springing from the base of the leaves on the current year's canes). It exacerbates the very problem of shading that it is intended to cure.

The unflappable vine

Trim in Europe

These Egyptian vines of 3000 BC were planted in richly manured beds and trimmed high on pergolas. The quality of their wines is unknown.

A Year in the Vineyard

Every vineyard has the same essential annual routine, but there are scores of options open to the wine-grower as to how and when each job is carried out. This chart indicates some of the more important tasks.

The decisions of the growers will be dictated by climate, tradition, economics and the pursuit of quality. Over the past 20 years or so there have been enormous advances in the science of growing grapes. The results of academic research are now shared worldwide, so that progressive growers have an uncomfortable amount of often conflicting advice to ponder. The majority settle for the certainty of tradition, while staying alert to the new products and techniques that promise a less grueling workload.

1 WINTER

Pruning
There are four basic choices:
(a) *Cane-pruning*
(the most skilled)
(b) *Spur-pruning*
(easier and quicker)
(c) *Machine pruning*
(effectively spur-pruning)
(d) *Minimal pruning*
(effectively no pruning at all during winter)
Mechanical pruning is often followed by a certain amount of hand-pruning or "cleaning up."

2 SPRING

Planting
The optimum time for planting is in early spring, as the ground is starting to warm up yet still retains good moisture. If the rootlings are planted too early, the roots may rot; in the New World vines are sometimes kept in cool stores and planted in early summer.

3 SUMMER

Irrigation
This period of flowering and fruit-set is a critical time in which the vine needs warm and calm weather, and in which the intervention of the grower is limited. Irrigation will begin at this time in dry regions in the New World.

4 AUTUMN

Harvest
The choice lies between the speed and economy of machine harvesting (where the vineyard permits it) and the gentler, slower and more controllable hand-picking.

In all cases late pruning will delay the development of the buds and result in a more even bud-break.

In Champagne (far left) and Alsace (left) it is an accepted part of vineyard hygiene to burn the prunings from the vines in winter. Some growers leave them lying between the rows to decompose slowly and add to the structure of the soil – or the risk, say others, of harboring fungal diseases.

Foliage sprays
The first of the lime-sulfur sprays is applied at woolly-bud stage (as the buds swell and soften) to guard against fungal disease. Organic growers or those wishing to minimize spraying will still accept the use of these sprays and of Bordeaux mixture (a solution of copper sulfate, lime and water).

Working the soil
There is an increasing recognition of the choice between the traditional agricultural practice of plowing the soil, and of leaving it untilled – relying in the latter case on the use of herbicides to control unwanted weed or excessive grass growth.

In frost-prone areas, a billiard-table-smooth, bare surface between the vines allows air circulation and hence protection against frost. Organic growers, however, encourage a variety of plants to grow there, thus providing a natural food chain (protecting the grapes) and adding nitrogen to the soil. Biodynamic viticulture is increasingly found in Old World and New World alike.

Canopy trimming and training
Directing and, later in the season, limiting the exuberant new growth is of critical importance in establishing the balance of the vine and achieving appropriate exposure of the grape bunches to sunlight. Traditionally a skilled job performed by hand, it can now be done by machines that can lift wires and shoots or weave support strings through the canopy.

Vine maintenance
(a) *Foliage sprays*
In cool, humid regions the vines must be sprayed to prevent botrytis attacking during flowering. Such attack destroys the grapes before they can begin to form.

The vines also need to be sprayed regularly against oidium and other mildews: Bordeaux mixture or systemic fungicides are frequently used. These latter chemical sprays are absorbed into the sap-stream of the plant. Unfortunately, fungal diseases rapidly develop resistance to specific chemicals, making it necessary to vary the formula.
(b) *Trimming the vine*
Throughout the growing season the canes must be trimmed and the remaining foliage raised and attached to the trellis wires to allow the maximum sunlight to reach the leaves and grapes.

Working the soil
While the area under the vines will not be disturbed, traditional growers still lightly plow the soil between the rows of vines to prevent runoff and thus conserve moisture.

Pest control
Caterpillars, moths and, toward ripening, birds have to be controlled. Other pests to which vines and grapes are lost include rabbits, foxes, snails and, in Australia, kangaroos.

Post-harvest sprays
At approximately 50 percent leaf fall, a spray is applied to kill mildew spores that would otherwise establish themselves on the vine over winter.

Working the soil and applications of fertilizers
Traditional growers will work manure and fertilizers into the soil and bank the soil up under the vines – thereby also protecting them from frost. The choice lies with the type and amount of fertilizer. On steep sites, to counter any runoff, the soil may be brought back up the hillside.

Vineyard maintenance
Between the end of harvest and the commencement of pruning, much vineyard maintenance is carried out: prunings are removed – and either burned or chopped up and incorporated into the soil – and trellising is checked.

So different are the problems of balancing the metabolism of a typical New World vine on a high-potential site that academics and growers have gone back to basics, analyzing the influences at work so that they can study them one by one. Mechanization appears to be the first step toward a solution.

Australia: brutally radical ...

In the early 1960s, Coonawarra in South Australia was the testing ground for a completely radical experiment, lasting until 1979. The sequence of events was: first, the abandonment of all soil working and the use of herbicides to create a billiard-table-smooth and completely bare vineyard surface between the vines; then the introduction of mechanical harvesting (by no means a world first, although a relatively early one). Next, mechanical harvesters were adapted to perform the function of a mechanical pruning machine; finally came the implementation of what is euphemistically called "minimal pruning," which in reality means no winter pruning at all.

... but wonderfully cheap

The cumulative effect of putting these techniques and practices to use was to reduce the cost of producing each ton of grapes (including picking), in an area renowned for making some of Australia's finest wine, to a quarter of the cost of producing the same quantity using traditional methods – hand-pruning, summer training, some cultivation or grass mowing and hand-picking.

From an economic viewpoint, therefore, these techniques have everything to commend them. As one might expect, however, the implications for quality are much less clear, and analysis of the rationale and effect of each viticultural step explains why.

Old hat to till?

Working the soil is a time-hallowed practice with strong emotional overtones. It starts in the home garden; there is something intensely satisfying in the sight of a freshly turned plot, the moist, dark brown earth proclaiming its fertility, worms burrowing indignantly downward from the unwelcome light, weeds vanquished and lying in limp heaps beside the beds. Similarly, the sight of a freshly worked

Mechanical harvesters have many virtues: not least the fact that they can be converted to hedging machines in winter and "prune" a whole vineyard in no longer than it takes to remove its grapes.

vineyard, weeds and grass removed, the vines in soldierly rows and bright green canopies in stark contrast to the brown soil, brings a feeling of deep satisfaction.

Soil satisfaction

And yet, working the soil with modern tractor-drawn equipment can be and often is very destructive. To start, every time a conventional tractor is driven along a row of vines, it compacts the subsoil, and the tractor tires necessarily run over the prime root zones. Working the top 12 inches (30 cm) of the soil does no more than hide the problem underneath. Of course, tractors cannot be eliminated from vineyards, although the lightweight, over-the-vine tractor common in France has advantages: its tires run down the middle of the row, and the compaction is less. Biodynamic vineyards have also seen the return of the horse. Equally undesirable, conventional cultivators destroy the all-important structure of the topsoil in which the fine feeder roots of the vine are so active during the growing season. In its undisturbed state, the soil builds up an active ecosystem with bacteria, worms and other organisms all helping to create nutrients and nitrogen for the vine to use. Paradoxically, undisturbed soil can also be much more effective in capturing water falling on its surface, be it from rainfall or irrigation. It establishes a capillary action that sucks the water downward, and surface evaporation is also less than that from worked soil.

If the decision is taken not to work the soil in any way, the question then arises of what to do with the weed and grass growth. Weeds vary from a mere visual nuisance to serious competitors for moisture and nutrients. Apart from specialized applications with organic farming, they need to be eliminated. The almost universal solution is to establish a weed- and grass-free band directly under the vine canopy, and these days herbicides are widely used to do this. After several years' application the top inch or two of the surface soil becomes sterile, and occasional weed growth is easy to control.

A Napa Valley grower favors an eco-friendly solution: sowing mustard between his vines and plowing it in as "green manure."

Machine pruning

Mechanical pruning is now so widely practiced that it has almost ceased to be controversial. The basic technique calls for the vine to be hedged by horizontal and vertical cutter bars, so that the pruned vines look like endless rows of hedgehogs. This process only works, though, where the vines are trellised at a constant height that is within the working range of the pruning machine. It also necessarily involves the vines being spur-pruned rather than cane-pruned. Traditionalists predicted at first that the vines would strangle themselves and die. They do not, although experience does show that a certain amount of cleaning up by hand pays off.

The initial reaction of the vine to machine pruning is to produce much higher yields; these eventually settle back and production then tends toward smaller berry and bunch weights, which help counterbalance loss of quality.

Minimal pruning

While minimal pruning has fallen out of favor, a hybrid, partially mechanized system is common. The first pass through the vineyard is by machine in a process called pre-pruning. This cuts all the canes from the year's growth 12 inches (30 cm) or so above the permanent, spur-pruned cordon. "Pulling off" the severed canes can be done quickly by unskilled labor, leaving the hand-pruners a clear field, markedly increasing their speed. In all except small vineyards, pneumatic pruning shears are used, with half a dozen pressurized leads rolling out on spools from the tractor-driven compressor at the end of the rows. On a quiet winter's day, there is

No vineyards are lovelier than the alleyways of pergolas that surround the fields of the Minho in northern Portugal. Their vinho verde *does not call for very ripe grapes: freshness and an acidic bite are guaranteed by growing them in the shade of their own canopies in a picturesque polyculture with vegetables and maize.*

something almost hypnotic in the *hiss-snick* sound of each cut as the pruners work along the rows.

Vines on fertile soil, supplied with everything they need to grow heartily, can become like spoiled children. They will establish a massive root system loaded with carbohydrate reserves, grow excessively and smother their own grapes (and next season's latent buds) in dense shade. Such vines will produce a relatively low yield of grapes (as little as the "magic" number of 3.3 tons per acre/45 hl per ha), but their wine will have low color intensity, a high pH, high malic acid content, low flavor and only moderate alcohol content.

"California sprawl"

Some call this phenomenon "California sprawl": when a vine dedicates most of its superabundant energy to growing leaves and canes, and only a small part to growing and ripening grapes. It is a no-win situation because however the vine is pruned, the result will be more or less the same.

How, then, does one satisfactorily control vigor in a high-yielding New World site, and how does one measure (or quantify) the success of such control? One of the answers has been to increase the planting density from the traditional 600 to 900 vines per acre (1,500 to 2,250 per ha) to around 1,350 vines per acre (3,300 per ha). But in practice this has a negligible effect on vine vigor. It may well result in a more efficient land use and, coupled with an appropriately complex trellis, may result in an increased yield of higher-quality grapes, but it is not an answer in itself.

Vigor control

On the contrary, very close planting on fertile sites can lead to a vicious circle of furious growth, leading to an impenetrable canopy of shade where few buds receive any worthwhile light. The few that grow just add to the mass of sappy vegetation.

Too much shade

Leaves properly exposed to sunlight have a much higher photosynthetic capacity than those that are shaded, leading to higher levels of sugar (carbohydrate) in the vine's system. Conversely, shaded shoots borrow sugars from elsewhere in the vine (including the grapes) to acquire energy for their growth. Buds that have been shaded in the previous growing season are less likely to break (or shoot) the following spring, and if they do break, are likely to be significantly less fruitful. Flowering and fruit-set are also impaired. It is thus not hard to understand why a shaded canopy will be less productive than one that is well exposed.

And as we have seen, shade also plays a major role in reducing grape quality. Shaded leaves and shaded bunches produce thin, soapy wine that has aberrant flavors, excessively herbaceous in the case of Semillon, Sauvignon Blanc and Cabernet Sauvignon, overly peppery in the case of Syrah (Shiraz) and so on. The incidence of botrytis, powdery mildew and downy mildew also increases sharply.

One answer to the problem was to go in the opposite direction and plant the vines as widely apart as 10 feet by 10 feet (3 m by 3 m), 450 vines per acre (1,110 per ha). This allows the grape-grower to control vine vigor naturally by exposing to the light a sufficient number of buds upon an appropriately designed trellis. The so-called "big vine" theory is, however, less attractive than it once was.

Australian viticulturist Dr. Richard Smart says that the ideas that a struggling vine makes the best wine and that low yields give highest quality are widely held in Europe:

A struggling vine

> *A common feature of both struggling vines and low-yielding vineyards is that, associated with lower vigour, the canopies have a good microclimate, i.e., most leaves and bunches are exposed to the sun. It is my belief that many of the quality attributes of low-yielding, struggling vineyards can be explained by this fact.*

Quantity vs. Quality?

Or can they be compatible?

No wine-grower will seriously attempt to deny that there is a relationship between quantity and quality. Every era of wine growing has acknowledged the fact; the assumption is built into almost all systems of wine law, and obvious extreme examples of what the French call *faire pisser la vigne* are known to all wine-lovers.

Wine-lovers also believe, even if they have no scientific proof, that the sensation of intensity and depth in certain very old wines that still live on from the early years of the 20th century, or even before, derives at least in part from the tiny yield (by modern standards) of their vineyards. Whether for good reasons or bad, most of the established vineyards throughout the world used to yield only a quarter of what they produce today.

Bordeaux in the 1980s   Yet the relationship is not a simple one. In the words of Bruno Prats, former owner of Château Cos d'Estournel:

> *If a mathematician were to study the relationship between the quality of the last 10 vintages of Bordeaux* [he said this in 1989] *and the volume of the harvests, he would inevitably conclude that the bigger the harvest, the better the wine.*

Within reasonable limits, in other words, when all goes well in a healthy vineyard, both quantity and quality increase.

Burgundy in the 1920s   When it comes to longevity, though, these words from Etienne Grivot, a highly respected and conservative grower in Vosne-Romanée (whose wines these days are superb), give a rather different perspective:

> *In 1980 I tasted many of the wines in our cellars. The wines of the early 1970s were then very nice, but are no more. But the 1929 was incredible; it is and always was very young and fresh, with big fruit, perfect color, good acid and great elegance. We also have some villages-appellation wine from 1952 which tastes younger than our 1980, with more body. So for me my first objective is to make wine from good fruit. And with the fruit of 50 years ago even if there was a lot of rot it would be impossible to make bad wine because production was so small, and the potential was so big. Even if you extracted only 40 to 50 percent of the potential of the fruit it was enough to make a good wine. Today you are working with a much smaller potential but much better technique. In the old days, with all their difficulties and mistakes, they still made great wine.*

Lip service to limits   There is – and one suspects there always will be – a certain lack of reality in the discussion about yield, and about the relationship between quantity and quality. Producers of wine that aspires to anything above the status of *vin ordinaire* all pay lip service to the necessity of limiting production. An increasing number in both the Old World and the New go further and talk of the need to reduce it. Yet there is a gap between the theory and the reality; all over the world yields are increasing, although the rate of increase has abated.

The quality ladder

In the simple world of jug wine, *vin ordinaire*, or what Australians call "Château Cardboard," yield is of little account. So long as the grapes are able to reach satisfactory sugar levels, the more the merrier. But then comes a distinction that is much less clear, and where yield is intensely debated: that between wine that is merely good, and wine that deserves to be called great.

Those who produce great wine, those who buy and consume it, those who write about it and most of those who read about it need no persuasion that it is a world apart from good wine, even *very* good wine. Many of those who make good or very good wine seek to deny that the gulf really exists. They ascribe it to clever marketing or Gallic romancing. Those who cannot afford to buy great wine tend to be equally dismissive – particularly if they have never tasted it.

Gallic romancing?

The wine professional who, over the years, tastes several thousands of good, very good and great wines (many in blind tastings) knows that there is indeed a difference, and that it cannot be explained by marketing alone. Certainly, labels (and reputations) have a powerful influence; confronted with a bottle of Château Latour or Romanée-Conti, you have to be brave and very experienced (or naive and exceedingly foolish) to criticize it. What is more, one can (and should) draw upon the knowledge of bloodlines in assessing such wines in their youth.

So the perception engendered by the label *is* important in establishing the difference. But there is more to it. The makers of great wines almost invariably invest more time and money in the process, if only because the price at which it sells means they can afford to. Certainly, there have been periods when great estates have fallen temporarily into decline, but these have been the exceptions that have proved the rule.

The French rule of thumb is that you cannot make great red wine if the yield exceeds 3.7 tons per acre (50 hl per ha). It brings forth vociferous protests from New World growers and from more than a few who make what ought to be great wine in the Old. This chapter is concerned with justifying the proposition. However yield is measured, there is no question of relating it directly to quality. As any student of elementary logic will tell you, the fact that great wine is made from a yield not greater than 3.7 tons per acre (50 hl per ha) does not mean that all 3.7-tons-per-acre yields will produce great wine.

The measurement of yield

Yield is usually measured either in tons of grapes or hectoliters of wine. The conversion factor between the two is not entirely simple. One ton of grapes at normal maturity will yield between 500 and 675 liters of juice. The range depends on three things: the size of the berries (and hence of the bunches), what type of press is used and how heavily the must is pressed. In a low-yielding vineyard, the berries will usually be smaller, with a higher ratio of stalks, skins and pips to pulp – in other words, there will be less juice available in each pound of grapes. As the berry and bunch size goes up, so does the relative proportion of juice. A yield of one ton per acre is equivalent to about 13.5 hectoliters per hectare (hl per ha).

Even the handmade wines of the great Bordeaux châteaus vary widely in yield from vintage to vintage. Since the 1980s, top growths have often found themselves with far more grapes than they want, and have to resort to thinning the bunches in midsummer.

An almost inane example is a 7.5-tons-per-acre (100 hl per ha) crop reduced by hail and rot to 3.7 tons per acre. Another rather more realistic example is a 3.7-tons-per-acre crop produced from virus-infected vines in an ailing condition; another is a crop produced from an old vineyard in which one-third of the vines are dead (or missing altogether), a fifth are barren, and less than half are producing; another is a crop produced by vines suffering severely from drought.

Less can be worse, too

The yield-quality relationship (if it exists) is not a simple linear one. As one dips below 3.7 tons per acre it by no means follows that there will be any increase in quality. It may be maintained, but more probably it will decrease, reflecting vines that are either diseased or excessively stressed. Very old vineyards also complicate the question: the chances are that many of their vines will be either decrepit or even missing. A helicopter flight over long-established vineyards is very revealing. Some have so many gaps that the yield-per-vine of what is left must be alarmingly high to maintain even the 3.7-ton standard.

Quality plateaus

As the yield exceeds 3.7 tons per acre, the implications are very different. There is a strong and respected school of thought that says that once the yield exceeds this amount, quality immediately reaches a level that can – with appropriate viticulture and canopy management – be increased to 7.5 tons per acre without any further significant drop in quality. Like the primary benchmark of 3.7 tons per acre, this secondary plateau will prompt a spirited response from some quarters, though it too has to be qualified and expanded. There are many variables that have to be taken into account, of course, including grape variety, clonal selection, rootstock selection, vine age, soil status and

Tight, narrow-row planting in Alsace (right) is typical European philosophy of letting vines compete with, yet shelter, one another. In total contrast, the Madonna vineyard in California's "high-potential" Carneros region (far right) has rows up to 10 feet (3 m). In spring the vineyard looks strangely empty. By vintage time the wine canopies will almost touch across the rows.

site potential, vine health (nematodes, viruses and phylloxera) and use of fertilizers, fungicides and herbicides.

Of these, the most significant is grape variety, and most particularly (as we shall see later in the chapter) whether it is white or red. It seems to be generally accepted that the quality of white wine is much less susceptible to deterioration through yield increase; certainly most winemakers aspiring to make great wine would support this view, suggesting that yields 10 to 20 percent higher than for red varieties will give wines of equivalent quality. The challenge to this proposition comes from vineyards such as Le Montrachet, whose average yield is half that of most of the other white Burgundy appellations, and whose wine has a wonderfully distinctive power and flavor.

Even when it comes to red grapes and wines, there are significant and commonly agreed variations. Pinot Noir is the most sensitive of all varieties to increased yields, readily losing color and flavor. Syrah (Shiraz) reaches a certain point and then abruptly collapses. The most resilient is Cabernet Sauvignon, with its naturally small berries and thick skins, which provide stout resistance to excessive water from any source. Petit Verdot is in the same class.

Relative sensitivity

Not even the First Growths of Bordeaux have escaped the net of significant increases in production (only a small part of which may be explained by increases in vineyard area). The period of 1945 to 1949 was one of unusually low yields. The most obvious reasons are that the vines had been starved of fertilizers during and immediately after the war; that all replanting came to an end with the onset of the

Bordeaux yields up

Controlling the yield to maintain quality

The yields permitted under appellation regulations (between 2.2 tons per acre (52 hl per ha) for a Burgundy *grand cru* and 3.7 tons per acre (50 hl per ha) for a Mâcon) are regularly exceeded by up to 50 percent. Even a traditionalist such as Bruno Prats is able to say with a straight face:

In my view, the ideal qualitative vineyard remains that of the Médoc, founded on very poor soils, with a high plantation density. It can produce yields of 40 to 60 hectoliters per hectare of extremely refined wines, as long as the vines are old. This is not a controversial statement.

How can it not be controversial when the commune appellation limit is 3 tons per acre (40 hl per ha) and yields 50 percent higher are routine? First, regular dispensations are granted by the authorities in "abundant" years. Second, plots with excessive yield are routinely declassified. So great has the increase been that "serious" proprietors regularly send workers into the vineyards in July and August to "bunch-thin," or cut off a significant proportion of the unripened crop – a job not relished by the staff, whose pride is in nurturing the grapes.

---

war; and that the timing of the massive replanting after phylloxera meant that the majority of the vineyards were not at this stage fully mature. Add it all up, and the results were low-yielding vines, subeconomic by the standards of today, but capable of producing great wine even at artisan level, let alone First Growth.

On the other side of the page there have been a number of "advances" since 1945. The well-run modern vineyard should have 100 percent of its vines either actually or potentially bearing a roughly equal crop per vine, in total contrast to the situation 50 or 100 years ago. Before questioning whether this is indeed a perfect situation, how has it occurred? Briefly, through clonal selection of vines certain to crop well and regularly; through rootstock selection, which can (according to some views though not others) support higher-than-desirable yields; through a successful war on viruses; through use of fertilizers; through better canopy manipulation; through the use of highly effective fungicides and insecticides; and, finally, through the economic imperative that says the producer cannot afford the luxury of a dead, diseased or infertile vine.

A warning note If all this seems positive, Peter Sichel sounded a warning note:

> *Clonal selection is a major concern. Clonal selections have been primarily for health, and some attention has been paid to color, sugar, acidity, balance and that kind of thing. But there has been very little work done on clones that more or less transcribe the character of the soil. That worries me, because if we are not careful, it seems to me – although remember I am not a technician on this kind of thing – it will be easy to develop clones that have a lot of color, a lot of personality, but which will completely dominate the soil-character aspect of our wines, and that – quite apart from the problem of excessive yields – people seem frighteningly unconscious of this danger of the clone dominating the soil.*

The German debacle

Yield changes in Germany have exceeded all others. Since the 19th century, yields have risen from 1.3 tons per acre (17 hl per ha) (the average for 1870 to 1879) to 7.7 tons per acre (104 hl per ha) (the average for 1970 to 1979). Prodigious yields, even up to 30 tons per acre (400 hl per ha), have been obtained; 50 is routine in some areas. In the 19th century (and earlier), German Riesling from the Rhine Valley was regarded as the longest-lived of all table wines and was frequently sold when 50 or more years old, with 100-year-old bottles not uncommon. In 1830 at Hochheim, 1775, 1776 and 1748 were the "fine old vintages" commonly offered. Price lists published in the latter part of the 19th century show that the top Rhine wines cost more than Bordeaux First Growths or the finest Champagne.

More wine, less taste The all-encompassing malaise that overcame German wines in the 1970s and 1980s, notwithstanding some great vintages, can be ascribed to many things. The deliberate lowering of quality thresholds by the new national wine laws in 1971 is fundamental, but excessively complicated labeling, unpredictable shifts of fashion between sweeter and drier wines, and (paradoxically) the success of "reliable" brands such as Blue Nun have all played a part. But to most observers, the root cause lies in the dilution and attenuation of flavor intensity and structure brought about by the prodigious increases in yield.

Happily, the great estates have become aware of this just in time. Today a top wine from the Rüdesheimer Berg or Johannisberg will have a similar yield to a Bordeaux *cru classé*. Yet it will take decades to undo the damage caused by past overproduction.

Yields have risen in the New World just as they have in the Old. The figures for Australia show the same dramatic escalation since 1945, from less than 1.5 tons per acre (20 hl per ha) to more than 6 tons per acre (80 hl per ha) in 2004. However, these figures are averages for all regions. Thus the Riverland of South Australia yields over 10 tons per acre (140 hl per ha), the Hunter Valley 3.3 tons per acre (45 hl per ha), the Yarra Valley and Tasmania about 3.7 to 3.9 tons per acre (50–52 hl per ha). But the debate becomes more complicated: what is an acceptable yield and how do you limit it when your high-potential vineyard is so fertile that the sky is the limit?

Australia: up *440*%

Dr. Richard Smart goes straight to the heart of the problem:

> *Most New World vignerons select vineyard sites that are too high in potential to give them top-quality wine, yet they all want it.*

We saw some of the means used to limit yields (and the reasoning behind them) in the previous chapter. Here it is sufficient to accept that, in the New World, just as in the Old, yields in most vineyards have overreached their potential to make outstanding wine. (There are exceptions, though: the great California Cabernet Sauvignons from the dry-land vineyards on the Rutherford Bench and Penfolds Grange from South Australia are good examples.)

Perhaps a cautionary note should be sounded here. There is a vast gulf between supermarket wine – made in large quantities in wineries that look more like oil refineries, bought and sold for, and to, a market largely driven by price, store position and colorful convenience packaging – and super-premium wines. At the other end of the scale, and wherever in the wine-producing world you look, the top of the quality/price pyramid is very small. Even Burgundy has only 1 percent *grand cru*, 11 percent *premier cru*, then 23 percent communal appellations (e.g. Chablis, Nuits-St-Georges, etc.), with two-thirds (65 percent) enjoying only regional AC-Bourgogne or Bourgogne Aligoté status – the stuff of supermarkets.

If out of all of this you sense a feeling of crisis and confusion, you are not far wrong. What, in broad terms, has happened is this: since the start of the 20th century, growers have gained access to a large number of scientifically derived techniques and tools previously undreamed of. As these became available, growers enthusiastically adopted them with minimal consultation with winemakers, and even less consideration for the style or taste of the wine. This trend extended well beyond grapes; the story of the breeding in California of the perfect tomato, a perfect sphere that was of a constant size, that would withstand packaging and transportation without bruising or marking, that would ripen perfectly when gassed in a cool store and that had absolutely no taste, is but one example.

Back from the abyss?

Somewhat grudgingly, the growers were forced to agree that the winemakers should have some say. Trial batches of wine were made, and full chemical analyses undertaken. The growers were still interested primarily in increased yield, but they began to accept that the chemical composition should not suffer unduly. The next step forward was the admission that perhaps the wine should be tasted. The problems here were (and are) that the tastings tended to be of one experimental wine against another, and of very

Grudging agreement

young wines at that, conducted by technocrats or winemakers with limited vision. There was little or no attempt to place the wines in a broader context, either in terms of history or in terms of absolute quality. Now, the final phase has been reached; winemakers of all ages in all parts of the world are tasting wines and assessing grapes in an appropriately broad context.

Yield and white wines

If one does taste wines in the appropriately broad context, how does one draw conclusions about yield and its influence on quality? First, as previously noted, white wines are less obviously affected by increased yield, and most varieties can produce at least slightly higher yields than red grapes without appreciable loss of quality. The basic reason is simple enough: the skin of the grape, which plays a central role in red winemaking, plays almost no part in white winemaking. The white grapes are either pressed immediately after they have been crushed or are pressed as whole bunches. The latter technique reduces the extraction of color and flavor from the skins to an absolute minimum. Only in Alsace, Bordeaux (white) and parts of the New World (mainly with Chardonnay) do we find any deliberate attempt to extract flavor from the skins of white grapes, and then on a limited basis. Since it is the ratio of the pulp to skin that changes (by increasing) with higher yield, the proportionate loss of skin content is understandably less important.

Less important does not mean unimportant, however. One only has to look at the German experience with Riesling. As we have seen, as yield goes up, the tendency is for bunch and berry weight to increase. This in turn leads to higher pH, lower acidity and lower total flavor content at a given sugar level. In terms of taste, this means lower flavor intensity, less total flavor and softer wine that will not age so well. A young wine made of grapes from high-yielding vines will lack entirely the length of flavor of its low-yield counterpart; it will be less profoundly fruity and have less of the character of its variety. As it rapidly ages, the light, crisp, fresh fruit of its youth (if it was particularly well made) will fade, leaving a wine that is flabby, soft and rather empty on the palate. Such varietal character as it may have once had will have all but disappeared.

Yield and red wines

Red wine derives all of its color and a great deal of its flavor from its skins. It is perfectly possible, though it takes care, to make white wine from red grapes by pressing them before fermentation has had a chance to start (the use of Pinot Noir for Champagne is the best-known example). Assuming normal red winemaking, the most obvious diminutions with increased berry size (the usual result of higher yield) are in color, in stability of color and in "structure," derived from tannins and acids. Quite obviously, too, flavor intensity will be less.

But much depends on the winemaker's response. Doubtless he or she will seek to extract more from the grapes of high-yielding vines; if he or she is very skillful, that additional level of extraction may partially compensate for the inherent weakness. What is technically called overextraction results from less skillful winemaking. The result is a tough, hard, tannic wine in which the fruit will never have the aroma or flavor to balance the tannins; by the time the latter soften, the fruit will have gone. It must be said, though, that it is easier still to overextract concentrated, low-yield grapes.

The point of balance

The searching questions are: how much is too much, and how does one tie in sensory appreciation to a given yield? Even for a single small vineyard with a single grape variety there will not be an immutable or precisely predictable figure for maximum quality, and even less will there be a necessary correlation between yield and quality from one year to the next. As Bruno Prats has pointed out, many of the best vintages in Bordeaux during the 1980s happened to be the highest yielding. Turn the coin over to the New World, and some of the worst vintages have been drought-ravaged, low-yielding years in which flavor is either diminished or over the top, with cooked, jammy fruit, excessive tannins and so forth.

The focus returns to a vine in balance, both in terms of its architecture (the ratio of grapes, leaves, canes, wood and roots) and in terms of the growing season.

Plague and Pestilence

Enemies of the vine

Nature has a way of balancing things, and the attempts of the human population to interfere with its course can bring unpredictable consequences. Plants, animals, diseases and predators can live in perfect equilibrium in one environment; alter one element and the balance tips. As Australia's experience with the rabbit and the cane toad shows all too clearly, some of the greatest dangers arise when a creature is introduced into a new country.

The rich family of American grapevine species evolved over the millennia in temperate climates that encouraged the growth of downy mildew and oidium (aka powdery mildew or *Uncinula necator*) and in soils that harbored large colonies of the microscopic louse called phylloxera. In a Europe ever curious about the exotic plants and animals of the Americas, Australasia and Asia, it was inevitable that American vines would be introduced as novelties. With the wisdom of hindsight, it was also inevitable that they would bring with them the American

A coven of diseases, old and new

Even in the dry climate of Crete, antifungal sprays are necessary; in the New Worlds, air-conditioned cabins replace the face mask, providing comfort as well as protection.

diseases to which they had built up a near-total immunity. The European grapevine, *Vitis vinifera,* in contrast, had no such immunity, and fell prey with devastating rapidity.

Anthracnose

It is not easy to identify all the diseases of the vine that preexisted the American invasion, or be certain when they first appeared. The most significant was anthracnose, which some observers have suggested was active in Roman times. It develops in conditions of high humidity and warm temperatures (70°F/21°C), and causes dark stains on the leaves, shoots and grapes. It seldom causes problems now because the treatment (spraying the plants with copper sulfate, lime and water, or "Bordeaux mixture") is the same as that used for downy mildew, which is far more active.

Botrytis cinerea

Botrytis cinerea has been known since ancient times. Botrytis is a fungus that grows on the skin of the grapes. After several weeks of growth it punctures tiny holes in the grape skin that allow moisture (i.e., water) to escape. Under ideal conditions the mold does its work gradually, over a prolonged period, and as the water from the grape evaporates, sugar and acid in the juice will increase until they almost double their original concentration. For botrytis to work in this way very precise conditions are required: cold and dry nights to slow down the growth of the mold, and warm, humid midday temperatures between 59°F and 77°F (15°C to 25°C) to promote its growth. Under these circumstances, what the Sauternais call *pourriture noble* and the Germans *Edelfäule* produces the great sweet table wines of the world.

The grapes of Château d'Yquem. Botrytis cinerea rots their skins grape by grape, concentrating the juice to extraordinary intensity of sweetness and flavor.

If conditions are too dry or too cold, the mold will not develop. In Germany, 2003 was such a year; it was too hot and too dry. Many Beerenauslese and Trockenbeerenauslese wines were made, but with minimal influence from *Edelfäule*. The concentrated sweetness came from the grapes singly dehydrating into near-raisins. If conditions are excessively warm, humid and wet, on the other hand, the mold grows too quickly, and rapidly degenerates into gray mold: *pourriture grise*. It may also be accompanied by black rot, a disease of American origin that thrives at temperatures of around 70°F (21°C). The result is total loss of the crop: nothing can be made of it.

Botrytis is included here as a disease because it is a major problem (if left unchecked) for makers of dry white and all red wines. What is more, it can (and frequently does) attack the vine at flowering, leading to the outright death of the bunch before the grapes have even begun to form. Systemic sprays therefore have to be used in the cool, humid regions that are prone to attack in spring. A small degree of botrytis in white grapes, however, may not be a bad thing, even when making dry wines such as Chardonnay: it accentuates and adds to the complexity of the total flavor.

Prophylaxis in the vineyard

In red wine, botrytis is always unwelcome. And the problem is that it will attack red grapes as readily as it does white, respecting neither plot boundaries nor the prayers of the vigneron. It is especially harmful to red wine color, lightening it and leading to premature browning. European growers have to deal with a percentage of rot (noble and ignoble) in almost every vintage; sulfur dioxide added to the crushed grapes is the standard response, and where the level of infection is minor, all is well. Prophylaxis in the vineyard is the better answer. There is hope, but no certainty, that years such as 1963, 1965 and 1968 will never occur again. In these years the red wines of Bordeaux and Burgundy were all but totally destroyed by mold.

The golden years

Other pre-American diseases were relatively minor, and in 1850 the general health of European vines was excellent. The productive life of a vine was generally recognized to be 70 to 80 years, and regeneration was an easy matter: simply bury a cane in the ground, leaving its tip exposed, and a new vine identical to its parent would take root. This technique of layering (or *marcottage)* is still practiced in those parts of the world where phylloxera and nematodes are yet to invade. Especially in a mature vineyard, it was the most effective way of replacing a single vine, as, if a rootling was planted, the competition from the surrounding vines often severely stunted its growth. (It is for this reason that, in Europe, rather than replant on a vine-by-vine basis, whole sections of vineyard are removed and replanted together.)

The consequence of such good health was that the vine could ripen its crop fully in most years, and the vigneron could wait until late in the season until picking, without the threat of oidium and mildew. French viticulture was entering a golden age. In 1855, Napoleon III presided over the Paris International Exhibition, which gave rise to the Bordeaux classification of that year. The 1858, 1864, 1865, 1869, 1870, 1874, 1875 and 1878 vintages were of such fabulous quality that well-preserved bottles still provide vinous nectar today; between 1850 and 1875, France's total vineyard area increased in size by 500,000 acres (202,500 ha).

Further scourges

Oidium

Around 1850 (some say 1845, others 1854) oidium, or powdery mildew, arrived from the U.S. Alarming crop losses of up to a quarter of the potential harvest were the result. It took 10 years to find the right treatment, but, once discovered, powdered sulfur dusted on the vines proved an enduring antidote. Oidium seemed to be a mere hiccup in a triumphant progress. But far worse was in store. In 1869, Professor Westwood of Oxford University was to write the following words:

> In the month of June 1863, I received from Hammersmith a vine leaf covered with minute, gall-like excrescences, "each containing," in the words of my correspondent, "a multitude of eggs, and some perfect Acari, which seem to spring from them, and sometimes a curiously corrugated coccus."

Phylloxera

This was the first description (in Europe) of *Phylloxera vastatrix*, the tiny louse that was to change the face of European viticulture forever, and many would say for the worse. And rather than leave that suggestion in the air, as it were, it is not for the reason that Professor George Saintsbury and others averred – namely that grafted vines per se were inferior to ungrafted vines. That myth is comprehensively answered by countries such as Australia, in which grafted and ungrafted vines exist side by side, and no one believes or suggests there is any necessary quality differential. The causes of the change for the worse are far more complicated, as we shall see.

Downy mildew

The last of America's unfriendly contributions to European wine growing was a

Phylloxera vastatrix

The effects of phylloxera eclipsed all other viticultural disasters when it arrived in Europe, doubtless carried in with botanical specimens brought from the U.S. by plant collectors. This tiny insect attacks the roots of *vinifera* vines, injecting them with poisonous saliva. With a healthy international trade in vine cuttings, and no effective quarantine, the insect found its way all over Europe, to South Africa, Australia and New Zealand, as well as California, by the end of the 19th century.

new and aggressive form of mildew (known as "downy" to distinguish it from the "powdery" oidium) that appeared in 1878. By this time, the scientists were alert. Within only four years Bordeaux University had brewed the cure, a bright blue mixture of copper sulfate and lime, known to this day as "Bordeaux mixture," which is sovereign against fungus diseases of most kinds.

Viruses in the vineyard

One might think this litany of afflictions was enough, but an even more sinister attack was being mounted against the vines of Europe. Vine viruses had been in existence for thousands of years: descriptions from Roman times leave no doubt of their existence. But it is clear that their incidence was not severe, nor is there any evidence of spread from infected to healthy vines.

The need for universal grafting to combat phylloxera changed the situation radically. Many of the American rootstocks brought into Europe for this purpose were (and are) carriers of viruses without showing any symptoms. In their apparent innocence they introduced two devastating viruses, "fan-leaf" and "leaf-roll," to the vineyards of the world. Grafting onto infected rootstocks dramatically increases the risk of viral infection, and one of the main concerns of modern-day plant breeders is to ensure their rootstocks are virus-free.

If one takes the combined effect of oidium, mildew, viruses, young vines and some pretty indifferent weather, it is hardly surprising that the average quality of French wine slumped between 1878 and 1899. To lay the blame at the feet of the American rootstocks, as many have done, is only indirectly justifiable. As for viruses, there is no cure: prevention through clonal selection and, perhaps, genetic engineering are the only answers.

Above: *American rootstocks have a variable but limited tolerance to lime in the soil. Too much prevents their uptake of iron salts, leading to chlorosis and yellowing leaves.*

Right: *Reddening vine leaves with green veins indicate a viral infection. Many old vineyards are infected without suffering unduly, but heat treatment of propagating material to destroy viruses in new vines is now standard practice.*

There remains the threat of Pierce's disease, yet another American harbinger of doom. Endemic throughout Texas and Florida, it swept across the United States, over the Rocky Mountains, through southern California, to Anaheim in Los Angeles (it was originally called "Anaheim disease"). The cause is a bacteria that is spread by small winged insects called "sharpshooters." The bacterium breed in reeds and other streamside vegetation, so three things are needed: water, the bacteria and the vector (the sharpshooter). Perhaps for this reason it has not become a worldwide problem – although there have been suggestions that it has arrived in Europe. The implications (in Europe, as in California) are chilling, for – unlike phylloxera and nematodes – there is no known answer, other than the removal of the infected vines. The eradication of reeds and their attendant insects from all wine regions is a proposition that makes mere root-grafting look like child's play.

Pierce's disease

The United States of America, California particularly, was ravaged by a new outbreak of phylloxera in the early 1990s. A new and destructive mutant (they call it "phylloxera type B") destroyed vines with more ferocity than the familiar form. Phylloxera traveled across the Rocky Mountains from the east in about 1870, only a few years after its appearance in Europe, at much the same time as it arrived in Australia. Given the complexity of its life cycle, it is hardly surprising that there should be different biotypes, and it is suggested that at this time it was a relatively mild version that arrived in California. Ignoring the experience of grafting gained in France, Californians adopted *Vitis rupestris* hybrid rootstocks (ARG1, AXR and 1202) to counter the first invasion, which the French had earlier discarded because of their relatively low resistance, and which left the vines once again vulnerable to attack. An alternative theory to that of the mutant development of type B is that there was a fresh infusion of phylloxera from the east, including the more active biotypes that had traveled to Europe a century before. The Napa Valley alone faced a cost of $1 billion to replant up to 80 percent of its vines using more phylloxera-resistant roots.

California and phylloxera type B

Australia has been through it, too. In 1875 phylloxera was identified at Geelong, just to the west of Melbourne, one of Victoria's leading wine areas. Notwithstanding that grafting had been identified as the solution, the government of the day ordered the wholesale eradication of all infected vineyards. When the louse appeared at Bendigo in central Victoria in the 1880s, the same orders were made. Two flourishing wine regions disappeared overnight, and it was almost 100 years before vines reappeared in these areas. The rationale was to protect the wine industry in northeast Victoria, but in vain. By 1900 it had taken a firm hold there. This time, at least, grafting was preferred to compulsory eradication.

The Australian phylloxera invasion

Phylloxera stopped at the Murray River. It has never penetrated South Australia, thanks to stringent quarantine precautions. And although it was active around both Sydney and Brisbane, it has similarly never affected the Hunter Valley. Even more surprising (and inexplicable) has been the escape of the isolated Chateau Tahbilk, in the Goulburn Valley of central Victoria, where Syrah (Shiraz) vines planted in 1860 remain defiantly in production, among adjoining plots long since devastated by phylloxera and replanted on grafted rootstocks. (You can purchase a special bin wine made solely from these vines.) Here, at least, there is an explanation: the old Syrah is planted on sandy soil through which phylloxera cannot travel – it prefers rocky or clay soils that crack in dry weather.

The Chileans frequently like to claim that theirs is the only country in the world producing wine from "pre-phylloxera" vines, which is actually untrue. It is certainly a viticultural paradise in which diseases of all kinds are virtually unknown. But others include the whole island of Cyprus, part of Hungary, sandy seaside vineyards at Colares in Portugal and in the Midi, and a whole catalog of areas, big and small, where phylloxera has not (so far) installed itself.

Chile: a vine-grower's paradise

When the vines have survived every threat and are laden with ripening fruit, it is the turn of the birds and wasps to destroy the crop. At Coldstream Hills in the Yarra Valley, Victoria, vulnerable areas away from the winery have to be netted against attack.

New Zealand and South Africa

New Zealand shows how vulnerable vineyards remain. Notwithstanding all the knowledge of quarantine procedures and of phylloxera's life cycle, and notwithstanding the watery barrier of the Cook Strait separating the North and South Islands, it took little more than a decade for phylloxera (long active in the North Island) to arrive on the South Island, at Marlborough. Viruses, too, are endemic in New Zealand and South Africa, and it is only in the past few years that South Africa has had access to Chardonnay vines that are not heavily virus-infected.

If we are to return to a golden age similar to that of the 19th century, it will be because we have eliminated viruses and (through genetic engineering) built in resistance to oidium and mildew. Whether this can be done without compromising varietal character, nobody knows. What is certain is that it will not be through the development of more powerful fungicides; both past and present tell us that chemical control is not the way to go.

Irrigation

A necessary evil?

Irrigation is one of the more emotive words in viticulture, and hence one of the least understood; there is nothing like a touch of good old-fashioned prejudice to stand in the way of truth. The French ban its use in most appellation zones (it is permitted in parts of the Midi), and out of that ban stems a surprisingly widely held view that irrigation and quality are incompatible.

The vine, like any other plant, demands a certain amount of water during its growing season. How much will depend on factors such as growing-season temperatures, wind speed, humidity, sunshine hours and inherent vigor (influenced by clone, rootstock, variety, soil and cultivation), to name but a few.

A certain amount of irrigation is necessary for vineyards in all of Australia's wine regions. The only large vineyard established there in the last 35 years without it is in the Hastings Valley on the New South Wales coast. It must also be remembered that in a country such as Australia, wide climatic fluctuations occur. In wet years there may be little or no need for irrigation, but in drought years the need becomes acute. New World growers have therefore developed a simple litmus test: look at the grass by the roadside during summer; if it is green, there is no need for irrigation. In most of Australia you may be assured that it is brown.

The situation in most French vineyards – certainly in Bordeaux and Burgundy – is entirely different. Ignoring for the moment climate change and vintages such as 1989 and 2003, rainfall and humidity in the growing season supply the vine naturally with most, if not all, of the moisture it needs. What is more, the structure of the soil and subsoil of areas such as the Médoc has excellent moisture-retention capacity.

But as in all matters viticultural, there are no absolutes, no simple rules of thumb. The widely held theory is that if you deny a vine easy access to water it will send its roots deep in search of it, and in so doing find flavor-enhancing nutrients that surface roots cannot collect. At best, this is a deceptive half-truth. Conversely, no grower in search of maximum quality wishes to have to rely on irrigation. He or she will be more than happy to have it available as a fallback, but would prefer the vine to find its water naturally. Nature, though, is unpredictable. Ask any farmer anywhere in the world about the weather and you will receive a long and detailed dissertation about the shortcomings of the current season.

Viticultural research has increasingly shown that the timing of irrigation is as important as its extent. Two of the most vulnerable periods are flowering and *véraison*: the time at which grape color changes and cell division stops. Too little water during and immediately after flowering will result in poor fruit-set and in berry-shatter (the tiny berries simply fall off), while too little water up to and during *véraison* will lead to reduced berry size (not necessarily a bad thing).

As always, there are choices and there are consequences. Irrigation can be used to increase yields, by promoting growth of bigger berries, bigger bunches and more bunches per vine, without any adverse effect on the crude chemical measurements of sugar, acid and pH. Indeed, these measurements may be better than those of grapes produced from vines with less or no irrigation. If the aim is to produce white wine for sale in cask, jug or flagon, there is no question: this is the way to go. But

Water of course – but how much?

The limestone soils of Jerez that produce the finest sherry are admirable sponges for winter and spring rains (there is none in summer) if they are tilled to open the surface.

Irrigation for yield

The great advantage of drip irrigation is precision. Each vine has its own water supply and a measurable amount goes only where it is needed – drip by drip.

white wine is far less critical than red. Similarly, as the quality aspirations of the grower increase, the situation becomes more complicated.

Most modern irrigation systems use drip feeders, one dripper per vine, emitting precisely controlled amounts of water, usually between $\frac{1}{2}$ and 1 gallon (2 to 4 liters) and four liters per hour. These saturate an inverted cone-shaped area directly under the dripper. Where irrigation is used simply to increase yield, the vine becomes entirely dependent on this supply and develops a compact root system confined to the area wetted (close to the surface). In consequence, it may be necessary to introduce nitrogen and other minerals needed for the balanced growth of the vine through the irrigation system. It becomes, if you wish, a kind of hydroponics (or water culture), as far removed from the romantic notion of the struggling vine as one could imagine, but allowing the grower an almost godlike control.

In the 1990s two advanced irrigation techniques were developed in the New World. The first was regulated deficit irrigation (RDI), which imposed a soil-water deficit just before or after *véraison*, measured by tensiometers buried in the soil, typically at two different depths. The result was higher concentrations of anthocyanins and phenolics, leading to an improvement in wine aroma and taste. The sting in the tail was a reduction in berry size, berry numbers and hence yield, particularly when water was short before *véraison*.

Partial rootzone drying (PRD) is an even more sophisticated technique. It involves watering half the vine's roots with normal quantities (the quantum determined by tensiometer measurement in this zone) and withholding water from the other half. The two sides are then switched on a two-week cycle. The wet half supplies adequate water to the whole vine canopy, while the dry side reacts by synthesizing various chemical signals that command the vine to slow its vegetative growth. The results are a smaller canopy with fewer lateral shoots; undiminished berry and crop weights with better exposure to light and ventilation; half the water usage compared to normally irrigated vines; and similar improvements in grape and wine quality to those observed with RDI.

The poor quality of grapes grown under conditions of excessive irrigation is the indirect, rather than the direct, consequence of overwatering. The vine simply grows out of balance: the canopy becomes far too big for the crop, the fruit is then shaded, and the grapes ripen very late, if at all.

Furrow, flood and spray

Drip irrigation is the most controllable system, also the most efficient and the most sparing of water. But there are others. The most ancient form of irrigation – furrow or flood – is practiced in countries such as Chile, with the snow-capped Andes providing an inexhaustible (and essential) water source in a bone-dry summer. In the Langhorne Creek area of South Australia, the Bremer River is deliberately diverted in late winter to flood the vineyards, providing subsoil water reserves that last right through the summer. Then there is overhead spray irrigation, particularly suited to very dry climates in which mildews are not a problem, but doubly useful in areas subject to spring frosts. If a frost threatens, the sprays are turned on and the ice forming on the buds will insulate them from temperatures below freezing point.

Laissez-faire

In regions where the growing-season rainfall (and soil moisture reserves) is usually enough to keep the vines growing and ripen their fruit, there will inevitably be years with too much rain. In these vintages the crop will be diluted in flavor, will not ripen properly and will probably be affected by rot. Red wines will suffer most, and may be a far cry from the noble quality implied by the label. However, given normal or below-average rainfall, and assuming frost or hail have not intervened, the classic regions of Germany, France and Italy produce wines of such quality that the ban on irrigation becomes irrelevant. If a continuation of the extreme weather patterns of 2003 were to occur, attitudes might change, but not soon.

Spray irrigation has its own advantages. Although it uses more water, it cools the whole vineyard, and in spring doubles as a protection measure against late frosts. On freezing nights it can be used to coat the tender new shoots with a layer of ice to protect them from subzero temperatures.

Through empirical observation of vines, grapes and wines, we have already arrived at the proposition that 3.7 tons per acre (50 hl per ha) represents the maximum yield for red wines of the finest quality. The norm for irrigated vineyards is to exceed that level, in some instances by a wide margin. But reduced irrigation can restrict yield to almost any level one cares to choose. The real question is whether by so restricting yield, quality will be improved.

To take an extreme example, vineyards in many parts of Australia (whether or not irrigation is available and used) may suffer acute water stress late in the growing season: the leaves dry up and fall off and the vine stops growing. Even where favorable winter and spring growing conditions and fertile soil have set the vine off to a flying start, things can go badly wrong. Despite a strong canopy and crop potential, if the water supply fails and no reserve is available, the vine's photosynthetic activity will abruptly halt. The French call this condition "apoplexy."

It takes a skillful grower, to use irrigation to balance quantity against quality. He or she must know precisely what is happening in the soil surrounding the rootzone. Moisture-measuring devices (tensiometers or gypsum blocks) give a fairly accurate picture. The grower's decisions then have to be carefully weighed, using his or her experience of the particular vineyard. Restricting water supply before *véraison* can, if judged correctly, advantageously slow down the grapes' growth. Similarly, it is possible to promote ripening and simultaneously limit the weight of the bunches by restricting water after *véraison*. "Deficit irrigation" can produce grapes of very high quality if skillfully used, but the risks of miscalculation are high, and the consequences entirely counterproductive.

A technique developed in the early 2000s uses superfine mist sprays over the canopy to drop the microclimate temperature by 9°F to 18°F (5°C to 10°C) during the hottest parts of the day, a technique especially useful in the Australian Riverland, where the dry climate reduces the risk of mildew and botrytis to a minimum.

In a perfect world, irrigation would not be necessary. Exactly the right amount of spring and summer rain, followed by three weeks of warm, dry weather leading up to vintage, would produce grapes as good as the *terroir* and grape variety allow. In the real world, there will almost always be too much or too little rain. There is not much the vigneron can do about too much, but if there is too little, irrigation is preferable to inaction. In the final analysis, the controlled use of water in a vineyard is the one and only element of climate within the control of the wine-grower.

Irrigation for quality

Apoplexy

Mechanization

Simply a question of time?

The Industrial Revolution of the vine

Gradually at first, then gathering speed, and now seemingly unstoppable, the Industrial Revolution has at last reached the vineyards of the world. There have been two dress rehearsals: first, the introduction of the horse-drawn plow; second, that of the tractor. These innovations had a radical effect on the way vines were planted, and in particular on the pattern and density of the planting. However, the mechanization of today and tomorrow is something far more fundamental.

There will always be pockets of resistance, indeed corners where not even the plow will reach. It is hard to imagine any form of mechanization (other than helicopters) coming to the near-vertical face of the Bernkasteler Doktor or the terraces of Côte Rôtie. How long it will take for the Industrial Revolution to cross the conservative thresholds of the *grands crus* of Bordeaux and Burgundy, though, is an open question. Or, indeed, will organic and biodynamic practices reverse the trend?

Moreover, the choices made for vineyards producing supermarket or popular wines will be very different from those made by the custodians of great vineyards. Much of this chapter deals with the former, which account for 95 percent of the world's wine production.

The old adage was "where plows can go, no vines should go." It referred to such land as the astonishing terraced slopes of the Rhine and Mosel (right) – and the old belief that meager soils meant better wine.

In Europe, the pool of cheap labor provided by Portugal, Spain, Romania and Albania is drying up. In Australia, equal pay for men and women led, with peculiar irony, directly to the development of mechanical pruning. For women are by far the best vineyard workers on time-consuming jobs such as pruning and summer training, and if wage justice were taken to its logical conclusion they should have been paid *more* than men, not less. Equal pay was thrust upon them, and thousands lost their jobs forever as a result.

If robots can build motor vehicles, they can certainly perform the far simpler task of caring for vines. And just as with the motor industry, the cost efficiencies of the automated producers sooner or later force change on the more conservative – or force the less efficient out of business.

Extending the automobile analogy, exotica such as the Rolls-Royce and Lamborghini may well always be handmade – and sold for a price that reflects that care and cost. But what about the Mercedes-Benz, BMW, Lexus and Cadillac? More and more automation, less and less need for hand finishing. This is the future for wine, too. And at the so-called beverage end of the industry – casks, flagons, jugs, *vin ordinaire* – automation and mass-production techniques have been in use since the days of Henry Ford and his Model T.

Mechanization starts the day the vine is planted. Broad areas in the New World are planted by tractor-drawn devices that open up the soil, allow a seated operator to drop in the vine, and then close up the earth immediately afterward. The time and cost savings relative to planting by hand are huge, and the results are better because greater accuracy is possible. In fact, modern technology will have made its mark well before the vine was planted: lasers can be used to level the land with perfect precision, and vine rows established with equal care; computer-controlled drip irrigation will have been installed in advance, and the vines given an exactly measured quantity of water within hours of planting; the soil may have been fumigated against nematodes; and herbicides will ensure they begin life without any competition from grass or weeds.

In its first and second years, the modern New World vineyard may still need some hand labor. From this point on, mechanization can take over. Not only can the vines be mechanically pruned, but all the canopy training and trimming during the growing season can be mechanized, too. To this end the machines of the future – being developed simultaneously in Italy, Australia and the United States – are designed on a modular basis: a single mechanized basic frame can be quickly converted by interchanging spray unit, pruning and harvesting modules, providing three machines for the price of two or less. There are also French-designed machines that lift up the foliage in summer by clipping the movable foliage wires together, exposing the fruit underneath to sunlight. New Zealand has pioneered mechanical leaf-plucking machines to perform a similar task by removing excess leaves from around the fruit.

Whether or not the vineyard is mechanically pruned is a decision taken on grounds of cost and quality. The options, including minimal pruning, have been considered in previous chapters, but it is hard to imagine the greatest vineyards, either in France or anywhere else, opting for anything so imprecise as a hedgecutter. Pneumatic pruning shears are their compromise with mechanization.

Mechanical harvesting is another matter. Used in conjunction with hand-pruning, it has few disadvantages. Great advances were made in the 1990s and the early years of the 21st century in machine design (and operation). Contamination by leaves and fractured canes can be reduced to very low levels, and walking through a vineyard after it has been picked will show minimal disturbance of the canopy (other than the absence of grapes).

No more cheap labor

Is handmade best?

The march of the machine

Mechanical pruning

Mechanical harvesting

Right: Working in the cool of the night in the Napa Valley, a mechanical harvester looks like a fire-breathing dragon.

Below: The antithesis of mechanical harvesting: stackable plastic boxes for hand-picked grapes. The fruit is not damaged even by its own weight in these deluxe containers.

Cheaper, quicker, cooler

Cost is the most obvious advantage: a third to a quarter that of hand-picking if done by an independent contractor, less still if the grape-grower has a large enough area of vineyards to justify owning a grape harvester. Speed is another: mechanical harvesters can operate 24 hours a day, ensuring that large areas can be harvested rapidly before a change in the weather (or after if rot is developing), and that in hot regions grapes can be harvested at night, taking advantage of cooler temperatures and lower grape-sugar levels. This makes processing – particularly of white grapes – very much easier, and significantly reduces the need for, and high cost of, refrigeration.

... or a long, hot wait

In large vineyards, speed has a second implication for quality: reducing the time-lapse between harvesting and the grapes arriving at the winery. The typical method of hand-harvesting in the New World is to pick into buckets, tip the grapes from buckets into a tractor-drawn skip, and then either tip this into a larger bin on a truck or lift several skips progressively onto the truck. Either way, there can be a long, hot wait in the sun. The jostled and squeezed bunches break, their juice runs into the bottom of the containers, and oxidation gets to work. Mechanization of this process does not avoid breakage of the grapes, but significantly reduces the time over which oxidation can occur.

Controlled oxidation

In the early days of mechanization in the vineyard, mechanical harvesting, according to conventional wisdom, was suited to red grapes but not to white. The assumption was that any oxidation of white grape juice caused by breakage of the grapes too long prior to fermentation was necessarily a bad thing. Obviously, under hot and possibly dirty conditions, it was and remains a serious matter. But nowadays it may be, within limits, actually sought after: controlled oxidation is preached and practiced by winemakers in various parts of the Old and New World alike. They take no risks, though. They strictly limit oxidation to the level and timing they want by using field processing stations or by rushing the grapes to the winery, protected by a dusting of sulfur dioxide.

There are exceptions

At most points from planting to harvesting choices exist: neither size nor commitment to quality necessarily precludes mechanical options. But certain grapes, and certain wines, do. In Champagne, the bunches are always pressed whole; mechanical harvesters cannot cut whole bunches. Many Burgundians and other makers of Pinot Noir are equally adamant they must have at least a percentage of whole bunches and/or stalks in the must, once again precluding mechanical harvesting. The selective picking of grapes with noble rot for Sauternes does likewise. In the press, moreover, unfermented grapes without stalks tend to become a congealed mass: stalks and stems keep the mass open enough for the juice to drain out.

The other extreme

The most luxurious alternative to mechanical harvesting is the use of small stackable picking baskets usually containing 20 to 30 pounds (9 to 14 kg) of fruit, which are filled by the picker and transported without further movement or decanting to the winery. White grapes in hot climates may be stored in their baskets in a cool room overnight and crushed the following morning when they are thoroughly cooled (to 41°F/5°C or thereabouts). This is the gentlest possible handling option, more gentle than one usually finds in even the greatest French vineyards, where the common practice is to pick the grapes into baskets for the pickers to tip into a *hotte* on the back of a worker who walks through the rows, and for the contents of the *hotte* to be tipped into a tub, tray or other larger container that will be taken back to the cellar by tractor or horse, finally to be tipped into the destemmer or (if white grapes) press.

The use of sophisticated sorting tables – sometimes in tandem, one before the destemmer, one after – is increasingly common in the top châteaus. There may, indeed, be more trained workers at the sorting table than in the winery proper. The high prices routinely commanded for the best wines allow costs such as these to be easily absorbed, with an ongoing cycle of self-fulfilment.

From vineyard to winery

Rapid transit from vineyard to winery is always important. In most small European vineyards this is an academic problem: distances are typically measured in meters rather than miles. In the New World distances can be, and frequently are, measured in hundreds of miles. The time from harvesting to processing may be over 24 hours, which is not of undue moment with sound red grapes free of rot, but can give makers of white wine a serious problem. The delay in processing amounts to involuntary skin contact with the juice. When used by choice in the winery, this can be very beneficial. When imposed on the winemaker in an uncontrolled situation, it can lead to some strange results.

Ancient craft or technical excellence?

Anyone who has planted a vine, watched it grow, picked its crop and made its wine feels the deep satisfaction of the ancient craft. The more the process is mechanized, the less that personal satisfaction. But 95 percent or more of the world's wine has not been made traditionally for a long time. Much of it has become a mass-produced beverage, little different from beer or spirits. Quality, though, lies not in the facts of handcraft or mechanization, but in their application – and, increasingly, in the sheer technical excellence of the machines themselves.

IN THE WINERY

Making the Wine

Winery equipment and how to use it

The line between the vineyard and the winery is not as absolute and clear-cut as it might seem at first sight. The winery – and much of its equipment – is but a passing phase in the transition from grape to wine, and as demonstrated by the grapes stored in clay jars, it is not even essential for that. The battery of equipment to be found there cannot of itself guarantee quality, create identity or forge style. These things come primarily from the grapes and the winemaker's imprint on them: the skill with which he or she manipulates the winery tools and imposes his or her thumbprint is the key.

The first tool to be found in most wineries is the crusher, an invention of the late 19th century. It is sometimes called a crusher-destemmer, in deference to the two quite separate functions it performs: crushing or splitting the berries to liberate the juice and then removing the berries from the stem of the bunch. Most crushers pass the bunches through a series of rollers first (to crush the berries), then separate the stalks with beaters revolving within a slotted cage: the already crushed berries drop through the slots and the stalks are ejected through the open end of the cage.

Some crushers destem first (and are known as destemmer-crushers), while most modern versions – in whichever configuration – have adjustable rollers that permit the winemaker to select anything from virtually whole berries to fully crushed grapes.

In many parts of the world (notably Champagne), makers of sparkling wine, and an increasing number of makers of high-quality white table wines, bypass the crusher altogether, placing the whole bunches directly into the press. The pressing process is much slower as a result, but the juice yielded is clearer and finer.

Makers of certain red wines using carbonic maceration techniques may also wholly or partially bypass the crusher – the most obvious examples being Beaujolais winemakers, who incorporate some whole bunches or use *pigeage* (foot stamping) for part of the *cuvée*.

New World makers of white wine who have chosen to crush the grapes may well pass the must through a device called a "heat exchanger" on its way to the press.

A battery of tools

Crusher-destemmers

Opposite: *Most of the world's wine today is made in plants as romantic as an oil refinery. Grapes look vulnerable and out of place in such a harsh industrial environment, yet nothing need necessarily be lost just because the scale is big.*

Cooling the must

The heat exchanger is an intestinelike contraption, with an inner tube (through which the must passes in one direction) and an outer tube (through which freezing cold brine solution – methylated spirits and water – passes in the other direction) arranged in a series of folds, with a single entry and exit point for each of the two tubes. The effect is instantaneously to reduce the temperature of the must.

The press

It is the timing of the use of the next major piece of equipment – the press – that so differentiates the making of white and red wine. Red wine is "made" – in the sense of the conversion of the sugar to alcohol, the transition from grape juice to wine – before the press is used; with white wine it is the other way around.

Whether or not a crusher is used, and whether or not skin contact is employed, white grapes will be pressed before fermentation begins. But with the exception of the unique, purpose-built Champagne presses, modern airbag presses can (and probably will) be used for both red and white wines.

Méthode ancienne

These days there are several different types of press. The most numerous (particularly in small wineries) are the basket presses; the 20th century introduced electrically driven hydraulics to apply the pressure, but the principle remains precisely the same as it was for the preceding 400 years. The "old press" at the Clos de Tart was built in 1570 and remained in use until 1924; and Robert Drouhin of Beaune used a press of similar antiquity in the 1980s to make small quantities of Burgundy using, in all respects, the *méthode ancienne*.

The traditional basket press was built in an upright fashion, with a solid plate descending on the grape skins, forcing the juice between the slots or gaps of the vertically arranged (and bound) pieces of wood forming the circular basket or cage. (The Champagne press works on the same principle, except that it is much shallower in proportion.) Basket presses are very much back in favor for New World red wines, especially Syrah (Shiraz).

... sideways into the 20th century

The first major development of the 20th century was to turn the cage over on its side, allowing it to revolve, and to mechanize (and ultimately computerize) the whole process. Vaslin of France was one of the major developers of this system.

The pneumatic, or airbag, press is in a sense a further development of this configuration. Instead of a plate moving along inside the cage toward a fixed end, or of two plates converging, a bag running along one side or section of the press is

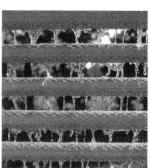

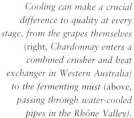

Cooling can make a crucial difference to quality at every stage, from the grapes themselves (right, Chardonnay enters a combined crusher and heat exchanger in Western Australia) to the fermenting must (above, passing through water-cooled pipes in the Rhône Valley).

inflated, pressing the skins against the cage. Because of the larger surface area under pressure, the grapes are pressed more gently, with less mincing and little or no chance of breaking the pips or unduly compressing the stalks (in either case liberating undesirable forms of tannin).

A yet further development has been the tank press, in which the external barrel is enclosed, other than for exit ports for the juice, theoretically offering a fully enclosed vessel that can be filled with gas so as to exclude oxygen. The majority of airbag and tank presses are nowadays made by Bucher.

Making the pips squeak

The last type of press is found only in very large wineries, and then is used only to make lesser-quality wine. It is the continuous press, which, as its name implies, extrudes the pressed skins (or *marc*) continuously from one end as fresh must is introduced at the other end. It is very efficient in terms of time, but significantly harsher than the "batch" presses. If pips squeak, it is in one of these machines.

Fermentation vessels: from vat ...

The introduction of stainless steel has revolutionized the vessels in which fermentation takes place, particularly for white wines. The traditional vessels – still widely used in Germany and Italy, for example – were made of oak (or cherry, chestnut or walnut), with parallel sides and the planks running vertically. These vats were not intended to impart any wood flavor to the wine, and were used for many decades (if not hundreds of years), gradually building up tartrate deposits that should have been (although sometimes were not) cleaned off. In such open vats the red grape skins can easily be "punched" back into the juice (on which they float), either by bare foot or by a disc on the end of a pole. This method of fermentation is used only for red (and fortified) wines and, while labor-intensive and seemingly archaic, it is still strongly favored by some excellent winemakers.

... to tank

With the 19th century came slate or cement vats, followed by enamel, glass or ceramic-lined vessels of similar shape, usually rectangular (or square) and installed in series in a permanently fixed position. Stainless steel is now replacing these worldwide. It introduces greater hygiene, facilitates in-place temperature control of fermentation and allows for all sorts of automated or mechanized agitation methods – two of the last being the Ducellier-Isman Autovinifier of Portugal and the Potter fermenter of Australia. The systems are

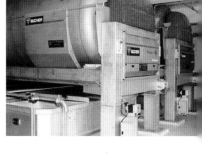

The traditional Champagne press (left) is used to press whole bunches, its large surface area and shallow depth facilitating the gentle extraction of clear juice with low phenolic levels. The modern Vaslin-Bucher pneumatic press (above) will treat either whole bunches or destemmed/crushed grapes, and can be set within a wide range of pressures.

Above: A New World refinery? No, a modern winery in Calastri, Sicily, with towering banks of stainless-steel fermenters and individual computer-controlled refrigeration, but all needing to be scrupulously cleaned.

many and varied, the least automatic being the simple draining of juice from the bottom valve of the vat and pumping it back over the top of the cap.

The development of the sideways-mounted press almost certainly gave birth to the idea of the "rotofermenter" (one of the proprietary brands being Vinimatic). Here the fermentation vessel is installed on its side and can be rotated to agitate the must; it is a potent piece of machinery, capable of quickly extracting massive color and flavor of a certain kind. Used with sensitivity and discretion it is a valuable tool; used insensitively it produces curiously hollow, hard wines. A variation used in Burgundy (Drouhin is a major exponent) employs interior revolving paddles, with the drum remaining fixed.

Filters ...   Both before (in the case of white wines) and after fermentation there is a range of machines designed to clarify grape juice or wine. There are four basic types: first, the centrifuge; second, pad or cartridge filters; third, earth and rotary filters; and fourth, cross-flow filters relying on osmosis.

Filtration is a highly technical affair. If this were not enough, it raises more emotion than almost any other aspect of winemaking, and is a subject we revisit later. The role (and use) of small oak barrels for fermentation and maturation is also discussed later, and so passed over here.

... and pumps   From this point the winery may contain numerous tools that are of interest only to winemakers and the technical journals – except for the ubiquitous must pump, which is considered essential by most but scorned by a few, who set up their wineries so that they can rely entirely on gravity, and so return to the mists of winemaking time.

The basic process of present-day winemaking is explained by the diagrams on pages 88–9, 114–7, 140–1, and 176–7. At every stage of the process, different options are available to the winemaker. Even given identical grapes it is these options that determine to a large extent the final quality, and certainly the individual style, of what is finally bottled.

The winemaker's job

In one sense it is easy to depict the winemaker as a mere quality-control officer, whose job it is simply to protect the quality of the grapes while nature turns them into their predestined kind of wine. As we have seen, in the classic French view, *terroir* (first) and climate (second) determine character, and it is not for mere mortals to interfere with nature. Protect what it gives, by all means; enhance it with care and discretion, perhaps; but under no circumstances seek to change it. Grapes and wines have a preordained status in life, and it is a form of vinous blasphemy to challenge that established order.

Conservative

The winemakers of the New World meanwhile exuberantly challenge that assumption, and all things implicit in it. That challenge, as well as increasing internationalism in all aspects of winemaking and wine marketing, has in turn led to a qualified reappraisal by the Old World of some of its cherished beliefs, and to a strong reaffirmation of others.

Tactical

Out of all of this has come a much greater understanding, and deliberate rather than automatic use of the options available: devices that primarily affect character and style, and not necessarily quality. It is of course true that scientific knowledge greatly helps the winemaker in selecting options, for he or she does so fully understanding why the consequences occur rather than simply relying on empirical observations (possibly handed down over the generations).

Indeed, scientific knowledge has created many of those options. It ensures a measure of control over virtually all winemaking procedures undreamed of 50 or even 25 years ago, and is a powerful aid in the development of new techniques (and hence of new flavors). Just as importantly, it all but eliminates the potential for the spoilage of wine in the winery, and equips the winemaker to deal effectively with poor grapes, whether affected by rot or mold, or simply lacking flavor.

With more thoughtful and precise vineyard management, the winemakers of this century should have significantly better grapes to work with than their 20th-century counterparts. If this happens, it will facilitate a trend to natural winemaking, in which the role of chemicals of all kinds in vineyard and winery will be progressively diminished. This, at least, will be the path for fine wine: wine of the kind that most readers of this book will want to drink.

The making of jug wine or *vin ordinaire* may well go down a rather different path. Perversely, "natural" winemaking can be much more costly than other methods, and certainly involves more sophisticated equipment. Manipulation may well become more important rather than less. One example is the making of wine with artificially reduced alcohol content. Heaven forbid that we should ever see a low-alcohol Corton-Charlemagne, but it seems probable we will see more and more low-alcohol jug wine sold in the supermarkets of the future.

Luddite views get us nowhere – even in winemaking. Modern technology will continue to produce better equipment. Membrane (pneumatic or airbag) presses produce more and clearer white wine juice; computerized control of temperatures and sophisticated refrigeration equipment mean that the winemaker can perhaps even close the winery on Sunday; improving filtration methods are reducing the already minimal use of chemical sterilants and antioxidants. And the list goes on.

Reasonable

If the term "modern" suggests superiority or immutability, it has no place in the context of this book: all it can hope to do is provide a snapshot of the philosophies, practices and attitudes of winemakers and wine-drinkers at the start of the 21st century. These have no special status; they are no more correct than those who have preceded them or those who will follow.

National Attitudes and Regional Characters

Jacques of all trades?

One of the immemorial cartoons shows a tubby, beret-wearing Frenchman busy filling bottles labeled "Beaujolais," "Burgundy," "Côtes du Rhône," "Bordeaux" and so on from a single cask in the back cellar, and out in front his wife offering the eager customers their choice (at suitably differing prices). It was born of an age in which there was a vast difference in the real articles, but not a great deal of knowledge about that difference, and when deceptive practices were a great deal more common.

Now there is ever-increasing knowledge about the actual (or theoretical) differences in character among the wines of the world, knowledge that raises one of the burning questions of our time. Are we in danger of moving toward universal "styles" of wine that obliterate or significantly blur the all-important regional differences between otherwise similar wines? Will our French cartoon take on a new and altogether different meaning?

Chablis

A test case

Chablis is a good example of the blurring of a distinct regional character. The classic description of Chablis likened its aroma to that of gunflint, the taste to sucking river pebbles. It was (and still is) regarded as the ultimate shellfish and seafood wine, austere, crisp, long-lived and bone-dry; in other words, very different from the white Burgundy of the Côte d'Or. Yet today it is sometimes not easy to tell the difference between a glass of Chablis and the majority of white Burgundies. Is this a good or a bad thing? Why has it happened? And how does it relate to the broader issue of wine around the world?

The differences between a Meursault or Montrachet, a Chablis, a California, an Italian, and an Australian Chardonnay are due to the interaction of *terroir*, climate, viticultural practice, winemaking practice and philosophy: the last a rather vague but nonetheless crucial factor partly reflected in viticultural and winemaking practices, but also reflecting the tastes, and even the structure, of the society in which the wine is made and principally drunk. Of the interacting factors, *terroir* and climate are largely (but not entirely) immutable: soil pH may be ameliorated by lime; soil structure may be improved by gypsum; soil drainage may be installed; trace elements may be added; and fertilizers are widely used. Climate may be softened by anti-frost devices; wind by the introduction of windbreaks; canopy microclimate by sophisticated trellising and vine-training techniques; and last, but by no means least, irrigation can permit viticulture in otherwise impossible climates (California's Central Valley, Australia's Riverland, Chile, and so forth) or ameliorate the impact of unusually warm and dry vintages such as that encountered in Europe in 2003. But at the end of the day, and when the particular bottle of wine has reached the peak of its power, the *terroir* and climate will have placed their mark on the wine, and the greater the quality of that wine, the more pronounced will be its birthmark.

It is of fundamental importance to the French (and to a lesser degree the Germans, the Italians and the Spanish) that the influence of *terroir* be enhanced rather than diminished, for only in that way can the special monetary value attaching to their great appellations be protected and justified. The scarcity factor is vital in this context. But how much of the traditional character of Chablis is in fact due to *terroir* and climate, how much to the intervention of man?

William Fèvre was Chablis' staunch conservative, insisting on the importance of geology to the flavor of the wine – but untraditionally aging it in new oak.

The traditionalists of Chablis, with the now retired William Fèvre at their head, insist that the soil – the celebrated Kimmeridgian chalky clay – was (and is) crucial. They regard as dastardly upstarts the modernists, headed by Jean Durup of the Domaine de l'Eglantière, who over 20 years have successfully urged the authorities to redraw the Chablis map with far wider boundaries well outside the Kimmeridgian zone. They blame the appellation authorities for any loss of true Chablis style.

Up to a point the traditionalists must be right, recent though the changes are. One can, after all, taste the difference between the *grands crus*, the long-established *premiers crus* and such newcomers as Vaudevey. But to put it all down to the *terroir* is plainly not right. In the past 30 or more years there have been major changes in the way Chablis is made. The majority of winemakers now ferment their wine in stainless steel with inbuilt cooling mechanisms, rather than the oak favored by winemakers such as William Fèvre and François Raveneau. Deliberately induced malolactic fermentation is now par for the course, softening the naturally high acid, smoothing out the tart edges and producing fuller wines. Better spray regimes, better viticultural practices and a run of warm vintages have produced cleaner, riper grapes with higher alcohol levels. Digressing for one moment to look beyond Chablis and take in Burgundy as a whole, it is more than possible the overall vintage conditions through the second half of the 1990s up to 2005 will be seen as a turning point 10 or 20 years hence. In 2005 Jean-Pierre de Smet of Domaine de L'Arlot observed: "In the last five years I have chaptalized once, in 2001; not so long ago, it would have been the reverse."

Jean Durup embodies the progressive school in Chablis, pressing for wider boundaries and playing down the role of the soil.

Most significantly, the levels of sulfur dioxide used in winemaking have been sharply reduced. The high levels, in excess of 200 parts per million, commonplace 30 or more years ago were responsible for stripping the wine's initial color and preserving it as a pale green-yellow for decades; they inhibited or prevented the malolactic fermentation; they invested the wine with a Peter Pan quality, which meant it often needed 20 years to reach its best; and they undoubtedly contributed to those celebrated gunflint and river pebble characteristics.

Different – but better?

The result is that Chablis is now riper and softer, showing more pure fruit characteristics, cleaner and less long-lived. It is in some respects less complex and less aggressive, but is better balanced. If it is aged in new oak, it can be confused with a Côte d'Or wine of similar age. One irony is that Monsieur Fèvre, who so passionately believed in the soil, was also the grower who used the most new barrels. Nonetheless, there are at least half a dozen growers – Raveneau, Michel, Dauvissat, Laroche and a few others – who do make wines of distinctive character.

These exceptions apart, Chablis has indeed come closer to the Côte d'Or in becoming more user-friendly, requiring less patience and developing into a technically much better wine. Whether it is better Chablis, and where the dividing line between anonymity and individuality should be drawn, is less clear.

Appellation control: a sense of order

Simply because the French have been more disciplined in their approach to making and marketing wine, they have long since outdistanced their most natural competitors, the Germans and the Italians. They have established a clearly defined and equally clearly differentiated appellation system that not only enshrines the varying types of wine, but also establishes a social structure extending downward from royalty to nobility to bourgeoisie to peasantry – and woe betide any who seek to challenge their preordained status in life. The rigidity of the system has its dangers and shortcomings, but it has some potent advantages, not the least being stability. Wine can be a complex and intimidating subject for ordinary consumers, and a degree of certainty and predictability (be it real or imagined) is an obvious advantage.

Quality: divine right?

That stability is built partly on history, partly on a clearly articulated philosophy – and the cynic would suggest on a presumption of inherent superiority. It also has (or had) an exceedingly narrow and parochial base, which has facilitated the most

The First Growth Château Lafite broke spectacularly with tradition in the 1980s by building a magnificent circular underground chai for barrel storage. The Médoc tradition is for long barns at or slightly below ground level.

microscopic examination and exploitation of tiny pieces of land (obviously beneficial) but inhibited a broader understanding of the world of wine beyond.

The 126-hour week

The emphasis has always been placed on *terroir*, which has justified a basically fatalistic approach to grape growing and winemaking. A striking example of this attitude is the story told of Château Margaux immediately after the great First Growth was bought by the late André Mentzelopoulos. One Sunday late in the 1978 vintage, while working in Paris, he telephoned the château to check on the progress of the fermentations. Receiving no answer, he chartered a plane and flew to the château, finding it indeed untended. His widow, Laura, recollected that, "He thought it was inadmissible that employees closed on Saturday and came back on Monday during fermentation, which lasts only three weeks of the year." For his part, the *maître de chai*, who was responsible, pointed out that the fermentations were slowing down with no risk of overheating, but admitted, "We weren't used to having a person of that caliber around, and we didn't follow the vinification as closely as we do now." Not only do the wineries of the United States, Australia, New Zealand and South Africa routinely work a seven-day week during a vintage, which will extend for six to eight weeks, but they will equally routinely operate night shifts taking over from day shifts, and senior winemakers accept an 18-hour day as part of their job.

France is rapidly becoming a battleground between natural, noninterventionist grape growing and winemaking, and high-technology wineries that permit, though do not force, manipulation of must and wine on a previously undreamed of level. Looked at through the prism of the better (by no means only the very best) châteaus of Bordeaux, the unprecedented prosperity that has followed in the wake of the 1982 vintage and the arrival of Robert Parker has seen massive investment in and refurbishment of wineries: Château Gazin in Pomerol and Château Malartic-Lagravière in Graves are two examples among countless others. Ultra-sophisticated temperature control of stainless-steel or wooden vats, microoxygenation (or microbullage) machines to soften tannins and concentration machines (vacuum or reverse osmosis) are standard equipment in the nouveaux riches châteaus.

Yet on the other hand is the move to organic/biodynamic grape growing, the near-automatic reliance on natural yeasts for both primary and malolactic fermentations, and a reluctance to fine or filter the wine. Many Burgundians prefer

Spain's most influential modern bodega is the house of Torres at Pacs, near Vilafranca del Penedès, in Catalonia. The Torres family has startled the world with wines unlike any Spain has ever made.

to avoid filtering their wines. And the Burgundian (and Muscadet) practice of keeping the wine on its lees in the barrel (and even stirring up the lees at intervals) also has its genesis in the creed of nonintervention, or following nature.

If all this paints a picture of France as a land of stubborn traditionalists, it only tells half the story. The emblem and embodiment of scientific rationalism is Bordeaux's famous professor of oenology, the late Emile Peynaud. Peynaud has been characterized as hero and as villain, as savior and as destroyer. His critics tell the (probably apocryphal) story of the expert given an unknown wine to comment on, and whose response was: "I can't tell you what the wine is or where it came from, but I can tell you it was made by Professor Peynaud." The supporters of Professor Peynaud would simply say that all he sought to do was give the winemaker a better understanding of, and greater control over, all aspects of winemaking; if chemical and bacterial reactions take place in the course of making the wine (and they do), those reactions should be planned and their consequences understood. If there is a problem with this approach, it is that it takes much of the mystique out of winemaking, and exposes impotence or incompetence for what it is. And by eliminating the chance consequences of bacterial contamination, oxidation, acetification or whatever, it is perfectly true that the wines made under Peynaud's control exhibited a degree of family resemblance: they are devoid of major technical faults.

Michel Rolland has since assumed the mantel, his influence even greater, thanks as much to the adulation of some American critics as to that of his French (and other) clients. Rolland is seen by some as the "Great Satan" for his enthusiastic endorsement of microoxidation, or microbullage. In Burgundy, the often misunderstood Guy Accad enjoyed a spectacular, if brief, role in the 1980s, advocating extended prefermentation maceration, partly to make up for deficiencies in the vineyard and grapes.

Fully understood, science does not mean the end of individuality or enforce the making of sterile, squeaky-clean wines. Giotto proved his skill by drawing a perfect freehand circle; Picasso showed in his early realist period that he had the ability to portray nature as precisely as any artist. Once winemakers have mastered the basic skills and techniques, then of course they may eschew them. It is an entirely different thing to ignore technique simply because it is not available in the first place – or because you do not understand it.

Rationalism: Professor Peynaud

Michel Rolland: the new prophet

The new-oak syndrome

Almost as important as the professor in shifting French thought has been the emergence of the cult of oak in Bordeaux and (to a slightly lesser degree) Burgundy. New oak barrels have always played a role, of course; the greater the estate, the greater the role. It was a wholly symbiotic, if partially unconscious, relationship: the highest-quality grapes produced the most intensely flavored wine, readily able to absorb the flavor of new oak without becoming in the least subordinated to it. The result was spontaneously recognized as exceptional, and commanded a price that amply repaid the proprietor for investment in new barrels. Lesser wines were perceived as simply that: they were accorded hand-me-down barrels, and the price became suitably modest. In periods of decline, one of the things that typified a poorly performing classed-growth château was that it spent less on new barrels.

The catalyst for change came largely from California. In the 1960s, intelligent and active winemakers such as Robert Mondavi started visiting France regularly, tasting the wines of the great producers, watching their techniques and asking questions – in particular, questions about their barrels. Those early inquisitors must have concluded that the French were being more than usually uncooperative, for all but the most general questions went unanswered. Just as milk comes from bottles or cartons, oak comes from the cooperage. But which forest? If the winemaker knew, he was not about to tell. In truth, he almost certainly regarded the question as stupid and unnecessary: the barrels had been supplied by the same cooperage for generations, and they were always satisfactory because the cooper knew the style of wine in question very well. As for how the barrels were made – with low, moderate or high "toast" – clearly these were the questions of a madman.

The kiss of oak

Since then the field of inquiry has extended to issues of air-drying versus kiln-drying; tight- versus loose-grained oak; and to a detailed correlation between those questions and toast, oak type and wine style. Look at any dissertation on the classed growths of Bordeaux today and you are certain to find reference to the amount of new oak used each year. Yet when Edmund Penning-Rowsell wrote his seminal work *The Wines of Bordeaux* in 1969, nowhere did he mention the use (or absence) of new oak. Quite modest châteaus have built high reputations by giving their wines the kiss of oak; not to mention regions whose wines a mere decade ago would have been sold anonymously in bulk.

Tastes in evolution

The battle between new technology and the traditional, sensitive, non-interventionist approach to winemaking has been joined, and will run for many years. It is true that winemakers do not have to use the battery of equipment at their disposal; it is most valuable in lesser vintages.

It is clear that the American influence has had a major impact on wine style and taste. It demands the deeper the color, the richer the fruit, the more generous the tannins, the greater the amount of new, high-toast oak, the better. This has put at extreme peril the close bond between the winemaker, his *terroir*, his vines and his grapes, built up over centuries, and resulting in an intuitive approach to winemaking with a cornerstone of *typicité*.

Italian idiosyncrasies

The Italians have gone down their own idiosyncratic and, at times, undisciplined path. The noble growths of Italy were few and far between. Even more so than in France, wine was (and is) a simple necessity of life, made casually and consumed without introspection. Almost everywhere you go in Italy there is a flourishing regional wine industry (there are 232 officially recognized DOC and DOCG zones), many places using indigenous grape varieties of obscure history that grow nowhere else in the world. Winemaking in Italy is every bit as rich and ancient – indeed, much more ancient – than that of France: the Frescobaldi family of Tuscany traces its wine lineage back to 1300, and this is a relatively recent date in the full 4,000-year perspective of Italian wine history.

Despite (perhaps because of) the ubiquitous nature of winemaking across the country, certain patterns appear. Over a long period of time Italians have come to expect dry white wines that are exceedingly pale in color, almost devoid of any aroma and largely lacking any recognizable varietal flavor. Served fully chilled, these are acceptable food wines: they perform the function of water, but have the advantages of being antiseptic and alcoholic. Looked at more critically, and compared to the white wines of other parts of the world, what aroma they have is not very pleasant, they are often exceedingly hard on the palate and have a chalky or bitter finish. The reasons are: the preponderance of Trebbiano (there are 250,000 acres/100,000 ha of this high-yielding but eminently undistinguished variety); the surprisingly widespread lack of refrigeration for white wine fermentation; and a real dislike of the fruity flavors that can be obtained from any white grape variety. Thus extreme juice oxidation, originally unplanned per se, became standard practice.

This approach is popularly supposed to have been modified for varieties new to Italy, notably Chardonnay. Yet arrange a blind tasting of French, Californian, Australian and Italian Chardonnays, and the Italians will still stand apart. They will no doubt have their supporters – Angelo Gaja in Piedmont commands spectacular prices for his – but the majority of non-Italian judges would have no difficulty in spotting the difference.

Leaders of modern Italy

The style and overall quality of Italian red wines are rather less challenging and, most would agree, decidedly more satisfying. Whereas gimmicky bottles (and some brilliant label designs) have made Frascati, Soave, Verdicchio and such wines commercially acceptable, if not entirely successful, red wines such as Brunello, Barolo, Barbaresco and Chianti *riserva* need no apology. Tuscany and Piedmont have emerged as regions where Italian technological flair has finally got to grips with wine. But once again it is necessary to stress that these are the tip of a very large iceberg, still bearing no resemblance to the raw, often fizzy and rough reds consumed within a year of vintage and close to the village where they were made.

Despite the differing climates, *terroirs* and grape varieties lying behind the best traditional Italian red wines, there was a common theme: they were aged for long periods in large, neutral wooden vats (cherry, chestnut, walnut or oak) and given further bottle-age before release, this approach being based on the need to overcome formidable tannins.

Revolution 1992

Over the past 30 years the already bewildering complexity of Italian wines has become tangled enough to drive a critic to drink. Enthusiastic planting of the classic varieties (notably the Cabernet family and Chardonnay) has been followed by equally enthusiastic use of new small oak barrels (the wooden *barrique* is enough to add several dollars to the price) and the emergence of several Italian equivalents of Professor Peynaud. The result was a profusion of nonconforming *vini da tavola* rejoicing in exotic names and frequently stunning packaging, selling for far more than the theoretically better DOC and DOCG wines, and tasting like a Franco-California hybrid. The Tuscan Cabernet Sassicaia started it all. By 1990 the situation was out of control. In 1992, the government had to rewrite the rulebook to contain the revolution.

Spanish parallels

Rioja is Spain's one classic red wine region with an unmistakable style of its own. Structurally, Riojas are not dissimilar to the best traditional Chiantis, the main difference being that American oak casks give them their characteristic vanilla-and-lemon flavor. The winemaking methods and philosophies, however, also run on parallel paths – blending grapes, then softening their tannins and lightening primary fruit by maturing for several years in oak. In Rioja, as in Italy, the current trend is to shorten the time in barrel and to encourage fresher, crisper fruit flavors. There is an increasing number of boutique wineries, such as Bodegas Roda, investing enormous care in the vineyards and no-expense-spared, gravity-fed wineries, then maturing the wine in French, not American, oak.

United States

The white wines of Germany, Alsace and the Loire Valley come under the microscope in the next chapter; for now the attention swings to the New World, and

From basic to classic

first to the United States (and thereby principally to California).

Californian winemaking philosophy has passed through a series of metamorphoses since the repeal of Prohibition. Initially it was concerned almost entirely with fortified wine production, in precisely the same way as Australia was. Its next phase started in the 1950s with the emergence of table wine as a serious commercial category, but largely fashioned from the same ignoble grape varieties as had been used to make fortified wine. Then in the 1960s the classic varieties, now becoming the international varieties, were rediscovered. Cabernet Sauvignon, Chardonnay, Sauvignon Blanc, Chenin Blanc, Johannisberg Riesling, Pinot Noir and Merlot changed the face of American winemaking forever. Rapid planting began in California, but soon spread – with varying degrees of success – to scattered regions right across the country.

The initial response was one of wonder and adulation on the part of winemakers and consumers alike. The more powerful the aroma, the bigger the flavor, the

The Barelli Creek vineyard in the Alexander Valley of Sonoma County encapsulates the beauty of this region, with its rolling countryside and intricate patches of native forest so different from the monoculture of the Napa Valley floor. Every corner of Sonoma brings a fresh and different vista.

higher the alcohol, the better. These were strange wines, soulmates of the waddling finned monsters churned out by the Detroit carmakers, and of the society that nurtured Marilyn Monroe. America's crush on size continued into the 1970s. Many attribute its partial demise to an article by *New York Times* wine critic Frank Prial.

Prial's (and many others') complaint was that these wines were clumsy, one-dimensional and just too darned strong; that they were varietal caricatures that could not be drunk with any pleasure, and least of all with food. So the era of "food wines" was born: wines in which dominant fruit flavors were toned down in a search for subtlety and complexity. Part of the stimulus for change came from improved viticulture: the massive, heavily shaded, traditional Californian vine canopy had meant that flavor ripeness did not occur until very late in the season, by which time potential alcohol levels were 14 percent or more. For some growers at least, better canopy management meant better grapes at lower alcohol levels.

Just too darned strong

There are those who would say defeat has been snatched from the jaws of victory. The ascendance of Screaming Eagle (Napa's answer to Bordeaux's *garagistes*), producing tiny amounts of opaque-colored, densely fruited, oaked and extracted wines, with 15.5 to 16 degrees of alcohol a requisite badge of honor, is an incontrovertible fact of life today, as is the influence of Robert Parker.

The changes in the winery saw the enthusiastic adoption of French (and Italian) winemaking techniques. Juice oxidation, barrel fermentation and full malolactic fermentation were adopted as normal practice for Chardonnay; the quest to tame the tart grassiness of Sauvignon Blanc adopted some of the same techniques, and blended it with Semillon in imitation of white Bordeaux. The prime subject for postgraduate research at the University of California at Davis became the changes in Cabernet Sauvignon's tannin structure when macerated for periods of 10 to 25 days after first fermentation. Then Merlot, followed by Cabernet Franc and afterward Petit Verdot, began to be blended with Cabernet Sauvignon, first experimentally, then as a matter of course.

The "choices" and "consequences" will be looked at in greater detail in the following chapters, but one is bound to ask whether the pendulum has swung too far. Has obsession with technique and theory led to wines that have lost the ability to capture the attention of the drinker, to effortlessly beguile the tongue?

The Australian love affair

Australia's experience certainly suggests the answer is yes. Here there is an unashamed and uncomplicated love affair with primary varietal fruit flavor, augmented by sometimes profligate use of oak. Both white and red commercial wines may be accused of simplicity, but above all else they are user-friendly. They are positive in their aroma and flavor, yet neither demanding nor intimidating. The white wines are spotlessly clean, and the majority of the Chardonnays are at their best within 18 months of the harvest. The red wines are soft, fruity and much, much lower in tannin than their California counterparts. While most repay cellaring, and a few demand it, they are nonetheless easily enjoyed when they are first released, usually at two to three years of age. At the top end, single region/vineyard wines have become steadily more sophisticated.

Australian winemakers achieve their results by meticulous attention to detail (in common, it must be said, with their equally fastidious and technically skilled American counterparts). But Australian ideas are different. While basically designed to protect a core of varietal fruit flavor, the techniques (and the underlying philosophies) vary widely according to the variety and desired style. These are discussed in the following two chapters.

The Australian approach to red winemaking shows a similar emphasis on varietal and fruit flavor. Barrel fermentation is almost as widely practiced as extended maceration (after fermentation), and the only concern about alcohol is that it may be too high (rather than too low). Australia also has a wine midway in style between Pinot Noir and Cabernet Sauvignon: Syrah (or Shiraz, as it is called there) gives wines diverse in style (according to climate), but that are mostly soft and round in the mouth.

New Zealand schools of thought

The rate of change in New Zealand has been even greater as it successfully sought to play catch-up with Australia after giving the latter a 10-year start. Sauvignon Blanc has always been its ace in the hole, and changes here have been incremental. It is Chardonnay that has been transformed, as we see on page 213. In the wake of Chardonnay, Pinot Noir is emerging as a wine of world class.

Millstones and milestones: South Africa, Chile and Argentina

South Africa has been making wine for far longer than any other New World country, but also had to free itself from the dead hand of the KWV, the decades of sanctions and endemic virus problems. An annual Tri-Nations Test Match (2003, 2004 and 2005) between Australia, New Zealand and South Africa, and an earlier head-to-head challenge held in South Africa in 1995, suggest that South Africa still lags behind the other two countries at the top end of the scale. However, its commercial success in the United Kingdom in the past five to ten years has put it firmly on the international map.

Chile's wine industry of today is barely 25 years old. Free from phylloxera, with a benign climate married with limitless snowmelt irrigation water, cheap labor, new wineries and the big four varieties (Sauvignon Blanc, Chardonnay, Merlot and Cabernet Sauvignon) dominating plantings, it has no distracting baggage to worry about as its exports stretch from Beijing to Moscow, London to New York.

Over the past 80 years, Argentina has managed to find every conceivable way of neutralizing its vast natural resources and precipitating one economic and political crisis after another. It is and always has been a world-ranked wine producer and consumer, albeit with little interest in export markets prior to the 1990s. With its varied terrain and climate (*terroir*, if you wish), it ranks with the Iberian Peninsula as a sleeping giant. Malbec is its key to awakening and striding the world stage. Indeed, many knowledgeable observers believe its potential is much greater than that of Chile.

New Zealand provides the newest landscape for the vine. Within a single decade, its Sauvignon Blanc became the world's favorite. The Te Mata estate at Hawke's Bay on North Island has the longest history – over a century – but its stunningly original architecture expresses an entirely new ethic. Te Mata emulates California, specifically Sonoma, with one of New Zealand's most successful red wines yet: a Cabernet and Merlot blend.

Light-Bodied White Wines

Choices, consequences and techniques

One way of regarding the enormously wide spectrum of white wines, deriving from different grapes, different climates and soils, and different winemaking techniques, is to see Riesling as the epitome of the most aromatic, least full-bodied, most transparent and brilliant in flavor, most reflective of its *terroir*. Its great rival, Chardonnay (few people would deny that they are the world's two greatest white wine grapes), then stands at the other end of the spectrum, epitomizing dense, full-bodied, multifaceted wines that derive much of their personality and individuality from the way they are made and aged – and, above all, from the oak of their barrels.

A continuum of characters   In between lies a continuum of characters, from the lightly aromatic (close in style to Riesling), to the merely neutral, and onward to the grapes that react in a similar way to Chardonnay to winery techniques.

The aromatic grapes and wines begin with Riesling, Gewürztraminer, Sylvaner, Welschriesling, Grüner Veltliner, Muscat Blanc à Petits Grains and Müller-Thurgau (along with the rest of the family of German-bred *Vitis vinifera* hybrids). Then there are a number of white varieties that, like the aromatics, are usually made without oak influence and bottled early in their life. These include Chasselas (the

From the Rüdesheimer Klosterberg vineyards, the view sweeps down toward Rüdesheim, then on across the Rhine to the vineyards of Bingen and the Nahe Valley beyond.

principal grape of Switzerland), Chenin Blanc, Aligoté, Colombard, Marsanne, Roussanne, Melon de Bourgogne (better known as Muscadet), the Trebbiano of Italy and the Rkatsiteli of Eastern Europe.

Of all these, Riesling stands out as the classic variety. Yet its hold on the hearts and minds of the world's wine-drinkers is curiously uncertain, and infinitely weaker than it was 100 or even 50 years ago. Rhine wines have a longer history in international trade than any other white wines. When, in the 18th century, almost all the best German vineyards were planted with Riesling, their quality soared, and they became eagerly followed by discriminating drinkers around the world. Even France acknowledged the unique qualities of the great Rieslings of the Mosel, and, to the British, "hock" (meaning Rhine wine) and "Mosel" were household words in just the same way as Chardonnay is today.

German wines of the 19th and early 20th centuries were intense, long-lived and basically dry. After World War II, and particularly the great 1959 vintage that produced many sweet wines, the taste for sweetness developed, and various technical means were found to keep German wines from fermenting to dryness or to resweeten them before bottling. The 1970s, however, saw a powerful reaction against sweetness in the German domestic market. Suddenly, *trocken,* or very dry wines, were in vogue.

As the fashion for *trocken* and *halbtrocken* wines emerged, much was made of the suggestion that these dry or near-dry wines were merely a reversion to the style of the golden age of German winemaking. The flaw in this argument is the radically different nature of the grapes; 120 years ago the average yield was 1.3 tons per acre (17 hl per ha), compared to as much as 10.4 tons per acre (140 hl per ha) today, and alcohol levels were significantly higher. So whatever the German enthusiasm for the modern *trocken* wines, it is not generally shared by the rest of the world, which sees most of them as charmless, thin and hard. The realization is dawning that German wines need to be of far-above-average quality to be balanced and satisfying without a little residual sugar. A dry Spätlese may well be highly enjoyable to drink, but a bone-dry Kabinett wine is usually a meager creature. Better to add sugar, French-style, to make a plain *Qualitätswein*, which then at least has the substance to be satisfying.

The subject of German wine quality is a minefield of politics and paradoxes. The very selection of Riesling seems perverse: as a late ripener it seems an illogical choice for the German climate. Early-ripening Chardonnay would have been more suitable, one would have thought. Yet Riesling's peculiarity is that it can, and indeed does, achieve intense flavor ripeness at as little as 10 percent alcohol – even, on occasion, as little as 7 percent.

The German approach to winemaking is based on the qualities Riesling can achieve in cool climates where full ripeness is the exception. Alcohol is regarded in a quite different light. The measure used to differentiate quality categories is "potential alcohol" – which, of course, includes residual sugar.

The emphasis in German Riesling is all on freshness, on fruit and on a balance between sweetness and acidity. Alcohol imparts its own sweetness; if it is reduced, the logical result is unfermented sugar. For this reason many observers think German Riesling finds its ultimate expression in Auslesen (*see* page 235) from the Mosel (and its least expression in *trocken* wines). It is the fine Rieslings that we are concerned with here.

The winemaking options for Riesling, though, are limited; there are only minor differences in the way it is made in Germany, Alsace, South Africa, California or Australia, yet, as we have seen within Germany alone, the resulting wines differ from one another quite considerably. The reason lies partly in philosophy, but largely in climate and *terroir*.

German Riesling

Sweet or trocken?

Cool but ripe

Making White Wine

CRUSHING

The first stage of controlled vinification is to crush the grapes and release the pulp and juice, making them easier to press. A key decision at this stage is whether or not to remove the stems. Left with the grapes, stems allow juice to drain more freely during pressing. Whole-bunch pressing of white grapes is increasingly common where winemakers seek to avoid phenolics and strive for finesse.

PRESSING

Cooling
Delaying fermentation until after pressing is essential. Where the ambient must temperatures are high, the juice is cooled by pumping it through "must chillers."

Pressing
White wine grapes are always pressed. Better-quality juice results when pressing is gentle. If too aggressive, the pips and stems break, and bitter astringent flavors that overpower those natural in the grapes are released. Good results are achieved with pneumatic presses, which are now replacing traditional vertical wooden ones. Both types yield juice of the highest quality and also enable the separation of different-quality pressings.

Settling
The juice is drained from the press into settling vats where the skin, pip and stem fragments remaining in suspension after pressing will settle to the bottom of the vat. The clean juice is then racked into separate vats ready for fermentation to begin. Centrifuging can also be carried out at this stage to clarify the wine, but it is an aggressive process, removing all the larger particles in the must, even yeast cells. It is often carried out when cultured yeasts are to replace natural ones for fermentation.

FERMENTATION

Traditionally in oak vats (increasingly favored for many high-quality wines), white wine is now more often fermented in stainless-steel vats, which enable easier regulation of yeast activity through temperature control. Prolonged fermentation at cool temperatures protects primary fruit characteristics and ensures the conversion of all the sugar to alcohol. After fermentation, some winemakers choose to leave their wine in contact with its lees (yeast sediment), which adds both flavor and freshness to the wine, retained by bottling it without delay.

Dark arrows indicate critical stages; lighter arrows show optional ones.

MALOLACTIC FERMENTATION

To soften astringent acidic flavors and to add complexity, a second, or malolactic, fermentation can be encouraged (it may occur quite naturally or be brought about artificially). This converts harsher malic acids to softer lactic ones. Where retaining acidity in the wine is important (e.g., in warmer climates where the grapes gain greater sugar and fruit flavors at the expense of their natural acidity), this second fermentation is prevented by removing the yeasts and proteins needed to initiate it.

MATURING

Clarification
Filtration, centrifuging or fining with bentonite clay (which "collects" remaining yeasts, proteins, grape-skin particles, etc., and precipitates them to the bottom of the vat) is used to prevent unwanted malolactic fermentation and any further yeast activity once all the sugar in the wine has been converted to alcohol. It also removes substances leading to "off tastes." With clarification the wine gains stability; the processes used for this stabilization, however, are quite aggressive, and many believe they lead to flavor loss. Clarification is completed by removing tartrates from the wine. Modern wineries now use thickly insulated stainless-steel vats for cold-stabilization. By cooling the wine to around 25°F (−4°C), tartrate crystals, which may otherwise form in the bottle, precipitate and fall to the bottom of the vat. In Germany this process traditionally occurred in large oak *Fuder* situated in cellars cool enough for tartrates to precipitate out at ambient temperatures.

After stabilization, the wine may be bottled immediately or matured first in oak barrels.

Maturing in oak
Maturing white wine in new oak imparts flavors that can overpower wines of more subtle character, but that add depth and complexity to others. Older barrels give more moderate flavors and are an option often favored in Burgundy.

FINISHING

Bottling
During bottling, cleanliness is essential; any bacterial activity, which may be encouraged by warm temperatures – especially when the wine is later transported or shipped for sale – is prevented by passing the wine through a fine filter. Some producers bottle the wine straight from its lees after fermentation to retain yeast character and freshness (even a slight spritz). Others, particularly in the New World, inject carbon dioxide (CO_2) at the bottling stage for the same effect.

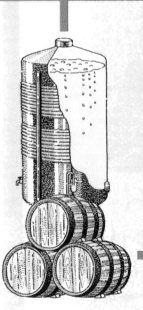
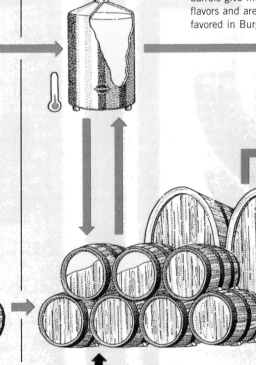

The grapes come first   The German attitude to winemaking is very simple and straightforward, ever emphasizing the grapes, ever downplaying the role of the winemaker. Grapes from Germany's Riesling vineyards (the best of which are often on steep slopes) are almost invariably hand-picked, and those from better estates are hurried to be processed with as little damage to their skins as possible; freshness of juice is seen as crucial. On less perfectionist properties a certain amount of maceration of skins and juice in the collection containers is not uncommon, due to tight packing or even semicrushing. The crushed must is taken directly to the press (pneumatic presses are now standard), and subsequently care is taken to select only free-run and light pressings for the better wines. Levels of sulfur dioxide are more moderate than in former years, as the usually low ambient temperatures of both the grapes and the cellars give a measure of protection against oxidation at this stage. Most winemakers are unconcerned about slight yellowing (or even browning) of juice, indicating a touch of juice oxidation. They are wary, though, of the implications of botrytis in dry or semidry winemaking – in particular its tendency to bind sulfur and thereby neutralize its protective function.

The juice is cold-settled overnight. Centrifuge pumps are sparingly used; filtration of the juice is even rarer. Because of the minuscule lots that the fine estates are often dealing with (for example, the famous house of J.J. Prüm of Wehlen in the Middle Mosel released 60 cases of its 1975 Auslese Long Gold Cap, 225 cases of its 1976, and 30 cases of its 1982 – and none at all in the intervening years), fermentation vessels (usually stainless steel, sometimes old oak) are small, and the low cellar temperatures mean that fermentation usually proceeds quite slowly at 54°F to 59°F (12°C to 15°C), initiated by either cultured or wild yeasts. While this last choice is very personal to the winemaker, the very top estates almost invariably allow their "wild" yeasts to do the job.

Harmony and charm   Frequently, particularly in the typically German large oval casks called *Fuder*, and in cold, damp cellars (which are the rule rather than the exception), fermentation peters out before all the grape sugar is converted to alcohol, leaving the slight degree of natural sweetness that gives the wine great harmony and charm. To preserve the sugar at this level, the wine is racked and sulfured immediately at the end of fermentation, and may be sterile-filtered. It will be fined (if necessary) with a variety of fining agents, and racked once again. The former German custom of keeping the wine for two, three or even more years in cask to soften its harsh acidity has all but disappeared with current methods of acidity adjustment. Where once Rieslings were prized for savory, sappy intensity and almost limitless endurance (they withstood even quite severe oxidation; some were prized for brownness and almost sherrylike qualities), today what is asked of them is bouquets of floral perfume and palate-tingling freshness.

Süssreserve   Perhaps the most contentious German practice is the use of *Süssreserve*: sweet, unfermented must added after fermentation and immediately before the final filtration and bottling. This "back-blending" (as the Australians describe it) is legal for all grades of QmP wines, on condition that it is made from grapes grown in the same vineyard or region and of the same grade as the wine to be sweetened. In other words, *Süssreserve* of Spätlese quality must be used for Spätlese wine, and so on. The level of addition is also limited by reference to the natural alcohol of the wine. But while much German wine, from slightly to moderately sweet, is made with the help of *Süssreserve*, the finest estates refuse to use it, much preferring the fermentation to remain just short of complete, and then stabilizing the wine as necessary.

The nature of acidity   The great German Rieslings have exceptional intensity of fruit flavor, deriving directly from the vineyard. Yields for these wines (when made as Kabinett or Spätlese) seldom exceed 4.4 tons per acre (60 hl per ha), with much lower yields for Auslese and the sweetest wines. They are intensely aromatic and flowery, with a little botrytis frequently adding complexity, their sweetness (be it slight or marked) combining with the always perceptible acidity to give impact to the fruit flavor. In no other wines is the nature and degree of their acidity so essential to quality. The Germans distinguish between *Weinsäure* (tartaric acid, which stimulates the palate attractively) and *Apfelsäure* (harsh-tasting malic acid). It is the difference between these two, and the vineyards – sheltered and south-sloping, or wind-chilled and shady – that create the crucial difference that provides the fundamental criteria for quality in German Riesling.

Alsace Riesling

The Alsace winemaker consciously endeavors to make a Riesling as different from that of Germany as the laws of chemistry and biochemistry will allow. The German strives for fruit and finesse, the Alsatian for power and strength. To the former alcohol is unimportant, to the latter it is all-important. Sweetness is almost an embarrassment, however high the price the top growers seek for their luscious Vendange Tardive and Sélection des Grains Nobles. The amount of sweetness tolerated in such wines is a mere fraction of that which a German winemaker looks for; the amount of alcohol correspondingly much higher. A Grains Nobles, the sweetest category of Alsace wine, is much more like Sauternes in strength and body than anything made in Germany.

Alsace lies in the rain shadow of the Vosges Mountains, where summers are typically long, sunny and dry, with France's second-lowest average rainfall. Riesling makes the greatest wines, but not by the margin it does in Germany. The

Dark clouds over the Vosges Mountains contrast starkly with the sunny vineyards of Alsace. The vineyards of the whole region are protected by the peaks and forests of the Vosges. They provide the rain shadow that gives Alsace its hot, dry summers.

The Hugel family, headed by much-loved Jean, in front of the St. Catherine cask in the Hugel cellars in Riquewehr. Built in 1715, it is the oldest cask in the world still in continuous use.

grapes will usually be picked at higher sugar levels; to qualify as a *grand vin* (or better) the wine must contain 11 percent alcohol (although chaptalization is permitted, and practiced, whether the wine needs it or not). One feels that the Alsace Riesling is being brought up as a man – a Spartan, even. One of the few concessions to modern technology is the centrifuge, used to clarify the juice after 12 hours or so of rough settling. From this point on the aim is to subjugate the pretty, flowery characters of Riesling and to invest it instead with a dry, steely strength.

In such traditional family houses as Hugel, fermentation takes place in ancient wooden casks; in banks of towering stainless-steel fermentation vats in the cooperatives. Fermentation temperatures are nominally held at 68°F (20°C) but in practice go higher, particularly where precise temperature-control facilities are not available. These temperatures are much higher than those which (for example) Australian winemakers would use, 54°F to 59°F (12°C to 15°C), and burn out many of the fruity esters and flavors of the grape. In 1981, Marc Hugel (son of Jean Hugel) worked a vintage in Australia, and returned determined to experiment using much lower fermentation temperatures (around 57°F/14°C). His results yielded a wine that was incredibly aromatic and intense, a kind of perfumed essence that was unrecognizable as a wine of Alsace. Rumor has it that small percentages are from time to time blended into the wines of the house, but – with good reason – Jean Hugel, who is regarded by many as a spokesman for the whole Alsace wine industry, has not allowed any overt change.

Once fermentation has finished, and the wine racked off its lees, the Alsace approach is strictly noninterventionist. Filtration, fining, even pumping: all are kept to a minimum. The one enemy the winemaker is concerned about is oxidation (*see* pages 212–14), one that is comprehensively defeated. Fresh, bracing, firm and aggressive in their youth, Alsace Rieslings need time in bottle: the greater the vintage, the longer. Just as the finest 1990 German Spätlesen and Auslesen were reaching their peak in 2005, so were the top Rieslings of Alsace. And if one were to give those wines another 20 years, it is arguable Alsace would better stand the test of time.

Elsewhere in Europe true Riesling is greatly outnumbered by its ignoble namesake, Welsh or Italian Riesling. Where true Riesling is found – in northern Italy, the Czech Republic, Slovakia, Slovenia, a little in Austria and Hungary (and a very great deal in Ukraine and Russia) – local tastes divide between the German and the Alsace approach to winemaking. Italy is more Alsatian; Austria (and even more so the Czech Republic) incline toward the riper German style typical of the Palatinate.

Australian Riesling

In the 20 years of explosive growth in Australian vineyards and wine production since 1985, one variety stood still, a bystander in the shadows. In 1985, Riesling was the leading classic white variety; by 2005, its tonnage (46,560 tons/42,239 tonnes) was dwarfed by Chardonnay (458,775 tons/416,194 tonnes), embarrassed by Semillon (108,204 tons/98,161 tonnes), Colombard (98,146 tons/89,037 tonnes) and Muscat Gordo Blanco (61,694 tons/55,968 tonnes).

The aim is to produce a wine that is highly aromatic and intensely fruity, but that has minimal reliance on sugar. In general terms, the Australian (and now New Zealand) approach is strictly to protect the juice before fermentation, keeping it at 32°F (0°C); to "cold-settle," centrifuge or filter it to absolute clarity; to ferment it in stainless steel at precisely controlled temperatures; to arrest fermentation with a barely perceptible (to the palate) level of residual sugar, achieved by bringing the temperature of the wine down to 41°F (5°C) and sterile-filtering it; and to bottle the wine as quickly as possible, usually within three months of the end of fermentation. At no time will it be put in oak, new

or old, large or small. The sulfur levels will be kept as low as possible. The only chemical adjustment will be to the acid, with tartaric (and possibly a little malic) acid added during fermentation and adjusted (if necessary) at bottling. In New Zealand it may be necessary to go the other way, and reduce natural acidity, as in Germany, but this is not common.

Riesling (like the other aromatic varieties such as Gewürztraminer) has high levels of monoterpenes responsible for the delicate but intensely fruity bouquet of its young wines. As the wine ages, these transform into a range of aromas ranging from honey to lightly browned toast to kerosene, with a citrus and mineral background.

Curiously, Riesling came late to New Zealand, initially submerged under oceans of Müller-Thurgau. Its style is closer to Germany than to Australia, high levels of natural acidity almost invariably balanced by 10 grams per liter of residual sugar. The best are fragrant and piercing in fruit flavor.

However bumpy the ride of Riesling has been in Australia, it pales in insignificance compared to that it has experienced in California, although its nemesis in each country is (or was) the same: Chardonnay. From 3,950 acres (1,600 ha) in the 1970s and early 1980s, plantings soared to 55,600 acres (22,500 ha) before plunging back to a little over 2,475 acres (1,000 ha). The market for dry Riesling (known in California as Johannisberg Riesling) collapsed, and today production is largely limited to late-harvest styles that, given enough botrytis, can be exceptionally concentrated, complex and luscious.

Other states are according the variety rather more courtesy. Washington State Riesling is a promising adolescent, although some observers see the wines as living off their flowery aroma and failing on the palate, with the hard, slightly green, herbaceous flavors that seem to be associated with unripe pips. Those of Oregon are quite different; the more humid and slightly warmer growing conditions produce grapes with high sugar levels and balanced acidity. The result is wines with lime-juice aroma and flavor, offset by the suggestion of bath powder that certain German wines evoke, and frequently enriched by a light infection of botrytis. There should be a future for these wines – as there should for the burgeoning Rieslings of regions as disparate as New York and British Columbia.

Above left: *Modern presses (these are airbag presses at Stag's Leap in the Napa Valley) mean gentler, more controlled and often faster pressing.*

Above right: *Refrigerated tanks at Montana Wines' Riverland winery. In New Zealand (and Australia) the Riesling approach is to ferment under strictly controlled temperatures to produce aromatic, fruity wines.*

New Zealand

Riesling in the U.S.

A time of reckoning

Aromatic White Wines

This choices-and-consequences chart illustrates those stages in the winemaking process in which the options chosen by the winemaker will fundamentally influence the taste and individuality of the final wine. The example is of light-bodied, so-called aromatic wines, epitomized perhaps by Riesling. Not every stage of the process is indicated: for that the reader is directed to the white wine process chart on pages 88–9.

Aromatic wines strive for finesse. They are deliberately made light in flavor, relying on fruit in the absence of oak overtones, and balancing sweetness with acidity. An important decision is whether to blend several grape varieties or produce a single-grape varietal wine. Beyond the broad division of sweet or dry, there are discernible regional differences in varietal character, reflecting the climate and soils as well as the vinification methods. Changing tastes also lend their weight: the trend in recent years has been toward drier, fresher wines. All of these factors need to be taken into consideration when choosing grape varieties and winemaking techniques.

1
IN THE VINEYARD

Choice of grape variety
(a) *Single variety*
(b) *Blend*

The choice of grapes largely turns upon the decision whether or not to blend. Riesling, the finest of the aromatic varieties, is seldom blended with other varieties, although Riesling/Traminer blends had a brief period of popularity in Australia. Simply because of the style of the wines – aiming at finesse, elegance and clarity – the complexity offered by blending is only rarely regarded as important.

2
CRUSHING AND PRESSING

Juice handling
The very name "aromatic" means that, apart from certain countries such as Italy, the usual practice is to protect the juice from oxidation by the addition of sulfur dioxide, which may be added in the crusher, in the press or as the juice is placed in the vat for settling.

3
FERMENTING

Right: Hunawihr's most famous vineyard, Clos Ste-Hune, grows particularly fine Riesling. Alsace is the only wine region in France in which the Riesling grape is permitted.

Far right: Temperature control in the fermentation vat is more essential than ever for aromatic wines, as grapy aromas are easily lost as the temperature rises.

Method of picking
(a) *By hand*
(b) *By machine*

The initial belief that delicate white wines could not be made from machine-harvested fruit has long since been proved false. In California and Australia, speed of harvesting and the ability to harvest during cool nighttime temperatures have more than compensated for damage to the grapes. In Germany and Alsace, almost all the grapes are picked by hand because of the limitations of steep slopes and the need to be selective.

Left: *Growers aiming for high-quality wine use a very sparing hand in applying fertilizers.*

Crushing and pressing
For almost all aromatic white wines, grapes are pressed immediately after crushing. For top-quality wines, only the free-run or lightly pressed juice is used.

Juice clarification
Juice must be clarified before fermentation, and this can be achieved by natural cold-settling, by filtration or by centrifuging.

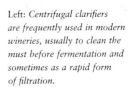

Left: *Centrifugal clarifiers are frequently used in modern wineries, usually to clean the must before fermentation and sometimes as a rapid form of filtration.*

Yeast choice
Because the juice is frequently filtered, centrifuged or cold-clarified, and because of typically low fermentation temperatures, most makers use cultured yeasts.

Choice of fermentation vat
Old oak vats are still widely used in parts of Europe, but the advantages of stainless steel (sterility, temperature control) are increasingly recognized. If oak is used, it does not impart any flavor to the wine.

Fermentation timing and temperature
The length of fermentation directly relates to fermentation temperature. In the New World, it may last one month at temperatures of 48°F to 50°F (9°C to 10°C); Old World fermentations tend to be much warmer and quicker.

Termination of fermentation
For most aromatic white wines the fermentation is stopped while there is still a little unfermented sugar left in the wine. This is achieved by chilling the wine, racking it and adding sulfur dioxide. Others – typically in Alsace and Italy – are fermented bone-dry, and still others are sweetened after being fermented dry by the addition of grape juice (*Süssreserve*).

4
FINISHING

Filtration
In the New World, aromatic white wines are almost invariably filtered. In the Old World, filtering tends to be kept to the minimum.

Cold-stabilization
This process involves chilling the wine to just above freezing point to prevent the risk of tartrate crystals forming after the wine is bottled. This is standard procedure in all larger wineries.

Bottling
In most instances the wines are bottled immediately or shortly after the end of fermentation; by and large, nothing is to be gained by storage in tank.

Gewürztraminer

It seems that the Gewürztraminer is as difficult to vinify well as it is easy to recognize and remember. It is an early-ripening variety, prone to spring frost damage, yielding much less than Riesling, and demanding nice judgment to pick it at the right moment when its aromas are ripened, but before its acidity drops (as it does, rapidly). Alsace has the climate and its growers know the secret. It is a pink-skinned grape that needs quick but gentle pressing to keep the juice white and clear: any turbidity results in almost unpleasantly phenolic wine.

In other parts of the world, winemakers find themselves between the devil and the deep blue sea in handling this variety. If they are too restrained in their approach – picking the grapes a little too early is a prime cause – a pale, faintly spicy but rather anemic wine results. If they leave the grapes on the vine a little too long and lower the temperature of the fermentation vat a bit too far, an oily, pungent, coarse, tannic wine with a particularly aggressive finish and aftertaste is the consequence. On balance, though, it is better to wait for full ripeness and risk having to boost the acidity artificially than to pick too soon. The aim should be a lively, fresh, rose-petal scent leading to a clean, refreshing, lycheelike finish. The Alsace version is most convincing fully dry; the German is softer, fainter, sweeter and rarely as memorable. Few New World winemakers seem to have the temerity to offer it without a little residual sugar to mask a tendency to coarseness. If any region shows the potential to challenge Alsace, it is probably New Zealand.

The symbiosis between the stone and gravel terroir of Marlborough and Sauvignon Blanc came as a complete surprise to the pioneer of the region, Montana Wines, after it planted the first vines in August 1973.

Pinot Gris

Pinot Gris rejoices in more actively used synonyms than any other important grape variety, even though one of its most important *noms de verre*, Tokay d'Alsace, was outlawed by the European Union mandarins. It is known as Ruländer in Germany, Pinot Grigio in Italy, Pinot Beurot in Burgundy, Fromenteau in Champagne, Malvoisie on the Loire and Szürkebarát in Hungary. A comparative tasting of Pinot Gris from these countries will emphasize that it is versatile enough to produce light, dry wines (especially in northeast Italy), or wines as dense, broad and mouth-filling as any white grape can produce. That seems to have been the significance of its now-outlawed name "Tokay" in Alsace, where it achieves an almost oily, unctuous richness. This led a number of winemakers to bring in new oak in an effort to show the Burgundians what a real white wine should taste like. So far, at least, the Burgundians do not seem unduly worried – which simply reinforces the Alsatian view that the Burgundians know nothing about wine anyway.

If there is to be a newly fashionable white wine variety for the next generation, it could boil down to a choice between the erratic Viognier and Pinot Gris. (Australia might contribute Verdelho as a long-shot challenger.) Of the three, Pinot Gris has the best credentials: in countries as far apart as Hungary and New Zealand it makes a wine full of character, a wine that does not need new oak – and usually does not receive it, hence its inclusion in this chapter – but which can react synergistically with it, given the chance. Because of its robust, mouth-filling flavor,

it is one of those varieties that winemakers class as forgiving: a feature they promptly take advantage of. For the reality is that if you see a wine labeled Pinot Gris (or one of its synonyms), be prepared for any possibility; it may be a little sweet, it may be bone-dry; it may have a little oak, but by rights should have none; it may be succulent in flavor and texture, or it may be oily and bitter, or thin, hard and chalky; it may be white, yellow, bronze-copper or delicately pink in color; it may be very good or very bad.

Chenin Blanc

Chenin Blanc is a more predictable grape and produces a more predictable wine, but is very nearly as variable in style and quality as Pinot Gris. In South Africa (where it is very widely propagated as "Steen"), in the United States, Australia, New Zealand, Argentina and Chile, it usually makes a blandly fruity wine that is as inoffensive as it is unremarkable. When handled intelligently, as it often is in South Africa, it keeps a lively zing of acidity – but many versions are simply dull, semisweet middle-of-the-roaders. In utter contrast, along the Loire Valley in Vouvray, Montlouis, Anjou, Bonnezeaux, Coteaux du Layon and Quarts de Chaume, it produces wines of at times Olympian quality but that are understood and appreciated by only a few, and that are grossly underrated in consequence.

Longevity on the Loire

The most striking quality of Chenin Blanc wines is their longevity. The sweeter versions from Huet and Marc Brédif (the latter variously labeled *demi-sec*, *moelleux*, *doux* and – exceptionally – *liquoreux*, as in 1921) and from Moulin Touchais in the Coteaux du Layon can be magnificent between 50 and 100-plus years bottle-age. After decades in the wilderness (which is why the makers often have exceptional museum cellars), underappreciated and underpriced, these wines are now in demand, their price better reflecting their sheer class (and the expense of making them).

The making of Chenin Blanc in the great cellars of the Loire Valley is exceedingly simple: crush, press, partially clarify the juice, ferment in an assortment of stainless-steel, fiberglass and ancient wooden vessels with no more than a chilly autumn for temperature control, a limited degree of lees contact and unhurried (but not particularly early) bottling. No oak, no artifice, no sophistication. The magic lies in *terroir*, climate, *pourriture noble* (for the sweet versions) and, perhaps above all else, time in bottle.

The result is a wine that emerges like a butterfly from its chrysalis. It is hard, slightly chalky and obviously acidic when young; with time it achieves a honeyed complexity with all manner of flowers and fruits hovering in the background. No other region where Chenin is planted is as marginal, on such a high latitude, as the Loire (where the harvest is often the latest in France). Moreover, once off the skeletal soils of the Loire Valley, the utterly promiscuous yield of the variety deprives the wine of any real character. It is always difficult to know where to place such wines in a food context (particularly when they fall in the *demi-sec* to *moelleux* range), but for many the solution is the terrace, the apéritif role.

Muscadet

The role of Muscadet (aka Melon de Bourgogne) is altogether easier to define. It should be served as cold as possible with fresh oysters. If it is a good Muscadet, the aroma will be similar; if it is not so good, just leave the oyster shells in the sun for a few hours. From a winemaking viewpoint (if not all viewpoints), the chief interest of Muscadet lies in the fact that it popularized lees contact: the best Muscadets are invariably bottled straight from unracked barrels, or *sur lie*. Lees are principally composed of the dead yeast cells that have multiplied in their millions during fermentation, and that settle as a creamy mud at the bottom of the fermentation vat once the process is over. The lees are a potent natural antioxidant, and there is no question that they have a real role in keeping the wine fresh and crisp (and equally no question that they can contribute to some of the smelly off-odors in some of the more forgettable Muscadets).

Muscadet takes the process of lees contact further than in the making of any other wine except Champagne (where the use is different but essential nonetheless). It is of great importance, too, in the fashioning of great Chardonnay, but only for Muscadet do the winemakers dare bottle the wine, unracked and unfiltered, direct from its lees. Muscadet therefore begins its maturation in a reductive environment, undisturbed by dissolved carbon dioxide, and its slight *pétillance* stems directly from this. (In the New World, such *pétillance* may come from zealous protection with gaseous carbon dioxide designed to prevent any possibility of oxidation, and – in many cases – deliberately to provide a touch of spritz on the tip of the tongue.)

Grüner Veltliner

Finally, there is Austria's Grüner Veltliner; why, so far, other countries have not planted the variety is hard to fathom. Perhaps it has been found guilty by virtue of its association (in Austria) with Riesling, with which it shares many things in common, not the least its longevity. It accounts for one-third of Austria's grape plantings, producing its best in the Wachau. It ages superbly (60-year-old examples can be quite marvelous), its initial spicy/peppery edge softening as the wine takes on a mouth-feel and flavor disconcertingly similar to mature white Burgundy. It is made in similar fashion to Riesling, without elaboration or artifice.

Vinifera crosses

German vines for English vineyards

By no means does this end the list of white grapes whose winemaking is, or should be, a simple and rapid, if not hurried, affair – where the essence of the matter is to preserve the fruit from oxidation, ferment clean juice, stabilize it if need be and bottle it early.

The same rules apply to some extremely aromatic grapes and some almost scentless ones. The most aromatic are Germany's *vinifera* crosses such as Siegerrebe, Scheurebe and all the younger -rebes that threaten the integrity of German wine. England's vineyards may well benefit from the work of German vine-breeders: Germany's definitely do not.

The list of more or less neutral varieties is endless. The best that can be hoped of most of them is enough sugar and extract to make them taste and feel vinous, and enough acidity to give them the power to refresh. The archetype of such grapes is the grossly overplanted Trebbiano of central Italy (which answers the Italian demand for a cold drink with some strength but no flavor to wash down seafood). Just how fine a "neutral" wine can be is, however, illustrated by the best Swiss Chasselas (or Fendant), which offers texture and a most delicate hint of fruit.

On the fringes are such varieties as the Marsanne and Roussanne of the Rhône Valley: the Marsanne fat and weighty, the Roussanne more fragile but an excellent lively leavener of a blend. The two together, under the ideal conditions of the hill at Hermitage, can make a monument of a wine that slowly deepens in flavor over decades while remaining almost unbelievably fresh. Though barrel flavor does not usually enter into its composition, in truth this is the sort of full-bodied, multifaceted wine that is closer to the subject matter of the next chapter.

Wooded and Full-Bodied White Wines

Choices, consequences and techniques

Sauvignon Blanc

Sauvignon Blanc is a grape open to even more differing interpretations than most. At one end of its spectrum it makes featherweight, aromatic wines, rather like those that are particularly sharp and grassy from Germany and southern Austria. Lesser Loire Valley versions such as Sauvignon de Touraine are like this in moderate vintages. At the other end, ripened to almost tropical fruitiness and aged in oak, Sauvignon Blanc can play the role of the poor man's Chardonnay. Some would not even regard it as a quality grape, let alone as a classic variety. Viticulturally, it is much more temperamental than Chardonnay, tending to produce tiny crops one year, excessive crops the next. In the winery, winemakers can find themselves between the devil of excessive, rank, herbal varietal character and the deep blue sea of bland, oily mediocrity.

Where the Pouilly is Fumé

Few would disagree that Sauvignon Blanc finds its greatest expression between the towns of Pouilly-sur-Loire and Sancerre at the eastern end of the lower Loire Valley. Here ground-hugging vines planted at very high densities produce wine almost painfully crammed with flavor and intensity (to some it is indeed exceedingly distasteful). The magic occurs entirely in the vineyard, the benefits of *terroir* culminating in fine, chalky soils.

Sauvignon Blanc's singular flavor is at its most powerful in Sancerre. The vineyards rise on all sides of the village of Chavignol, one of the most sought-after in the region.

Winemaking methods and equipment vary from extremely primitive to adequate: hard pressing of the grapes, rough juice settling, minimal temperature control of fermentation, minimal postfermentation handling, and bottling when it suits the work pattern in the vineyard are the order of the day. Rarely would you find a single stick of oak – until recently, that is, for the new-oak disease is a highly

contagious one and the scene is now changing. But with exceptions (the large firm of de Ladoucette and a few cooperatives), most of the producers are small, and the money for expensive items like new barrels, or more sensitive equipment such as membrane presses, is simply not there.

In its contribution to the great sweet wines of Bordeaux (which we visit in due course), the role and stature of Sauvignon Blanc are undoubted. Its support role to Semillon in producing the dry white wines of Bordeaux has been rather less distinguished – not through any fault of either Semillon or Sauvignon Blanc, but simply through what could often only be described as diabolically bad winemaking. These were white wines made (apparently reluctantly) by makers of red wine using red-winemaking equipment and techniques to produce what everyone knew was second-class wine.

White Bordeaux

The most immediate and catastrophic consequences of such perfunctory winemaking were averted by massive doses of sulfur dioxide. Young white Graves used to reek of nothing but sulfur (and perhaps a little cabbage) for the first 10 years of their lives; thereafter the poor or mediocre vintages would simply rot away. Happily, the great vintages can slowly throw off the chains that bound them for so long and at 30, 40 or 50 years of age become fine wines. There was one winemaker, though, Claude Ricard of Domaine de Chevalier, who went to great pains, clarifying the juice before fermenting it by laborious barrel-racking. His wines were (and still are) splendid. But he was alone.

Strange as it sounds, it was an Australian initiative that changed this gloomy picture. In 1978, Len Evans from the Hunter Valley headed the team that bought Château Rahoul, an unknown property in the village of Portets in the Graves region. Their first vintage, 1979, was made by Brian Croser of Petaluma (South Australia), assisted by a Dane, Peter Vinding-Diers.

Croser applied his New World technology, cleaning the juice by cold-stabilization, chilling it at 32°F (0°C) until all solids were precipitated, and then fermenting at a moderate temperature. He also used indigenous yeasts, rather than a "safe" cultured strain, which imparted what Vinding-Diers calls "the signature of the farm." The immediate result was a cleaner, fruitier and altogether more attractive young wine than any Graves property had ever made.

In 1980, Denis Dubourdieu, of the Barsac château Doisy-Daëne, followed suit, soon joined by the *négociant* Pierre Coste of Langon, in this new wave in winemaking. Bordeaux's dry white wines had been given new life from the Antipodes. The 1980s saw "flying winemakers" bringing Australian technology to more and more areas of southern France to make young wines that tasted frankly of fruit.

"Flying winemakers"

Gone now is the excessive sulfur dioxide; in its place is selective use of skin contact, the cold-fermentation of relatively clear juice, and the judicious use of new oak, together with lees contact and many of the New World Chardonnay techniques. Wines of great fragrance, suppleness and intensity are the result; wines that produce a very credible alternative to those of the Loire Valley, particularly for those who prefer complexity to instant stimulation.

California instinctively emulates the white Bordeaux style. It shies away from the aggressive, almost wild Sancerre flavors. Nowhere is the American diffidence about full-frontal fruit flavor more apparent than with Sauvignon Blanc. A society that drinks swimming pools of Coca-Cola every hour, that indiscriminately throws fruit, waffles and maple syrup on the breakfast bacon and eggs, studiously avoids salt and substitutes sugar, takes all the flavor out of coffee, and invented the Waldorf Salad is inherently unlikely to enjoy the tart, herbal, gooseberry flavor of untamed Sauvignon Blanc. Robert Mondavi had the answer when he coined the label "Fumé Blanc" for a slightly oak-aged version that avoids all extremes. It has been widely and industriously imitated.

California's "Fumé Blanc"

New Zealand　　　New Zealand, in contrast, emulates the Loire and – most would say – takes its flavors to another dimension. The Marlborough district of the South Island is one of the clearest cut examples in the New World of a region with a homogeneous *terroir* and climate that is ideally suited to a particular variety (Sauvignon Blanc) and that could satisfy in all respects the French *appellation contrôlée* system. Other parts of New Zealand produce Sauvignon Blanc of quality, but not with the consistency or the panache of that of Marlborough.

Like California, New Zealand's winemaking techniques cover the full gamut from simple vat fermentation (most common) through to cool-room barrel fermentation (typically, a small percentage for back-blending). The differences lie in the vineyard, in the growing techniques and in the climate. On an issue such as this, there is no right or wrong; the Californians make one style, the New Zealanders another. On the evidence to date, the world at large strongly prefers the New Zealand version.

Other varieties

Semillon (Sémillon)

Semillon, Pinot Blanc and Viognier complete the transition to the market leader among full-bodied white wine varieties. Only in Australia does Semillon (here spelled without the *é*) make a great dry white wine on its own. Its shrine is the Hunter Valley, where it is best picked with a potential alcohol of 10 to 10.5 percent by volume, cold-fermented in stainless steel, and bottled within a few months of vintage – still water-white, timidly emitting faint aromas of grass, mineral and lemon, the taste even more subdued. Over the next 20 years it acquires a luminescent green-gold color, the aromas of honey, lightly browned toast and oak (though none is there), the weight and mouth-feel changing from ultra-light-bodied to medium-full-bodied. It is the ultra-chameleon of the wine world.

After a depressing few decades where Lindemans vacated the throne, bottle-matured Hunter Semillon (five to six years old when released) is once again the dominant force in the Australian wine-show system, with McWilliam's and Tyrrell's supported by smaller makers such as Brokenwood. The flow-on effect has been a revolution in the way the Barossa Valley is making its best Semillons, picking at 11 to 11.5 degrees rather than 13.5 degrees, and abandoning the use of oak.

Viognier　　　Viognier is a wonderful eccentric, producing wines in the northern Rhône that taste as if a truckload of gummy bears had been emptied into the fermentation vat. Here and there across the United States and Australia a few brave souls are seeing whether they can work something of the same magic with this, a notoriously awkward grape to grow, using a variety of winemaking techniques ranging from the deliberately rustic (Rhône) approach to ultra-sophisticated barrel fermentation. Unexpectedly, perhaps, it is its secondary use as a cofermentation partner with Syrah (Shiraz) that is underwriting its expansion in all corners of the globe.

Pinot Blanc　　　Pinot Blanc has long been taken for a first cousin of Chardonnay, and in parts of the Côte d'Or treated as such. Monsieur Ponsot, the mayor of Morey-St-Denis, makes a Pinot Blanc of enormous power and strength, using precisely the same methods as he would if it were Chardonnay. Perhaps the flavor is slightly less fruity and lingering, but it would take an ace taster to spot it. Odd vines and patches of Pinot Blanc persist in many old Chardonnay vineyards, and yet it is no relation. Pinot Blanc is a white mutation of Pinot Noir, thus a cousin (or sister) of Pinot Gris. Chardonnay comes from another "bloodline" altogether.

The great majority of the world's Pinot Blanc wines come from Alsace and (as Pinot Bianco) from northern Italy. Neither region treats it in the Chardonnay manner; instead, it is used as a rather high-yielding, gently fruity but generally rather neutral grape for quick-drinking wine. That of Alsace is attractively soft (without the steeliness typical of the region), while most Pinot Bianco is just Bianco. Picked early with high acidity, it provides the base for many Italian sparkling wines. Yet mention should be made of some growers in the northeast, particularly in Collio, who do make the most of its character.

In Germany, Pinot Blanc, known as Weissburgunder, has been used (in such warmer regions as Baden) mainly to make a softer and less aromatic alternative to Riesling, or to blend with overaromatic hybrids. Recently, more free-thinking German winemakers have given it a brief spell in *barrique* (the French term is modish) to produce something very distinctly alternative and almost shockingly un-Germanic – an excellent table wine nonetheless.

One hears little of Pinot Blanc in the New World. Chalone Vineyards in California makes the most upper-crust example, treating it like Chardonnay. As yet, Australia does not grow it, nor does New Zealand.

Chardonnay

And so we come to the grape that has forged such a close bond with oak that it is no exaggeration to say that a substantial percentage of regular wine-drinkers have little idea where the flavor of Chardonnay stops and that of oak starts. The more skilled the winemaker and the better the wine, the more difficult it will be to make the distinction. It has to be said that the winemaker has an unfair advantage with the extraordinary range of options available in handling this most flexible (and forgiving) of varieties, the selection of which will fundamentally affect the ultimate style of the wine (and the apparent role of the oak).

White Burgundy

Anyone who has shared a bottle of one of the very best white Burgundies (1978 Le Montrachet of the Domaine de la Romanée-Conti comes to mind) has tasted such perfection that it brings a touch of sadness: a feeling that one will never taste a greater white wine. (This is a feeling periodically experienced by a privileged few ever since Claude Arnoux wrote his panegyric for Montrachet in the early 1700s, so the sadness is quite illogical.) Complexity is the keynote of white Burgundy: complexity deriving from a series of fortuitous and planned inputs, which may be totally convincing and satisfying, or flawed and unsound – but it will be Burgundy.

Viewed in contrast with the convolutions and sophistications of New World winemakers, the traditional Burgundian approach to Chardonnay was simple, if not downright rustic. There was a conviction that they (the winemakers) were correct in everything they did: a Gallic confidence born of centuries of experience, and an indifference to what others may be doing, because those outsiders did not share their *terroir*. We use the past tense, for the younger generation of Burgundians, encouraged by such patrician figures as Vincent Leflaive and Robert Drouhin, are now traveling, working and comparing notes in California, Australia and elsewhere.

The result is that the face of white Burgundy is changing. Just as in Chablis (*see* page 76), care and attention to detail are making the traditional recourse to heavy doses of sulfur dioxide unnecessary and, importantly, unfashionable. The wines are becoming cleaner, softer, more forward and – some would say – more anonymous. The majority would say that they are also distinctly better wines, and that bottle-age will allow their *terroir* and true quality (or lack of it) to be expressed.

A greater threat to clear-cut vineyard identity comes from increasing yields. Astute judges have long pondered about the extraordinary concentration and flavor of Le Montrachet: specifically, how much derives from *terroir*, and how much from the lower-than-usual yields. But all things are relative. First, Chardonnay suffers far less from the effects of increased yield than does Pinot Noir (as indeed does any white grape compared to any red). Second, the Burgundians have certainly been blessed with a superb combination of *terroir*, climate and (by and large) clonal selection. The overall quality of the raw material – the grapes – is better than that of any other region in the world.

The winemaker using Chardonnay grapes can be likened to a sculptor: he or she starts with a mass of raw, moist clay. The greater the mass, the more profligate can be the sculptor in shaping the work; great chunks may be carved away without undue concern, for there will always be enough left to allow the last shaping and chiseling as the work takes its final form. It is something that many New World winemakers should realize, but do not. Blissfully unaware, it seems, that their mass

Chardonnay grapes arriving at the Robert Mondavi Winery in the Napa Valley. After being tipped from the "gondola" in which they are transported, an Archimedean screw moves the grapes into the winery.

Chardonnay

This chart illustrates those stages in making wine with Chardonnay in which the options chosen by the winemaker will fundamentally influence the taste and individuality of the final wine. Not every stage of the process is indicated; for that, the reader is directed to the white wine process chart on pages 88–9.

Chardonnay's varietal character is expressed in many forms: as the steely, acidic wine of Chablis; as a fuller-bodied, more buttery wine in southern Burgundy (gaining warm fruit characteristics in New World regions); and as a base wine for Champagne, to name a few.

Geographical variation in style is influenced by vinification techniques, but of key consideration everywhere is the emphasis placed on either simple primary fruit structure or on secondary fruit characteristics that develop as the wine matures. Balance of the two is very important. Using wood for fermentation or maturation and malolactic fermentation are also key influences on style, as is tradition: should Chardonnay be vinified to emulate a classic Burgundy, or should varietal character be expressed according to the region?

1
HARVESTING

Method of picking
(a) *Picking by hand*
Mandatory if the grapes are not going to be crushed before pressing. Only economically viable in smaller-scale vineyards such as in Burgundy and top New World wineries.
(b) *Picking by machine*
Almost a necessity in the grand-scale New World vineyards. Enables night harvesting when it is cool: a great advantage in hot regions.

2
CRUSHING AND PRESSING

Juice and must handling
(a) *Protective handling*
Adding a small dose of sulfur dioxide to the crushed grapes and cooling the juice protects it from oxidation and results in more color and primary grape flavor.
(b) *Unprotected handling*
Oxidation can be deliberate, to produce more complex, fuller wines. These age more slowly, but loss of primary fruit flavor must be accepted. This option eases the onset of malolactic fermentation. Cooling optional.

Above: Loved by growers and winemakers alike, Chardonnay is one of the most popular grape varieties – here growing for Champagne production in the Côte des Blancs.

Right: Chardonnay grapes destined for Robert Mondavi's winery in the Napa Valley, California. Chardonnays from this region are said to rival even top-quality white Burgundies.

Far left: Contoured vineyards in Napa Valley, California's most concentrated and prestigious wine county, now home to all the best grape varieties.

Left: Gallo Frei Ranch tank farm; winery or refinery is a question often asked, but technology and quality are not incompatible.

Crushing

The decision whether to crush or not depends on the kind of pressing (*see* pressing).

Skin contact

Will only follow protective handling. Increases phenol extraction from grape skins, leading to a more robust Chardonnay with fuller flavor. Extended contact (up to 30 hours) deepens color prematurely, and flavors may break up and become oily. A practice on the wane for all but the cheapest wines.

Pressing

(a) *Whole bunch*
Whole-bunch pressing is traditionally used for sparkling wine, increasingly used for table wine. Leads to very clear juice with lowest possible phenol levels; very finely flavored and structured wine results.
(b) *Crushed fruit*
A better option if full-flavored table wine is required or if grapes are relatively low in flavoring phenols in the first place.

Juice clarification

(a) *Nil*
(b) *Partial*
(c) *Total*
Normally nil or partial in Old World. If followed by cool fermentation, should lead to a richer wine. If followed by ambient fermentation is possible with abundance of flavor in the grapes or where a neutral wine is desired. Sometimes total in New World, followed by cool fermentation. Clarification is achieved by holding in a settling tank, filtering or centrifuging.

3 FERMENTING

Choice of fermentation vessel

The main choices are stainless-steel tanks, upright oak vats or oak barrels. The percentage of new or used barrels has major consequences for flavor.

Choice of yeast

Falls between wild, indigenous, feral (one and the same) or cultured (many strains available, each with specific properties).

Fermentation temperature

In the eyes of New World makers, the single most critical factor in determining style. Modern practice is to ferment Chardonnay very cool – at about 59°F (15°C) – to produce fruitier wine. Uncontrolled fermentation in a hot climate can rise above 86°F (30°C). Classic Burgundies are fermented in small barrels that maintain the cool temperature of the cellar.

Malolactic fermentation

Significantly softens and adds to the complexity of Chardonnay. It will be encouraged in cool-climate wines that might have excess acidity. Generally avoided in warmer regions where acidity tends to be low.

4 MATURING

Maturing in oak

The importance of oak selection is now widely understood. The options are between type of oak (forest of origin), new or old and the degree of toast. Maturation in oak following fermentation in oak results in much better integration of oak.

Lees contact

Originally a French technique, but now being widely used. Lees are a powerful antioxidant and add a creamy complexity to the wine. Some prefer lees to skin contact, though care must be taken to ensure they remain sweet. *Bâtonnage* (stirring) will accentuate the effects.

Maturation time before bottling

Ranges from three months to two years – the former if no oak is used or if wine is oak-fermented and a delicate wine is required. Temperature and humidity of the barrel-storage room are critical factors.

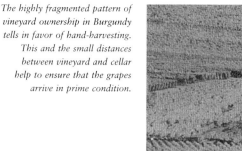

The highly fragmented pattern of vineyard ownership in Burgundy tells in favor of hand-harvesting. This and the small distances between vineyard and cellar help to ensure that the grapes arrive in prime condition.

of clay is very much smaller, they use Burgundian methods and thereby threaten (and sometimes altogether destroy) the integrity of their raw material.

Picking and crushing

The initial handling by the Burgundian is gentle and sensitive; while mechanical harvesting is on the increase, it has not yet reached – and may never reach – the great estates. The highly fragmented pattern of vineyard ownership in Burgundy, the relatively ready availability of labor, the sheer conservatism of the average Burgundian and the need to selectively discard moldy grapes in poorer years all tell in favor of hand-harvesting and against the use of machines. The very small distances between vineyards and cellar and the generally low ambient temperatures of autumn also help the grapes reach the winery in prime condition.

Crusher/destemmer

New high-tech crushers give the winemaker many choices enabling great control over the must. While whole-bunch pressing, retaining the stalks (the grapes in this instance bypass the crusher and are taken directly to the press), is very rare in Burgundy, so, happily, is the opposite extreme of skin contact: usually the must is taken directly from the crusher to the press and then pressed without delay.

Sulfur dioxide may be added at the crusher, at the press or as the juice is passed into the vat for settling, although the later the addition, the more the juice will have oxidized. Only a few winemakers are experimenting with wholly oxidative (unprotected) juice handling, a technique we look at in detail later in this chapter.

Barrel fermentation

The must is allowed to settle overnight, during which time most of the heavy solids (chiefly minute pieces of grape pulp) will fall to the bottom of the vat. The standard procedure is then to rack the still-cloudy juice into the barrels, and wait. If the weather is particularly cool, the juice may have to be warmed; ideally it should be at around 59°F (15°C) for fermentation to start.

Although most Burgundian winemakers prefer to rely on wild yeasts, they may resort to cultured yeast if there are problems with the fermentation getting started or finished (*see* pages 218–20 for a full explanation of yeast choice and consequence). Once it does start, it creates its own heat, and there is no further need to warm the cellar – indeed, quite the reverse. White wine fermenting in barrel will readily reach 72°F to 77°F (22°C to 25°C) of its own accord; anything higher or lower than this will be due to the ambient temperature. While the typical Burgundian cellar may naturally be very cold, if it is filled with fermenting *barriques* of wine, that ambient temperature will rise considerably, and wine temperature likewise. Refrigerated cool rooms are unheard of in Burgundy, so if winemakers want to reduce the fermentation temperature they must pump the wine out of the barrel and pass it through a heat exchanger – or possibly empty a number of barrels into a temperature-controlled stainless-steel vat.

Wild yeasts

Barrel fermentation of partially clarified juice at moderately high temperatures leads to a suppression of primary fruit aroma and flavor in the wine, although these will recover to an extent over a period of time, both before and after bottling. The texture and structure will be complex, although once again it will initially be hard and rough. For the system to work well, two preconditions must be satisfied: there must be a tremendous depth and intensity to the flavor of the grapes, and the wine must be given time in bottle (a minimum of two years, sometimes longer) for the component parts to marry, soften and evolve.

Wine made in this way from this type of raw material has the capacity to swallow the aroma and flavor of new oak. It is exceedingly rare to find a white Burgundy with the type of overt oak influence regularly encountered in the New World. One is tempted to instance Louis Latour's outstanding Corton-Charlemagne as an exception, but it is highly likely that a significant portion of its toasty, nutty aroma and flavor comes from the wine rather than the oak.

Lees contact is widely practiced in Burgundy; indeed, the lees are so highly prized that those from a great wine (such as Montrachet or Bâtard-Montrachet) may be transferred to a lesser wine to enrich or ennoble it (only, of course, once they have done their work with the parent). Regular stirring of the lees, or *bâtonnage*, is practiced weekly in the first few months, less regularly thereafter. With luck, a naturally occurring malolactic fermentation will then start shortly after the primary fermentation; with a great deal of luck it will finish before the onset of winter takes the temperature of the wine down to levels (41°F to 59°F/5°C to 15°C) at which the malolactic bacteria cease their activity. In this last event they appear to go into hibernation, and will spontaneously resume their activity the following spring as cellar temperatures rise once again. It was this observation, without any understanding of its chemical and biochemical origins, that caused winemakers to claim well into the 20th century that wine in the cellar stirred and came to life in response to the sap rising and buds bursting in the vineyard.

Lees contact

Burgundians do not like filtration, and practice it sparingly. It is perhaps less of an issue with Chardonnay than Pinot Noir, since the alleged color and flavor loss due to filtration is less apparent, and the risk of bacterial activity in the bottled (and unfiltered) wine is also substantially lower.

Filtration

The traditional white Burgundy was an extremely powerful, complex and long-lived wine. The relatively high levels of free sulfur dioxide early in its life gradually diminished and became bound, actually contributing to its complexity. The lush fruit, tamed by the winemaking methods, needed years to reassert itself. For the New World winemaker, smelling these wines could be an unnerving experience, with all sorts of sulfide, malolactic and botrytis influences at work. The modern style of white Burgundy is much cleaner: the juice has been clarified to a greater degree, sulfur levels reduced, fermentation temperatures lowered and

White Burgundy then and now

(mainly with the malolactic fermentation) cultured microorganisms used. The time in oak, too, may have been shortened and, although it is hard to draw any particular conclusion from this, the winemaker following this path will quite probably filter the wine.

New World Chardonnay: California

If Burgundians are finding new excitement and possibilities in the winery, their New World counterparts are finding many (though not all) of them in the vineyard. Tim Mondavi spoke these words 15 years ago; many things have changed since, but, if anything, they are even more apposite today than then:

> *Philosophically I think it's extremely important to recognize that we are beginning to understand we are raising a natural beverage from the soil and the climate we have; we are interacting with these, and pursuing the soil just as the Burgundians are pursuing the textbooks. The polar opposites of terroir and technology are coming together.*

The Californian approach to Chardonnay has undergone several profound changes since the variety became popular in the 1960s. The style of the early wines was massively alcoholic and strong, but monolithic in flavor and structure, with the characteristic hot, sweet burn of any high-alcohol white wine.

A revelation: oak

By the mid-1950s, though, a few producers were asking searching questions – and sometimes stumbling on the answers. Fred McCrea at Stony Hill began as early as 1951 taking infinite pains to make balanced Chardonnay. In 1956, Brad Webb, winemaker at Hanzell Vineyards in Sonoma, introduced French barrels for aging for the first time. His assistant, Bill Bonetti, recalled "our surprise when a barrel of Chardonnay must was left unattended, I confess by mistake, and fermented in the

Right: California's pioneering winemakers have been experimenting with Burgundian methods since the 1960s. They include barrel fermentation and consequently higher fermentation temperatures. The barrels in the foreground hold fermenting wine.

Below: The mission-inspired Robert Mondavi Winery.

barrel and turned out the best lot of all." Hanzell was the moment of discovery: the mysterious essence of Burgundy lay in marrying Chardonnay with new oak. But it took years to find out exactly how much – and we are still learning.

In most wineries, the emphasis was on new oak, the winemakers arguing that such a strong and forceful fruit base as theirs could support a high level of oak – and indeed needed it to provide complexity. The result was a massive assault on the senses; such wine was an exhilarating experience for the wine-lover who had not encountered it before. The difficulty lay in drinking a whole glass: the flavor built up and up. No one could actually drink the wine; least of all with food.

The standard approach in making these wines had been to use no skin contact; to carry out temperature-controlled fermentation in stainless-steel vats, followed by sterile filtration. Brilliantly clean wines were then taken to barrel, with no possibility of either lees contact or malolactic fermentation, and were bottled 6 to 15 months later. The result was wines as far removed from those of Burgundy as one could possibly fashion.

By the second half of the 1970s, the winds of change had started to blow, and they intensified in the 1980s. Winery practices changed first: barrel fermentation of cloudy juice, total lees contact, partial or total malolactic fermentations (increasingly the latter) and higher fermentation temperatures – indeed the full gamut of Burgundian practices, with only the high sulfur levels absent (and in fact reduced to an absolute minimum).

Change in the wind

Much of the pioneering work was done at Simi Winery in 1981. Specifically, the use of sulfur dioxide (and to a lesser degree ascorbic acid), usually added to the juice before and during fermentation, was stopped and was only used once the malolactic fermentation was complete. Parallel with this approach, the use of protective inert gases (carbon dioxide and nitrogen) was also abandoned until the fermentation was finished. After this point one or other of these gases was always used to protect the wine while it was moved around the winery.

Juice oxidation

The resulting wine had a lower content of flavoring phenols, lighter and fresher color that took longer to deepen, lower sulfur dioxide levels and aged more slowly. The question remains, of course, whether reduced phenols (and hence modified and reduced fruit flavors) are a desirable aim. As Simi's former winemaker Zelma Long herself readily conceded, they may not be desirable for all wines (particularly where the starting levels of phenols are in any event low) and may not be philosophically desirable for winemakers who place special value on primary Chardonnay fruit flavor.

Racking Chardonnay at Heitz Wine Cellars in the Napa Valley.

Lower phenol levels are also the consequence of another trend: the pressing of whole bunches, stalks and all. This technique, borrowed from sparkling winemaking, works well with high-flavored grapes, less well where flavor is naturally delicate. Once again, it was developed in California, but has since been taken up with enthusiasm by Australia for its top-end Chardonnays.

As the 1980s got underway, a few of the more perspicacious winemakers started thinking about their vineyards, adopting the catchphrase "growing wine" – an upbeat version of the old aphorism that "great wine is made in the vineyard." By the end of the decade, it was clear that progress had been slow in the Napa Valley; "California sprawl" (*see* page 49) was still evident everywhere: large, undisciplined vines surrounded by masses of dark green leaves, cascading to the ground from the relatively low, single-wire trellises. But in Oregon, as in Sonoma and Carneros, far more sophisticated viticulture was already the norm, and has since become so in the Napa Valley.

Growing wine in the vineyard

The aim of the new viticulture is simple: to grow a vine that is in balance, producing a modest crop of grapes that have been adequately exposed to sunlight, and that reach full flavor ("organoleptic ripeness," to use the jargon) at 22.5° to 23.5° Brix. The aim of the new winemaking is to produce wines with elegance, complexity, subtlety and – above all else – good mouth-feel (the last a predictable reaction to the sledgehammer wines of the 1970s). "Harmonization," according to Tim Mondavi, is the key:

> *We as a winery were once appropriately criticized for having too much oak in a number of our wines. All that has changed, with far less use of new oak and much more use of two-, three- and four-year-old oak. And it is not just the amount of oak, but the way the oak is used that has changed incredibly and led to much more subtle integration. Diminished sulfur and lees stirring have also helped produce a brighter-colored wine, more fragrant, with more honey in the aroma as well as suppleness in the mouth.*

As Zelma Long put it:

> *Winemakers still want power, but they are more interested in finesse and balance; they still want aromatics, but they are more interested in how the wine feels in the mouth. They are looking for wines that are more multi-dimensional, in which wood and fruit are integrated.*
>
> *Most California Chardonnays are distinguished by tropical fruit flavors – pineapple, banana – and some apple. I am trying to look for something beyond that, to get away from what is not only simple fruit but what is always the same kind of fruit. I am trying to find the other nuances of Chardonnay flavor – more of the stony/gravelly flavors – to bring another dimension, while still looking for concentration of flavor – and, of course, complexity.*

Chardonnay in Australia

One can always argue about starting points for fashion trends, but 1985 was a seminal year in Australian wine history, as the value of the trickle of exports exceeded that of imports for the first time in 45 years. The 20 years that followed saw Australia grow from minnow to whale; it was Chardonnay that was the spearhead for the first decade, Syrah (Shiraz) for the second.

In 1992, the tonnage of Chardonnay exceeded that of Riesling for the first time; by 2005 it was nine times as great.

Taste in flux

As discussed at various points in this book, an all-encompassing distinction has to be made between grapes grown for big-volume, popular wines, typically from warm-to-hot parts of Australia, and those grown in cool climates and destined for ultra-premium wines. For the former, yield is all-important, viticultural techniques standardized. For the latter, yield is restricted, hand-training of the vines in the growing seasons standard practice.

In the winery, tank fermentation plus oak staves or chips are used for the big-volume wineries. For the best wines, the more intelligent and skillful winemakers are making moves to pull back on fruit and introduce more complexity. Skin contact has been eliminated; oxidative juice handling is being selectively used, as is whole-bunch pressing; barrel fermentation is universal; cloudy-juice fermentation followed by some malolactic fermentation is giving greater complexity; and oak flavor is being more subtly incorporated.

"Dolly Partons"

Two radically different styles have emerged. There are the super-rich, relatively high-alcohol (13.5° to 14°), warm-climate wines made with some residual sugar and flavors of honeyed, peachy fruit. Variously likened to peaches and cream or Dolly Parton, they bloom lusciously but briefly, passing their best within two to three years. This is the Chardonnay style that has captured most attention overseas and – surprisingly – in the United States in particular, where the [yellow tail] (*sic*) brand grew from zero to 7.2 million cases between 2001 and 2005. The other style is far less obvious: usually cool-grown, with highly disciplined and selective

California has few vineyards more ideally sited or better maintained than the Joseph Phelps estate in the wooded foothills on the east side of the Napa Valley at St. Helena.

winemaker input (little or no skin contact, careful pressing and so forth). The wine takes three years to begin showing its potential, and evolves fully over a much longer period of time.

Chardonnay is grown almost everywhere *Vitis vinifera* will grow and ripen. To discuss all of its styles is not practical in anything other than an entire book on Chardonnay (of which there are a number). Suffice it to say that its current popularity will not be short-lived – it is a superb grape, capable of producing superb wine in an almost infinite number of guises – and to hope that the combined influences of *terroir* and healthy parochialism will defeat the dark forces of universalization.

Sparkling Wines

Choices, consequences and techniques

Champagne

Its history

Of the great wines of France, Champagne is the newest arrival. Champagne as a district has been making wine since early Roman times, and by the ninth century it had become sufficiently well established as a high-quality region for a distinction to be drawn between the wines of the Vallée de la Marne and those of the Montagne de Reims. From this time on it went from strength to strength: by the early 16th century, the wine of Aÿ had become so highly prized that it was said to be "the ordinary drink of kings and princes."

It was not until the 17th century, however, that the first sparkling wines made their appearance, and not until the early 19th century that Champagne came to be synonymous with sparkling wine. Neither were the numerous special techniques essential for making Champagne all discovered by one person (notwithstanding the extraordinary feats popularly attributed to Dom Pérignon), nor at any one time. The evolution of the present-day method of making clear sparkling wine using the second fermentation took over 200 years.

Its image

From the outset, Champagne has been blessed with a superabundance of extraordinarily talented and energetic marketers. Small wonder that so many books have been written about the subject, so rich is its anecdotal history. Those marketing and promotion skills remain undimmed to this day, making truly objective assessment or criticism of Champagne extremely difficult. On the one hand there is the knowledge that if one does a blind tasting of Champagne under neutral "scientific" conditions, comparing 20 or 30 Champagnes, what appear to be some quite unpleasant aromas and flavors will be detected in a few of the wines, while others free from fault will nonetheless fall well short of the top-ranked wines. Yet on the other hand, ask a wine judge when he or she last found fault with a glass of Champagne proffered in ordinary social surroundings and the answer is very likely to be "hardly ever."

Made to be drunk

Part of this stems from the fact that Champagne is made to be drunk. Now, that may seem a banal statement of the obvious, but not so much so when you realize a dedicated wine-drinker might savor the bouquet of a great Burgundy for 10 minutes before taking a first sip, and if sharing the bottle with a number of others, might take 30 minutes to consume a single glass. Champagne, even extremely rare and old Champagne, will seldom be treated like this. It will be uncommon for its bouquet to be given more than cursory acknowledgment, while to swill it ruminatively around one's gums is to turn one's mouth into a mini washing machine. Champagne is a wine that appeals to the broadest senses, rather than to the particular. It is the overall impression it leaves in the mouth after it is swallowed that matters most.

Its style

It is true that the greatest Champagnes are wines of extraordinary finesse, balance and above all else length of flavor; the intrinsic quality of these wines is on a par with the greatest of the still white or red table wines. And just as the Burgundians place special emphasis on the bouquet, the Bordelais on the palate and structure, so the Champenois claim the finish and, in particular, the aftertaste as the special feature of their wine.

Not that all Champagnes taste the same: there is a world of difference between a Pol Roger and a Krug, a Taittinger and a Bollinger, let alone between a vintage Champagne of one of the *grandes marques* and a nonvintage "buyer's own brand" from one of

the cooperatives. Yet the overall consistency of the quality and style of nonvintage Champagne from the *grandes marques* exceeds that of any other category of wine in any other region – an astonishing achievement, given the marginal climate in which the Champenois grow their grapes, and the fluctuations in supply and demand they so skillfully manage from both marketing and making viewpoints.

Champagne is France's northernmost vineyard region. Without the special properties of its chalk soil, free-draining and sun-reflecting, it would be a very doubtful area for ripening grapes.

Assemblage (blending) is the most critical stage of the long and convoluted process that makes the finished Champagne. It is the art that made Dom Pérignon the most famous oenologist of his day: indeed, perhaps the first famous winemaker in history.

Assemblage

Blending involves a detailed knowledge of the past, present and future of the materials, and requires highly specialized tasting skills that can see beyond the often hard, acidic, thin and chalky base wines that give only a barest glimpse of how they will taste once they have been blended, undergone the second fermentation, benefited from contact with yeasts during years of maturation on the lees and been adjusted for sweetness using *liqueur d'expédition*. The task demands the mental skills of a chess grand master as the literally endless permutations and combinations are considered. The blenders at Moët & Chandon typically have 300 different base wines from any one vintage to deal with. The possible permutations are beyond calculation.

One of the most fascinating, important yet shadowy aspects of Champagne is the use of "reserve" wine held from earlier vintages. It may be held in magnums (under slight gaseous pressure), in stainless steel or (less commonly) in oak. Houses such as

Reserve wine

Making Champagne

PRESSING

Making the finest Champagne depends first on attaining the purest possible must. This is achieved by harvesting the crop by hand, gently pressing grape bunches whole and ensuring that the contact between juice and broken grape skins is minimal. Many Champagne houses believe the traditional basket presses are the gentlest method of pressing. The large surface area of the press and small fruit loads ensure that must does not drain over crushed grapes, absorbing tannins en route. Pneumatic or bladder tank presses are also used, which exclude oxygen. They are much faster.

The juice is released from the press in order of quality. The more the fruit is pressed, the greater the tannin, pip and skin content. Better-quality wines are made from only the free-run and first pressings. Second pressings may be used, but for lesser wines.

Cooling
From the press, the must is pumped to small vats, each containing only one pressload of juice so that the choice in the final blend can be as precise as possible. En route the must may be chilled to prevent any bacterial activity and to stop fermentation beginning before *débourbage* (clarification) can take place.

FIRST FERMENTATION

Débourbage
Skin and other impurities can be settled out of the wine at ambient cellar temperatures, but a quicker and more thorough clarification is achieved by chilling to 23°F (–5°C). Purity, and therefore stability, can be increased by fining with bentonite clay. Many winemakers argue that if clarification at this stage is too thorough, the complexity of flavors in the wine will be reduced.

Fermentation
Once clarified, the wine is racked into clean fermentation vats. The size and composition of the vats are of key importance: small vats enable greater control of the fermentation, and stainless steel ensures cleanliness. However, two of the best Champagne houses, Krug and Alfred Gratien, still prefer to ferment their wines in old oak barrels.

Other important considerations at this stage include choice of yeast, chaptalization and malolactic fermentation. Cultured yeasts will usually be used, their effects on the wine being more predictable. The use of wild yeasts can be a gamble, though they may increase a wine's complexity. The wine's potential alcohol almost always needs raising and it is invariably chaptalized. Malolactic fermentation is encouraged as it softens and rounds the wine and adds to its stability.

After fermentation, the wine is once again stabilized before *assemblage* (blending): the most important stage of the *méthode champenoise* process.

Dark arrows indicate critical stages; lighter arrows show optional ones.

ASSEMBLAGE

Cold-stabilization

Suspended matter is precipitated out of the wine by cold-stabilization, preventing both the formation of tartrate crystals and any unwanted yeast or enzyme reactions that may impair the wine. It is then racked off the deposit and further clarified by filtering and fining.

Blending

Great skill and experience are required to create wine of a consistent and fine house style – nonvintage Champagne. Tasting after tasting will be set up, some wines of which will go in various proportions into the final blend. In years where the quality of the harvest is particularly high, a certain proportion will be used to make vintage blends (from only one year). In other years "reserve wine" is of more importance, and is blended in to maintain the house style.

Blending together numerous wines of different chemical properties encourages the presence of unwanted matter, and the wine must again be clarified. Producers aim to maximize purity and stability of the blend by a further period of cold-stabilization, filtering and fining. Gelatin is the most common fining agent used in Champagne. The wine then undergoes its third and final racking.

Liqueur de tirage

After the final racking, the wine is transferred to the bottling line. But before being bottled, a mixture of reserve wine, sugar and selected yeast culture is added to the base wines to stimulate a second alcoholic fermentation. Sugar is necessary in the blend because all base wines for Champagne are dry, and devoid of fermentable sugar. The type and amount of yeast used will vary according to the style of the Champagne.

Making Champagne (CONTINUED)

SECOND FERMENTATION

Champagne gains its sparkle by undergoing a second fermentation, this time in the bottle. As the sugar in the *liqueur de tirage* is converted to alcohol, Carbon dioxide (CO_2) bubbles dissolve in the wine, completing the transformation from still to sparkling. The thickness of the glass can withstand the pressure that builds up as CO_2 is produced. Metal crown caps are used to seal the wine during the fermentation. Keeping the temperature low slows down this process and results in smaller bubbles in the Champagne – one indicator of good quality.

Storage *sur lattes*
In most top Champagne houses the second fermentation and subsequent maturing of the bottles takes place in deep, cool chalk cellars. The aging period may last as long as 20 to 50 years. During this time the wine gains in creaminess and complexity through contact with its yeast sediment (lees). The bottles are stacked, separated by laths (*lattes*). The care in their stacking is to ensure that, should one bottle explode during fermentation, the others will be disturbed as little as possible.

Restacking and shaking of the bottles at intervals is carried out so that the sediment does not stick to the bottle, which would complicate clarification.

CLARIFICATION

Remuage
When secondary fermentation is complete, the lees remaining in the bottle must be removed. The bottles are transferred to wooden racks, then each bottle must be gradually riddled (tilted from horizontal to vertical) to encourage the sediment down into the neck of the bottle. Performed manually, this is painstaking work: skilled *remueurs* are employed to rotate and fractionally tilt the bottles until they are fully perpendicular and ready for disgorgement. The operation may last several months.

Gyropalettes
Using *gyropalettes* shortens the period over which clarification occurs to as little as a week. The principle is the same as *remuage* but mechanized and far more efficient. The bottles are stacked upside down on palettes and mechanically rotated every eight hours, which causes the sediment to spiral down to the neck.

Alginate beads
While technically proved on small-scale batches, logistical issues and costly machinery have led to the cessation of the beads project by inventor Moët Hennessy. Improved specialized yeasts have also played a part in simplifying traditional clarification techniques.

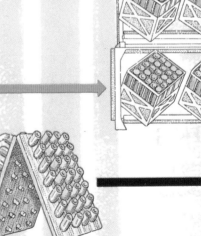

Dark arrows indicate critical stages; lighter arrows show optional ones.

MATURING

Once the yeast sediment has settled, finer Champagnes are matured for up to five years *sur pointes* (upside down). The flavor is further enhanced by contact with the sediment in the neck of the bottle. The disgorging process to remove the sediment is delayed as long as possible.

DISGORGING AND *DOSAGE*

Disgorging is essential but disruptive because it briefly exposes the wine to air, increasing its natural oxidation rate and thus (perhaps) reducing its aging potential. It requires extreme dexterity and speed to remove the crown cap and quickly dislodge yeast sediment from the bottle without losing any wine. Freezing the sediment in the neck of the bottle provides a much tidier and more efficient method. The pressure from the Champagne forces rapid ejaculation of the sediment when the crown cap is removed.

Dosage, sweetening with *liqueur d'expédition* (wine and sugar), is essential for most Champagnes, which at this stage may be quite acidic. Those that have undergone a long maturation will have been softened by contact with yeast sediment and may not need *dosage* – e.g., Brut Sauvage or very old RD – but they will need topping up with wine to fill the bottle after the removal of the sediment.

FINISHING

Immediately after the *liqueur d'expédition* has been added, the bottles are corked, automatically shaken to distribute the *liqueur,* and then labeled.

At this stage some wines will undergo additional "cork age." Most Champagne producers (and quality sparkling winemakers in other countries) believe a minimum of 12 months on cork after disgorgement is highly desirable. From this point on, it is simply a matter of personal choice; 30- or 40-year-old well-cellared Champagne from a great vintage is ambrosia from the gods for some, a strange curiosity for others.

Krug have reserve wines of up to 20 years old, although in diminishing quantity with age. They will usually be held over from vintage years and, tasted on their own, can be superb. A 60-year-old magnum of Bollinger reserve wine (made from 100 percent Pinot Noir) tasted in the 1980s was a memorable experience: nothing to do with Champagne, and more like an old (yet Peter Pan–fresh) white Burgundy; it had acquired the nutty creaminess of mature Chardonnay.

Reserve wines can be used at three stages in the making of Champagne. They can be incorporated in the primary ferment, then (most commonly and importantly) at the time of blending or *assemblage* along with the *liqueur de tirage*, and least importantly (because of the tiny volume) with the *liqueur d'expédition*. All the Champagne houses privately acknowledge that the quality and style of their reserve wines have a powerful influence on their overall house style, but tend to downplay this importance publicly.

Vintage Champagne: a shadow of doubt

Where, you may ask, is the mystery, where are the shadows? It lies with vintage Champagne. Under European Union legislation, 85 percent of the wine must be from the stated vintage year, which would allow generous incorporation of reserve wine. Under the *appellation contrôlée* of Champagne, the wine must be 100 percent from its stated vintage. It is a situation that one can imagine the Italians finding themselves in, and runs entirely counter to the precision with which so much of the affairs of Champagne are run. No one will officially admit it, of course, and strict proof of any breach would be very difficult to obtain, but reserve wines are customarily used in the blending of vintage Champagne – and to its great benefit – just as much as with nonvintage wines.

Making Champagne

The basic steps of Champagne-making appear on pages 114–17. Rather than repeat that explanation here, we shall focus on those aspects that affect the style of Champagne, and differentiate it from all other sparkling wines.

Terroir and the échelle des crus

The Champenois and the Comité Interprofessionnel du Vin de Champagne are ever alert to emphasize their unique combination of *terroir* and climate. However much the cynics or the jealous may seek to dismiss this as an empty piece of propaganda, there is something very special about the grapes grown in Champagne. Others may point to the progressive upgrading in the *échelle des crus* system (which classifies every tiny part of Champagne on a percentage basis from 80 to 100 percent) and to the extreme concentration of *échelles* at the top of the scale rather than the bottom. Cynics may scoff at the story that Dom Pérignon could tell from which vineyards otherwise unidentified grapes came merely by tasting them, and that he decided his blends by an early morning tasting of grapes left on his windowsill overnight. The fact remains that, over the centuries, the Champenois have decided which plots should be planted with Pinot Noir, which with Pinot Meunier and which with Chardonnay, and have then graded each vineyard or *cru* in the most detailed fashion imaginable. The ultimate fascination is that, having so minutely detailed their *vignoble*, they proceed to blend white and red grapes from across its length and breadth – although wines such as Moët & Chandon's luxury *cuvée*, named after Dom Pérignon, are made entirely from grapes with an *échelle* rating of 100 percent.

Whole-bunch pressing

The Champagne practice of taking whole bunches direct to the press goes back to the 17th century. The strict limitation of the yield of juice per ton of grapes, the shape and size of the traditional press and the low pressure under which it operates all predate scientific analysis (which totally supports the belief of the Champenois that these methods and controls produce juice of higher quality). We now know that free-run or lightly pressed juice is likely to have higher acidity, lower pH, fewer solids (paniculate matter from the pulp of the grape) and lower phenols (flavor compounds) than juice from grapes that have been passed through a crusher or been more rigorously pressed to produce a higher yield.

Left: *North- as well as south-facing slopes in Champagne produce grapes for the finest sparkling wines in the world.* Below: *The seemingly contradictory term "blanc de noirs" is just that: Champagne made from the very gentle pressing of black grapes.*

The advantages of fermentation in oak as opposed to stainless steel are still hotly debated, although only two of the better-known houses (Krug and Alfred Gratien) ferment entirely this way, and only one (Bollinger) does so partially. These three houses produce particularly big, rich and complex Champagne, and part of their style must derive from fermenting in oak. Oak barrel fermenting is far more costly and time-consuming than fermentation in steel; it may help induce malolactic fermentation; but since the barrels are all very old, there is no possibility of the pickup of any oak flavor per se, nor is there any likelihood of greater oxidation (fermenting wine protects itself under its natural blanket of carbon dioxide). The obvious difference is the inability to control fermentation temperatures precisely, as can be done with stainless steel, and the probability that these will exceed the 64°F to 68°F (18°C to 20°C) range normally found with stainless-steel fermentation.

Fermentation vats or barrels

The paramount importance of *assemblage* (or blending) is not in dispute. However, the synergy achieved by a master blender has its limits: the quality of the individual base wine components inevitably places some limits on what can be achieved. But given top-quality base wines and a skilled blender, a quite miraculous transformation takes place in the one to three years the wine matures in its bottle on the lees after the addition of the *liqueur de tirage*. It is customary in the New World to talk of the effect of "yeast autolysis," and in particular about the flavor of yeast. The French disparage such talk; quite correctly, they say that the aroma, flavor and texture changes that occur during the period of lees contact are not due simply to the presence of the dead yeast cells, and in particular that one cannot smell or taste yeast per se (or at least the dead yeast we are talking about here). What one is observing is a complex change in aromas, esters and flavors, partly due to the aging changes in the base wines, and only partly to the process of autolysis. While the changes are continual, and start soon after the end of the second fermentation, the effects on the aroma and flavor become progressively more apparent with time. Chemical analysis also shows that, after an initial burst of activity, a slowdown is followed by a buildup, giving technical strength to the appellation requirement of at least 12 months on the lees.

The taste of yeast?

Henri (right) and Olivier Krug (left) in the tasting laboratory, where so much time and skill is invested in choosing the base wines which will make Krug Grande Cuvée.

Champagne is kept fresh by its high concentration of carbon dioxide (CO_2), but the lees (so long as the wine has not been disgorged) bolster that freshness. It is this capacity (and the ever-continuing gain in complexity) that has given rise to the

Recently disgorged

super-luxury class of wines that have spent an abnormally long time on their yeast lees. Traditionally, these were curiosities reserved for special guests in Champagne: anyone who has been privileged to taste a 1921 Pol Roger disgorged that morning will need no persuasion that they take Champagne into another dimension. Bollinger, however, decided to commercialize such wines (albeit on a tiny scale), and to register a trademark, "RD," which stands for *récemment dégorgé* ("recently disgorged"). Like "Xerox," the expression "RD" has passed into general verbal usage to describe a product (or a process), but it can be used only on the Bollinger label. The label always states the precise date of disgorgement.

Partly because recently disgorged wines are served in Champagne within hours or days of disgorging, partly perhaps because Bollinger specifies the disgorgement date, a myth has grown up that these wines suffer some magical but evil decay once they have been disgorged. This is nonsense; any Champagne is (in a sense) at one point in its life recently disgorged. If the wine is extremely old when it is disgorged, it is most unlikely to have any need or capacity for further improvement, and if it was cellared in Champagne, it will have been stored under perfect conditions. The natural conclusion is that it should be drunk before movement, inappropriate storage or other misfortune can occur. But it will not decay; other things being equal, a 50-year-old Champagne disgorged 10 years ago will be much fresher than the same wine disgorged at its normal time, i.e., 47 years ago.

Cava

The Spanish cava wines made in the Penedès region of Catalonia are the most widely known around the world after Champagne. The reason is very simple: with a production of some five million cases each, Codorníu and Freixenet, the two largest houses, are both over three times larger than Moët & Chandon (with a mere 1.5 million cases). In the wake of a European Union ruling banning the use of the term *méthode champenoise* on wine labels, cava as a name has become even better known, and (somewhat cynically) has been given the trappings of an *appellation contrôlée*. It has nominal geographical boundaries (conveniently drawn around all the cava producers), prescribes the production methods (almost identical to those of Champagne) and prescribes the grape varieties.

The cava producers spare no effort, time or expense in making their wine. Their cellars are massive and massively impressive; their technology is excellent (Codorníu invented the *gyropalette*); and the packaging of the wine leaves nothing to be desired. The wine, unfortunately, does – and not merely in comparison to Champagne. Its problem is that where Champagne is delicate, cava is (with rare exceptions) lead-footed. Certainly it has great complexity and abundant flavor, but the remarkable combination of intensity and elegance that is the hallmark of Champagne is nowhere to be found.

The reasons lie partly in the climate (and possibly soil), partly in the grape varieties and partly in the indefinable pulse that beats in the heart of Champagne. The climate is simply too warm: lying on the same latitude as Tuscany. The three principal authorized varieties – Xarel-lo, Macabeo and Parellada – are beloved of the Spanish and well suited to the climate, but they will never produce a wine in the style of Champagne.

Spanish investment in the latest winemaking technology means more cava is produced than any other sparkling wine in the world.

Italian bubbles

Nothing could be less like Italy's usual ascetic style of dry whites than Asti: this is grapes in a bottle, with the fruit flavor intensified by the bubbles. For the dust-dry, chalky quality of Italy captured in bubbles you must go to the Veneto, where Prosecco is a venerable tradition. Both Asti and Prosecco are usually vat-fermented. Altogether more serious are the new-generation *méthode champenoise* wines made from the "right" varieties (Pinot Noir and Chardonnay) by winemakers such as the Trentino-based Ferrari, Ca' del Bosco in Lombardy or Villa Banfi in Piedmont. The Italians are exceedingly proud of their achievements, which are technically excellent. But seriousness alone does not make a wine great, and some find more charm in the frivolity of Asti.

A challenge to the prodigious volume of the cava producers comes from the German producers of Sekt, a logical development for a country best suited to producing wine with low natural alcohol, high acidity and a modest level of fresh fruit. Small quantities of the best Sekt are made using the *méthode champenoise*; most is made by the Charmat process in vat. The top Sekts from 100 percent Riesling are thoroughly enjoyable: cheerfully fruity, not at all too sweet, entirely natural, and there is no pretence that these wines emulate Champagne.

France has other sparkling wines of some class and interest. Blanquette de Limoux lays claim to being the first sparkling wine of modern times: its history begins over 100 years before Champagne. Originally it was a *pétillant* wine made by the *méthode rurale* – in essence, the first half of the *méthode champenoise* (it does not go to the trouble of removing the lees). It is now made by the *méthode champenoise* – and in substantial quantities. The grapes are the local Mauzac, Chenin Blanc and (increasingly) Chardonnay, grown in the hills behind Corbières, above Carcassonne. For New World palates used to clean and clearly delineated styles, the history of the wine is of greater interest than the wine, which tends to bitterness and a hard, chalky, lemony cast. Adding Chardonnay has changed the style considerably, and it will presumably continue to evolve.

Other wine regions, notably Burgundy and Alsace, are also making sparkling wines, known as *crémants* to set them apart from Champagne.

The sparkling wines of the Loire Valley – based primarily on Chenin Blanc, although Chardonnay is of increasing importance – were almost as famous as those of Champagne in the latter part of the 19th century. Three Champagne houses (Alfred Gratien, Bollinger, and Deutz and Geldermann) have significant operations there, although the major production comes from a number of cooperatives. A few *pétillant* wines continue to be made and, like the *mousseux* versions, can be quite superb with 20 years or more of bottle-age. Some of the *mousseux* is made by the *méthode champenoise*; most, however, is produced by the Charmat process (*see* page 235).

The importance of the right varietal base (Chardonnay, Pinot Noir and, less importantly, Pinot Meunier) has been handsomely demonstrated in California, Australia and New Zealand.

Both California and Australian sparkling wines have gone through several phases of development. Until the 1970s in California and the 1980s in Australia, base wines were fashioned from everything and anything other than Pinot Noir or Chardonnay. In Australia, varieties typically used for better wines were Ondenc, Semillon, Chenin Blanc, Colombard, Trebbiano and Riesling, with the red component usually absent but extending to Syrah (Shiraz) and Cabernet Sauvignon when present. The approach was to pick at sugar levels similar to those of Champagne grapes, but, because of the warm climate, they were harvested while very green, with distinctly lower acidity and, most significantly, much less flavor intensity. Winemakers found themselves in a cleft stick: if the grapes were allowed to become too flavor-ripe, the finished sparkling wine became very coarse and rank in flavor; if the winemaker judged the material to perfection, and if the wine was given three or four years on the lees (and extra bottle-age thereafter), it could attain a balance, a rich complexity similar to that of the best cavas – a glowing color and a nutty, biscuity flavor that certainly filled the mouth, but which could never claim elegance or finesse.

The next phase was the discovery (in both California and Australia) that Pinot

Noir grown in warm climates produced execrable table wine. By default, as it were, it was diverted to production of sparkling wine, although it was noticeable that the much more compliant Chardonnay did not initially accompany it; the Chardonnay was in too much demand for table wine, a fact saying much about the attitude to sparkling wine that prevailed at the time in both countries.

The new wave   Change came with the third phase and the development of vineyards purposely established for sparkling wine production: Chardonnay and Pinot Noir in cool climates, such as those of Carneros and the Central Coast of California, Australia's southern Victoria, the Adelaide Hills, Yarra Valley, Macedon Ranges, Tasmania (of rapidly increasing importance) and the South Island of New Zealand. This led to a further discovery about Pinot Noir: whether climate, *terroir*, the particular clone or a combination of all three is the cause, it performs less well and less predictably than Chardonnay in fashioning top-quality New World sparkling wines. Pinot Noir seems to engender a certain toughness; one might expect it to blend synergistically with the far softer, creamier Chardonnay, but it has tended not to. Pinot Meunier is even less successful and is sparingly grown; its tendency to rapid development in sparkling wine is even more pronounced, with a strong, yeasty, beef-broth aroma and flavor developing within 18 to 24 months.

California   The style of the best California sparkling wine is arguably closer to that of Champagne than are Australia's versions. The differences between Australian and California sparkling wines track those of their table wines. Domaine Chandon in the Napa Valley is widely recognized as being the most reliable large producer, and manages to make wines with length, flavor and good mouth-feel. The long-established (indeed pioneering) Schramsberg maintains a rich (though dry) style that seems to express Napa values perfectly, while Iron Horse, lean and racy, seems to do the same for cooler Sonoma. Others can have aromas just as strange and off-putting as the less convincing efforts of Champagne: in the mouth they tend to be rather ungenerous, hard and chalky. Once again, it seems at least some of these deficiencies stem from inappropriate viticulture in inappropriately warm areas; the French-owned wineries have been surprisingly slow in moving to the cool climate of Carneros, although Taittinger has left no one in any doubt about its views with the establishment of Domaine Carneros and its unfortunate "château."

Australia   Any discussion of sparkling wine in Australia has to differentiate between low-priced, big-volume beverage wine that is tank-fermented, and high-quality, bottle-

Despite a very different climate from that of Champagne, Seppelt's has been refreshing Australia with its sparkling wines from Victoria for generations. Only in the past few years has Australia grown Pinot Noir and Chardonnay to make a deliberate imitation of Champagne.

fermented icon wines made in much smaller quantities. The fact that both are fashioned predominantly from Chardonnay and Pinot Noir is barely relevant. Increasingly, the finest sparkling wines are made from Tasmanian grapes, with Macedon, the Yarra Valley and Adelaide Hills other super-premium sources.

Domaine Chandon in the Yarra Valley shares with Moët & Chandon a wine style that emphasizes midpalate softness without compromising a crisp, clean and long finish. Its methods of achieving this have evolved and changed over 15 years, as have the sources of its grapes. As a consequence of targeting even cooler regions than the Yarra Valley (including Tasmania, the high Strathbogie Ranges and the Upper Yarra), a weighted average of 30 percent of the base wines are taken through malolactic fermentation, with Pinot Noir to the fore. Care is now taken to avoid bronze coloring in the key *cuvées*, which are brighter straw yellow.

Moët & Chandon in Victoria

New Zealand is a serious producer of seriously good sparkling wines, the epicenter being Marlborough, the varieties Chardonnay and Pinot Noir. The relative absence of Pinot Meunier is not a cause for grief; the top-end wines are given at least two years on the lees (following bottle fermentation, of course) and have all the complexity one could wish for. This complexity in no way threatens the delicately poised yet intense fruit-derived flavors of the best wines.

New Zealand

Deutz Marlborough Cuvée, the outcome of a joint venture between Montana and Deutz and Geldermann (now part of Louis Roederer) in 1988, is generally recognized as the fine and elegant leader of the sparkling band. At the opposite style extreme is Cloudy Bay's Pelorus (Cloudy Bay is part of LVMH), somewhat akin to Bollinger or Krug on vinous steroids, so rich and chewy is it. Since 2000, the style has been slightly refined, but is still a startling mouthful. In between these extremes are a dozen or so wines of great quality and style, including Corbans Amadeus Classic Reserve, Daniel Le Brun Vintage Brut (and others under the Le Brun label) and Domaine Chandon Marlborough Brut, orchestrated by Domaine Chandon Australia.

Sweet Table Wines

Choices, consequences and techniques

Ancient sweet wines

Sweet wines have a very much longer history than dry ones. The wines of the ancients, of the Near East, of Egypt and classical Greece were almost certainly made as sweet as possible – and as concentrated. The Greeks, at least, always drank their wine diluted with water (sometimes seawater), hot or cold according to the season, and usually flavored with herbs and spices. Under these circumstances it may seem surprising that they made such fine distinctions between the qualities of the various regions of Greece, and especially of the Aegean Islands.

What vines Italy grew before its colonization by the Greeks were probably all high-trained up trees. The grapes could rarely have ripened enough to give sweet wine. Hence the ancient tradition in Italy that low-trained and staked vines were a Greek importation, and that sweet or strong wines were in the Greek style.

Madeira Fumé?

The Romans resorted to concentrating their grape juice by boiling it before fermentation. They also frequently "smoked" their wines by stacking the amphoras in a loft above a furnace. The result must have been a sort of "Madeira Fumé." Certainly it indicates that they accepted (even encouraged) oxidation. Once oxidized under the right conditions, the wine was stable (no wine is more stable than Madeira) and could be kept indefinitely.

But another reason emerges for their liking for sweet wines, as concentrated as possible (and frequently laced with pepper, spices and honey). They were the traveler's insurance policy against wines too foul to drink or vinegary *posca* at inns along the road. The Romans were indefatigable travelers, and it was their custom to carry their own additives to make tavern wine more palatable.

Keeping it sweet

Today there is no problem in adjusting the sweetness of any wine, strong or weak, to any desired level. Fermentation can be stopped before the natural sugar is exhausted by a number of methods. The two most common are adding sulfur dioxide and fine filtration to remove the yeasts. Sweet must can then be "back-blended" into dry wine with no risk of refermentation.

The ancient civilizations of the Near East and the Mediterranean fermented their wines in earthenware jars, usually buried to the neck in the ground (a practice still common in Georgia and just surviving in Cyprus). Sweetness and strength were the qualities they looked for.

Before the age of technology, the only natural method was to ensure such a high degree of sugar that the yeasts suspended activity. This was achieved either when the fermentation produced about 16 percent of alcohol or, in intensely sweet must, long before. In Greece and similar climates, super-sweet grapes were easily achieved. The simplest methods were to pick them and leave them piled in the sun to raisin, or to hang them under roofs to shrivel with a similar effect, or, more painstakingly, to go around the vineyard twisting the stalk of each bunch to restrict the circulation of sap, and then wait for the juice in each grape to slowly concentrate. There are examples of these methods still in use today (*see* pages 135–6).

These warm-climate methods are not possible in cooler and more humid regions. Grapes left on the vine to overripen will simply rot. But there is more than one kind of fungus that makes a meal of a grape. One in particular has an entirely benevolent effect. How this "noble" rot, the celebrated *Botrytis cinerea*, was first discovered and put to use is the subject of various legends (*see* page 130).

None of the stories is very convincing – the last least of all. For a start, *Botrytis cinerea* was known and described in Roman times, and in all probability goes back further still. Second, anyone who has grown grapes in a region in which botrytis occurs knows it is an ever-present phenomenon. In some years the level of infection will be minor, in other years quite high, and in others still it will totally invade the crop. Third, while the vignerons of 200 or 300 years ago may have lacked microscopes and a knowledge of biochemistry, they were acutely observant, and it seems very unlikely they would not have made the connection between botrytis and a wonderful rich flavor in their white wines. Finally, all are agreed its effect has been known in Hungary since the mid-17th century. Why would that knowledge have remained a secret?

Besides, the Loire Valley, Bergerac and Sauternes had made celebrated sweet wines since the mid-1600s at least. In a 1666 court case involving the owner of Château d'Yquem and several of his tenants who wished to pick their grapes too soon, it was noted that, "It is not customary in Bommes and Sauternes to begin picking before 15 October." In most years botrytis must have taken a firm hold by this time. In those years when botrytis laid low (it depends on a degree of humidity) they probably tried to make similarly sweet and concentrated wine by leaving the grapes to overripen, Greek-style. The 2000 vintage is an example of Sauternes being denied the benison of botrytis. You can taste the difference – but not so clearly that the wines are not obviously Sauternes.

To present-day eyes, grapes heavily infected with botrytis are not exactly attractive. A heavy web of greenish gray mold, with short hairs growing outward, covers the grapes; each grape has partially or totally collapsed, and, if handled, readily exudes sticky juice and a cloud of mold spores. Extracting the juice from the crusher and press can be exceedingly difficult because the high juice viscosity and sugary-slippery nature of the skins make pressing difficult and the jamlike consistency of the must almost impossible to pump. What is more, the must has an evil-looking, murky black color: the brilliant green-gold color that emerges at the end of fermentation is scientifically explicable, but to the eyes of the layman – like those winemakers of former centuries – it seems a miracle.

The benison of botrytis

Château d'Yquem represents perfectionism on a scale not even attempted in any other vineyard. It can take 10 multiple passes around the 220-acre (90 ha) vineyard to pick the vintage. Each vine produces only one glass.

Sweet Table Wines

This choices-and-consequences chart illustrates those stages in the process for making sweet wine in which the options chosen by the winemaker will fundamentally influence the taste and individuality of the final wine. Not every stage of the winemaking process is indicated: for that, the reader is directed to the white wine process chart on pages 88–9.

Sweet table wines are made from grapes that have dehydrated and the juice concentrated sufficiently for sugar and acid levels to rise significantly above normal. This might occur naturally in the vineyard or can be induced artificially in the winery. Other methods of producing sweet wine are to concentrate the juice after crushing and pressing or to add grape concentrate to dry wine to sweeten it.

1

IN THE VINEYARD

Botrytis cinerea
A cryptogamic fungus that occurs under warm and humid conditions. The spores settle on the skin of the grape, which exudes moisture and shrivels, and the juice becomes more and more concentrated. This has the effect of producing intensely sweet juice. Sauternes and German Trockenbeerenauslese are produced from botrytized grapes.

Freezing
Partially botrytized grapes are left on the vine until the December or January frosts occur, then they are picked at dawn while still frozen. As the water in the grapes turns to ice, sugar and acidity in the juice that remains become increasingly concentrated. This method is used principally in Germany to make Eiswein, in Canada likewise.

Raising
Supersweet grapes can be achieved by twisting the stalk of each bunch of grapes to restrict the circulation of sap and concentrate the juice. Rarely carried out now, but was popular in the 18th century in Italy and Provence. Severing the whole cane sustaining the bunches ("cordon-cut") is, however, used in various parts of the world.

2

IN THE WINERY

Concentrating whole grapes
(a) *Freezing*
Partially botrytized grapes are frozen to produce an Eiswein variant in California and Australia.
(b) *Artificially induced botrytis*
Grapes picked at normal maturity are placed on racks in a temperature-controlled room, then sprayed with botrytis spores. Alternating cool and warm air is blown over the grapes to simulate ideal conditions in the vineyard. After two weeks, the grapes shrivel, leaving concentrated juice.
(c) *Raising*
Grapes are picked and left in the sun on straw or wooden trays to raisin, or are hung under roofs to shrivel. In the Jura in France, the wine is called *vin de paille*, in Italy *passito*, in Germany *Strohwein*.

Concentrating crushed and pressed grapes
(a) *Osmotic concentration*
An experimental technique that is being used as a means of bypassing the need for chaptalization.
(b) *Freeze concentration*
This commercializes the principles underlying the production of Eiswein. A coil or hollow plate through which chilled brine is continuously pumped is placed into the vat. An ice block gradually forms, which is then lifted out of the vat, or the concentrated juice is pumped out, leaving the ice to melt.

Adding grape concentrate to wine
In this instance the wine is fermented dry and then *mistelle* (grape concentrate) is blended in to sweeten it.

Above: *A hydrometer: an instrument for measuring the sugar concentration in sweet wines.*

Left: *Harvesting nobly rotted grapes at Château d'Yquem. It takes several passes through the vineyard to select completely rotten grapes. Pickers may use scissors or just forefinger and thumb to coax off individual berries, leaving others to become more concentrated in sugar.*

In Greece, grapes are spread out on sheets to dry beneath the hot sun – a raisining technique that goes back to classical times.

Rollercoaster Attitudes to sweet white wines have fluctuated wildly, especially in the 20th century. Having been extremely popular in the 19th century and the early decades of the 20th, the status of these wines declined precipitously in the years after World War II. By the end of the 1950s, demand for Sauternes had diminished to the point where Sauvignon Blanc, Semillon and Muscadelle were pulled out and replaced by Cabernet Sauvignon and Merlot; even a château as famous as Château d'Yquem was compelled to introduce a near-dry white wine, which it calls simply "Y" (pronounced *Ygrec*).

Glorious wines, fabulous prices Such lack of interest – and such prices – underline the fact that the greatest sweet wines of the world have almost always been made because of the owner's (or the winemaker's) passion, rather than for a reasonable profit. A brief period of glory in the 19th century saw the Russian Czars pay fabulous sums for Château d'Yquem, while the Austro-Hungarian, Russian and Polish nobility did the same for Tokay *Eszencia*. Once the sharply diminished yield and the ever-present risk of the partial or total failure of the vintage are taken into account, the seemingly high price per bottle shrinks alarmingly. The 220 acres (90 ha) of vineyard produce 8,000 cases on average – if one ignores the years in which no wine at all is made under the Château d'Yquem label. A 220-acre (90 per ha) New World vineyard would routinely produce 45,000 cases of premium wine, perhaps more. Or, to look at it another way, the maximum permitted yield under the *appellation contrôlée* for Sauternes is a very low 1.9 tons per acre (25 hl per ha); that of Château d'Yquem is only one-fifth of a classed-growth Bordeaux château.

Making Sauternes

Thanks in part to the luster of Château d'Yquem, Sauternes has usually been acclaimed as the greatest of the sweet wines, whatever the merits of German Trockenbeerenauslesen or Tokay *Eszencia* may be. As the chart shows (*see* pages 126–7), sweet white wine can be made in many different ways; here we will follow that of Sauternes, with Château d'Yquem as the model.

Tris and grains rôtis There are multiple choices at the time of picking. The traditional, time-consuming and very costly pattern of multiple passes through the vineyard, or *tris*, is still practiced at Château d'Yquem. The number of *tris* will depend on the vintage: in 1972, 11 *tris* over a period of 71 days failed to produce any wine worthy of the name d'Yquem; in 1976, two *tris* over 22 days were sufficient to produce a classic wine; the average between 2000 and 2004 inclusive was six *tris*. If quality is the prime concern, repeated *tris* are mandatory. The object is to harvest only those grapes that are fully affected by botrytis, known locally as *grains rôtis*. Those affected by gray or black rot are cut off and discarded. Those still unaffected or only partially affected are left for a later pass – and so on, for however long and however many *tris* are necessary.

This is not only highly skilled work, but exceedingly slow: as few as two or three berries may be removed from a bunch, dislodged by a finger or with the closed tip of the cutting shears. The picking rate is one-twentieth of that for dry white wines, where whole bunches are picked with virtually no selection involved.

Under the relentless pressure to control costs, multiple passes are steadily becoming less frequent in Sauternes. The least satisfactory shortcut is to restrict the harvest to (say) two *tris*, for no further selection to be made, and to rely on chaptalization to increase sugar levels. An optional approach is to sort the harvest on tables in the *chai*; the 1979 harvest at Château Padoun in Barsac (then owned by the Australian Len Evans and managed by the Dane Peter Vinding-Diers) was dealt with this way. Every bunch was cut with, of all things, nail scissors, the botrytized grapes going into one *cuve*, the unaffected grapes going to another (to make a dry white wine). There is evidence this method was used in bygone days; its disadvantage is that it reduces the amount of sweet wine that may be made from any given vintage because the unaffected berries are not given the chance to develop botrytis on the vine.

Left: *Handmade wine begins in the vineyard: botrytized grapes at Yquem are picked one by one; extracting juice from them is exceedingly difficult. Less oozes from a modern press than the old basket press (below).*

Château d'Yquem uses both traditional vertical basket presses (albeit in a new stainless-steel format) and pneumatic bag presses, the latter brought into play where the grapes are heavily botrytized. If the basket press is used, the process may be repeated three or four times, the sugar level increasing progressively. This press will yield only three barrels a day; the juice from the successive pressings will have been blended before going to barrel.

Pressing

The combined juice of the pressings is run directly into barrels without clarification or settling. The only quick method of clarifying juice of this density is by a device known as a rotary drum vacuum filter, and Château d'Yquem finds no need of such gadgetry. Fermentation of extremely sweet musts can be very difficult: stories are told of German Trockenbeerenauslesen taking two years to partially ferment, and of Tokay *Eszencia* not fermenting at all. This is not what one would expect, because sugar is a food that yeasts devour with gusto; however, at extreme sugar levels (63° Brix or above) fermentation is to all intents impossible, while even at 45° Brix it proceeds slowly, and will necessarily leave around 18° Brix of unfermented sugar.

Fermentation

In fact Château d'Yquem aims to harvest its grapes at 36° Brix, which at the end of fermentation leaves about 13.5 degrees of alcohol and around 125 grams per liter residual sugar unfermented. Normally fermentation will continue until the alcohol level reaches 16 degrees, but a combination of the high background sugar, a substance called botryticine (a form of antibiotic) and the addition of sulfur dioxide act together to limit the alcohol to 14 degrees.

Château d'Yquem uses 100 percent new oak every year for barrel aging, and the wine remains in wood for three and a half years before it is bottled. During this time it will have been racked 15 times, and fined once or twice, but never filtered. During the spring of the following year the process of *assemblage* will commence, and will continue through the summer. During this time every cask will be evaluated: depending on the success of the vintage, a considerable number (never less than 10 percent, often much more) will be declassified and either sold in bulk or (in the case of semi-dry Sauvignon Blanc) used in making the dry white wine "Y." The *assemblage* will also have to arrive at the right balance between Semillon (usually 80 percent) and Sauvignon Blanc (20 percent), the latter usually having lower residual sugar.

New oak

Good new,
wonderful old

Because of the extraordinary care Château d'Yquem takes at every stage of its winemaking, it is not surprising that the resulting wine swallows up both the new oak and the sulfur dioxide, with the consequence that even a relatively young d'Yquem is a totally enjoyable experience to drink (in 2005, for example, the 1997 was flawless, utterly seductive and delicious). A 1985 tasting in Australia of 50 vintages from 1899 onward (the event spanned an entire day) simply proved what anyone with any experience of the wine already knew: even the weakest vintages improve for 10 to 15 years, the good vintages for 20 to 30 years, while the great years can live (if not improve) for a century or more.

Sauternes below
d'Yquem

What may be called good Sauternes from the other *crus classés* of the region are made in similar fashion. There has been a modest but distinct revival of interest in the style, and considerable investment in a number of the next tier of châteaus. There has also been a proliferation of special *cuvées* made in favorable vintages, while cryoextraction has proved invaluable in lesser years. More careful use of sulfur dioxide and more careful handling of grapes, must and wine alike, have resulted in wines that can be enjoyed far earlier than those made in bygone decades. Cheap Sauternes are just that: bland, soft, tropical-flavored (pineapple and apricot) wines at their best; thin and awkward at their worst. No fine Sauternes is ever inexpensive, as no wine in the world is more costly to produce.

Edelfäule

Trockenbeerenauslesen

Sauternes is challenged by Germany's Beerenauslesen and Trockenbeerenauslesen: the peak of the pyramid of wines, starting with Spätlese, from selected riper grapes in which botrytis is fully developed. A unique comparative tasting of Château d'Yquem and Schloss Vollrads' Trockenbeerenauslesen in the late 1980s demonstrated that the two have virtually nothing in common except sweetness. It is simply not meaningful to compare them side by side: all it does is demonstrate that some tasters will prefer Sauternes, others Trockenbeerenauslesen, and that in any given vintage, one may excel, the other may disappoint.

The differences are all too obvious. The grapes in Germany are grown in a much colder climate, in places on near-vertical slopes of schist; a single high-yielding variety (normally Riesling) is used, rather than a blend of low-yielding grapes; the clarified juice is fermented exceedingly slowly; and new oak (or even near-new) is never used. Trockenbeerenauslesen must be made from grapes harvested with a potential alcohol of 21.5 degrees (more than all but a handful of exceptional and rare Sauternes ever attain), yet the chemical analysis of the two styles could hardly

Botrytis legends

The first concerns Tokay. In 1650, the vintage at the castle of Tokaj was delayed on the pretext of an expected Turkish attack; by the time they were picked, the grapes were rotten on the vine – revealing the extraordinary effect of botrytis. For their part, the Germans have always regarded the discovery of botrytis as theirs, and typically are able to pinpoint the date (1775), the place (Schloss Johannisberg) and the people (J.M. Engert, the vineyard manager, and the prince-abbot of Fulda). Mr. Engert always had to obtain the permission of the abbot before starting the harvest, but in 1775 his messenger was

inexplicably delayed between Fulda and Johannisberg. By the time he returned with permission to pick, the grapes had all become moldy, but with nothing else to do, they were harvested – and produced a miraculous wine, allegedly unlike anything previously encountered.

Another legend relates how the German-born owner of Château La Tour Blanche (a Sauternes château) brought back the secret of botrytis from the Rhine in the 1830s and showed the Marquis de Lur Saluces of Château d'Yquem how to recognize and handle botrytized grapes to make the great sweet wine for which Château d'Yquem promptly became famous.

be further apart: Sauternes will typically have 14 degrees of alcohol, 9° Brix residual sugar and 6 grams per liter of acidity; for Trockenbeerenauslesen, the figures will typically be 6.5 degrees to 7.5 degrees of alcohol, 25° Brix residual sugar, and 10 grams per liter of acidity. The structure of the Sauternes, in other words, rests on alcohol and sugar, the Trockenbeerenauslese on sugar and acidity.

Grape by grape

The grapes, principally Riesling, are hand-picked in much the same way as in Sauternes. A grower making Spätlese and Auslese wines looks to the average must weight, or degree Oechsle (the German version of Brix), to categorize the resulting wine. For Beerenauslese and Trockenbeerenauslese wines the regulations speak of the picking of individual berries. Whether it is berries or bunches that are picked depends both on the state of the grapes and on the perfectionism of the grower. But laborious, repeated pickings of the vineyard are essential, even though the extreme case where (in the Rheingau) 100 pickers took two weeks to gather enough grapes for 300 liters of juice is very unlikely to happen today.

Barrels in the bedroom

The grapes are crushed and pressed (with the usual difficulty), and the juice clarified by chilling (and sometimes the addition of enzymes); sulfur dioxide is added at the crusher and at the press. Because the climate is so cold, no cooling of the fermentation is ever required; on the contrary, it may be necessary to warm it slightly. Tales are told of winemakers taking their treasured little barrels of Trockenbeerenauslese into their bedrooms – if not actually their beds – to keep the fermentation going. The sweeter the must, the slower and more reluctant the fermentation; since an active fermentation generates its own heat (and thereby, metaphorically, adds fuel to the fire), a slow one will not generate any significant warmth, and the winter may virtually stop it until the following spring. As with Sauternes (and, indeed, all sweet wines), malolactic fermentation does not occur – and just as well: depending on the bacteria, malolactic fermentation in a wine full of sugar can be quite disastrous, producing extreme levels of volatile acidity.

Eiswein

Fermentation will be stopped at the chosen time by cooling and by adding sulfur dioxide. The wine will then be racked and, after fining, racked again. In past times German wines, both dry and sweet, were matured in large oak casks for exceedingly long periods. Now the practice is to bottle them as quickly as possible to minimize oxidation, and to sterile-filter to ensure subsequent stability.

Eiswein (or icewine) is made from grapes that have been frozen on the vine, and are picked at dawn while still frozen: a picturesque scene involving mufflers, fur boots, lanterns (or car headlights) and many a draft of hot white wine and sugar from a kettle. Failing the onset of botrytis in the vineyard, a German grower has one last chance to salvage the remaining unpicked grapes and make sweet wine. He or she has to wait for them to freeze solid.

There are some who believe these are the finest of all the German sweet wines. Botrytis will have played a much lesser role; if all the water content in the juice had been removed by botrytis, the grapes would have been picked before the deep December – occasionally January – frosts that trigger the making of Eiswein. If there is little or no water, there is nothing to be gained from the freezing. So the Riesling flavor is usually much purer; and a feature of all great Eisweins is their superb, tingling acidity and extraordinary length of flavor.

Since 1982 an Eiswein has had to be made from must (or juice) with the same degree Oechsle as a Beerenauslese, and is labeled simply as Eiswein. Before 1982 there were grades of Eiswein, the most common being Spätlese Eiswein and Auslese Eiswein. Beerenauslese Eisweins were known but were uncommon, Trockenbeerenauslese Eisweins exceedingly rare. The 1982 regulation was much criticized at the time. Many growers felt that Auslese Eisweins had the best balance, and many also feared that the new mandatory must weights would seldom be achieved in practice. By chance, 1983 produced an unprecedented quantity of high-quality Eisweins that easily complied with the regulations, and the criticisms were silenced.

Extremely luscious, high-quality icewine is consistently made in Canada, in both Ontario and British Columbia. The principal producer, Inniskillin, uses a number of different varieties, and even makes a sparkling icewine.

Frozen grapes

Little has so far been written about the making of Eiswein, and one account (suggesting that the grapes are crushed and pressed and the ice skimmed off the top of the vat) is patently wrong. In fact, the grapes are simply pressed as whole bunches, and the ice remains with the skins in the press. Some secondary skimming could take place in the unlikely event of ice re-forming in the vat, although as freezing the juice (a method used in the New World) is forbidden, the amount of ice collection will be minimal. From this point on the winemaking practices will be the same as those used for Trockenbeerenauslesen, Beerenauslesen and so on.

Tokay

The history of Hungary's great sweet wine, Tokay (in the English and French spelling: the Hungarian for the place is Tokaj, the wine Tokaji), goes back long before any known history of Sauternes, or German Auslesen designated as such.

This quintessence of Hungarian taste suffered many buffetings in the 20th century. The Russian Revolution of 1917 removed one of its prime markets; the 1919 Treaty of Versailles shrank Hungary to a fraction of its former size; and for 40 years after the Second World War the Communist command economy obliged growers to churn out immense quantities of, with few exceptions, turgid wine. Many pre-Communist bottles survive, however, as witness to its former greatness; 300-year-old bottles have proved magnificent and there are many excellent survivors from the early 20th century. Since the early 1990s first-class wines have been made again; as they mature, the fabulous potential of the region is coming back into focus.

Shriveled grapes for making Tokaji Aszú Eszencia yield a minute amount of juice, concentrated to the consistency of molasses.

If accounts of the making of Tokay read like something from the Brothers Grimm, with buckets of this being poured into barrels of that, it is because no fully accepted new formulation has been officially agreed to succeed the ancient measures of sweetness and quality. The great sweet Tokay wines are called *aszú*; *aszú* means dry – as in grapes dried on the vine, either by botrytis or desiccation. Sweetness is measured in the number of (notional) *puttonyos*, or buckets, of *aszú* grapes added to a given quantity of (dry) wine, three being the minimum and six the maximum.

There are three grape varieties in the vineyards – Furmint, Hárslevelü and Muskotály (Muscat de Frontignan) – much in the same way as Sauvignon Blanc, Semillon and Muscat in Sauternes. Furmint is aromatic, lively, with high acidity (and has recently been shown to make excellent dry wine). Hárslevelü offers body and different aromas. The proportions are typically 65:30:5. The harvest is one of Europe's latest, traditionally starting on October 23, by which time autumn mists and relatively reliable autumn sunshine (the climate is sharply continental) should have induced a high level of botrytis infection, especially in the Furmint.

The harvest is by hand, starting with a single pass through the vineyard (sometimes followed by others), separating botrytis-shriveled grapes from those still full of juice, which are taken straight to the press-house to make a strong (often 14 degrees) dry wine, while *aszú* grapes are stored. At this stage a tiny quantity of juice is expressed from the stored *aszú* by its own weight: juice that can have a sugar content as high as 90 percent. This is *Eszencia*, a fabled liquid that can scarcely be induced to ferment at all.

After years of storage in glass jars (such sweetness drys out barrel staves to the point that the barrel starts to leak), it may reach 3 percent alcohol, but alcohol is scarcely the point in an essence so sweet and high-flavored. A very little of the very best is sold, at a very high price; most is used for blending. *Eszencia* from the 1880s tasted in 2006, though almost black in color, was still intensely fresh and fruity. In many cases *Eszencia* was fortified with brandy to make more of a drink of it.

The process unique to Tokay is to add the immense sugar content of shriveled grapes to wine that has already undergone fermentation. This was misunderstood by some of the French companies who invested in the region in the 1990s, who looked for a wine more like Sauternes by using unfermented must instead of wine. It seems, however, to account for the unique Tokay flavor. The *aszú* is steeped in the wine (or must) for between two and five days. Must, being an aqueous solution, extracts less sugar and flavor from the *aszú* than the alcoholic solution that is wine. In the Royal Tokay winery, which we will use as the model (Hugh Johnson was among its founders and maintains an interest), the procedure is as follows.

At harvest time the *aszú* is stored in bins under refrigeration while the base wine is fermented at 61°F to 64°F (16°C to 18°C) for up to 25 days (after must settling for two to three days). Lots of wine and *aszú* from different vineyards are fermented and stored separately. The wine is settled and racked and then mixed with *aszú* at the rate of 2,500 to 3,000 liters of wine to 3 tons (2.7 tonnes) of *aszú* in three stages, 1,000 liters at a time, each batch run off after two days (sometimes longer) without pressing. The three batches differ in analysis, the first normally the richest in sugar and extract, and are fermented separately, the best qualities in once-used barrels of the local Zemplen oak, in sizes from 250 to 500 liters, for up to six months, the least concentrated in tank for six to eight weeks. Although dilution of the base wine with a near-equal quantity of *aszú* almost halves its alcohol content, the second fermentation only generates 2 to 3 degrees of alcohol, resulting in a wine that stops fermenting with a very high sugar content at about 10 to 11 percent of alcohol.

After this time, with the sugar content determined by the richness of the *aszú*, the wine is refrigerated, fined with bentonite, filtered and dosed with sulfur dioxide and moved to barrels in the deep cellars at 50°F (10°C). The barrels are filled to the bung and kept full over the full aging period of not less than three years (and not

Bottles in Tokay cellars are stored upright, not horizontally. Their corks are replaced every 10 to 15 years. Bottles have survived from the 17th-century origins of Tokay in extraordinarily good condition.

more, these days, than five). The cellars, cut deep in tufa, have a humidity of 85 to 98 percent and a thick coating of *Cladosporium cellare*, a white mold that soon turns black and houses a microflora beneficial to the aging wine, though in precisely what way is not clearly determined. In the past some cellarmasters left a headspace in their barrels to profit by what is known as *darabbantartás*, the effect of microflora akin to *flor* in sherry, but acting in cold cellars very much more slowly than *flor* in warm bodegas. *Darabbantartás* was beneficial to the stronger, drier wines made with no distinctive or separate *aszú* picking and known as *Szamarodni*. It is found to create volatile acidity and rancid character in fine *aszú* wines.

Renaissance of Tokay

After 15 years of the so-called Renaissance of Tokay, a number of companies are producing light-colored wines with obvious analogies to Sauternes, some of them still using must for the second fermentation and sufficient sulfur dioxide to avoid the browning associated with naturally oxidized *aszú*. These wines have much less of the classic Tokay character in their youth, although their analysis is very similar to classic wines and age may make them more typical.

What was once the *puttonyos* measure, and is still used on labels, is now more akin to that of German Auslesen, with a minimum and maximum sugar and dry extract content defining each category. A three-*puttonyos* wine has a minimum sugar content of 60 grams per liter and maximum of 90. A minimum dry extract of 21 grams per liter is also required by law. A four-*putt* wine has 90 to 120 grams of sugar, five-*putts* 121 to 150 and six-*putts* 150 to 180, with a 10 percent excess allowable (though no one is heard to complain if a six-*putt* wine exceeds 200 grams.) With each *puttonyos* number the dry extract minimum also rises by 5 grams, so that a six-*putt* wine has a minimum dry extract of 40 grams per liter. Wines richer than six-*putts* qualify as *Aszú Eszencia*, with sugar levels rising from 181 to 450 grams per liter and dry extract in proportion.

The unique character of Tokay, however, is in the total balance between sugar, alcohol, dry extract and acidity. Alcohol levels remain low, typically in the region of 10 to 12 percent by volume, sugar is far higher than in, for example, Sauternes: Château Yquem normally has 14 percent alcohol and 120 grams of sugar. More would seem too sweet. It is the acidity of Tokay, deriving in the first place from the Furmint grape, that balances what seem absurd sugar levels to give the wine a clean, and sometimes astonishingly long, finish. A great six-*putt* wine, Mézes Mály (a single vineyard) from 1999, has 10.6 percent alcohol, 234 grams of sugar, 12.9 grams of acidity and 63 of dry extract.

Such wines are unique on earth, fresh and clean to drink when bottled, developing aromas of dried fruits over 15 or 20 years, then moving on to a panoply of more developed aromas. It is rare to meet one too old at any age.

Austria

For many years, the world at large has undervalued all dessert wines except (but even sometimes including) Sauternes and the great Rhine and Mosel wines. This can be the only explanation for the general neglect of Austria's potential. In the Burgenland, Lower Austria, Beerenauslesen and Trockenbeerenauslesen (and Ausbruch, which is somewhere in between) are regularly made with relative ease and in prodigious quantities. If most of them lack the celestial finesse and extraordinary acid balance of the greatest German Rieslings and Hungarian Tokays, they are nonetheless dessert wines of superb quality.

The Loire Valley

It is also true that the makers of the sweet wines of the Loire Valley might equally well claim that their wines are not given the recognition that is their due.

The sweet wines of Anjou, Bonnezeaux, the Coteaux du Layon, Vouvray, Montlouis and Quarts de Chaume can be absolutely superb. The 1921 Marc Brédif Vouvray Liquoreux ranks with the other monumental sweet wines of that extraordinary vintage (notably various Trockenbeerenauslesen and Château d'Yquem). In more recent times, 1947, 1959, 1987 and 1989 have produced unctuous Loire wines of great power, breeding and longevity. Properly cellared, the sweetest *liquoreux* wines of those latter two years will live for at least another 30 to 40 years from now (in 2005, a tasting of nut-brown 1872, 1885 and 1892 Moulin Touchais, of Coteaux du Layon, suggested perfect cellaring conditions might double that life expectancy). Loire sweet-wine terminology is sometimes in dispute, but there are five grades (in descending order of sweetness), namely *liquoreux*, *doux*, *moelleux*, *demi-sec* and *sec*, with the sweetest two exceedingly rare, and the distinction between *moelleux* and *demi-sec* nebulous.

The making of these wines is almost Germanic in its simplicity. Multiple passes through the vineyard are necessary for *moelleux* or sweeter wines. After crushing, pressing and clarification through either settling or filtration, the wines are fermented in stainless steel, enameled vats or, rarely these days, old oak at moderate (64°F to 68°F/18°C to 20°C) temperatures. They are racked, fined and (usually) filtered before being bottled in the following spring, normally in April. It is left to

Warm, airy lofts provide the means to achieve super-concentrated grapes, whatever the weather. Italy's vin santo is a product of grapes raisined by this method.

bottle-age to work the miraculous transformation from a rather chalky, hard youth with a layer of simple sweetness superimposed, to the supple, complex and lingering flavor of maturity. The fruit flavors that then emerge range the full gamut from apricot to lime to peach to pineapple, but with no one character dominating, and with a honeyed envelope tinged with a touch of *crème brûlée*, suggesting that these wines are almost a meal in themselves. Most agree that their predestined role is as a privileged apéritif.

Botrytis in the New World

California and New Zealand (in particular) and, to a lesser degree, Australia produce Riesling – and a little Gewürztraminer – with extreme levels of botrytis-derived sweetness. The majority are made from naturally botrytized, vine-ripened grapes; spraying racks of previously harvested grapes with botrytis inoculum has largely gone out of fashion.

South Africa's famous Nederburg wines, developed by Gunter Brozel, and primarily based on Chenin Blanc (but again with other varieties, including Weisser Riesling and German crosses such as Bukettraube and Kerner), achieve extraordinary levels of complexity and near-overwhelming sweetness.

Wine from raisins

The same applies to sweet wines made from grapes left to raisin in the sun. The abbé Bellet, writing between 1717 and 1736, reported that in Italy and Provence sweet wines were made from grape bunches, the stems of which were twisted, and which were then left to ripen on the vine. This labor-intensive technique was the same as that used for the legendary Constantia of the Cape in the 18th and 19th centuries. Cane-cutting is the modern-day equivalent: the fruit-bearing cane is cut near the trunk or old wood, and left on the vine until the grapes shrivel.

The principal wines made by drying grapes today are *vins de paille* and *vini passiti* (notably *vin santo* and Amarone red wines from the Veneto, in Italy). For the *vins de paille* of the Jura the grapes are air-dried on mats or trays in lofts for three months, then crushed, pressed and fermented in oak casks. They are matured in wood for at least two years and, just as with Tokay, oxidation plays an important role in producing a golden brown–colored wine with a honeyed, toffeelike mid-palate, finishing off with a tangy bite.

Scant respect is paid to Commandaria, the liqueur wine of Cyprus, today, but few wines have such direct links with the ancient world. The grapes, black Mavron or white Xynisteri, grown in gritty sand in the foothills of the Troodos Mountains above Limassol, are picked onto mats (or sheets of plastic) and laid out beside the vines. One or two weeks of September Cyprus sun is enough to shrivel them. Donkeys are still used to carry the fruit-laden mats down to the press house, where red and white grapes are pressed separately. A minority still ferment in rotund earthenware jars buried to their rims in the ground.

There is little Commandaria made to a high standard, but samples of fresh wines from Keo in Limassol have proved to be intensely sweet and clean with 14 percent of alcohol. There is real potential for quality here. The usual practice is to age them for some years in old barrels in the open air until they are thoroughly oxidized.

Sweet Semillon

In the unlikely environment of Australia's Riverina region (often called the Murrumbidgee Irrigation Area), best known for large yields of near-hydroponically grown grapes, and home to McWilliam's, De Bortoli and Casella – of [yellow tail] (sic) fame – a de facto *appellation contrôlée* has evolved since 1982. In that year De Bortoli made a luscious botrytis Semillon (now called Noble One); there are now over a dozen producers of high-quality botrytis Semillons – the grapes are picked at the end of May or early June: up to four months later than normal maturity. The best are barrel-fermented in a mix of new and used French oak, reaching a peak within a few years of vintage, but capable of living much longer.

Light-Bodied Red Wines

Choices, consequences and techniques

The idea of lighter-bodied and fuller-bodied red wines is familiar to every drinker, even if he or she has never tried to pin down exactly what it means or which wines fall into which categories. For the purpose of this book, three categories of "body" are proposed. The first and the last should be more or less self-explanatory: clearly a Beaujolais *primeur* is a far lighter wine (though not necessarily a less alcoholic one) than a classed-growth Bordeaux. What lightness means here is absence of solid structure, of tannins and "extract"; the more of these elements a wine contains, the fuller-bodied it is.

The medium-bodied category is possibly the most contentious, since wines from any of the groups will fall naturally into it under certain conditions. Bordeaux of a cool, wet vintage will belong here (or may even be light-bodied), while outstanding Beaujolais from a great year will certainly have enough extract and aging potential to be classed as medium-bodied. Thus the quality of individual wines and vintages will often displace them from their "typical" categories.

Most difficult of all to place are Burgundy and other wines made from Pinot Noir. They regularly run the gamut from near-rosés to full wines with both flesh and muscle on their bones. They are placed in the medium-bodied category, the subject of the following chapter, because, while a Richebourg or a Chambertin

Beaujolais, the quintessentially light-hearted red before it was launched into international stardom, was bought by the barrel by the bistros of Lyon and Paris. It is prized for its softness of flavor, sappy smell and thirst-quenching appeal. Chiroubles (below), is one of the crus of Beaujolais.

may have great intensity of flavor and bouquet, it will not have the strong tannic structure of the full-bodied group. That is the grace and mystery of Pinot Noir.

The obvious profundity, complexity and longevity of the full-bodied red wines (chiefly but not entirely fashioned from Cabernet Sauvignon and its relatives) lead one to think that light-bodied reds are somehow inferior – or, if not inferior, certainly less serious. With that impression goes the assumption that it is easier to make a light-bodied red wine. Both impressions are incorrect. Making the wine is every bit as challenging, and, if the winemaker surmounts the challenge and has started with the appropriate grapes, its quality can be every bit as good.

Types of light-bodied red wines: rosés

Rosé wines could be classified as either tinted whites or very light-bodied reds, depending on their origin and vinification. They are something of a hybrid, borrowing part of their vinification technique from standard red winemaking, part from white. In terms of style and weight in the mouth, they are commonly closer to white wine than conventional red.

Choice of methods

Rosé wine can be made in any one of five different ways, or variations of them:

(i) White and red wines are blended: the usual method of achieving the color in rosé sparkling wines (even Champagne), in some European *vins gris* and in occasional cheap New World rosés.

(ii) Red grapes, crushed or (better) uncrushed but broken, are chilled and allowed to macerate for between 12 and 48 hours before the juice is drawn off (by static draining rather than by pressing) and then cold-fermented in the same fashion as a white wine. With broken or barely crushed grapes, this is known as the "bleeding," or *saignée*, method, the remaining must producing a more concentrated wine; this is the most commonly used method in the New World. With crushing but very little maceration it produces America's "blush" wines.

(iii) Whole bunches of red grapes are pressed, and the free-run and very lightly pressed juice is fermented without the skins. This is essentially a European method that gives rise to a very pale-colored wine, or *vin gris*.

(iv) Crushed grapes and juice are fermented together for one to three days before the juice is run off. A traditional European method.

(v) Red wine is heavily fined to remove tannins and is color-stripped by treatment with active carbon; this is last-resort winemaking producing a poor wine, with economics the sole motivation.

Choice of wines

Tavel in the southern Rhône Valley is arguably still the best-known specialist in rosé, but increasingly lives on the strength of its reputation rather than the quality of the wine in the bottle. Most Tavel is made by the prefermentation maceration technique, using uncrushed grapes, and produces a wine with a distinctive orange, onion-skin tint, high alcohol (a minimum of 11 degrees is required, but the wine often reaches 13) and signs of oxidation that rob the wine of freshness. The best winemakers are changing their methods to produce a wine with brighter color, more aroma and fresher, crisper fruit; they are achieving this through better temperature control, better use of sulfur dioxide and careful handling of the wine between the end of fermentation and bottling. The many enjoyable rosés of Provence are made more or less in the Tavel fashion.

In terms of volume sold, Mateus and other Portuguese rosés have a greater following than Tavel and Provence. They are bland, quite sweet, slightly carbonated at bottling to give them refreshing fizz, and should be served chilled. If subjected to critical sensory analysis, the conclusions will not be flattering. Spain, on the other hand, produces elegant, fresh, dry rosé in Navarre, based on Garnacha.

Ideally, any rosé should offer the flavor of fresh grapes in a clean wine with a

Tavel, west of the Rhône, produces wines from the same grapes as Châteauneuf-du-Pape, its neighbor across the river. But there the similarity ends: the best Tavel rosés, unlike the macho papal reds, are made as light, crisp, and refreshing as possible in the warm conditions.

refreshing cut of acidity or a little tannin. Not surprisingly, the tastiest are made from the tastiest grapes: usually Cabernets and Pinot Noirs. Anjou on the Loire has a long tradition of making very pale (and often oversweet) rosés from Cabernet Franc. The rare French rosés from Pinot Noir can be seductive. Marsannay in the Côte d'Or produces such a wine in tiny quantities. For a more plentiful (and much cheaper) source, St-Pourçain-sur-Sioule in central France is the place to look.

New World rosés are made in a radically different mold. The typical Australian or California rosé will be a vivid light purple-red to bright pink color, with not a hint of orange or onion-skin in its makeup. The bouquet will be extremely fresh and fruity. Ultraprotective winemaking techniques are used throughout, entirely excluding oxygen, using cold-fermentation in stainless steel and bottling at the earliest possible date. In the opening decade of the 21st century, an unexpected development occurred in many parts of the world: rosé came back into fashion. What's more, high-quality Grenache, perhaps with a jab of Syrah (Shiraz), usurped early-picked Cabernet Sauvignon as the variety of choice in countries such as Australia, producing both bone-dry and faintly sweet versions. Pinot Noir also became more common.

Reds from the Loire Valley

St-Nicolas-de-Bourgueil is generally reckoned the fullest and sturdiest of a group of three appellations, followed by Bourgueil and then Chinon. The minimum statutory alcohol requirement of 9.5 degrees gives the clue to the style of these Loire Valley wines, made at the western end of the Touraine region from Cabernet Franc (and up to 10 percent Cabernet Sauvignon). More than most wines, they prove that lightness of body does not mean lack of intensity. The very cool growing conditions have a number of implications: low alcohol, low tannins, intense

Making Red Wine

CRUSHING

The old way was to tread the grapes, or to remove the berries from the stalks by hand, sometimes rubbing them down a corrugated surface. Increasingly, the choice these days is between crushing and then destemming the bunches, or to bypass the crusher and simply destem the bunches, keeping the berries largely intact. The latter choice is often taken for Pinot Noir and also for Syrah (Shiraz); the former for Cabernet Sauvignon. The whole-berry route allows berry-by-berry inspection on slow-moving sorting tables.

FIRST FERMENTATION AND MACERATION

Fermentation vats were traditionally made of oak. Many still are, but stainless steel has the advantages of being easier to cool and easier to clean. High uncontrolled fermentation temperatures burn out the fruit flavors in the wine, but can also promote greater color extraction from grape skins, so a good temperature balance is essential. The length of maceration, the period during which the juice is left in the vat in contact with the grape skins, depends on the depth of color and tannin required in the wine. During maceration, the wine may be pumped over the surface of the cap, or the cap may be pushed down manually or hydraulically with a plate on a pole or ram; foot-stamping (*pigeage*) is still used by some makers of Pinot Noir, and in the Douro in open fermenters.

Carbonic maceration

Carbonic maceration is an alternative fermentation process in which the fruit is allowed to ferment spontaneously under a protective layer of carbon dioxide (CO_2). The weight of the grapes is sufficient to crush the fruit and release the juice, known as free-run, without mechanical pressure. The resulting wines tend to be softer and less astringent than those fermented in the traditional way, so this method is well suited to grapes that normally yield hard, acidic wines. Wines made by carbonic maceration are usually for drinking young (for example, Beaujolais Nouveau) and do not respond well to aging.

PRESSING

Pressing the grape mass, or pomace, occurs after the free-run wine has been removed from the fermentation vat. This process is not as important for red wines as it is for white, and in fact is not always carried out at all. "Press wine" is high in tannin and coloring pigments. At the discretion of the winemaker, a percentage of it may be blended with the free-run wine to add tannins, character and longevity.

Dark arrows indicate critical stages; lighter arrows show optional ones.

MALOLACTIC FERMENTATION

This process is almost always encouraged in red winemaking. It is a secondary fermentation in which malic acid is converted into lactic acid and carbon dioxide (CO_2). It softens the acidity of the wine and, once complete, adds to its complexity and stability.

In many European cellars, the wines will mature for six months before the malolactic fermentation commences (in the spring following vintage).

The merits of a quick malolactic fermentation at the end of the primary fermentation or a slow, delayed one can be the subject of intense debate.

MATURING

Maturation in oak
High-quality red wines today are almost always matured in oak. Oak contributes vanilla and woody tannin flavors. For how long the winemaker ages the wine in barrel is one of the crucial decisions, arrived at by regular tasting.

Racking
The wine is racked every few months by transferring it to a clean, sterile barrel, gently aerating it and leaving any sediment in the bottom of the old barrel.

Fining
The object of fining is to clarify the wine. The fining agent (usually egg white or bentonite clay) is poured onto the surface. As it sinks through the wine, it carries any solids to the bottom of the vat.

Filtration
The final option before bottling is whether or not to filter. Passing the wine through a fine filter guarantees (or should guarantee) its stability and "brightness" even under fairly adverse conditions. But some winemakers believe it strips the wine of its character.

FINISHING

Before bottling, the wine should be completely stable. It remains vulnerable to oxidation and contamination until the cork goes in. Mechanical bottling lines account for 95 percent of modern bottling. It is important to fill the bottles to exactly the right level to allow adequate room for the cork.

Right: *Chinon, on the river Vienne, one of Touraine's three red wine villages (along with Bourgueil and St-Nicolas-de-Bourgueil), in a region dominated by whites. Cabernet Franc, the principal grape in the reds of the Loire, makes soft, fruity Bourgueil (below), which has echoes of both Bordeaux and Beaujolais.*

aroma, crisp acidity, but (in quality terms) only a few vintages in which the grapes achieve their full potential ripeness. The vintage of 1961 was famously good; 1989 produced wines that were still full of life 15 years later.

Making Touraine reds

The wines are made by mainstream red wine methods: the grapes are crushed and destemmed, with a standard fermentation but little maceration once the fermentation is over. The winemakers accept that robust tannins and dense color are neither feasible nor indeed desirable. Aging is in small to medium-sized oak barrels and vats that are neither new nor ancient. A low percentage of the smaller barrels may be replaced each year. Barrel aging may extend for a surprisingly long time – up to three years – with regular racking over that period.

Beaujolais

The image of Beaujolais has suffered enormously since the 1980s. The quick money to be made from the flood of Beaujolais Nouveau encouraged growers to sharply increase yields, hoping the weather would hide their greed. Sometimes it did; most times it did not. A celebrated libel case against a small magazine that dared to describe the execrable quality of much Beaujolais only worsened the situation. Yet Beaujolais at its best is the most gloriously fruity and aromatic of all red wines. Its freshness and exuberance (and the ever-increasing amount of wine made as Nouveau) mean it is not taken seriously, which is no bad thing, for it is a wine to be swallowed rather than sipped, enjoyed in high spirits rather than analyzed and dissected. Some critics go even further, following in the footsteps of a legendary English author who gained his knowledge of the region by looking out of his train carriage window as it passed through. It deserves a closer look. If the wine list of a strange restaurant in a strange place looks depressing or unduly expensive, Beaujolais is often the safest haven.

Most books pass rather airily over the precise methods used to make Beaujolais, seemingly regarding it as insignificant. In fact, it is of fundamental importance in shaping the unique style of the wine, and is subject to a number of variations.

The Nouveau phenomenon has, happily, run its course, but Beaujolais remains in dire straits. Both domestic and export sales have plummeted since 2000, and were it not for Georges Duboeuf's steadying influence, the situation might be even worse. In 2005, Duboeuf was producing 40 million bottles a year, most of it purchased as fermenting wine from growers. Duboeuf's operation is a mix of highly skilled use of high technology and sustained public relations in all of its many important markets.

Carbonic maceration must have played a role in the making of the first wines consumed by our early ancestors, if the legends are true that grapes, stored in clay pots for winter, spontaneously fermented. It is thus curious that scientific knowledge of its chemistry is recent, and came about by chance. In 1934, a French research team set about developing methods designed to keep table grapes as fresh as possible between the time they were picked and the time they arrived on the table. One of the techniques tried was the storage of grapes at a temperature of 32°F (0°C) under a cover of carbon dioxide. After two months it was found that they had become gassy and fizzy, with a strange but not unpleasant taste. Unfit for sale as table grapes, they were made into wine, which was likewise considered to be pleasant but unusual.

Research initiated by Professor Michel Flanzy (and continued since) shows what happens after a grape is harvested and placed in a container filled with carbon dioxide. The berry is alive, in the sense that it can (and does) initiate enzyme-triggered changes in its chemical composition. The first change is the consumption by the berry of its stored carbon dioxide, which it needs to stay alive. Enzymes then attack the sugar in the berry, turning it to alcohol and producing more life-sustaining carbon dioxide in the process.

If carbon dioxide is readily available from the surrounding atmosphere, the berry will also absorb it from this source. The fermentation that thus occurs within the individual cells bears no relationship to normal fermentation. It is neither triggered by nor proceeds with yeast. Over a one- to two-week period (shorter at higher temperatures, longer at lower temperatures), up to 2 degrees of alcohol accumulate inside the berry, at which point the alcohol effectively kills the berry, and the intracellular fermentation ceases.

During that fermentation period, though, glycerol, methanol, ethyl acetate and acetaldehyde will have been produced in significant quantities, along with a range of amino acids. It is these substances that give wines made using carbonic maceration their characteristic lifted, pear-drop bouquet.

Carbonic maceration is employed in several different guises. The full-blown *macération carbonique* process sees the vat entirely filled with whole grape bunches. The bigger the vat, the greater the weight pressing on the bunches at the bottom, which will then split and exude juice. Either wild or cultured yeasts (the latter deliberately added) will cause this juice to start fermenting, giving off carbon dioxide that then fills the vat and protects the bunches higher up in the vat from oxidation and acetification, and that also progressively raises the temperature.

Thus two fermentations will be going on simultaneously but independently: the intracellular fermentation in the intact berries, and the alcoholic fermentation in the juice and split berries. As the alcoholic fermentation proceeds, the skins of the grapes in the bottom half of the vat will become softer (if the fermenting juice is pumped over the top of the vat, the change will be more widespread), and more and more bunches will collapse, so that the bottom third of the vat will be filled with fermenting wine.

At some point between three and seven days, the fermenting wine will be run off, and the remaining must will be pressed. The free-run component will have little residual sugar (depending on how long it has been fermenting) but the must (with a high percentage of intact berries) will still be rich in sugar. The two parts will be combined and the fermentation will conclude fairly rapidly – extended perhaps for a few days by chaptalization, but the essence of Beaujolais relies on a quick, relatively warm fermentation.

An alternative method – also used in Burgundy – is to fill a third to a half of the vat with whole bunches, and then top up the vat with crushed grapes. Once again, the two different fermentations will proceed concurrently, and the subsequent winemaking does not differ greatly from the full *macération carbonique* method.

In both cases malolactic fermentation occurs naturally and quickly. A carbonic-maceration wine has a higher than usual pH and more amino acids: both provide a favorable environment for malolactic fermentation – which is fortunate, given the

Carbonic maceration

In the vat, the "compote" of unbroken grapes undergoes carbonic maceration – a spontaneous fermentation process during which the berries feed on their own store of sugar, releasing carbon dioxide.

Parallel ferments

Nouveau

speed with which Beaujolais Nouveau must be made and bottled.

Beaujolais Nouveau is made in much the same way as Beaujolais. The principal difference is that the must is pressed early (after only three days), resulting in fewer phenolic flavoring substances being extracted. It is also quite certain that, whatever the appellation, the best grapes are used for Beaujolais, the least good for Beaujolais Nouveau. As soon as Nouveau has finished its malolactic fermentation it will be racked, fined and filtered; within weeks (if not days) it will be on the market.

Beaujolais proper follows a slightly more leisurely path. In recent years, there has been a tendency to embellish the richer *crus* (notably Moulin-à-Vent and Morgon) with new or used oak. While used by Georges Duboeuf and a few quality-conscious winemakers, this is a debatable trend, for it may confuse the issue (and the consumer). Duboeuf has an arrangement with tonnellerie Dargaud & Jaeglé to supply shaved two- to four-year-old barrels. In good years, the rich fruit can be enhanced by a touch of oak; in lesser years, it is an inappropriate intrusion.

But oak apart, the emphasis remains on the exuberant fruit of the Gamay grape. Winemaking techniques are designed simply to stabilize and clarify the wine, not to embellish that which needs no embellishment, nor to give it complexity that will blur the clarion call of the fruit.

Thermovinification

A number of producers – most prominently Duboeuf – use thermovinification, flash-heating part of the unfermented juice to 140°F (60°C) or more in the manner of Château de Beaucastel. The juice is then yeasted and added back to the fermenter with the main portion of whole bunches and untreated juice.

Chianti

Chianti, along with its legitimate and illegitimate offspring, is such a moving target that categorizing it as light-bodied is as open to challenge as treating it as medium-bodied. It can in fact be either, although what it is not is full-bodied. There are differing weights and styles: Chianti, Chianti Classico and Chianti *riserva*. There are also highly skilled and dedicated producers, there are unskilled and unscrupulous winemakers, and there are great vintages and there are poor vintages. Then there are the challenges of the new-wave *vini da tavola* (VDT) and, since 1992, *indicazione geografica tipica* (IGT), made in Tuscany – in Chianti, indeed – but refusing to be bound by the dictates of the DOCG. The Italian view of things is fluid at the best of times, and significant implications for traditional Chianti are emerging from the techniques used in making the new VDT and IGT wines. The Chianti of yesterday was very different from that of today; it is certain that the Chianti of tomorrow will be quite different again.

Ancient vs. modern

The changes have come thick and fast in Chianti, and in particular Chianti Classico. When both Chianti and Chianti Classico were granted DOCG status in 1984, the principal change to the formula established by Baron Bettino Ricasoli in the middle of the 19th century was the right to use 10 percent of "other" recommended or authorized grapes. In practice, the 10 percent was Cabernet Sauvignon, Merlot and (later) Syrah (Shiraz), but the incorporation of 5 to 10 percent Canaiolo and 2 percent Malvasia remained obligatory.

For the simple Chianti DOC promulgated in 1967, other recommended grapes included Trebbiano, Colorino, Malvasia Nera and Mammolo, further fortification coming in the form of up to 15 percent–strong wine or must from more southern regions. The 1984 grant of DOCG to Chianti achieved little or nothing to enhance its status (or its quality).

Searching for Sangiovese

In 1996, the Chianti Classico DOCG was changed once again to distinguish it from other Chianti subzones, and to allow 100 percent Sangiovese wines to use the Classico appellation (and *riserva*). The use of Canaiolo and Malvasia became optional (with a ceiling of 10 percent, but effectively zero) while the use of other recommended or complementary varieties (effectively French) grown within the region was increased to 15 percent (since raised to 20 percent).

Of even greater significance for the future was the 1988 launch of the Chianti

*San Gimignano lies just outside
the zone of Chianti Classico. The
new Italian wine laws of 1992 are
a determined attempt to preserve
the integrity of regional traditions
while allowing scope for
ambitious winemakers with
ideas of their own.*

Classico 2000 Research Program. Its aim was to identify the best clones of
Sangiovese, the best rootstocks, optimum planting densities and preferred canopy-
training systems. Trial blocks of numerous specific clones were planted between
1989 and 1996, and from 1993 dedicated microvinification laboratories
established. In 1995, organoleptic and analytical tests started, and by 1999 the first
conclusions were drawn, the most important being the identification of four
superior clones (two selected by Paolo di Marchi of Isole e Olena), and vertical
spur-pruning as the best training method. By 2000, it was estimated that 30 percent
of Chianti's vineyards had been replanted, and the hope is that by 2010 the figure
will be close to 100 percent. Then another 10 to 15 years will have to pass before
the ultimate quality of Chianti Classico can be determined.

The French question

The question that will continue to be debated as to how much Cabernet Sauvignon,
Merlot and/or Syrah should be used. There is no limit to the amounts incorporated
with Sangiovese and sold either as a VDT or IGT wine, and there should be no objection
to this. The market will determine demand and, hence, price for such wines.

How much Cabernet, etc., should be used in Chianti Classico is an altogether
different question. The high-water mark of adulation of variety at the expense of
terroir and the varieties indigenous to that *terroir* has passed. Now the aim is – or
should be – to find points of difference, not similarity. Sangiovese properly grown
in Tuscany has both unique *typicité* (the Italians call it *tipicità*) and inherent quality
of a high order. Turn the coin over, and you find that the numerous and ongoing
attempts to match that quality (forgetting *typicité*) in the New World have been
dismal failures. Sangiovese may be an easier proposition to grow than Nebbiolo,
but that is not the issue. Sangiovese should be seen to be the king of Tuscany, all
other varieties – Italian or French – no more than the king's courtiers.

Rioja

Many of the issues confronting Chianti also confront Rioja. Specifically, should
the wines be subjected to long cask aging, which gives complexity, smoothness
and softness, but which also oxidizes and subjugates the fruit? And what role
should oak play in shaping the taste of the wine? On the latter point, Rioja is

Chianti

This choices-and-consequences chart illustrates those stages in the winemaking process in which the options chosen by the winemaker will fundamentally influence the taste and individuality of the final wine. Not every stage of the process is indicated; for that the reader is directed to the red wine process chart on pages 140–1.

The making of Chianti, perhaps Italy's most famous red and the mainstay of Tuscan viticulture for centuries, was in danger of becoming a complacent business. Tuscany now ranks with Piedmont in terms of innovation, but also in rediscovering the special qualities of Sangiovese.

1
IN THE VINEYARD

Choice of grape variety
(a) *Sangiovese 75–100 percent*
(b) *Canaiolo 0–10 percent*
(c) *Trebbiano/Malvasia 0–5 percent*
(d) *Other optional reds, including up to 15 percent Cabernet Sauvignon*

Varietal choice is one of the most hotly debated issues in Chianti today. One school of thought lays maximum emphasis on Sangiovese and denies the value of

2
FERMENTING

Fermentation timing
(a) *Long: 2–3 weeks*
(b) *Medium: 7–10 days*
(c) *Short: 3 days Vinimatic*

Choice of fermentation technique is vitally important in determining wine style. Long maceration extracts all available tannins and accentuates the tendency of Sangiovese to bitterness; it necessitates long cask maturation and (probably) the need for further maturation in bottle to allow the wine to soften. The midcourse produces wines with good balance, complexity and fruit, but perhaps not the same longevity.

Above: *The "pomace" is what remains after pressing grapes – the residue of skins, pips and pulp.*

Right: *Fruity, fresh Chianti for local drinking may still be bottled in bulbous flasks (fiaschi), either covered in straw or plastic, but the more tannic, serious Chianti, intended for aging, goes into Bordeaux-style bottles that can be stacked.*

incorporation of other varieties, particularly white. It is strongly opposed to Cabernet Sauvignon, which robs the wine of its *typicité*. The other school argues that the blends give the greatest complexity and that the marriage of Sangiovese and Cabernet Sauvignon is a synergistic one.

Left: *The American-owned Villa Banfi at Montalcino in Tuscany is one of the most technologically advanced operations in Europe. The pneumatic presses, like the entire winery, are computer-controlled.*

The recent move to short fermentation (usually associated with Vinimatic fermenters) produces a very fruity, very soft, brilliantly colored *nouveau* style.

Governo

The use of the *governo* technique (adding must from 5 to 10 percent of grapes that have been left to dry and concentrate to vats of normally fermented wine in order to cause a refermentation) is subject to trend. While a handful of producers insist it should be used in *riserva* wines, most limit its use to Chianti made to be drunk young, where it freshens the wine with the touch of gas it creates and gives the illusion of a little sweetness through the glycerol it produces.

Malolactic fermentation

While most independent observers regard the softening effect of malolactic fermentation as highly desirable, some makers are still prepared to leave its occurrence to chance. Most, however, encourage it and seek to complete it quickly after the end of fermentation.

3

MATURING

Choice of oak

(a) *French* barriques – *old and new; increasingly preferred*
(b) *Tuscan chestnut – old and new*
(c) *Large old Slavonian oak*
(d) *No oak*

Next to the impact of Cabernet Sauvignon on Tuscany, the influence of new oak is largely used with discretion and sensitivity in the making of Chianti (but not so much so in the making of *barrique vini da tavola* or IGT wines). Oak choice is usually linked with fermentation choice: long fermentations with large old oak maturation, shorter fermentations with new small oak. Some winemakers reject oak in almost any form, preferring concrete or glass-lined tanks.

Maturation time

(a) *Very long: 3–9 years*
(b) *Medium: 1–2½ years*
(c) *Short: 3–6 months*

Once again, there is a link: long maturation in large, old neutral oak; the shortest in new *barriques*. This in turn links back to fermentation: a fresh, fruity wine low in tannin can be much improved by oak tannins.

Fining and filtration

The continuity continues: very long-vatted wines that have been racked many times are less likely to need fining (and are also less likely to be filtered because of the philosophy of the maker) than those that have spent a shorter time in oak.

Bodegas López de Heredia, one of the great bastions of Rioja tradition, ferment and age all their wines in oak – the minimum is three years.

moving in the opposite direction to Chianti, yet the new thinking in each region has a similar aim. Riojans have not (so far) burdened themselves with the complication of adding Cabernet Sauvignon or Syrah (Shiraz); the old Cabernet vineyard of the Marqués de Riscal is the one exception. All other Rioja reds are made from all or some of Tempranillo (typically 75 percent), Garnacha (25 percent), Graciano (2.5 percent) and Mazuelo (2.5 percent). As in Chianti, some of the new-wave producers are using 100 percent Tempranillo in their top wines, and for good measure using French, not American, oak. Rioja has always indulged in winemaking on a grand scale. An indication is that a bodega must have a storage capacity of 83,000 cases and at least 500 *barriques* before it can apply for permission to export its wines.

In the majority of bodegas the grapes are crushed and fermented in a wholly traditional fashion, with temperatures peaking at 86°F (30°C) or more and finishing within three tumultuous days. The must is then allowed to macerate for seven days before being pressed. Thereafter the handling of the wine will depend on its grading or appellation, determined by the Rioja *consejo regulador* (set up in 1926). In each grade the wine may be either *clarete* (lighter-bodied and of lower alcoholic strength: between 10 and 11.5 degrees), or *tinto* (darker, fuller-bodied, higher in alcohol). *Tintos* are today far more frequently encountered than are *claretes*. During their long sojourn in barrel, the wines were traditionally repeatedly fined with egg whites and repeatedly racked, but a less rigorous regime is used with the current shorter oak aging. Cold-stabilization, pasteurization, and filtration are all options open to winemakers before bottling; pasteurization is the most contentious, although it is not clear whether or how it affects the wine.

While easy to enjoy when first released, the longevity of the best wines has been underlined by a series of recent auctions at Christie's and Sotheby's in London, where 30- to 80-year-old Riojas have brought high prices from aficionados.

Ambivalence in oak

The oak used is still usually American, a strange twist given the fact that most American wine producers prefer to import their oak from Europe. What is more, having selected this highly perfumed and flavored oak, many Rioja winemakers traditionally went to extremes to tone down its flavor. New barrels are washed with hot water to reduce the flavoring compounds, then further seasoned with lesser wines. Once used for top-quality red wines, the lengthy maturation and consequent pickup of oak aromas and flavor would be balanced by egg-white fining. Despite these apparent efforts, the oak does give the wines a marked vanilla-lemon perfume and flavor: a hallmark of the Rioja style. Another is the suppleness and smoothness of the texture; as a consequence of the fining and the very long cask- and bottle-age given to the wines, the tannins are extremely soft. This unusual lightness of structure has historically made Riojas the first-choice reds of Spain.

The small family firm of Bodegas Muga in the Rioja Alta claims to be the only producer in the region to use American oak exclusively for both fermentation and maturation.

The aging regulations for Rioja

Red wines	Maturation before sale
Sin crianza	Usually labeled *cosecha*; has no aging in wood.
Crianza	One year in oak. Should not leave the winery until the third year after the vintage.
Reserva	Three years between cask and bottle, of which one year must be in oak. Sold at least four years after vintage.
Gran Reserva	Two years in oak and three years in bottle, or vice versa. Should not leave the winery until the sixth year after the vintage.
	Note: *Reservas* and *gran reservas* can shorten the time in barrel, but must then be bottle-aged for an additional period twice as long as that by which the barrel aging was shortened.

Medium-Bodied Red Wines

Choices, consequences and techniques

No grape makes the choices open to a winemaker more critical than the Pinot Noir. Curiously, this was not always so. Traditional English texts on wine tend to stress the "masculinity" of Burgundy when compared with the supposed "femininity" of Bordeaux: the precise opposite to our present categorization of Burgundy as medium-bodied, Bordeaux as full.

Burgundy, in truth, has changed through the years. In the 18th century the high fashion was for Volnay, so pale and light that it was called a *vin de primeur* – bottled in December and drunk before the next harvest. In 1728, Claude Arnoux wrote:

> [Volnay] produces the finest, the liveliest and the most delicate wine in Burgundy … its grapes are so delicate that they cannot abide the [fermenting] vat more than 12 to 16 or 18 hours, because if they are left in longer, [the wine] begins to taste of the stalks … This wine is only a little stronger in color than *oeil de perdrix*.

Later in the 18th century, and throughout the 19th, the fashion swung in favor of the *vins de garde* of the Côte de Nuits (above all Chambertin): wines that were deliberately made as strong as possible, with honey added (until Monsieur Chaptal introduced beet sugar), and vatted for long enough to make them fully red and relatively tannic.

These were the wines that gave Burgundy its "masculine" reputation, and that were easy to "cut" with dark Rhône wines for export. In the last four decades of the 20th century, and extending into the 21st century, the pendulum swung wildly, initially favoring ultralight-bodied wines, excused on the grounds of purity and (misplaced) respect for *terroir*. True, the wines were not adulterated, but they were made from overcropped vines, the vineyards bombarded by sprays of all kinds. Yields have now been pulled back; there has been a dramatic move to organic (and some biodynamic) viticulture; and the best wines absolutely reflect their *terroir* with

Pinot Noir in Burgundy

Oeil de perdrix

Vins de garde

The temperamental Pinot Noir was born in Burgundy, selected and perfected by the Cistercian monks of Cîteaux in the Middle Ages. It reaches its apogee in the village of Vosne-Romanée, where the sea of vines laps right up to the walls of the growers' houses.

that deceptively silky and fragrant ease of great Burgundy. Once again, however, a caveat: there is still far too much poor Burgundy made by growers who have no understanding of the storm clouds ahead, and who neither know nor care about the problems facing Bordeaux and parts of the Midi.

The color of
Pinot Noir

The Pinot Noir grape differs from all other important dark-skinned varieties of *Vitis vinifera*. It has fewer coloring pigments (anthocyanins) and is more prone to oxidation; it has fewer flavoring substances and fewer tannins; and it is liable to lose a significant proportion of these during vinification. For these reasons, too, Pinot Noir is especially sensitive to climate and to its treatment in the vineyard – and in particular to overcropping.

In the cellar

The choices – and the arguments – start the moment the grapes come into the winery. Should they be crushed with the rollers on conventional spacing? Should they simply be destemmed with the berries left intact (or as intact as possible)? Should whole bunches go into the fermenting vat, or should the entire fermentation start with nothing but whole bunches?

The choice adopted will have a major impact on style, much less so (if at all) on quality. Some makers, knowing their vineyards intimately, will always follow one course, arguing (if they need to) that this will most clearly reflect the *terroir*. Others may elect to significantly change the percentages of crushed/destemmed/whole-bunch grapes according to the vintage, using more whole bunches in warm, dry years that allow the stalks to partially lignify (or go brown) and thus avoid green tannins. This approach, the maker argues, will optimize complexity without subverting *terroir*.

The next decision to be taken is whether it is necessary to run off part of the free-run juice. When yields were at their zenith, but the consequences were becoming apparent, it was common to run off up to 20 percent before fermentation commenced.

The scarcely spectacular middle slopes of the Côte at Vosne-Romanée are Burgundy's most precious parcels of Pinot Noir. Here, the Domaine de la Romanée-Conti conjures quite extraordinary intensity, complexity, depth and sheer beauty from its delicate grapes.

The very best winemakers concede that it is basically an unsatisfactory choice, stemming from an excessive crop in the first place, and while it gives better color and greater concentration of flavor, it also leads to an imbalance in the must. Relative to wines from optimum yields, the resulting wine will be lower in acidity, less aromatic and fruity, higher in tannin and have a higher pH. In extreme cases, they can have an unnaturally "thick" character. Nonetheless, if the crop has been excessive, it *is* the lesser of two evils, though "bunch-thinning" (*see* page 154) is the best solution of all in abundant years.

Where traditional vats (open or closed) are used, conventional wisdom considers warm-to-hot fermentation temperatures (86°F to 90°F/30°C to 32°C) to be most effective in extracting color from Pinot Noir. But there are those who believe that color is best extracted in the absence of alcohol (i.e., before fermentation), that aroma and flavor come with fermentation, and that tannins come from the maceration afterward. Either way, winemakers of Pinot Noir in Burgundy and elsewhere are convinced that it is desirable for fermentation to reach a relatively high temperature.

Extracting color

The one exception lies with the use of the sideways-revolving Vinimatic vats, which quickly and effectively (perhaps too quickly) extract maximum color and flavor from all grape varieties, Pinot Noir included. Indeed, it is easy to overextract material from the grapes this way; care must be taken to avoid doing so.

Chaptalization was considered quite essential to the making of Burgundy regardless of the naturally available sugar in the grapes. This view was first challenged by a few iconoclasts such as Hubert de Montille in Volnay, but he has many companions these days. As yields have come down and viticultural practices improved out of sight, sugar levels have increased markedly – even in vintages such as 2004. Add in the impact of (apparent) climate change, and both the frequency

Chaptalization

Pinot Noir had no place in Spain until the house of Torres, already famous for magnificent Cabernet blends with traditional Catalan grapes, planted it in the highest vineyards of Penedès. The Torres barrel cellars, sturdily traditional, give little idea of the innovative scope of the company.

and degree of chaptalization are diminishing. Its proponents say quite simply that "it is for the feel in the mouth": an oblique reference to the fact that, particularly if it is added progressively in small amounts toward the end of the primary fermentation, it "stresses" the fermentation and leads to an increase in glycerol.

Oak – a matter of taste

The conservative view is that new barrels are not only unnecessary for the production of fine Burgundy, but may positively harm it. If the oak is of the wrong type, if it is clumsily handled or if the wine is not sufficiently strong and rich, then oak may indeed detract from the wine's character (or fail to help it). But it is fundamental to the making of all of the wines of the Domaine de la Romanée-Conti, all of the *grand* and *premier cru* wines of Méo-Camuzet and Domaine Dujac and many other great winemakers who use all-new barrels every year. At the end of the day, it is a matter of taste, although the double new oak regime used at Domaine Laurent seems to be directed to the American market more than any other.

The final bone of real contention is filtration: many of the top producers are implacably opposed to it, and no scientists or biochemists seeking to establish that it has no long-term adverse effects on color or flavor will change their minds. Indeed, the antifiltration camp often even avoids pumping Pinot Noir wherever possible, relying on gravity or gas-pressure movement. What is clear is that some unfiltered Burgundies do not react well to being exported. Tranquil life in a cool Burgundy cellar is one thing; shipment in hot climates is another. Heat can trigger unwelcome bacterial activity, leading to off-odors, cloudiness and the development of high levels of the spoilage yeast known as *Brettanomyces*.

At the risk of gross understatement, one can say that, for Burgundy, the simpler (and more conventional) the winemaking process, and the less new oak involved, the simpler the wine. Commune and classification (*grand cru*, *premier cru* or commune) will then impose another layer of quality and character. But distinctions of *cru* are in a different category from those of winemaking technique: one must try to imagine a three-dimensional scale to understand the pattern. When one then looks at the performance of Pinot Noir in other parts of the world, even those skeptical about the meaning of *terroir* have to admit that there is something very special about Burgundy; a magical combination of *terroir*, climate and tradition.

Filtration

New World Pinot Noir

In Europe, Burgundy has no challengers. There are marketable Pinot Noirs from Italy's South Tirol; a serious attempt by the house of Torres in the high Penedès of Catalonia; some too often anemic and overoaked Spätburgunders from Germany; and usually frail Pinot Noirs from Sancerre and Alsace; but none of these approaches the triumph of the Côte d'Or (and, to be fair, its neighbor, the Côte Chalonnaise). It has been left to the New World, and principally three countries – the United States, Australia and, increasingly, New Zealand – to throw out a challenge to Burgundy. Only a few select regions and a few select winemakers within those regions have produced Pinot Noir of real style and merit, but what they have achieved in more recent vintages holds great promise for the future, particularly with better clonal selection, increasing vine age and greater experience in handling this most temperamental variety.

New World methods of making Pinot Noir vary even more widely than those of Burgundy, while paying due regard to what Burgundy is doing. The Californians and Oregonians have progressively moved away from whole-bunch fermentation (finding the tannins from the stalks too astringent) and compensated by using a longer period of maceration at the end of fermentation. Some are justifiably cautious about the amount of new oak they use, and if there is a criticism, it is a tendency to "undermake" the wine rather than the reverse. The decision not to filter has become very fashionable – even if it means having to accept cloudy wine. Australasian methods are similar, the principal difference being greater use of a percentage of whole-bunch fermentation, and intolerance of cloudy wine.

Since the first edition of this book, much has changed in the New World. In California, the ridgetop vineyards of the Sonoma Coast have joined the Russian River as truly impressive producers, Santa Barbara on the Central Coast matching wine for wine. In Australia, Tasmania has matured into a fully fledged competitor with the regions circling Melbourne (Geelong, Gippsland, Mornington Peninsula, Macedon Ranges and Yarra Valley). But the biggest changes have come in New Zealand, where Marlborough, Nelson, Christchurch, Canterbury and most notably Central Otago (all in the South Island) have joined Martinborough/Wairarapa (at

The Oregon climate, as uncertain as that of Burgundy, appears to be ideal for Pinot Noir. In a statement of faith, Robert Drouhin, the leading Beaune grower/négociant, has planted 100 acres (40 ha) in the Dundee Hills. These rotary fermenters in his Oregon winery are the same as he uses in Beaune.

Pinot Noir

This choices-and-consequences chart illustrates those stages in the winemaking process in which the options chosen by the winemaker will fundamentally influence the taste and individuality of the final wine. Not every stage of the process is indicated: for that the reader is directed to the red wine process chart on pages 140–1.

Pinot Noir is a difficult but alluring grape. No other *vinifera* grape displays such genetic variation, which creates problems for grower and maker alike. Clonal selection is vital in the battle against viral menace. Bunch-thinning has proved beneficial in improving the quality of the fruit. Responding happily in Burgundy, which produces the finest Pinot Noir wines in the world, it sets a real challenge for quality winemakers in the New World. Plantings in Oregon, cooler parts of California and Australia confirm that the grape is best suited to cooler, marginal climates.

1 IN THE VINEYARD

Bunch-thinning
Removing a percentage of bunches from the vine in order to reduce the crop is common. The quality of Pinot Noir is particularly compromised by excessive crops. In the New World, removal of the shoulder (or wing) of each bunch is also practiced in some of the best vineyards.

2 CRUSHING

Crushing options
(a) *Whole bunches (some or all)*
(b) *Destem only*
(c) *Partial stem*
(d) *Total crush*
(e) *Stalk return*

Whole-bunch fermentation takes additional time and space in the winery and demands open fermentation vats and *pigeage* (by foot or pneumatic ram), but results in complex, aromatic wines. Destemming without

3 FERMENTING

Choice of yeast
Choice lies between wild or cultured yeast; Burgundians overwhelmingly prefer the former, arguing that it gives greater complexity and subtlety. For a more general discussion on wild yeast, *see* pages 219–20.

Choice of fermentation vat
(a) *Open*
(b) *Closed*
(c) *Vinimatic*

Determined by the choice made at the crusher. Extraction of color and flavor from the must is aided by pushing down the cap of *marc* into the fermenting juice by foot or by automatic plungers, or by pumping the must from the bottom of the vat up over the *marc*. The Vinimatic is an

automatic vinifier that was transiently popular, but is now mainly used in the production of lesser red wines.

Temperature choice
Almost all producers believe Pinot Noir must reach 86°F (30°C) during fermentation, but give different reasons – some say for color, others for aroma and flavor.

4 MATURING

Choice of oak
(a) *Type of oak*
(b) *Percentage of new oak*

Well-chosen oak, handled in the right manner, is of fundamental importance for the greatest Burgundies. Good Burgundy (and Pinot Noir) can be made without new oak, but lacks the complexity of the greatest wines.

Lees contact
Not an uncommon practice in Burgundy. Similar to lees contact with Chardonnay, except that stirring is not usually practiced. As long as no off-characters develop, it can be very beneficial in adding weight and complexity to the wines.

Period in oak
Decision will depend on the percentage of new oak, the weight of the base wine and the style sought by the winemaker. It is easy to spoil Pinot Noir by leaving it in oak for too long.

Method of picking

(a) *By hand*
(b) *By machine*

Machine picking limits the options of the winemaker, and in particular precludes whole-bunch fermentation. It is rarely used in the production of quality Pinot Noir.

Clonal Selection

Much work has been done in Burgundy to identify superior clones. The New World has adopted this with enthusiasm, with specific use of identified clones (e.g., 113, 114, 115, 776, 777), while in Burgundy there remains a preference for *sélection massale*, or a generic mix from existing vineyards.

Left: There is a high premium on undamaged grapes, since damaged ones begin to oxidize immediately. Time is of the essence in getting the picked grapes to the winery before they can spoil.

crushing is widely used; fermentation is initiated faster and green tannins from the stems are avoided. A partial destem offers some of the advantages of both (a) and (b). Fully crushed and destemmed grapes give good color but may lead to somewhat coarser tannins.

Juice runoff

Running off part of the juice before fermentation commences in order to concentrate it has become common practice in high-yield years. The end result is not as good as bunch-thinning, as the pH will rise, making it more difficult to achieve balance and silky mouth-feel.

Prefermentation maceration

Extracts color and tannin from the pomace. Frequently takes place in Europe because the reliance on wild yeasts and the fairly high level of sulfur additions mean that fermentation takes three to four days to commence. Can be significantly extended by chilling the must and adding more sulfur dioxide.

Above: Using a basket press results in a "cake" of solid matter. This can be used as cattle feed or vineyard fertilizer.

Chaptalization

Usual in Burgundy but forbidden in Australia. Undoubtedly it adds roundness and fatness to the texture of the wine. Since the mid-1990s, the overall use of chaptalization in Burgundy has decreased significantly.

Maceration choice

(a) *Postfermentation maceration*
(b) *Partial barrel fermentation*

Conventional approach calls for 5 to 12 days postfermentation maceration to extract soft tannins; a minority prefers to finish the fermentation in barrel, relying in part on the subtle oak tannins that are extracted.

Malolactic fermentation

(a) *Early (inoculated)*
(b) *Late (natural)*

More or less standard practice. Malolactic on lees adds an added dimension to Pinot Noir, but may give off-flavors. Traditionalists argue that late, naturally occurring malolactic fermentation also gives added complexity. Early will require a warm 59°F to 68°F (15°C to 20°C) barrel storage area.

Below: The ultramodern fermentation plant at Pacs del Penedès, owned by the house of Torres. Torres has invested in the latest wine technology as well as introducing some of the classic French varieties, Pinot Noir included.

Fining

Gentle fining – usually with egg white – is often used, sometimes as an alternative to filtration, sometimes in addition. It removes excess tannins, but must be used with discretion or it will detract from the character of the wine.

Filtration

Burgundian dislike of filtering is spreading to the New World. However, some unfiltered Burgundies may react to heat during export, which can trigger cloudiness and off-odors.

the southern end of the North Island) as producers of excellent to outstanding Pinot Noir when the weather gods permit.

It is, though, a grape that remains a great enigma: the ultimate challenge. Confirmed Cabernet Sauvignon drinkers may never understand or appreciate it; something which causes Pinot-philes no concern at all. For better or worse, there simply isn't enough great Pinot Noir to satisfy existing demand: it would be a disaster if it suddenly acquired the popularity of either Chardonnay or Cabernet.

Italian red wines

Italy produces such a profusion of red wines, made in diverse climates and using everchanging techniques, that all attempts to classify and parcel them neatly for overseas consumption have failed. The eternal Achilles' heel of wine is that it is complicated, it intimidates. Italy achieves levels of complication and intimidation unparalleled in any other country, even Germany, partly through its own efforts but largely because of the accidents of its long history. The consequence is that its red wines are far less well known and appreciated than they should be. The selection here is but a small and inevitably arbitrary one.

Some might say it is typical of Italy that some of the greatest and most of the poorest wines share the same birth certificate, which, if not quite alleging illegitimacy, certainly denies nobility. It is no less appropriate that it should have been the noble Marchese Mario Incisa della Rocchetta who, in 1948, started it all by planting Cabernet Sauvignon on the family estate at Bolgheri on the Tuscan coast. He called his wine Sassicaia, which from the start bore no comparison with any other in Italy. His nephew, Marchese Piero Antinori, recognized just what Sassicaia foretold, and took it – and its relatives – onto the world stage. The first Antinori creation was Tignanello, a blend of Sangiovese with a little Cabernet that remains his best known of all. Pure Cabernet Sauvignons, Bordeaux blends and pure Sangioveses followed in its wake in spurts and dribbles, it seemed, from the baroque fountains of every noble Tuscan *fattoria*; all failed to conform in one way or another with the DOC rules. It has been easy to deride the DOC system, but they were desperately unlucky: the system was promulgated in 1963, just a few years before the new wave of viticulture and oenology swept over the country. To all intents and purposes, the DOC regulations could have been written 100 or 200 years earlier and scarcely been more outmoded.

The significance of the new upmarket *vini da tavola*, and, since the passing of the Goria Law in 1992, *vini tipice* under *indicazione geografica tipica* (IGT), extends right across Italy, and has meant radical changes in both vineyard and winery. In the vineyard, the changes are obvious enough: the planting of French varieties often at the expense of traditional Italian grapes. In the long term, the changes in the winery may prove even more significant, for they represent changes in attitude – in philosophy – which will alter the face of Italian wine forever.

Trends away from tradition

The methods used to make these wines are not unusual; it is the difference in approach that contrasts with that of traditional Italian red winemaking. The traditional way was to take varieties naturally high in acid, tannin and potential alcohol, and ferment them in such a way as to extract every available particle of flavor and tannin. Having created a vinous monster, the winemaker would then seek to tame and soften it by prolonged aging in large old Slavonian oak vats, with oxidation as a principal weapon in the armory. The wines had a certain balance, and sometimes made a very memorable bottle, but did nothing to highlight the most desirable characteristics of the grape variety or region concerned.

Barrique-*aged* vini da tavola

The introduction of new oak in the form of Bordeaux-style *barriques* forced a complete change. Instead of three to five years in oak, the period was reduced to 12 to 18 months. This had a doubling effect: instead of tannins being reduced by the process of oxidation and aging (and deposited in the barrel in the form of heavily stained tartrates), they were boosted by the tannins extracted from the oak. And new oak inevitably introduces another dimension of flavor and complexity (which traditionalists, of course, dislike). Taken together, these changes meant that the wine being taken from the vat had to be less tannic and more fruity if any semblance of balance was to be achieved by the time it was bottled.

Winemakers started to play down the vigor of their fermentation and macerate the wine for shorter periods afterward. They also introduced grapes calculated to have a softening effect: most obviously Merlot and Cabernet Franc, but (surprisingly) even Cabernet Sauvignon. In such wineries, fermentation (which may incorporate a percentage of whole bunches or berries) takes place in stainless-steel vats with inbuilt temperature control, and typically lasts between a week and a maximum (including maceration) of two. Malolactic fermentation is artificially encouraged and finishes soon after the primary fermentation. Only then is the first sulfur dioxide added. Whether the wine is then matured entirely in new or near-new oak *barriques* or whether it will also spend some time in the traditional old oak vats (called *botti*) will depend on the winemaker. In all, it may spend between 15 months and two years in some kind of oak after fermentation.

While still producing its splendid Chianti Classicos, the Castello di Ama, near Radda in the heart of the zone, is as uninhibited as any Tuscan estate in its experiments with foreign grapes. Its vini da tavola *include Chardonnay, Merlot, Sauvignon Blanc and even Tuscany's most promising stab at Pinot Noir.*

While the French-*barrique*-aged *vini da tavola* originated in Tuscany, and while they are more common there than elsewhere, the use of *barriques* has spread across the length and breadth of Italy. The passing of the Goria Law in 1992 gave their use (via IGT) even greater opportunities than previously. As experience with the use of *barriques* grew, most of the early clumsy and excessive oak influences were toned down. But Italy is no different from any other part of the wine world; wines constructed around the aroma and flavor of oak, and not that of the *terroir* and grape, continue to be made and purchased, often at high prices.

The Tuscan wines fall most neatly into the medium-bodied category. They do so whether they are pure Cabernet Sauvignon, pure Sangiovese, blends in which Sangiovese is dominant or blends where Cabernet Sauvignon takes the lead. These wines are fragrant and supple; where Cabernet Sauvignon is dominant, it is gently herbaceous, but never tannic or astringent. While they will improve with bottle-age, they do not positively need it: five to seven years from vintage will see them reach their plateau of development, however long they may remain on that plateau thereafter. Rusticity or *typicité* have no place in these wines: sulfides, volatile acidity and oxidation are conspicuous by their absence, and those aromas and flavors that are present are the result of very deliberate winemaking decisions.

This highlights the tension between tradition and opportunity. In some ways Italy provides an interface between the New World and the Old. In 1992, Piero Antinori had no doubt that the advantages outweighed the disadvantages:

The second Risorgimento?

> I must say that while I admire French wines greatly, I consider myself privileged to be operating my business in Italy rather than France. It is so much more exciting to be in Italy, where so many things are changing, rather than to be in a rigidly established situation, even if it be at the highest level as it is in France. For many centuries, Italy has been a producer of quantity rather than quality, for that is what the consumer wanted. Then it suddenly all changed, and in the last 20 years we have had this sort of revolution. Producers and customers have both discovered the enormous potential Italy has for quality wines of kinds we have never attempted before.

However, he does not see Chardonnay and Cabernet Sauvignon engulfing Italy:

> In the long term, I see the future of Italian wine lying more in our own varieties, provided we are able to improve them through clonal selection, which I am sure we can. I believe in our varieties because we have such an ancient viticultural history and tradition. The world is being invaded by Chardonnay and Cabernet Sauvignon, but the consumer will want a

wider choice, which Italy can provide with its traditional varieties. This does not mean there is no place for Chardonnay and Cabernet Sauvignon in Italy; clearly there is. There are regions where certain grape varieties have a real history and tradition, and these should be maintained and protected. There are other regions without a significant history, rather like California or Australia, and in these regions Chardonnay, Sauvignon Blanc and Cabernet Sauvignon should play an important role.

The northern Rhône – Syrah (Shiraz)

The wines of few regions fit less tidily into the categories of medium- and full-bodied than those of the northern Rhône. The best wines of Hermitage, Côte Rôtie and Cornas are full-bodied, the wines of the best producers made in the great vintages emphatically so. Such wines explain why Hermitage and Côte Rôtie were rated as among the finest, if not *the* finest, in mid-19th-century France – why Professor George Saintsbury wrote of an 1846 Hermitage as

"The manliest French wine"

> *One of the three or four most remarkable juices of the grape, not merely that I ever possessed, but that I ever tasted … It was the manliest French wine I ever drank.*

Moving down the appellation scale to Crozes-Hermitage and St-Joseph, or taking the wines of less exalted winemakers from lesser years in Hermitage, for example, the wines become medium-bodied. We look at the vinification techniques and options for all the wines of the northern Rhône (to avoid duplication) in this chapter, but discuss the qualities of the full-bodied wines in the next.

Northern Rhône winemakers are as idiosyncratic and as definite in their views as any in France. The extreme example is Marcel Guigal, who has broken with convention so far as to taint (as a few still see it) his exquisite Hermitage and Côte Rôtie super-*cuvées* with new oak. Such things may pass in Italy, where he could even (at the expense of his DOC) have added Cabernet, but the discipline of the French appellation system strongly discouraged such outrage. Nobody, however,

Right: *Terraced vineyards at Cornas, in the northern Rhône. Cornas, sheltered from the mistral, grows Syrah of a more consistent ripeness than anywhere else in the northern Rhône.*

Below: *La Chapelle, from the hilltop vineyard of the house of Jaboulet, overlooking the Rhône, is consistently one of the finest wines of Hermitage.*

challenges Syrah's supremacy in the region, nor, at the end of the day, the magnificence of Guigal's La Mouline, La Landonne and La Turque. Even the varieties that are officially permitted to soften its ruggedness (Marsanne and Roussanne in Hermitage) are less used today as winemakers learn to handle the mighty Syrah on its own; however, the use of Viognier with Syrah in Côte Rôtie has become de rigueur.

Yet because Syrah reigns unchallenged, and because it is a variety that normally has intense color and flavor, the winemaking choices become less vital than the differences in *terroir* and the vintage. The most important recent development after the use of new oak is the increased use of carbonic maceration, and here its effect is significantly less marked than it is in Burgundy and Beaujolais.

The enormous production of the southern Rhône, the plethora of unfamiliar grape varieties and the years of prostitution of the Châteauneuf-du-Pape label have all helped to obscure its superlative quality. As with the northern Rhône, there is also considerable diversity of style, nowhere more so than among the wines of Châteauneuf-du-Pape.

Only in Burgundy does one find such a bewildering array of options and sub-options for the winemakers as in Châteauneuf-du-Pape. Only in Burgundy can one find in a single appellation such a gulf between the great and the execrable, such diversity of style within a given level of quality. But Burgundy permits only one grape in the vat; Châteauneuf-du-Pape allows 13. Whether this is accumulated tradition or in fact a viticultural insurance policy is not clear. Grenache is always the dominant grape; Cinsaut, Syrah, Mourvèdre, the white Clairette and/or Picpoul are other essential varieties.

The greatest wines of the best years (and poor years are relatively rare in this warm, dry climate) are full-bodied by any standard, but they are made only by a small handful of conservative producers (headed by the Perrins of Beaucastel). Taken as a whole, Châteauneuf-du-Pape can be said to fall fairly into the medium-bodied category. These wines can be incredibly rich on the midpalate, but the tannins seldom have the astringent authority of the true full-bodied red wine. That

The southern Rhône

Châteauneuf-du-Pape

Ancient bush-pruned Syrah vines baking in the sun of the southern Rhône appellation of Gigondas.

Father Marcel (left) and son Philippe Guigal (right): generational change has had no impact on the justifiably great reputation enjoyed by the wines of this enormously successful business.

richness comes from a number of factors: the warmth (aided and abetted by the stony *terroir* that traps the heat of the day and radiates it through the night), the generally low yields (the appellation allows only 2.6 tons per acre/35 hl per ha); and the resultant high alcohol of not less than 12.5 degrees, the legal minimum – the best growers, however, are happy with 14.5 degrees.

The possibilities are a mathematician's delight and a draftsman's nightmare. If one simply looks at the choice of fermentation methods, the permutations and combinations become obvious. A Châteauneuf-du-Pape may incorporate a percentage of all of the following fermentation methods: carbonic maceration, destemmed whole berries, destemmed crushed berries, whole bunches (without carbonic maceration), crushed but stemmed bunches, and crushed and destemmed fruit. But what is more, differing treatments may have been given to some or all of the grape varieties incorporated into the blend and, of course, those varieties may be up to 13 in number.

There are the usual choices – and arguments – about the subsequent maturation and handling of the wine. By far the greatest amount spends between 18 and 30 months in very large old oak vats (or *foudres*) or in waxed-cement or glass-lined steel vats. The effect of storage in such containers is minimal: there is obviously no flavor pickup; oxidation will be at a minimum simply because of the size of the container; and precipitation of tartrates and other sediments will be slow, but nonetheless sufficient to allow most producers to indulge in their aversion to filtering their wine (and a lesser number to fining it). Neither new oak nor used Burgundian *barriques* show signs of making any real inroads here, nor should they. But in such a pervasive atmosphere of conservatism (for even the "new" vinification methods are merely a collation of diverse techniques of long standing) there are always exceptions: Château de Beaucastel eschews filtration, uses traditional fermentation methods and ages its wine in old oak – but uses a sort of "flash pasteurization" technique on the grapes as they leave the crusher as a means of extracting the maximum color and flavor from the skins by rapidly heating them to 176°F (80°C), then cooling the must to 68°F (20°C) before fermentation starts.

These are all wines driven by fruit and by their formidable alcohol (usually not less than 13 degrees). Since alcohol does not diminish, but fruit flavors do, the wines fall into two distinct camps: those that should be drunk at two to six years of age, and those that will live for 20 or 30 years.

Gigondas

The wines of Gigondas are as unpredictable as those of Châteauneuf. Almost every producer has a different idea about proportions of different grapes (although under the appellation regulations Grenache must account for at least 65 percent), and vinification methods vary likewise. Just to add a touch of spice, one of the best domaines, Les Gouberts, has taken to using new oak for its top *cuvée*, in the knowledge that the smell of oak is worth dollars.

Australian Syrah (Shiraz)

The only vineyards outside of the Rhône Valley to grow the Rhône varieties in large quantities have for 150 years been those of Australia. Appropriately, the motherlode of six cuttings was collected from the Hill of Hermitage by James Busby in 1831, with original plantings in the 1850s (Barossa and Eden Valleys), 1860 (Goulburn Valley) and 1880 (Hunter Valley) still in all-important production, with many more vineyards spanning the next 125 years. Having thrown off a short-lived challenge by Cabernet Sauvignon in the early 1990s, Syrah (Shiraz) is by far the most important red grape variety, accounting for almost 25 percent of all plantings (red and white).

Making Shiraz

An overwhelming proportion of Australia's red grapes – and Shiraz is no exception – are harvested free of rot or mold. The grapes are almost invariably crushed and destemmed, and fermentation is started immediately with cultured yeast. Stainless-steel fermentation vats are used; the most common are semi-enclosed, and either use devices called "header boards" to keep the cap of skins submerged, or autovinification (*see* page 179) in a Potter fermenter. Some wineries use open vats and either punch down the floating cap with rods or pump juice drawn from the bottom of the vat over the cap periodically to wet and partially submerge it, a traditional technique used all over the world or, finally, use header boards to keep the cap submerged and periodically rack off all the juice and return it over the top (Penfolds Grange is made thus). Fermentation temperatures are usually controlled between 64°F and 77°F (18°C to 25°C).

Penfolds, Blass and Hardys, along with a number of smaller wineries, press all or part of their Shiraz musts before primary fermentation is complete (at 1.8° to 5.4° Brix), and move the still-fermenting wine to barrels, where the primary fermentation will finish, often in conjunction with the malolactic fermentation (initiated by inoculation while the primary fermentation is still going on). The alternative is the more traditional extended maceration at the end of fermentation (sometimes used for part of the wine, part being barrel-fermented). *Choices in ferment*

Almost all quality wine is matured in *barriques* or hogsheads; American oak was the traditional choice and remains so for classics such as Grange, but there has been a concerted move toward French oak for other top-quality wines, particularly those from cooler regions. While most red wines are fined and/or filtered, there is some trend away from filtration, largely driven (one suspects) by marketers and exporters to the U.S.

Regular-quality wines undergo malolactic fermentation in vats, and are filtered and moved to barrels as inert wine around July, about four months after the harvest. The barrels will be turned "on the shive" (with the bungs submerged to a "two o'clock" position to avoid oxidation) and the wine left to mature until July of the following year, when it will be racked, blended, filtered once again and then bottled. *"On the shive"*

The better wines will have received far more attention and work. The malolactic fermentation will have taken place in the barrel; the barrels will be kept with their bungs at 12 o'clock and topped up every week or two; and they may be racked three or four times. This handling is much more costly, but produces a more textured, supple wine. The minimum-handling techniques produce a strangely sterile, "undermade" wine.

Just as in the northern Rhône, Shiraz responds to the differing effects of climate and *terroir* – although in the Australian view, climate has a much greater role. The Hunter Valley (with the warmest climate, much hotter than that of the Rhône) produces a wine that is often quite tough, tarry, and tannic in its youth, but which softens over 20 years into a velvety, gently earthy wine of sometimes remarkable elegance.

The Barossa Valley is (nominally at least) home to Penfolds Grange. Grange is made from 60- to 120-year-old, dry-land, bush-pruned vines that yield a mere 1.5 to 1.9 tons per acre (20 to 25 hl per ha). The grapes are picked at 22.5° to 24.5° Brix – not an alarmingly high degree of sugar, resulting in 13.5 percent alcohol (*see* page 237). To compensate for the fact that the wine is partially barrel-fermented, extra tannins are added in powdered form in the fermenter, and it spends 18 months in all-new American oak hogsheads. *Barossa: home of Grange*

The result is a massively concentrated and flavored wine that is not sold until it is five years old, immature under 10 (but unfolding thereafter), and that can be magnificent after 20 to 35 years. Even at that age, the incredibly rich cassis/berry-fruit flavors and sweet vanilla extracted from the oak sustain the wine.

The quadrupling in Shiraz plantings between 1996 and 2005 was accompanied by a marked increase in the cool-climate style, redolent of pepper, spice and red fruits, and in the emergence of Heathcote as the center of central Victoria Shiraz. Here, stupendously luscious, supple wine, with Viognier an increasingly common handmaiden, is grown on 500-million-year-old Cambrian greenstone soil, which just happens to have weathered into a vivid, red ocher color: a harbinger of the dense, purple wines that result.

Northern Rhône: Syrah

This choices-and-consequences chart illustrates those stages in the winemaking process in which the options chosen by the winemaker fundamentally influence the taste and individuality of the final wine. Not every stage of the process is indicated: for that, the reader is directed to the red wine process chart on pages 140–1.

The vineyards of the northern Rhône cover a 40-mile (65 km) stretch running from Vienne to Valence, with the finest wines coming from well-exposed terraced vineyards overlooking the river. The granite-based soil allows the grapes to produce wines of an almost unrivaled intensity of bouquet and flavor.

Above: Water-cooled stainless-steel fermenting tanks make the task of controlling temperature far simpler, but mean major investment on the part of the winemaker.

Right: Temperature of the fermenting grapes in an open vat is continuously monitored. If the temperature inside the vats gets too high or low, there is a danger of the fermentation "sticking."

1 IN THE VINEYARD

Choice of grape variety
(a) *100 percent Syrah (Cornas and Crozes-Hermitage)*
The differing weight and intensity of Cornas (intense and powerful) and Crozes-Hermitage (much lighter) highlight the importance of site and *terroir*.
(b) *80 percent Syrah, 20 percent Viognier (Côte Rôtie)*
Viognier gives aroma to the bouquet and a little extra fruit to the palate, but lightens the color and structure. Those who do use it (including Jaboulet, Delas, Champet and Duclaux) do so at only 4 to 5 percent. Guigal uses 11 percent in La Mouline.

2 CRUSHING

Crushing options
(a) *Whole bunches*
Crushing whole grape bunches with their stems by automatic *pigeage* is used by a number of major makers, including Chapoutier and Chave.
(b) *Partial crush or destem*
Jaboulet prefers partial crush, partial whole-bunch (60 percent) with pumping over. Guigal

3 FERMENTING

Carbonic maceration
This practice, where fermentation begins inside the grape itself, yields wine full in flavor and bouquet. It has become more popular over the last 20 years, but tends to produce wines "semi-*nouveau*" in style that are best drunk young.

4 MATURING

Maturation
(a) *Old oak vats*
Traditionalists strongly argue for their use of old oak, believing that any interference with the flavor of Syrah brought about by the use of new oak is undesirable, reducing or obscuring the *typicité* of their wines.
(b) *Used Burgundy* barriques
Aging in one- to two-year-old Burgundian casks is favored by many of the better Rhône producers, sometimes in conjunction with old oak for part of the maturation period.

(c) *85 percent Syrah,
15 percent Marsanne and
Roussanne (Hermitage)*
The use of Roussanne and
Marsanne in Hermitage is less
common these days. Their effect
is similar to that of Viognier in
Côte Rôtie, although they are
less overtly fruity.
(d) *90 percent Syrah,
10 percent Marsanne and
Roussanne (St-Joseph)*
Once again, the white varieties
are not much used, although
permitted up to 10 percent.

*The sight of new barriques is
increasingly common, with
Guigal the leader of this band.
Others, such as Chave, show
new small oak.*

destems but does not crush.
(c) *Total crush and destem*
Total crushing and destemming
used by lesser appellations, and
tends to produce wines lacking
in complexity.

Below: Remontage, *the system
of pumping juice over the grapes
during fermentation to extract
the maximum color and flavor
from the solids.*

Choice of fermentation vat

(a) *Stainless steel*
The cooler fermentation
temperatures possible in
stainless steel can enhance
fruit flavor and freshness in
Syrah. Not yet widely adopted.
(b) *Old oak/concrete*
In the alternatives to stainless
steel – wooden or concrete vats –
temperatures can rise above
95°F (35°C), giving burned,
jammy flavors. Control of
high temperatures will be
attempted with cooling coils
or by pumping over.

Fermentation time

Long fermentation and
maceration (three weeks) are
partly responsible for strength
and depth of structure.
Short fermentation (10 days)
is used for lighter styles –
including those given
carbonic maceration.

(c) *New oak*
Some have successfully
introduced new oak –
particularly Guigal, with his
prestige bottlings of Côte Rôtie.
Others have followed, but not
on the scale of Guigal.

Maturation period

(a) *Short (one year)*
The prime exponent of relatively
short oak maturation is Jaboulet
with its Côte Rôtie and
La Chapelle Hermitage, which
are matured in used Burgundy
barriques.
(b) *Long (3 to 3.5 years)*
Guigal gives his top wines 3 to
3.5 years in new oak *barriques*,
which adds a major dimension
to their flavor and structure.
(c) *8 to 24 months*
Most winemakers adopt an
18- to 24-month midpath.

Clarification

(a) *Fining*
Barrel maturation and
racking eliminate the need
for this process, but those
who choose to clarify use
egg white.
(b) *Filtration*
Similarly, filtration is
infrequently used; Jaboulet
is the principal proponent.

Full-Bodied Red Wines

Choices, consequences and techniques

The distinguishing feature of a full-bodied red wine is the authority it has on the finish. In its youth this authority is frequently astringent and aggressive, and even though the wine may be high in alcohol and have a strongly flavored and constructed midpalate, it will be the finish that dominates – and that must soften before the wine becomes a pleasure to drink. One of the key issues confronting the maker of such wines (and ultimately the consumer) is whether such youthful toughness should be encouraged, tolerated or discouraged. In the simplest terms (for it is but one indicator of a more complex issue), how much tannin is too much tannin? Increasingly, too, the question is whether or not the tannins are ripe. In field assessments of ripeness, winemakers are no longer content just to chew the skins and pulp of the grapes, but also crunch the pips (and inspect them to see whether they have turned brown).

Bordeaux and the Cabernet family

Few wine-lovers anywhere dispute the proposition that the greatest full-bodied red wines of all are those of Bordeaux, and above all of the Haut-Médoc. Rather more might wonder how the overall standard of the wines of the last half of the 20th century will look from a standpoint 50 or 100 years hence – but then, that same question is raised about every generation of children or wines.

Growing a mixture

Bordeaux's growers can certainly select one or more of the varieties in the vineyard at the expense of others, but they would hesitate to alter the proportions of Cabernet Sauvignon, Merlot and Cabernet Franc with which time and custom have endowed them. To some extent the varietal mix is the persona of the property: a château is what it grows. It needs a brave owner to tamper with his or her inheritance. But it is also true that if growers thought they could ripen Cabernet Sauvignon reliably every year, the role of the other varieties would diminish in importance. Merlot is grown in the Médoc and Graves partly as a form of insurance (it ripens earlier and is thus less susceptible to autumn rain), and dominates St-Emilion and Pomerol because the heavier clay soils of those regions will ripen Cabernet Sauvignon only in exceptional vintages. If these limitations did not exist, arguably the function of Merlot, Cabernet Franc, Petit Verdot and Malbec would be a support role to balance the structure of the Cabernet Sauvignon according to the dictates of the particular vintage. Not that anybody in Pomerol would agree, of course.

Concentration machines

In the last 15 years of the 20th century, concentration machines found their way into all châteaus able to afford them – and almost all were. They operate either on vacuum operation or reverse osmosis, in either case removing water (but little or nothing else) from the must. The theory is they are used only in years of abundant yield, but cynics suggest they are employed more frequently. What they will not do is remove moldy characters from the must: they may indeed increase those characters by the very fact of concentration. Such devices are usually kept well hidden from the probing eyes of American wine critics.

Throughout this book, the focus is on the fine wines of each country, region and style. Overall, there is little point in talking about beverage, or supermarket, wine falling in the "fast-moving consumer goods" (FMCG) shopping basket. But the situation in Bordeaux in the first decade of the new century demands some discussion of the yawning gulf between the position of the makers of the best Bordeaux wines and that of the least (or lesser).

The run of generally excellent vintages between 1982 and 2005; the Robert Parker/*Wine Spectator* influence; favorable world economic conditions; new technology (arguably); and the Michel Rolland factor (arguably) have brought unprecedented prosperity to the best-known châteaus of the region. This in turn has brought investors with seemingly limitless finances to purchase and then upgrade vineyard and winery practices alike, or allowed long-term owners the same ability. We shall return to some of these factors shortly.

At the top, swimming with money

At the other end of the spectrum, there are literally thousands of producers in the lesser parts of Bordeaux – most obviously but not restricted to the Entre-Deux-Mers – who are, to all intents and purposes, bankrupt. The wines they are making are no worse than those of 10, 20 or 30 years ago, but what was acceptable then is not acceptable now. New World wines made from ripe grapes and without any technical fault (nor necessarily any great character, but that is another matter) are dramatically different from the thin, green and often faulty wines carrying the Bordeaux AC or Bordeaux Supérieur AC.

At the bottom, bankruptcy

While the domestic market for these wines lingers on (but declining by 7 percent per annum, partly due to the French *Loi Evin* directed to reducing wine consumption), export markets are closing fast, saying the wines are not saleable no matter how low the price. Removal of 25,000 acres (10,000 ha) of vines may give some temporary relief, as will the subsidy trough until it, too, is sucked dry.

At the other end of the scale, globalization of the world's wine markets and a vastly increased flow of information and critical review have led both to greater competition and greater sophistication in the marketplace. In the vineyard, the outcomes have been entirely beneficial. A swing to organic growing practices, reduced use of fertilizers and systemic sprays, propagation of lower-yielding clones, shoot-thinning early in the season, bunch-thinning (green harvest) at *véraison* and early removal of bunches affected by rot or mildew have all resulted in lower yields of riper grapes.

The new sophistication

Sophisticated sorting tables – a section vibrating, installed both before and after the grapes are destemmed – are increasingly found. Green, moldy or shriveled grapes are methodically removed. Effective selection at this point eliminates or reduces the need for concentration, be it by old-fashioned juice runoff or modern reverse osmosis or vacuum concentration. It also answers the criticism that all you achieve by concentration applies equally to sound and moldy flavors.

The most modern wineries (Château Malartic-Lagravière is a conspicuous example) have endeavored to eliminate pumping the must or grapes prior to fermentation. There the sorted berries fall directly into an 880-pound (400 kg) vessel (looking like a Sputnik) that is then lifted and positioned above the fermentation vat or tun; its base plate is opened, and the must falls into the vat. Another custom-made device, looking like a prehistoric insect, allows the cap to be broken by sideways rather than vertical pressure when (finally) juice is pumped over during fermentation.

Precise, computer-monitored control of fermentation temperatures, rare in the 1970s and early 1980s, is now universal in the better wineries. Its arrival coincided with a large-scale swing away from old wooden vats to stainless-steel fermenters. Interestingly, even though temperature control is less easy to manage, there is a distinct move back to oak vats – not for oak flavor, but to aid the work of oxygen in a ferment, and to diminish reduced aromas and flavors.

The First Growth Château Lafite epitomizes the difficulty of classifying red wines by their body. Its wines are tannic and sinewy in structure, living as long as any great Médoc, yet usually relatively light or delicate beside its rival Pauillac First Growths, Latour and Mouton-Rothschild.

In the same vein, microoxygenation has swept the scene since its invention in 1990. While its primary use is to soften otherwise harsh tannins in finished red wine, it can also be used to build the yeast population in the early stages of fermentation and aid clarification of finished wine, eliminating or reducing the need for filtration. Finally, it can also counteract reduction. With the *en primeur* tastings of Bordeaux red wines in March/April, six months after vintage, assuming such huge commercial importance, the benefits of microoxygenation are all too obvious. (The technical aspects of its use are discussed on page 224.)

Microoxygenation

While there is and always will be finessing at the edges, fermentation techniques in Bordeaux vary little. Destemming is universal, crushing common, most fermentations rely on indigenous/wild yeasts tolerant of modest additions of sulphur dioxide; unless there is active intervention to heat or cool the must, fermentation will commence after a lapse of two or three days. The temperature will be allowed to rise to a maximum of 84°F to 86°F (29°C to 30°C) – some will intervene earlier – and the wine will be pumped over two or three times a day for varying periods.

As the fermentation begins to subside, progressive chaptalization (notwithstanding climate change, still very much part of the Bordeaux landscape) will take place over several days, extending primary fermentation up to six days after initiation. Thereafter, the must will be allowed to macerate for anything from 7 to 21 days. The wine will then be pressed, and allowed to settle prior to being taken to *barrique*. The percentage of new oak will vary from one-third to 100 percent, the choice of oak type often left to the cooper, although in many châteaus a surprising number of coopers will have supplied barrels, perhaps to give a de facto mix of oaks, while also keeping the coopers on their toes.

Malolactic fermentation will normally take place the following spring – a hazard for the *en primeur* tastings, but avoided by more adroit makers ensuring the tasting *assemblage* barrels have completed "malo," as it is called for short. There is a progressive *assemblage* of the individual barrels over the year following the vintage, even though the wine will not be bottled until 6 to 12 months later.

The process will not only "marry" the components, but also allow the internal classification into the first wine (under the name of the château), the second wine (with a different name, though shown as produced by the château in question) and in some instances a third wine, which may be bottled and sold with attribution to the château or sold as a so-called "clean-skin" (no label) or sold in bulk. Fining and filtration are carried out on an as-needs basis, although increased awareness of *Brettanomyces* has led to greater use of filtration.

While there is no doubt about the Cabernet Sauvignon–dominant wines of the Médoc and Graves belonging in the full-bodied category, there is scope for much more discussion when it comes to the Merlot-dominant wines of Pomerol and St-Emilion. The latter are softer, sappier, can be more fragrant and tend to mature more quickly.

The central feature of the wines of Bordeaux is their structure. Just as the Burgundians consider the bouquet of prime importance, the Bordelais are principally concerned about the way the wine tastes and feels in the mouth. They see this as driving everything else: the bouquet, the finish and the aftertaste. This is built around the variety (most obviously Cabernet Sauvignon), the vinification (particularly postfermentation maceration), and the use of new oak.

The reason why these wines are revered around the world is the extraordinary harmony and balance they achieve with age. The question of when to drink is an intensely subjective one. It is hard to imagine anyone (even the French, who prefer to drink their red wines younger than do British or American consumers) suggesting a 1982 Bordeaux is anything other than superb at 20 years of age.

California Cabernet Sauvignon

The Cabernets of California are widely accepted as the finest in the world outside Bordeaux. In 1979, when Baron Philippe de Rothschild joined forces with Robert Mondavi to produce Opus One, it seemed that the ultimate compliment had been paid to the Napa Valley. Christian Moueix managed to reinforce it when he laid the foundation for Dominus in the early 1980s. Even the producers of the greatest red Bordeaux look with admiration (even awe) at the spectacle of "their" Cabernet ripening so perfectly, seeming year after year to offer the opportunity to make the sort of great wine Bordeaux sees perhaps once in a decade.

The Californian approach to Cabernet is closely modeled on that of Bordeaux. As with Chardonnay, avant-garde winemakers have sought to go beyond the simple expression of fruit and *terroir* to seek the subtlety and nuances that seem to flow so easily from the hands of Bordeaux's winemakers. Changes in philosophy – and with philosophy, technique – have closely paralleled those developed for Chardonnay, but in the case of Cabernet have tended to focus on the quantity and the quality of the tannins. While many Californians would disagree, most outside observers found the tannin levels of California Cabernets from the 1970s and early to mid-1980s unacceptably high and aggressive.

There is no doubt that the face of California Cabernet Sauvignon has changed, that the wines are more supple and harmonious in the mouth, that the best are magnificent. But to say that the tannins are better balanced, softer and riper than they once were begs the question. The real issue is whether the starting point is valid: is the Bordeaux tradition of long maceration after the fermentation really the best winemaking method for grapes grown in the warm, dry Napa Valley climate, often on low-yielding vines with minimal assistance from irrigation? It may very well be – as most Napa vignerons assert – that the tannins extracted later in the maceration are softer and more supple.

The cult Cabernets

The other issue to emerge progressively through the 1990s was that of the typically mountain-grown cult wines (personified by Screaming Eagle) routinely tipping the scales at over 15 percent alcohol by volume, and much loved by critics such as Robert Parker. Matched with a mountain of charbroiled steak on a midwinter's night, these wines have their place. They have also proved a useful investment for the early movers.

Australian Cabernet Sauvignon

Australia's and California's Cabernets are as different as their Chardonnays. Australia has a wide range of climates and soils in which Cabernet Sauvignon is grown, but the wines emerge with a surprisingly broad homogeneity of style. With the exception of a few badly made, overextracted wines (usually from very small wineries), all Australia's Cabernet Sauvignons are far softer, far fruitier and far more accessible than their California equivalents. The winemakers might be accused of making wines that are simple and unsophisticated. The reality is that the wines taste almost directly of their

If the southern hemisphere has a "First Growth," it is Penfolds Grange. But Penfolds, based at the Nuriootpa winery in the Barossa Valley, produces a range of red wines in which the qualities of South Australian Cabernet and Merlot as well as Syrah (Shiraz) find their fullest expression.

Cabernet Sauvignon and blends

This choices-and-consequences chart illustrates those stages in the winemaking process in which the options chosen by the winemaker fundamentally influence the taste and individuality of the final wine. Not every stage of the process is indicated: for that, the reader is directed to the red wine process chart on pages 140–1.

Cabernet Sauvignon is considered by many to be the best grape variety in the world. It is the easiest to grow and harvest, and adapts admirably to different environments, Old World and New. It is *the* grape of the Médoc, producing some of the finest red Bordeaux. A very high ratio of pip to pulp makes it extremely tannic. It is usually blended, especially with Merlot, to soften the tannins, and needs aging in oak and in bottle. Cabernet Sauvignon has a natural affinity with oak; top estates leave their wines in new oak *barriques* for up to two years.

Above: A fermentation vat being emptied of its frothing contents. Right: Winemakers go to great lengths to clarify their wines. Particles of tannins or anthocyanins left behind after fermentation need to be removed if the wine is to be clear and bright. Fining is carried out in traditional wineries by using a natural coagulant – here, beaten egg white.

1 IN THE VINEYARD

Choice of variety
Choice of grapes may be imposed by climate or *terroir*, or may be that of the winemaker seeking to balance the structure of pure Cabernet Sauvignon, usually with Merlot, Cabernet Franc and Petit Verdot.

2 CRUSHING

Crushing options
(a) *Crush and destem*
(b) *Whole berries*

Crushing and destemming are almost universally practiced in Bordeaux, but with the use of modern crushers with adjustable rollers, a percentage of whole berries can be used in some ferments.

3 FERMENTING

Choice of fermentation vat
(a) *Traditional oak/stainless steel*
The choice between traditional upright oak vats and stainless steel has important implications only if temperature regulation is required, because only the stainless-steel vats are temperature-controlled.
(b) *Open plunging/closed pump-over*
Open fermentation with hand-plunging is perhaps old-fashioned, but gives good color and tannin extraction. Closed tanks are widely used, either with a "floating cap" or with the cap held submerged by boards.

4 MATURING

Choice of oak
The choice between new or used oak, the type of oak and the degree of toast is a key issue in determining taste and quality. Nevers or Allier are most widely used. The better the grapes, the more oak the wine can sustain, in which case there will be a greater use of new oak.

Bunch-thinning

A practice that is standard in high-yield years. Removing a percentage of grape bunches from the vines will produce a smaller crop, which will make more intensely colored and flavored wine.

Method of picking

Machine picking is an option in almost any vineyard – size and terrain permitting – because Cabernet Sauvignon grapes are invariably crushed, so it is not critical that they remain whole at harvest. However, it does preclude the use of sorting tables

Must concentration

Traditionally achieved by running off juice immediately after crushing. For the wealthy wineries, vacuum concentration or, better still, reverse osmosis machines provide a superior outcome, the latter able to also remove taints and molds.

Prefermentation maceration

This stage frequently takes place in Europe (whether or not it is a matter of choice) because the reliance on wild yeasts and the sometimes high level of sulfur additions mean that fermentation takes two to three days to commence. This maceration extracts color and tannin from the pomace.

Choice of yeast

The choice lies between slower-acting wild yeasts or more predictable cultured yeasts.

Above: *Color is extracted from Cabernet Sauvignon grapes by spraying the fermenting must over the cap of skins.*

Temperature

Most makers choose a 77°F to 84°F (25°C to 29°C) range in Bordeaux, slightly lower in the New World. With the strong structure of Cabernet Sauvignon, temperature control is not critical.

Chaptalization

Almost invariably carried out in Bordeaux, seldom in the New World. A process that is necessary if the sugar content of the grapes is too low, owing to unfavorable weather during the vintage cycle.

Postfermentation maceration

Standard practice in Bordeaux, California and Italy; common but not invariable in Australasia. The aim is to extract more tannins and to soften those tannins already present.

Malolactic fermentation

Invariably improves the quality of red wine by lowering the acid level and adding to the complexity of the flavor, and so is systematically encouraged. The only choice lies between starting the process with cultured bacteria or relying on natural triggers.

Maturation period

Prolonged maturation of bygone years is now seldom practiced; 15 to 21 months is the most common period.

Racking frequency

Racking aids clarification and softens the wine. This might be carried out as frequently as every month for the first few months.

Fining

In Bordeaux, fining takes place toward the end of the maturation period in order to clarify and stabilize the wine. Elsewhere it may only be used for excessively tannic or heavy wines.

Filtration

Filtration before bottling is generally practiced in Bordeaux and universally in the New World.

Five generations of growers and winemakers at the Cantina Aldo Conterno in Monforte d'Alba have helped to establish the classic Piedmontese style of tannic Barolo, astringent Barbera and mouth-filling Dolcetto. But here, too, the style is changing as new technology and new grapes move into this ultratraditional region.

Making Australian Cabernet

fruit: the varietal flavors come through clearly, and so does the influence of *terroir*.

Australia's success in increasing exports twelvefold since the first edition of this book has made it patently obvious it should maximize the potential of Coonawarra, its Cabernet Sauvignon jewel in the crown. It is still in the course of doing so, but the best wines from this region have improved out of all recognition, the litmus test coming in the form of wine-show results (reliable indicators in Australia).

The primary agent for change has been vastly improved viticulture: lower yields and better phenolic ripeness. Fermentation techniques for top-quality Cabernet Sauvignon do not vary greatly: fermentation of fully crushed grapes around 77°F (25°C) with pump-overs two or three times a day. Maceration time after fermentation varies enormously: from none to 40 days. Frequently there will be an ultimate *assemblage* of parcels of wine picked at varying times and vinified quite differently. Some such Cabernets are partly fermented in barrel; all the good ones are aged for a while in new oak. It is quite common to find barrel fermentation in American oak followed by aging in French oak (or vice versa). After 15 to 21 months' maturation, and several rackings, the wine will be sterile-filtered and bottled.

More downmarket Cabernet Sauvignon from less exalted regions is fermented (in

Angelo Gaja has been the Gorbachev of the revolution that is sweeping through Piedmontese winemaking. He angered and amazed many Italians by introducing classic French grapes and oak barrels to the region, but has maintained his reputation by insisting that the venerable reds of northeast Italy deserve more recognition as being among the world's great wines.

stainless steel) with oak chips augmented by microoxygenation (*see* page 224) for an instant touch of class before being racked and then filtered "star-bright." A certain amount will receive a perfunctory period of barrel aging in four- or five-year-old oak; tannin and acid will be adjusted, and the wine bottled after the minimum of handling.

Top-of-the-range Cabernet Sauvignons (and Pinots and Syrahs) are handmade in precisely the same way as at a top French château or California winery. This means hand-pruned vines, hand-picked grapes (with rigorous selection), careful crushing, fermentation in small vats, either maceration after the fermentation or the fermentation finished in barrels, extensive use of new French oak, a deliberate choice between exposure to air or total protection from it, racking, the possible elimination of lesser barrels and high-quality packaging.

Piedmont: Barolo and Barbaresco

A variety of minor, and some major, revolutions are recorded in these pages, but perhaps the modernization that has swept through Piedmont in Italy in the past 25 years amounts, for those who know its wines, to the most epoch-making of all.

Piedmont is the perfect place to examine the dilemma winemakers face in weighing up the relative values of tradition and new technology. There is no question that,

Piedmont

This choices-and-consequences chart illustrates those stages in the winemaking process in which the options chosen by the winemaker fundamentally influence the taste and individuality of the final wine. The example is Piedmont, home to some of the best of Italy's native grape varieties. Not all the stages in the winemaking process are shown: for that the reader is directed to the red wine process chart on pages 140–1.

Piedmontese traditions are strong, adhering to the old viticultural concepts. Typically, the vineyards occupy hills, not plains, and yields have been sensibly restrained. Despite this strong wish to preserve the heritage (the native Barbera and especially Nebbiolo grapes have long occupied the best vineyards, even with the introduction of foreign varieties), the application of modern technology and growing acceptance of external influences, such as the use of French *barriques*, have meant that new styles of wine are emerging – a direct reflection of choices made in the winery.

Hygiene standards and control of temperature during fermentation have been revolutionized by the introduction of stainless-steel vats, even in such redoubts of tradition as Piedmont. Wine matures more slowly in steel than in wood barrels.

1
IN THE VINEYARD

Grape variety
The Nebbiolo grape produces Piedmont's classic wines, Barolo and Barbaresco, and is the region's most prestigious variety – the optimum choice for many growers, and usually allocated the best south-facing vineyard sites.

2
FERMENTING
Choice of fermentation vat

(a) *Stainless steel*
Fruit aroma and flavor can be retained by keeping must temperatures low during fermentation. Stainless-steel vats allow such control, usually maintaining temperatures at 73°F to 84°F (23°C to 29°C). This is an option now widely favored by modernists and traditionalists alike.

(b) *Old oak vats*
Now less likely to be used for Piedmont wines because of the lack of temperature control. This can lead to considerable loss of the fruit flavor that many see as vital for counterbalancing the Nebbiolo's inherent acidity. Aside from the initial expense in investing in stainless steel, oak does retain a slight advantage in that it can contribute to the wine's complexity.

3
MATURING AND FINISHING

Maturation time
(a) *Long maturation*
    (up to four years)
Traditional makers favor long maturation for their wines, relying on time to mellow high tannin levels – especially those caused by lengthy maceration and oak fermentation.

(b) *Short maturation (Barbaresco: nine months minimum; Barolo: one year minimum)*
Other winemakers give freshness and fruit flavor priority, these being better achieved by maturing for shorter periods.

Other varieties making full-bodied Piedmont reds include the widely planted Barbera, also used for 100 percent varietal wines, and chosen for its acidity and its high-yielding reliability.

Harvesting

(a) *Early*
Piedmont's wine-growers currently favor higher acidity, more pronounced grape flavors and less tannin than formerly: achieved by harvesting grapes at optimum balance in terms of ripeness and of flavor. Essentially, this means picking earlier.

(b) *Late*
More traditional Piedmont growers might seek to obtain high alcohol and high tannin levels, so harvest as late as possible (October to November) to allow the buildup of sugar and anthocyanins.

Below: *Contrasting starkly with the shining steel vats, oak botti (the large ones) and barriques for maturing wine. French oak casks are increasingly being used to age Italian wine, giving new dimensions to the classics and opening new vistas for winemakers.*

Postfermentation maceration

(a) *Prolonged (up to one month)*
(b) *Short (10 to 12 days)*

From the winemaker's viewpoint, the shortening of the maceration time must be as significant as controlling the fermentation temperature. Not only is the amount of tannin diminished, but the possibility of oxidation over the longer period is also reduced. The resulting wines are more supple and balanced, though still retaining strong tannins when compared to other wine styles. It is quite possible they will not have the same longevity, however.

Degree of malolactic fermentation

(a) *Immediate and total*
Control of malolactic fermentation is best achieved by using temperature-controlled stainless-steel fermentation vats. These enable wines to be held at warm temperatures (68°F/20°C) after their first fermentation to ensure a quicker onset, control and completion of the malolactic process. Once finished, the winemaker can apply protective sulfur dioxide to achieve a cleaner, fresher and more stable wine.

(b) *Delayed or incomplete*
Complexity and softness in a wine are often achieved by slow malolactic fermentation, but if left to run its course naturally (as would happen in oak vats in Piedmont), there is a risk that it will draw to a halt before all the acid has been transformed. In such cases, malic acid remaining in the wine may cause unwanted sour flavors.

Maturation vessel

(a) *Old Slovenian oak/chestnut*
Choice of maturation vessel is swayed by the tannin content desired. The addition of as few wood tannins as possible to the already abundant grape tannins present in Piedmont reds is ensured by using large oak vats for maturation. These are the traditional choice.

(b) *New barriques (for part or all of maturation)*
Some winemakers take the view that oak tannins are complementary to grape tannins,

so promote aging in new barrels. Similarly, wines undergoing shorter postfermentation maceration may also be seen to benefit from contact with new oak.

(c) *Barolo maturation*
Barolo must age for at least three years in total, *riserva* for four-and-three-quarter years with minimum time in oak specified opposite.

(d) *Barbaresco maturation*
Barbaresco must age for 21 months, *riserva* for 45 months.

Blending and bottling

(a) *Wines from many sites (house style)*
Blending wines from different sites used to be the most common approach. This produces wines of distinctively differing house styles.

(b) *Individual* cru *bottlings (from a specific site)*
Single-vineyard bottlings (or at least from the same delimited subzone) are now the standard practice for virtually all the top-quality Barolos.

viewed by international standards – the perfect, universal palate-in-the-sky as judge – the new Barolos and Barbarescos are better wines. But are they better Barolos? Are they better Barbarescos? Certainly, the debate is far from over, with producers from both camps convinced of the correctness of their chosen courses. Experience suggests, though, that a grape with so marked a character as the Nebbiolo, growing in soils and a climate as distinct as those of Piedmont, will eventually assert its traditional style.

Fault or character?

The Piedmont chart on pages 172–3 indicates the two fundamentally different approaches to the making of Barolo and Barbaresco. The modern approach, most famously espoused by Angelo Gaja with Barbarescos and the Ceretto family with their Barolos, produces more internationally acceptable styles of wine. One does not have to be an aficionado of Nebbiolo or the wines of Piedmont to understand and enjoy them. The traditional approach tolerates a degree of toughness, a touch of volatility, some tarry, farmyard characteristics and slight oxidation: the underlying strength and durability of the wine can carry these blemishes when young, and allow them to meld with age into a matrix of such complexity that to identify or complain about the faults seems churlishly pedantic. Growers such as Bruno Giacosa, Aldo Conterno and Bartolo Mascarello are unashamed traditionalists, and have no shortage of buyers prepared to wait for 20 years or more before thinking seriously about drinking the wine.

The avant-garde style emphasizes fruity freshness and urges that technical faults should not be condoned simply because they are "typical." It categorically denies that its wines will not age with grace, pointing to better chemical composition and the absence of any bacterial activity and spoilage. Traditionalists believe the aromas they are accustomed to are the essence of Nebbiolo in their soil; they do not distinguish between fault and character. While these wines were once supported and judged by parochial regional markets, the judgment of today is increasingly international in perspective.

Hermitage and Côte Rôtie

In deference to tradition and Professor Saintsbury, a chapter on full-bodied red wines should also include Côte Rôtie and Hermitage from the Rhône Valley. The world heavyweight class contains other champions: Vega Sicilia from Castile, Brunello di Montalcino from Siena, even that sublimated blackstrap Priorato from Catalonia. But for a model of body, strength and complexity – delicacy, even – outside the world of Mouton and Latour, one must turn to the great wines of the northern Rhône. Because new oak has not traditionally been used in fashioning them, it is (or was) possible to see their layers of fruit-driven flavors, and equally to see the changes that occur as the wines evolve in bottle. *Terroir* is all-important: whether one is comparing Hermitage with Côte Rôtie, or the three rival Côte Rôtie vineyards, La Landonne, La Turque and La Mouline, the differences are consistently observable. But this is no rustic backwater simply relying on *typicité* and historical reputation: the influence of the winemaker is no less observable.

The grapes of Hermitage: Syrah (Shiraz) from the steep slopes of the northern Rhône achieves a concentration and structure that puts it among the world's most individual red wines.

Marcel Guigal in Côte Rôtie has emphatically demonstrated that Côte Rôtie and new oak can make a spectacular impact. Not all winemakers have followed precisely in his footsteps; some of the best producers in Hermitage, in particular, have continued to eschew the use of new oak. As in other parts of Europe (and the New World), the use of new oak has led to more winemakers following the example of the house of Jaboulet and shortening the time the wine spends in oak (be it new or old) before it is bottled.

The very nature of the vineyards – the steep terrain, the schist-rock soil – and the climate have protected the integrity of the grapes to an uncommon degree. What has changed most of all is the celebrity of these wines. First the English, then the American market "discovered" the stature of wines that have been in their midst – remarkably consistent, marked on every map, indeed situated alongside what might be described as France's main highway – for centuries. Those who have drunk and loved them for years must wince at what fashion has done to their prices. The compensation is that if they are profitable, they will improve. It was always thus. Fine wines can only be – have only ever been – made for discriminating markets.

Fortified Wines

Choices, consequences and techniques

There is no catch-all definition of fortified wine except that at some stage in its creation its alcoholic strength is increased by the addition of grape spirit. Fortified wine did not come into existence until the 17th century, when distillation was commercialized (first by the Dutch). Port, which most regard as the best example, took its present form around 1775 (as did Champagne). As late as 1754 the British merchants in Oporto complained about "the habit of checking the fermentation of the wines too soon, by putting brandy into them while still fermenting; a practice which must be considered diabolical, for after this the wines will not remain quiet, but are continually tending to ferment and become ropey and acid."

"Fortified wine" means a wine containing alcohol that has been added and that is not simply the end result of the alcoholic fermentation. The amount added varies substantially, as does the stage at which it is added:

Fortification

(i) Before fermentation. Some wines are fortified before fermentation starts, and thus never ferment at all. A few table wines (called *vins de liqueur* in France) are made this way; they lack structural complexity and develop very slowly in bottle. Slightly more common are wines that are subsequently barrel-aged for many years. The most noteworthy are certain (though not all) Muscats and "Tokays" from northeast Victoria, Australia. These demand the addition of the greatest volume of fortifying spirit, as the final alcohol strength (18 degrees or more in the case of Tokays and Muscats, much less in the case of Sauternes-style wines) is almost entirely derived from addition.

(ii) During fermentation. All vintage and tawny ports and many Muscats are fortified during fermentation. Fortification in fact arrests fermentation. The timing of the addition and the calculation of the amount of spirit required are crucial in determining the final style of the wine. The misleadingly named *vins doux naturels* of southern France (most famously Muscat de Beaumes-de-Venise) are also fortified for the purpose of ending fermentation.

(iii) After fermentation. The best example of fortification after the end of fermentation is sherry. The degree of fortification is significantly less than for port, both because the natural alcohol level is higher and because the finished wine is generally lower in total alcohol.

The sterilizing and stabilizing effect of adding several degrees of alcohol to dry table wine has long been used to protect wines shipped in barrel. This caused great dispute in the late 19th century as Australian table wines started to make substantial inroads into the English market: arguments raged as to whether or not the wines were lightly fortified or achieved their very high alcohol levels naturally. The question was important because of a duty differential: although the Australian winemakers were adamant that they were able to achieve 16 degrees of alcohol with ease in areas such as northeast Victoria, the English authorities thought otherwise. The debate ended inconclusively, but a bottle of 1880s "Hearty Burgundy" from the famous firm of B.P. Burgoyne tasted in 1990 left no doubt that at least some of these wines were indeed fortified, even if only lightly.

Making Sherry

CRUSHING AND PRESSING

Drying

Grapes destined to sweeten or color wines are left to dry in the sun to increase their sugar content. The bunches are laid out in the open in long lines on *esparto* grass mats, protected at night by plastic sheets.

The modern practice is for the dried grapes to be lightly crushed and destemmed before pressing. In the past they would have been taken straight for pressing.

Pressing

Only in the last few decades has treading grapes in nail-studded boots in troughs (*lagares*) been gradually abandoned in favor of mechanical presses. Of these, the best quality is the batch type – either the horizontal or inflatable bag press. The alternative, the continuous press, incorporates long, sloping screws that produce must of different qualities by varying the pressure. The rules of the *consejo regulador* allow only 70 percent of the potential juice to be pressed from the grapes to make sherry.

The must is left for about 24 hours for solid matter to settle out before being pumped into the fermentation vats.

FERMENTATION

Traditional fermentation vessels are oak butts and huge Ali–Baba–type concrete or earthenware vats. Most bodegas now favor stainless steel or other modern materials, although barrels are still used.

The first stage, in which most of the sugar is transformed into alcohol, lasts for three days to a week and is quite violent. With the onset of the much slower secondary fermentation, a range of organic compounds evolves.

Ideally the temperature of the fermenting must should be kept below 77°F (25°C) for fino and below 86°F (30°C) for oloroso-style wines. At the end of fermentation (in late December or in January) the must falls bright, as suspended matter falls to the bottom of the tanks.

CLASSIFICATION

After fermentation is complete sherries will be classified into three broad categories: fino, oloroso and rayas ("inferior"). The fino wines are lighter and will develop into fino and amontillado styles, the olorosos are heavier, most of them destined to be blended with sweetening wines as "cream" sherry (although old dry oloroso can be superb).

As a result of this initial classification, the fino wines are fortified to 15.5 degrees, which is the optimum degree for the growth of *flor*, and the olorosos are fortified to 18 degrees. *Flor*, the yeast that forms like a skin on the surface of the wine, is indigenous to the Jerez region and imparts the distinctive aroma and flavor that is characteristic of fino.

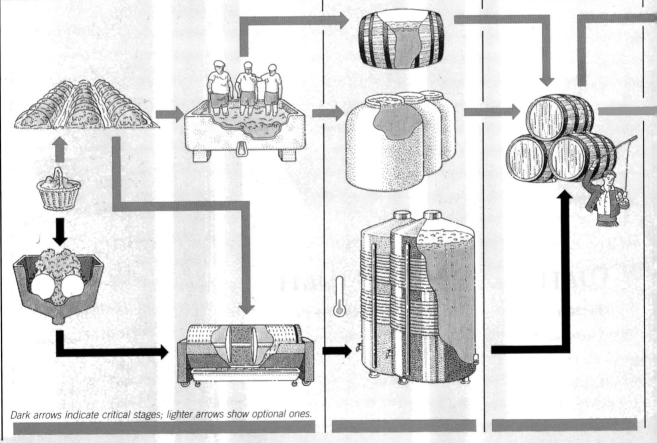

Dark arrows indicate critical stages; lighter arrows show optional ones.

SOLERA SYSTEM

At this stage the sherry may be put in a *criadera*, or young wine reserve, before it is taken to the *solera*.

The *solera* system ensures a consistency of style and quality by blending young wines with older wines over a period of three or four years. The *solera* consists of butts of wines of varying ages. The oldest, always at floor level, is the *solera* proper, and stacked on top are the second, third and fourth scales.

As the older wines are drawn off for blending or bottling, so the butts are replenished from the next in age and so on to the end of the series. The result is that younger wine refreshes each barrel on the way down and just enough nutrients pass down to the older wines to keep their *flor* alive (at least in the case of finos). No more than a quarter to a third of the wine will be drawn off at a time. The youngest butts are topped up with young wine of the same type, from a *criadera*.

The success of the system depends on the fact that the younger wines rapidly take on the character of the older wines to which they are added.

FORTIFICATION

The alcoholic degree of fino is reduced during its period in the *solera*. Having been fortified to 15.5 degrees, it is likely to be down to around 14.7 degrees by the time it is ready for bottling perhaps four years later. The practice is to refortify finos up to 15.5 degrees to 17 degrees.

Manzanilla, a vibrant and refreshing alternative to fino made at Sanlúcar de Barrameda, is bottled at, or slightly below, 15 degrees.

Oloroso sherries actually increase in alcoholic degree while they are in the *solera*. Without the covering of *flor,* they are exposed to air and very slowly evaporate, bringing them up to around 18 degrees to 20 degrees.

BLENDING AND CLARIFYING

All sherries are dry at this stage. Sweet sherries are made by adding sweetening wine. For dark cream sherries this is usually "PX": the sweet, dark, concentrated, fortified juice of the Pedro Ximénez grape. *Mistela*, the fortified raisined juice from Palomino grapes, is sometimes used for sweetening medium sherries.

Sherry is slightly cloudy when it is drawn from the *solera*, so it requires clarifying. Traditionally it was fined with egg white. The albumen attracted to itself suspended particles, which were then carried down to the bottom of the butt by adding "Spanish earth." This process is still used in smaller bodegas. In the larger, mechanized bodegas the wine is clarified by filtration.

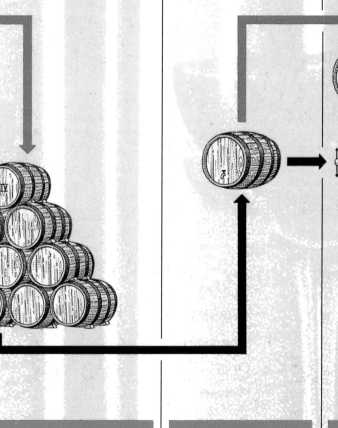

Port

If wine is fermented dry, and then fortified, it undergoes no risk at all; if it is fortified before the end of fermentation, the risks increase, as unfermented sugar may well referment; it was precisely this fact that caused the English merchants so much anxiety in 1754. However, adding 1 or 2 degrees of alcohol to wine that had completed its fermentation incurred no such risk, and it was thus that the wines of the Douro started their life. Fortification of the ferment started sporadically in the early 1700s, reached the current "formula" by 1775, but did not become uniform practice until around 1850.

All the grapes for port are harvested by hand. While Portugal does not have the vast agrarian labor pool it once enjoyed, the wild vineyards of the Douro – awe-inspiring with their size and palpable sense of history – are suited neither physically nor emotionally to mechanization. It may come, one day, but the fact that foot-treading in the *lagares* has survived (against all expectations) suggests that change will be slow.

Fermentation takes place either in the small *quintas*, or farmhouses, of the independent grape-growers or in the very much larger wineries of the port houses. Wines made up-country in the *quintas* are often still foot-stamped in the traditional manner. The *lagares* are like oversized granite spa baths that are filled with grapes to a little over knee height; these are then foot-trodden by teams of swaying workers who (especially in tourist-frequented *quintas*) are entertained during the monotonous hours by a band playing assorted drums, pipes, accordions and tambourines. This may seem like a cross between a cabaret and sheer primitivism, but it is a very effective way of producing high-quality wine, above all of extracting

color and tannin from the grape skins. The high quality of the wines produced in this way is also helping to preserve them from extinction.

The vast majority of port, however, is not trodden. The fermenting vessels that replace the labor of stamping are therefore designed to the same end: to extract all the pigments they can. The vats used by most of the major houses are called Ducellier autovinifiers; these work with a complicated system of pressure buildup and release driven by the carbon dioxide created during the fermentation. The violent agitation of the must promotes maximum extraction of color and flavor compounds over a short period of time. However, less aggressive fermentation methods are increasingly sought: submerged caps (held below the surface by header boards), allied with pumping over, Potter fermenters (of Australian design) and simple floating caps, also regularly pumped over, are among the methods gaining favor.

Autovinification

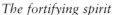

The fermentation is interrupted when about one-third of the sugar content has been converted to alcohol, the fermentation reaching approximately 16° Brix; the must is then pressed, and the wine is fortified to around 18 degrees. From this point on the wine can go in radically different directions, depending in part on the quality of the vintage, in part on the quality of the wine.

Many port-drinkers very reasonably assume that much of the character and quality of the wine derives from the fortifying spirit used. Nothing could be further from the truth. The Junta Nacional de Aguardente long held a monopoly on the supply of spirit to the port houses. What it supplied was distilled from cast-off wines from Portugal's southern vineyards or (less frequently) from the Douro. It is not called *aguardente* ("burning water") for nothing: it is raw and it is fiery. The

The fortifying spirit

sole aim of the houses in making their choice from the small range of samples available is to select the most neutral spirit. The limited effect of the Portuguese spirit was graphically demonstrated in 1904: little or no spirit was available from the government agency in that vintage, so the only alternatives were German spirit distilled from potatoes and grain, and small quantities of *aguardente* imported from the Azores. The vintage ports of that year, however, are still revered for their quality and style.

The fortification formula

The calculation of the amount of fortifying spirit to be used is unexpectedly complex and depends on many factors: the starting sugar content of the must, how much remains at the point of fortification, how much sugar is to be left and what degree of alcohol is required. It has to be remembered that the volume of spirit added is quite substantial and will dilute the sugar in the wine. Winemakers use either a complicated set of tables or a chart to gauge exactly how much to use.

Types of port

Port is unique in offering such a diversity of styles, ranging from ruby to tawny to vintage wines, from a more or less common starting point. "More or less" because, while the vinification method up to the point at which the future of the wine is decided will have been the same, certain vineyard sites and certain varieties will almost inevitably go in the same direction every year. The destiny of each lot of wine is decided on the basis of intensive and repeated tastings over its first 18 months. The best wines of the best years will be destined for bottling at 18 months as vintage port. Thereafter nothing but time and the dark bottle itself witness its transformation. Tawny ports, by contrast, are actively worked on in the shippers' lodges for years on end.

The maturation and blending of old tawny ports

During the first few years of its life, a tawny port will spend time in a variety of containers: stainless-steel vats, concrete vats, large old wooden vats and smaller (650-liter) casks. Once its career as a tawny port is determined, it will be transferred to the elongated casks called pipes (each with a capacity of 523 liters). For the first 10 years or so, the wines will be racked once a year; the ostensible reason is to remove the deposits that collect at the bottom of the pipe (and hence by degrees to clarify the wine and make it more brilliant), but the racking also accelerates the process of oxidation that takes place almost imperceptibly in the pipe. During the early years, the deposits will be a mixture of dead yeast cells, tartrates and various particulate matter of organic or bacterial origin. As the wine ages, the deposits lessen in volume and the racking takes place once every 18 months rather than once a year. The nature of the deposit also changes: it becomes almost entirely composed of polymerized anthocyanins (coloring compounds) that gradually precipitate, reflecting the progressive change from red to reddish brown to light brown to the final almost golden and luminescent hue of a very old tawny port.

Traditional terraced vineyards above Pinhão, pinned to the steep valley sides by banking up the rocky schist between the rows of vines to prevent the soil from being washed down the slope.

The color changes – and the chemical changes that they indicate – are inextricably bound up with the process of oxidation and the production of the aldehydes that give these wines their all-important *rancio* character (literally "rancid," but in this case referring to the nutty taste and brownish color the wines take on as a result of oxidation). At no point, however, should the flavor of oak play any part; port winemakers go to considerable lengths to ensure that the barrels are seasoned before they are put into use, and prefer older oak.

Apart from the deliberately oxidative methods used during racking, the aging wine may have additional spirit added. Normally, though not invariably, in the warmth of a port lodge the alcohol will evaporate more quickly than the water, leading to a reduction in the alcoholic strength. It may also be "freshened" by the addition of a percentage of young wine; it is quite possible for old, wood-aged wines to become stale, and it is preferable to freshen them in the cask rather than simply relying on the blending process.

Blending takes place shortly before the wine is bottled; port sees none of the gradual fractional blending of a sherry *solera*. Its mathematics are by no means simple. If a

10-year-old tawny port is to be blended, it will have a weighted average age of not less than 10 years, but it will by no means be half 15- and half 5-year-old wine. Rather it will be predominantly 10-year-old material, with a small quantity of much older wine and a little more 5- or 6-year-old wine: both the very old and the very young wine will have a disproportionate (if varying) influence on the blend.

Portuguese tawny ports, compared with their equivalents from other countries, are, above all, elegant: the spirit is much more evident than in those of other countries, not because it is stronger per se, but because the fruit is more delicate and fine. As in all of the great fortified wines, while the taste on the palate and tongue is sweet, the finish is dry. The sweetness should never cloy thanks to the complexity, which is summed up in the term *rancio*.

New World "ports"

South Africa, the United States and Australia are the chief winemakers of port-type wines outside Portugal. The signing of a long-negotiated wine agreement between Australia and the European Union in June 2005 heralded the end of the use of "vintage" and "tawny port" in that country. There being no market-acceptable alternative names, producers will have to rely on brand recognition, a successful strategy already employed with sparkling wines.

South Africa

The Cape has had a reputation for fortified winemaking since the great days of its dessert Muscat Constantia in the 18th and 19th centuries. The original Constantia disappeared a century ago (although it is being revived today). "Tawny port" has – to a limited degree – taken its place. The climate of Paarl is very warm to hot, and extremely rich, full-bodied and at times heavily sweet "tawny ports" are made there. These are even further away in style from those of Portugal than the Australian versions; they are mouth-filling, rich wines that rely on power rather than persuasion.

United States

More "vintage" than "tawny port" is made, but quality has remained surprisingly indifferent, given the range of available climates and the very high level of technological skill, not to mention the vast quantities of fortified wine made over the years. The United States wine industry was for decades based on fortified wine production. The "vintage ports" seem to suffer from extremely aromatic but rather unpleasant fortifying spirit, which obscures whatever quality or style the base wine may have had (which usually was not much, with Thompson Seedless or Sultana as the principal grape variety). There are one or two specialist winemakers today who are doing much better.

Australia

In 1960, 70 percent of all Australian wine was fortified, much of it of sherry style, but also large amounts of "port" of every imaginable style and hue. By the turn of the century, fortified wine was no longer a major sales category: small amounts of very high-quality tawny-style and even smaller quantities of very good if idiosyncratic vintage-style "port" are made, but most of the fortified wine sold these days is cheap "cream sherry." One notable exception is Seppelt, which produces a range of high-quality sherry styles ranging from fino to oloroso (though it will no longer be able to use those terms on its labels). Good though these are, they pale into insignificance compared with the port-style Para Liqueur, kept in cask until it is 100 years old and first released on the centenary of its birth. It is only topped up with the same wine taken from another barrel (the quantity steadily diminishes), so it is 100 percent of the stated vintage. Opaque brown, with a tinge of green, it is so viscous it pours like molasses, staining the glass when swirled, the flavor explosively intense.

Significant changes to the making of vintage-style "ports" occurred during the 1990s. Portuguese varieties have now joined Syrah (Shiraz) as the preferred base, and the level of sweetness has been brought back closer to the Portuguese model of 5° to 7° Brix. The consequence has been more elegant wines that will nonetheless repay a minimum of 20 years' bottle-maturation.

Port

This choices-and-consequences chart illustrates the principal stages in the port-making process in which the decisions taken by the maker fundamentally influence the taste and individuality of the final wine. Port is one of the most strictly controlled of all wines – every stage of its making is overseen by a body of statutory authorities.

Port is one of the great "processed" wines. The industry for which Portugal's Douro region is justly famous is based on long-established, unchanging blends on which the major houses have built their names. Despite increasing mechanization of some of the stages, there is no substitute for the skill of the winemaker in timing the fortification and in the assessment and blending of the port wine.

Quinta do Noval, perhaps the most famous of the quintas on the Douro, perched high above Pinhão. Old Noval vintages are among the most magnificent of all ports.

1 IN THE VINEYARD

Choice of grape varieties
Nine varieties are permitted to be planted, but only six are commonly used in the best vintage ports. While the selection of varieties is becoming more important, much more attention is paid to the location of the vineyard from which the grapes for vintage port come.

2 CRUSHING

Crushing
(a) *By foot*
Foot-stamping in open *lagares* is still used for a percentage of the finest wine from the best of the small *quintas* selling to, or owned by, the major houses.

(b) *By mechanical crusher*
Mechanical crushing is the alternative, and this is by way of a vertical crusher peculiar to the

3 FERMENTING AND PRESSING

Choice of fermentation vat
(a) *Lagar*
The traditional fermentation vat is the same granite or slate *lagar* in which the grapes are crushed. The must is broken up by workers using wooden implements.

(b) *Autovinifier*
The port autovinifier is a closed system whereby the must is forced up and over the cap due to the pressure created by carbon dioxide buildup during fermentation.

4 BLENDING AND MATURING

Assessment, blending and classification
The process of tasting commences in the Douro as soon as fermentation is finished, and continues in Vila Nova de Gaia after the wines arrive there the following March. At this point, the general style of the wine will be shaped, although its precise destiny may take years to determine.

Method of picking
Almost all the grapes are picked by hand; at the smaller, up-country *quintas* into square, woven cane baskets that are then transported to the winery by all manner of locomotion, and at larger *quintas* into rectangular steel skips to be taken by truck to the larger wineries.

Douro; stalks are not removed in a hot year, but most of them are in a cool year, when more grape acidity is retained and green, bitter, stalky tannins would overbalance softer fruit.

Left: *Treading grapes to the sound of a local band takes place in the cool of the night at the more traditional* quintas.

Below: *Vintage port is like Champagne in being virtually "made" in its bottle.*

(c) *Open tank with pump-over system*
Gentler and more widespread (as electricity becomes available in the Upper Douro), the open-vat alternative is a system where the must is sprayed over the cap by pump.

Fermentation temperature
Fermentation temperatures range between 79°F to 84°F (26°C to 29°C). The large surface area of the *lagares* and the frequency of the convulsions of the autovinifiers allow circulation of cooler air. With the open-tank system, the larger volumes of must need to be cooled.

Fortification
Grape spirit (*aguardente*) is added before fermentation has finished so that some of the natural sugars remain in the wine. The timing of this fortification is critical and involves the use of either a complicated mathematical table or the winemaker's intuition, developed over decades of experience, to ensure the correct level of sweetness remains.

Pressing
Either continuous presses or Vaslin-type plate-and-chain presses are used. Because of the color and tannin remaining in the partly fermented skins, pressing is always thorough – designed to extract every drop of juice. The pressings are always used in the finished wine because they add balance and complexity.

Wood aging and bottling
Vintage or vintage-style port will be bottled young – between 18 months and six years, then left to mature in bottle. Otherwise the wine will be wood-aged to produce a kaleidoscopic range of port styles.

Stabilization
Cold-stabilization of young wines destined for any of the bottle-aged categories is extremely important, as it removes the excess tartrate crystals that would otherwise form during maturation. The wine is cooled to 14°F (–10°C).

Clarification
Wood-aged ports may be lightly fined before being bottled, and gelatin is the most commonly used fining agent. Wines like old tawny may not need fining, having been racked many times during barrel maturation.

Madeira

The Madeira effect: ordeal by heat

The evolution of Madeira into the only fortified dessert wine that can challenge the greatest port is an epic of serendipity. First the discovery of the island, then its importance to transatlantic shipping, the long, tropical voyages of its modest wines to the Indies (West and East), and their arrival there as something far better than when they left are the happy chances that led to a unique way of making wine.

Madeira, though, is not one kind of wine, but half a dozen. What they have in common is their island origin, and the fact that, like the favorite wines of ancient Rome, they are baked in ovens as part of their "elaboration." The great bulk of Madeira today has no greater destiny than a sauce in a French kitchen. It is made of various grapes, but mainly Tinta Negra Mole, picked as early as August, fermented almost dry in concrete vats, then sweetened and fortified with unfermented must stopped by adding alcohol (known as *vinho surdo*), before being given three months in a 50,000-liter vat heated to 122°F (50°C) by a heating coil.

This is the most summary way of producing the Madeira effect. Fine Madeiras are made by variations on this method, the most important of which are selection, care and time. Four styles of Madeira are sold under the names of the grapes from which, in theory at least, they are made. In ascending order of richness, concentration and strength, they are: Sercial, Verdelho, Bual and Malmsey (or Malvasia). In practice, the supply of these premium grapes has been short ever since first oidium, then phylloxera, devastated the island's vines. It is normal for a certain amount of Tinta Negra Mole to enter into all except the very finest lots of wine.

Sercial and Verdelho are made as white wines, fermented after pressing, without their skins. Some Sercial vines are grown as high as 2,300 feet (700 m) above sea level; their grapes may not ripen until late October, with only enough sugar for a mere 8 percent alcohol. The wines are fermented to dryness, then fortified and sweetened (Sercial more fortified, Verdelho more sweetened) with *vinho surdo*.

Bual and Malmsey are crushed (they were formerly trodden like port), then fermented as red wines, skins and all, until the Bual has consumed at least half of its sugar, the Malmsey perhaps a third – when, again like port, their fermentation is

Space being at such premium on Madeira, vines are trained up pergolas, leaving the ground beneath their leafy canopy free for growing a second crop of fruits or vegetables. Pergolas also allow air circulation around the grapes – important in a warm and humid climate.

stopped by adding spirit. Originally this was cane spirit (Madeira grows excellent sugar cane); today it is grape spirit from mainland Portugal.

The procedure for a high-quality wine is then the same, whether a dry Sercial or a very rich Malmsey. At a total strength of 17 percent, it is run into 650-liter casks of American oak (known as scantling pipes) that are then stacked in an *estufa*, or hot store. The store is heated by hot-water radiators to a maximum temperature of 122°F (50°C) for between three and six months (six months at 104°F/40°C is a preferential treatment for a potentially top-quality wine). The effect is partly to caramelize the sugar in the wine while achieving the *rancio* effect by thorough oxidation. The wine is then allowed to cool very gradually and left to rest for a year or more while its destiny is considered. During this time it is racked by pouring from a height to give it a thorough exposure to oxygen.

The rancio *effect: ordeal by oxygen*

Very exceptional wines are kept apart, under observation for as long as 30 years before being offered as vintage Madeiras. The majority join an island variant of the *solera* system of fractional blending, deriving a good deal of their style from the well-aged oak butts that have held their predecessors for generations.

The late Noel Cossart's *Madeira, the Island Vineyard* is the standard work on the subject. He tells a curious story of how as a young shipper he had tried the experiment of blending Sercial, Bual and Malmsey together, having been told that by tradition the wines would not mix. He was happy with the result until the hogshead arrived at its final destination, Newcastle-on-Tyne, where it was found to have completely fallen apart: "One could draw off the Sercial from the top, the Bual from the middle and the Malmsey from the bottom."

In other respects, Madeira, after its ordeal by heat, is the most stable of all wines. It carries what appears to be a perilous load of volatile acetic acid and more than its share of aldehydes. But air cannot harm it. The greatest Madeiras have spent many years in cask, and often in wide glass carboys, in warm climates where they feed on oxygen – only becoming more concentrated and complex in the process. An old word for their penetrating quality was "eager." Michael Broadbent has used the word "swingeing" for the degree of acidity that keeps these relics immortally fresh.

Madeira

This choices-and-consequences chart illustrates those stages in the winemaking process in which the options chosen by the winemaker fundamentally influence the taste and individuality of the final wine. There are four principal styles of Madeira (ranging from dry to sweet), but differences in blending and aging create further diversity, as the classification indicates.

The original grape varieties for making Madeira – Sercial, Verdelho, Bual and Malmsey – have been joined by another: Tinta Negra Mole. This grape produces varying styles of wine, reflecting the site on which it is grown, and consequently emulating to different degrees the characteristics of the original four. (Sercial, Verdelho, Bual and Malmsey are styles of Madeira as well as grape varieties.)

Classification of Madeira
Sercial A pale, light-bodied wine with a nutty bouquet; darkens with age and softens. Sugar levels at 0.9° to 2.7° Brix and the driest of the wines, but particularly smooth.
Verdelho Golden when young, darkening with age until it reaches a deep green-brown. Medium-bodied and of medium sweetness. Full and quite dry with age, 2.7° to 4.5° Brix.
Bual Rapidly darkens and never less than medium dark. Fragrant fruit with an almost smoky complexity that mellows with age. Fully sweet, with 4.5° to 6.3° Brix.
Malmsey Dark in color, almost black with age, tinged with olive green. Enormously fruity, honeyed and luscious, with 6.3° to 11.7° Brix.
Finest, Choice, Selected (three years) Will typically be made from Tinta Negra Mole, the most widely grown grape. The basic Madeira with simply an indication of whether it is dry, medium, sweet, etc. No grape variety is specified.
Rainwater (three years) A three-year-old wine made from Verdelho. It takes its name from an 18th-century blend that accidentally included rainwater. Soft, easy-drinking style, usually medium sweet.
Reserve (five years or older) A blended wine of a number of vintages, the youngest of which must be at least five years old (after *estufagem*). The grape variety may be specified; if it is, it must contain 85 percent of that variety.
Special Reserve, Old Reserve (10 years or older) The same requirements as for Reserve, except that the youngest component will be 10 years old. Much richer in style and more complex.
Extra Reserve (15 years or older) As before, but with a minimum of 15 years.
Vintage Must be made from the noble varieties, have spent 20 years in cask after *estufagem*, and an additional two years in bottle. Must be 100 percent of the specified variety.
Solera A dying art, though once very famous. Only 10 percent can be drawn off and bottled at any one time and must be replaced by wine of similar quality. The date is that on which the *solera* was established and is not a true indication of the average age.

1 CRUSHING AND PRESSING

Crushing
(a) *Foot-crushing in* lagares
Still believed by the traditionalists to produce the finest wine but in fact it is now uncommon.

2 FERMENTATION AND FORTIFICATION

Fermentation vessel
Large concrete vats are normally used for fermentation, but some argue that better wines benefit from the "seasoning" effects of new oak pipes. By the time the wine has been heated, blended and bottled, though, much of the new oak flavor will have disappeared. Autovinification has also been introduced at some lodges, allowing constant pumping over, which enables increased extraction of color and flavor from the grapes.

3 CONTROLLING THE TEMPERATURE

Heating (*estufagem*)
Estufagem is the slow heating process by which Madeira's sugars are caramelized, resulting in its unique flavor.

(a) *By shipping* (vinho da roda)
The origin of the practice of maturing Madeira by shipping it around the world as ballast is lost in the mists of time, but the benefits of such prolonged heating were well noted by the mid-18th century, and this method was actually practiced until World War I.

4 FINISHING

Fortification
(a) *Initial fortification*
All Madeiras are ultimately fortified to 17 degrees alcohol. The amount of fortification for Sercial and Verdelho will be small (3 to 4 degrees), but this may be the first time these wines have received any spirit.

(b) *Further fortification*
Conversely, for fine Bual and Malmsey this may be the third

(b) *Mechanical crushing/destemming*
Widely adopted in the larger wineries, though for Madeira the choice of whether or not to crush or to destem is not believed to greatly influence the final product.

Pressing
(a) *Pressing before fermentation*
For Sercial and Verdelho wines, the grapes are usually pressed and the juice separated before fermentation begins – these are drier Madeiras, which benefit less from prolonged skin contact.

(b) *Pressing after fermentation*
Grapes for Bual and Malmsey wines are pressed after they have been fermented, their natural sweetness being complemented by grape-skin flavors.

Fermentation and fortification
(a) *Fermentation until dry*
To retain the grapes' drier characteristics, Sercial and Verdelho undergo total fermentation and are not fortified at this stage.

(b) *Fermentation arrested by fortification*
Bual will be fermented until approximately half the sugar has been converted to alcohol. Malmsey, the sweetest of the Madeira styles, will be fermented for only a few hours and retains virtually all its natural sugar.

Racking
The first grading of Madeira occurs after the wine has been racked off its fermentation lees. Each style is then classified according to its quality.

Fortification
(a) *Fine wines*
The addition of alcohol reduces the wine's vulnerability. Winemakers consequently choose to carry out most of the fortification of their highest-quality wines at this stage, raising alcohol levels to 17 percent. The sweeter base wines, not having undergone full fermentation, will require higher alcohol additions to reach this percentage.

(b) *Lesser wines*
Lesser-quality wines are not fortified at this stage as they are more prone to alcohol loss during the heating process that follows. The least alcoholic musts – Bual and Malmsey – do need some fortification, however, to increase their stability.

(b) *Storage under natural heat (canteiro)*
The modern equivalent is storage in south-facing lofts of winery lodges, resulting in the wine being heated to 113°F (45°C) each summer day, cooling overnight. The wine (in pipes) can be stored for up to 30 years (rare).

(c) *Pipe storage in heated sheds (estufas)*
The most common method for medium- to good-quality wines is storage in *armazen de calor* – special buildings heated by hot-water ducts – the best wines being kept for six to 12 months, at 104°F (40°C) and over, in high pipes that rise to ceiling height.

(d) *Heated vats*
Basic generic Madeira is heated in large ceramic-lined concrete tanks with built-in heating coils – held at 122°F (50°C) for three to four months. After this period, the wine is fortified, having lost much of its alcoholic strength during its rigorous heating.

Cooling
Gradual cooling is critical for all wines, but particularly for Sercials and Verdelhos, which at this stage will be most vulnerable, having not been fortified at all. Both oxidation and acetification are real risks.

Below: Vintage Madeira, much rarer than vintage port, spends at least 20 years in cask in the wine lodges in Funchal, the island's capital. Malmsey, the original of the four principal grapes, makes the richest wine.

stage of fortification: initially in the fermentation, adjusted after racking to 17 degrees and now again to compensate for the loss during heating. Old wines may need yet further fortification at blending and bottling.

Filtration and fining
The wine is either fined with gelatin or bentonite, or filtered, and then allowed to rest for 12 to 18 months before classification.

Racking and final classification
After the rest period, the wine is filtered and given a vigorous aerated racking; its fate is then determined and it will be stored according to its final destiny. It may spend as little as 18 more months in cask or over 50 years.

A practice unique to Madeira is to periodically uncork and decant into shallow dishes old vintage wines that have spent decades in bottle. Thus a Madeira from the 1870s might be decanted in the 1920s, and again in the 1950s. In each instance, the wine will be fully exposed to air, and will be tasted over a period of days, and possibly weeks, until it is once again saturated with oxygen and returned to bottle.

Sherry   The original purpose of fortifying port with spirits was simply to stabilize a very rich wine that traveled badly. The taste for a high degree of residual sugar evolved later, until stopping the fermentation at an early stage became standard practice. (*See* the sherry-making process on pages 176–7.) Added to a finished wine, one whose fermentation is complete, with no residual sugar, spirits have no such dramatic effect: they merely strengthen the brew and protect it from bacterial accidents. Dry sherries are the classic example of fortification for this purpose.

The inherent instability of sherry, at least of the finest natural dry sherries, determines the way these delicate and exquisite wines are made. "Delicate" may seem a strange word to use about a wine with 16 percent alcohol, but in hardly any wine is freshness so important as in true fino. Kept too long in bottle, or in cask under anything but perfect conditions, its extraordinary fragrance and vitality disappear and will not recover. An overaged fino may find a second life as an amontillado – but that is a different style of wine.

The fragility of sherry starts in the vineyard, with grapes of little flavor, low acidity and high pH. The sherry grape, the Palomino, makes poor, flabby table wines; only its performance under the special conditions of Jerez, in the stark, white, limy clay known as *albariza*, saves its reputation.

It is picked very ripe, because high natural alcohol is essential to its performance. Grapes intended for sweetening or coloring wine are left to shrivel slightly in the sun – which further lowers their already low acidity. Those for fino are pressed as rapidly as possible, but not until they have been dosed ("plastered" is the old term) with gypsum. *Yeso*, or gypsum, is an additive that has been used since Roman times. Today 2.2 pounds (1 kg) is added to each 1,540 pounds (700 kg) of grapes, whose must will fill one butt. *Yeso* is pure calcium sulfate, naturally present in the Jerez soil, but now prepared industrially. It reacts with potassium bitartrate in the wine to produce (insoluble) calcium tartrate, (soluble) potassium sulfate and valuable tartaric acid. The precise reactions that make *yeso* an essential ingredient of sherry are still being studied, but their effects include a more moderate rate of fermentation, increased acidity and the production of aromatic esters and ethyl tartrate. *Yeso* also encourages the growth of the vital yeast, *flor*.

The formation of flor   The all-important *flor* is caused by the growth of yeast cells on the surface of the wine within a few weeks of the end of fermentation. The same yeast (or one of the same yeasts) that triggers the primary fermentation (*Saccharomyces beticus*) is responsible for the growth of the *flor*. Initially specks, then islands of *flor* appear; these coalesce into a thin, continuous film that thickens and becomes wrinkled, changing in color from white to light gray and ultimately to brown. At this point, portions break away and sink to the bottom of the cask, and are promptly replaced by new, thin film. The "flowering" of the yeast normally occurs in spring and autumn, dropping in summer and winter – basically in response to changing temperature.

The effect of flor   Modern analysis has identified more than 100 volatile compounds affecting the flavor of sherry. The main ones are acetaldehydes, an integral part of the *rancio* character, and compounds called acetals. Under the action of *flor*, glycerol decreases, thinning the wine's texture to the gloriously crisp, dry flavor of fresh fino. A further effect comes from the autolysis of dead yeast cells that fall to the bottom of the butt. Only one other wine gains such character from its interaction with yeast: Champagne.

In the hot Jerez autumn, runaway tumultuous fermentation has always been a problem, leading to loss of both wine (spurting from the bungholes of casks) and a degree or more of alcohol. There is also likely to be a loss of valuable but volatile aromas. Although Jerez now has giant temperature-controlled vats in its bigger bodegas, new oak casks are its traditional fermenting vessels, still very much in use. It is the best way of maturing the casks and preparing them for later use in the *criadera*, the young wine nursery, and the *solera*, where the physical properties of oak are as essential as its flavor is unwelcome.

Much has been written of the classification of new sherries into styles, butt by butt, as they develop in the bodega. In practice it would be strange if a wine intended to be a fino, picked at the right ripeness in a vineyard known for finos, turned out to be an oloroso. Olorosos – stronger, broader and more pungent wines without the delicacy of finos – are fashioned just as deliberately. What is in doubt, and demands patient tasting and retasting, is the real quality of a given butt: whether it deserves to join a top-quality *solera* or should be kept for lowlier blending purposes.

The bodega of Antonio Barbadillo is the biggest in Sanlúcar de Barrameda, the original sherry-shipping harbor at the mouth of the river Guadalquivir. The district produces the freshest, most delicate fino sherries that take on the character known as manzanilla in the ancient bodegas of the town. The sea air gives manzanilla a slightly salty tang.

Oloroso wines are fortified using grape spirit to about 18 percent alcohol before joining a *solera*; finos, from their lower natural fermented strength, to 15 percent. More alcohol would not permit the growth of *flor*, which is a fino's essential distinction. Any *flor* growing on an oloroso is thus killed by fortification.

Under a vigorously growing protective layer of this unique yeast, the delicate wine is protected from oxygen and the attack of acetic acid. Without it, it would soon be vinegar. To keep *flor* flourishing, frequent refreshment with young wine is needed. A fino *solera* therefore is a relative hive of activity, with wines regularly being drawn off and the butts replenished, while an oloroso *solera*, its wines without *flor* protected by their fortification, needs very much more time to achieve maturity.

A *solera* is not the end of the blending process. Indeed, it might be described as the beginning. It is rare for straight *solera* wines to be sold without at least some further blending, because all *solera* wines are fully dry. Most commercial sherries are well-tried blends from more than one *solera*, adjusted to customers' tastes by a little sweetening with sweet wine (*dulce*) made either by stopped fermentation or added sugar. The chief exceptions to this further blending are top-quality finos and sherries now marketed as *almacenistas*, which are straight *solera* wines from individual growers' stocks. These unsweetened wines of wholly distinctive character are the ultimate expression of the region, and must be counted among the finest white wines in the world.

A *solera* is an aggregation of butts divided into equally sized stages, each stage containing sherry of different (steadily increasing) average age. For wines such as manzanillas that depend on freshness, there may be as many as 10 stages; for old, slow-moving amontillados or olorosos, there may be only five or six.

The solera *system*

Taking a five-stage *solera* as an example, the youngest wine will be in stage V (when the *solera* was in the course of establishment, that wine will have been young and of a single vintage year). The oldest wine will be in stage I. Sherry will be taken from stage I twice a year; on each occasion a little over 20 percent of the actual contents of each butt will be removed for bottling or blending. Expressed as a total of the wine in the *solera*, this represents 5 percent of the total on each occasion, or 10 percent a year.

The wine removed from stage I is replaced by an identical quantity of wine from stage II and so on up the chain. Stage V, the youngest, is in turn refreshed from a *criadera*, or "nursery," which could be described as a tributary flowing into the mainstream of the *solera*. The *criadera* is in turn run on the *solera* system so that its oldest wine is only slightly younger than the wine in the *solera* stage V. Only the youngest stage in the *criadera* is refreshed with *añada*, or new wines.

"Running the scales" of a *solera* is not just a question of taking around 95 liters from each butt in the higher stage and putting it in a butt in the next (lower) stage. If the wine is being removed from, say, stage IV and going into stage V, the wine drawn from each single butt in stage IV will be divided equally among all the butts in stage V, a tedious process but essential to guarantee the uniformity of the blend. In smaller bodegas, or with *soleras* of extreme quality, the process will be carried out using pitchers into which

the wine is gravity-siphoned and then poured through a perforated copper tube into the next stage: the perforations ensure the gentle passage of the incoming wine so as not to disturb either the *flor* on the surface or the lees on the bottom of the cask. In larger bodegas, the process will be done by gentle pumping, with the wine withdrawn being mixed in a vat and then pumped back to the next stage.

Choice of sherry style

Anyone who has visited Jerez and drunk fino – drawn direct from a butt chilled in a cool room overnight – at 11 a.m. in the sun-dappled, leafy courtyard of one of the bodegas, will know just what a glorious wine fino is. The wine is drunk, not sipped: the midmorning *tapas* (appetizers) simply add fuel to the fire. It underlines another unique feature of fino: it is best drunk straight from the butt; next best when consumed within days of being bottled; will not suffer unduly from a few months in bottle; but loses freshness progressively (and significantly) over the months thereafter. It is no more than an unfortunate recognition of commercial reality that the shippers decline to put legible bottling dates on their finos.

Fino
The wine is fundamentally shaped by the *flor*, and to a much lesser degree by its fortification: it has that "cut" to both its bouquet and taste that adds to its crispness, intensifies its dryness. It should be drunk slightly chilled in summer, and should be regarded as a first-class alternative to, let us say, a Chardonnay: after all, its alcohol is not so very much higher. It is also exceptional value for money.

Manzanilla
Manzanilla shares many similarities with fino, but it is made exclusively in the humid seaside climate of Sanlúcar de Barrameda (some distance from Jerez), which encourages the growth of a thicker layer of *flor* than that of fino. The result is a brilliantly refreshing style, slightly lower in alcohol and higher in acidity than fino. Its only drawback is the necessity of consuming it fresh, ideally within six months of bottling.

Amontillado
The extra age in butt, the significantly higher levels of aldehydes and the somewhat higher alcohol content (in the sherry bodegas, water loss through evaporation comfortably exceeds alcohol loss) – all act to give amontillados a nutty warmth on the midpalate, a

Far left: *A solera system in a Jerez bodega. In a solera, which could be described as a fractional blending system, wine is drawn from the oldest of a series of butts, which is then topped up from the next oldest, and so on. Each addition rapidly takes on the character of the older wine to which it is added, but the aging wine must be carefully chosen to match the old.*

Left: *Australia's most successful answers to the fortified wines of Europe are its creamy, long-matured sweet Muscats. The Brown Brothers' vineyards, in northeast Victoria, provide grapes for their most luscious liqueur Muscat.*

rounder, softer feeling before the cleansing dryness of the finish. If fino is the wine for spring or summer, amontillado is the wine for autumn (or a rainy summer's day). It should not be chilled, but otherwise treated in much the same way as fino.

Oloroso

Take out the *flor* influence, but add an extra dimension of *rancio*, and the many-layered complexity of oloroso takes shape. These are wonderfully intense and concentrated wines; if sherry aficionados are divided in their views as to which of the three styles they prefer, it is a question of personal choice rather than quality. If fino is the wine of summer, oloroso is the wine of winter.

Australian Tokay and Muscat

If any New World fortified wines deserve a place alongside the classics in this chapter, it is the limited production of liqueur Muscats and Tokays from northeast Victoria – particularly from the district of Rutherglen. Tokay is in fact made from Muscadelle, "Tokay" being a traditional (though incorrect) name for Muscadelle.

Making the wines

The very hot, highly continental climate of northeast Victoria allows the grapes to reach exceptionally high sugar levels in years when late vintage rains do not interfere: readings of over 36° Brix are achieved in the greatest vintages, though normally 27° to 29° Brix are considered adequate. Sweetness comes through simple dehydration and raisining: botrytis is not welcome, although it, along with even less welcome molds, sometimes makes its mark.

The grapes are crushed and destemmed (no easy task if they are raisined at very high Brix levels) and fermentation initiated with cultured yeasts. Depending on the starting Brix, the quality of the grapes (or must) and the desired style, fermentation may be arrested almost as soon as it has started or left until the must has 14° to 18° Brix unfermented sugar. The earlier the fermentation stops, the greater the spirit addition needed to produce the required balance – and the higher the cost of the wine.

The real magic comes with prolonged wood aging, often enhanced by storage at the top of corrugated-iron sheds to intensify the heat. The final wine is typically a blend of wines of different ages, with a core roughly the age of the finished wine.

Oak and Wine

Choices, consequences and techniques

The bond between wine and oak was forged by the Romans. No doubt all sorts of woods were tried over the centuries, and some – notably cherry, chestnut and walnut – remain in limited use in some European countries today. Oak has many features that make it perfect for use in the winery, some of which parallel its suitability for shipbuilding: high tensile strength, light weight, malleability and impermeability to water (or wine). The large barrels and vats fashioned from Roman times onward look primitive and clumsy by modern standards, but they did the only job that was expected of them: to act as vessels for storage or transport.

The role of the container

At some point fairly early in the history of the use of oak, winemakers came to appreciate and understand the softening and "complexing" effect of the slow and gentle process of oxidation brought about by the entry of oxygen through the working apertures of the barrel or cask and through the oak itself. In cellars of relatively low humidity, there will also be considerable evaporation of the wine, which, for reasons of economy, the winemaker may wish to prevent, but which in all except extreme cases will hasten the barrel-aging process and almost certainly improve the wine by slightly concentrating it.

In old oak vats (which the French call *foudres* or *demi-muids*, the Germans *Fuder* or *Stücke*), tartrate crystals will gradually accumulate and completely coat the inside of the vat. Apart from preventing any possibility of the pickup of oak flavor, and adding to the impermeability of the oak, the crystal lining helps precipitate the tartrate present in the new wine most recently placed in the barrel. In cold European cellars, winter partially cold-stabilizes the wine, something New World winemakers achieve (and, it must be said, achieve more completely) through refrigerated cooling to 32°F (0°C) or below in stainless-steel vats.

The larger the container, the slower will be the process of softening and oxidation. Over the centuries some countries and regions moved to smaller barrels – perhaps originally for transport, then for maturation, although initially not for fermentation. The distinction between fermentation and maturation is important: large oak vats (which have various configurations) can be used for both tasks, whereas the small barrels (*barriques*, hogsheads and puncheons) are only used for the fermentation of white, not red, wines (sometimes also for the final stages of fermentation of some red wines after they have been pressed).

It is only in the last 40 to 50 years that much attention has been paid to the other characteristic of oak: its ability, when new, to impart an extra dimension of flavor to wine. This characteristic has always been known, of course; the Italians, the Portuguese, the Spanish (in Jerez) and the Champenois went to considerable lengths to avoid it. When new pipes are introduced into the port lodges, mediocre quality table wine is made in them for two or three years before they are first used for vintage port. But in Bordeaux and Burgundy, the attitude was (and is) very different, with the flavor being prized; now the interest in the differing flavor characteristics of different oak types has become a matter of intense study.

The principal types of oak used are *Quercus alba* (from eastern North America), and *Q. robur* and *Q. sessilis* (from Europe). Within Europe, oak is harvested in and sold from a number of countries: French, German, Balkan and Portuguese oaks are the most common. French is by far the most significant, the all-important differences

Old barrels that have been used many times impart no oak flavor to the wine.

between its forests being the focus of attention in the New World. Sometimes it is suggested that oak finds its way from Baltic countries to be "re-badged" as French. With the unlocking of East/West trade, Baltic oak may well rise in importance, and act to stabilize the escalating prices of French oak.

Limousin excepted (briefly in vogue for use with Chardonnay in parts of the New World, notably the U.S.), French oaks are more subtle than American, German or Portuguese. But any winemaker using a significant amount of new oak knows there is disconcerting variation in flavor (and quality) between two barrels, even when the oak, the "toast" and the cooper are the same. With oak from different coopers, the variation can be even more marked. The reasons for the variation are many and varied. The growth rate of the tree is influenced by the climate and soil variations of the area, the density of the trees within the forest and the age of the tree. The slower the rate of growth, the tighter the grain and the better the flavor of oak in the wine. Chemical analysis shows that more desirable phenols are extracted from slower-growing oak. Another source of variation derives from the seasoning of the oak after it has been milled into green wood staves; staves can be machine-sawn or hand-split, the quality of the latter being significantly better. The variables are: seasoning for three years in stacks in the forest; for three years in the cooper's yard, which allows for periodic water spraying of the stack; and for 18 months to two years, followed by adjustment to bring the moisture content to the desired level of 17 to 18 percent. Kiln drying is a quick-fix method, but one not used by the best cooperages.

The buildup of tartrate crystals in a much-used cask needs to be checked – or the volume available for wine is reduced.

Making the barrels

Then there is the manner in which the casks are made. The characteristic oval or egg shape of the barrel means that the staves are bent by being heated. The wood may be heated by steam, by being immersed in boiling water or by being grilled over an open fire. French coopers have largely preferred to use the open-fire technique (a few immerse the staves in water before firing, a process called wet-fired), and it was from this that the realization came that the level of browning, or "toast," of the surface of the oak has a very significant effect on the flavor of the wine.

The effect of toasting

Tasting and chemical analysis have both increased our understanding of the effect of toasting. Seven principal aldehydes, 18 phenols and seven other aromatic compounds (principally lactones) have been identified as contributing to the oak aroma and flavor in wine. If the oak is slowly toasted over a small fire (rather than charred quickly over a hotter, larger fire), the aromatic aldehydes and flavor compounds are increased by a factor of many times. There are, of course, some winemakers (and some kinds of wine) for which more is not better, and not all barrels are made with medium or high toast levels.

New and used barrels

So far as the winemaker is concerned there is a very significant difference between a new barrel and one used for a second, third or fourth time. It is generally agreed that the useful life of a barrel in making quality table wine in which oak aroma and flavor are important is between four and six years. Since the cost of a new barrel is very high (around $850 for a *barrique* from a French cooperage in 2006) and its functional life as a container is 60 years or more, a number of lateral approaches have been tried. One of the obvious solutions is to disassemble the barrel, shave the staves, reassemble and re-fire it. The results have been satisfactory, but have their limitations. If the barrel is three or four years old, shaving will markedly improve it, but it will not emulate the performance of a new barrel. Another approach has been to use chips or finely ground shavings; if the quality of the oak is good, and if the chips are skillfully used (e.g., during primary fermentation), the result can be disconcertingly good. Yet another approach is to use "inner staves": planks of new oak placed in stainless-steel fermenters. But one cannot eliminate barrels; the other effects of barrel maturation are still essential to give the wine the appropriate texture. At some point, though, they will be passed on like clothes from an older sibling, serving in making lesser-quality table wine and ultimately in making fortified wine (quite possibly very good fortified wine).

Oak

The ability of wood to influence the smell and taste of wine was recognized only recently. Originally, oak barrels served primarily as vessels for convenient transport or storage using a material readily available. This choices-and-consequences chart illustrates some of the options available to those winemakers who introduce the effect of oak into the winemaking process and the way the wood adds to the flavor and aroma of the final wine.

The source of the oak and the tightness of the wood grain are critical to its quality, and vary according to the climate, the soil and the nature of the forest where the wood was grown. The way in which the barrels are prepared by the cooper, the number of times the barrels are used and their size are as important as the very fact of using oak to add complexity to the taste of the wine.

1

IN THE FOREST

Choice of oak type
(a) *French*
    Tronçais
    Nevers
    Allier
    Vosges
    Limousin
(b) *Other*
    Baltic
    Balkan
    Portuguese
    German
    American

Choice of oak type is of primary importance; *see* page 193 for the varying uses and implications of the choice. It should be realized, however, that the quality can and does vary greatly from cooper to cooper, and even from barrel to barrel.

2

IN THE COOPERAGE

Right: *New French oak barrels await filling in cellars in the Barossa Valley, South Australia.*

Far right: *The staves of a barrel are cut (or, better, riven) straight, then curved by being heated on a fire.*

Choice of grain
(a) *Tight grain*
(b) *Loose grain*

Given a choice, most makers would unhesitatingly choose the slow-grown, tight-grained oak in preference to the loose-grained oak, which gives a less subtle and fine flavor.

Left: *The state-owned Tronçais forest in the Allier in central France produces the most prized barrel oak on a 160-year rotation.*

Seasoning of oak
(a) *Time*
(b) *Air-dried*
(c) *Kiln-dried*

Once again, given an effective choice, it would be for air-dried oak seasoned for three to four years. In practice, the choice may not be available, or, if it is, becomes very expensive. Some winemakers accordingly buy and season their own oak, which they then send to the cooperage to be made up into barrels.

Method of making
(a) *Machine-sawn or hand-split staves*
(b) *Steam-bent, wood-fired or wet-fired*

Barrels made from hand-split staves are better in every way than those that use machine-sawn staves, but are more expensive. Similarly, barrels made over a fire are generally preferred to those made using steamed staves. In each case, the heat is necessary to allow the staves to be bent into shape.

Level of toast
(a) *High*
(b) *Medium*
(c) *Low*

If the barrel has been wood-fired, it is possible (indeed common) to select the level of toast or char. The choice is very much a subjective one, determined by the style of the wine the winemaker wishes to make. High-toast barrels give a distinctive spicy/smoky tang admired by some and not others.

3
IN THE WINERY

Choice of barrel size
(a) *Barrique, 224 liters*
(b) *Hogshead, 315 liters*
(c) *Puncheon, 450 liters*
(d) *Others up to 450 liters*

As a general rule, the smaller the barrel, the greater the extraction of oak flavor and the more rapid the development of the wine. For some winemakers this is desirable, for others it is not. Cost also enters the equation: the larger the barrel, the more economic it is.

New or old oak?
(a) *100 percent new*
(b) *Mixture of new and old*
(c) *100 percent old*

Once again, the choice is primarily determined by the philosophy of the winemaker (and the desired taste of the wine), and secondarily by considerations of cost. The strength of flavor of the raw wine, the period over which it is intended to age and conventional expectations of the final taste of the wine are all factors determining choice.

Storage conditions
(a) *Controlled*
(b) *Ambient*

The need to control temperature and humidity will vary from country to country, but the end result of cool, humid storage is not in doubt: better wine, all other things being equal. Cost is a limiting factor.

IN THE BOTTLE

The Chemistry and Methods of Analysis of Wine

The analysis of grape juice or wine enables the winemaker to determine what chemical adjustments should be made (normally the addition of acid, sulfur dioxide or sugar) and what treatments are necessary (filtration and cold-stabilization being two examples). The decision will be made using chemical indices, the four most commonly cited ones for dry table wine being: alcohol, acid, pH and volatile acidity.

Alcohol

Alcohol is produced by the fermentation of grape sugar, which usually accounts for 15 to 24 percent by weight of the must before the onset of fermentation (glucose, fructose and sucrose all having the same value or weight). All other things being equal, slightly less than half the sugar will be respired as carbon dioxide during fermentation, the remainder converted to ethanol (commonly called alcohol). Thirty years ago, it was sufficient to say that 1.8° Brix (1° Baumé) would produce 1 degree of alcohol. The table of conversion rates in the first edition of this book showed an even lower conversion rate: taking 10.1° Baumé as an example, it showed 9.4 degrees alcohol, 26.8° Brix producing 14.4 degrees alcohol.

The text did note, however, that "some yeasts can actually increase the alcohol by up to 5 percent." What was then of minor interest for researchers and a nonissue for winemakers has since become a source of extreme frustration and uncertainty for winemakers and (some) consumers in parts of the New World. In a nutshell, there has been a seemingly remorseless increase in alcohol levels, and disagreement on its causes.

On one issue there is total agreement. Cold-fermentations of white wines in closed or partially closed tanks, vats or barrels will result in a higher conversion rate of sugar to alcohol than much warmer red wine fermentations in open vats or tanks. Thus two very different tables are now given (on page 237), one for white wine, the other for red. The reason for the lower conversion rate is the loss (by evaporation) of alcohol during red wine fermentation that results from the interaction of open fermenters, pumping over and/or plunging the must, and the higher fermentation temperatures.

Opposite: *Patriarche Père et Fils in Beaune claims to have the biggest cellars in Burgundy with a history dating back to 1780.*

Reverse osmosis

The Old World quest for higher alcohol, for richer and softer wines, has been aided by the proliferation of reverse-osmosis and microoxygenation equipment, the first to strip water from the must, the second to instantly soften and polish the tannins. These ideas and aims have spread around the world. Finally, there is the issue of climate change, and the extreme swings in weather that accompany it – witness the 2003 vintage in western Europe.

So red wine alcohol levels have increased significantly. For some makers, for some styles and for some markets (such as the United States), alcohol is a badge of honor; the more, the better. In some New World countries, including Australia, the attitude is ambivalent and, ironically, reverse osmosis is made to stand on its head. While the addition of water per se is forbidden in Australia, it is as legal to remove alcohol as it is to remove water by reverse osmosis. Another alcohol-reduction technique is especially vigorous aerative pumping over the red-grape fermenting must, which results in the partial evaporation of alcohol.

The California-based Vinovation business of Clark Smith and the Australian Memstar joint venture of Messrs. Wollan and Baldwin have taken reverse osmosis to levels of extreme sophistication. Memstar is able to reduce (or remove) alcohol, water, volatile acidity and *Brettanomyces* with a mix of licensed and self-patented techniques, all based on the cornerstone of reverse osmosis. Here we are interested in the reduction of alcohol, and the discovery of the so-called "sweet spot": a quasi-umami point at which the wine has the best flavor and mouth-feel.

James Halliday participated in a tasting experiment involving a Pinot Noir that had an alcohol level of 15.2 percent, and the same wine stripped of 4 percent of its alcohol. By blending the two in various proportions, it was possible to taste the wine with 12 different alcohol levels. Two sweet spots, at 13.27 percent and 13.52 percent, emerged from the group tasting. Thus, in real-life reverse-osmosis procedures, it is highly desirable to taste the wine continuously as the alcohol is progressively reduced, rather than have a preconceived number. The one exception is the 14 percent alcohol level, which, if exceeded, gives rise to financial or other problems in certain parts of the world.

The situation with white wines, in particular Chardonnay, is even more problematic. The nonlinear table for white wines corresponds exactly with the practical experience of winemakers throughout Australia, and (we strongly suspect) elsewhere in the world. Witness the 2005 vintage in Burgundy. It is a synthesis of a number of factors that have yet to be comprehensively researched.

One piece of the jigsaw puzzle is the fact that, in the early stages of fermentation, the yeasts divert part of the sugar to build their populations and cell-wall thickness (biomass). Once the fermentation has reached 10 degrees alcohol (regardless of its potential level), the yeast population is sufficiently large, and thereafter all available sugar is directly converted to alcohol. However, this alone is insufficient to explain the increase.

Another piece is the time-honored but inappropriate use of Baumé (as opposed to Brix) as a measure of sugar. Baumé is a measure by weight of that portion of the juice other than water, while Brix directly measures the percentage of soluble solids in the juice. This becomes apparent in the phrase "apparent sugar," which is a measure of the nonfermentable grape solids (acids, etc.) in the juice.

Yet another is the problem of obtaining a true analysis of sugar from the juice or must. Many wineries rely on a hydrometer, a very inexpensive piece of equipment that is normally calibrated to give a true reading at 68°F (20°C), but which can be upset by all manner of things, most obviously gas or skins and pips in the sample. Sample error is indeed the answer most commonly given by researchers confronted by otherwise inexplicable conversion rates.

Next, it is well known that the efficiency of yeasts in alcohol production can and does vary significantly. Thus EC118 (a Lallemand yeast) is notorious for increasing

Portugal has progressed from an almost medieval wine culture two decades ago to some very modern facilities indeed. João Pires, at Pinhal Novo, just south of Lisbon, took the radical step of employing an Australian winemaker. Wine is not made in the laboratory, but accurate analysis is an enormous help.

white wine alcohol levels. Another commercial yeast developed by Maurivin converts only 84 percent of the sugar to alcohol, compared to 97 percent of the most efficient yeasts. The fascinating question is, what happens to the remaining sugar? The seemingly obvious answer is increased glycerol production, but in fact the levels are normal. It is a subject of ongoing research.

One might think that wild-yeast fermentations would result in lower alcohol levels, but this, too, is not so. It is not surprising, in fact, that the dominant wild yeast in the nearby environment should be highly efficient.

The alcohol produced does not have any flavor in the narrow sense, but does have an important impact on the taste and balance of the wine. It adds a sweetness and a roundness that can be felt as much as it can be tasted; characteristics that come into clear relief at the extremes. Thus a high-alcohol Chardonnay (14 degrees or more) will often seem to have unfermented sugar, so obvious is the sweetness. High alcohol may also give a slight burning sensation to the finish. At the other end, low-alcohol wines are characteristically thin. An even more dramatic illustration is the effect on a high-quality wine of standard alcohol content that has had 50 percent of that alcohol removed by reverse osmosis (*see* page 225). The wine so treated tastes extremely acidic (and thin), yet the acid content has in fact remained constant. The removal of the sweetening influence of the alcohol simply throws the wine out of balance – German makers of cheap Kabinett *trocken* wines take note.

Effect on flavor

The alcohol content of table wines is commonly increased (less commonly decreased). The principal method of increase is the addition of one of a number of forms of sugar to the fermenting wine: it may be refined beet sugar or cane sugar, or added as concentrated grape juice (grape sugar). The process is usually called chaptalization, taking its name from Jean-Antoine Chaptal, Napoleon's minister of agriculture, who formally sanctioned its use in 1801.

Methods of alcohol adjustment

Chaptalization

To raise the level of alcohol by 1 degree requires the addition of 17 to 19 grams per liter of sugar, which may not sound a great deal, but in reality quickly adds up: 88 pounds (40 kg) of sugar for a very small (3.3 ton/3 tonne) vat. Wines are sweetened during fermentation; with some winemakers deliberately (although technically illegally) adding the sugar in repeated small quantities toward the end, with the dual aim of extending the period of fermentation and of stressing it to assist the formation of glycerols.

In Europe, the European Union has issued regionally based regulations that govern the use of chaptalization. These lay down the minimum potential alcohol of the wine before chaptalization, the maximum sugar addition and the maximum alcohol content after chaptalization. In the coldest, most northern regions, chaptalization is permitted in every year; in the moderate central zones it is authorized in poor years; in the warm southern zones it is not permitted at all. In no case, however, may sugar and acid be legally added to the same wine – a rule that is as honored in the breach as it is in the observance, or dubiously circumvented by adding sugar to the must and acid to the fermented wine. In 2003, it was legal to acidify in Burgundy, but only if no sugar was added.

There are numerous misconceptions about the effect of chaptalization, the most common being it makes the wine sweet – that one can actually taste the sugar. Since it is entirely fermented, this is manifestly not so. But as we have seen, alcohol does give an impression of sweetness in the tactile sense; it is for precisely this reason that if one asks a Burgundian why he or she chaptalizes in the years in which sufficiently high natural levels of alcohol can be achieved without chaptalization, the answer will be "for the feel" – meaning the feel of the wine in the mouth. And like any winemaking technique, if used with discipline and sensitivity, it can very significantly improve wine quality; if used lazily or unintelligently, it can be positively harmful.

German wines designated as *Qualitätswein mit Prädikat* may not be chaptalized, but may have their potential alcohol increased by *Süssreserve*, provided it is made from grapes of the same quality and potential alcohol as the must being sweetened.

Concentrated grape juice

In Australia, a similar situation exists: the use of sugar is prohibited (other than in sparkling wine), but the use of concentrated grape juice is permitted. The drawback of such concentrates – particularly for red wines – is the diluting effect on flavor unless the concentrate is made from the same or similar red grapes.

This method of increasing alcohol simply commercializes (or industrializes) the principles underlying the production of German Eiswein: in any given solution, the water content will freeze first, leaving the other constituents in a concentrated form. When applied to full-scale wine production, a coil or hollow plate through which chilled brine is continuously pumped is placed into the vat holding the grape juice; a large ice block gradually forms, which is then lifted out of the vat – or the concentrated juice pumped out, leaving the ice to melt in place. This is a technique most suited to sweet white table wines, but has also been used to advantage with dry white wines.

Acid

Several different kinds of acid may be present in wine: tartaric, malic, lactic and citric acids are the most common. Tartaric and malic are the principal grape acids, and lactic acid is formed in the wine by the conversion of malic in the course of malolactic fermentation. If the wine does not undergo this fermentation (some white wines do not, almost all red wines do), lactic acid will not be present. Naturally occurring citric acid is present only in tiny quantities.

The effect on wine flavor

Wines that are deficient in acid taste flat and flabby; up to a certain point, acid both intensifies the taste and (with white wines) can even make the fruit flavor seem sweeter. Lactic is the sourest acid, followed by tartaric, citric and malic.

Adjusting acidity

In countries in which it is permitted, adjustment (up or down) is a simple matter. The real questions for the winemaker are how much to add, when to carry out the adjustment and which acid to use. For the consumer, the questions (and the commonly held misconceptions) are similar to those relating to chaptalization.

As a rule of thumb, acid correction is permitted in Europe when chaptalization has not been used, and is generally permitted in the New World countries. If nature (and appropriate viticultural techniques) permitted it, no winemaker would wish to adjust acid – or any other component of wine. But in the warmer regions of the New World, acid adjustment is as essential and as widely practiced as is chaptalization in the cooler parts of Europe. It is quite remarkable that as one crosses the equator or the Atlantic, sugar and acid undergo some mysterious alchemy that makes one perfectly acceptable in one country and frowned on, if not actually despised, in the other.

Major corrections – the addition of 1, 2, or 3 grams per liter of acid – are best made while the wine is fermenting. Opinions are sharply divided as to whether acid corrected at this time can ultimately be detected in the finished wine, but all would agree that the best results (in terms of taste) are obtained where the acid is added earlier rather than later. Those who say they can identify a wine that has had acid added claim the finish is harder (at an identical acid level) than a wine with only natural acid. In countries such as Australia the argument is a suspicious one, because virtually every wine will have had acid added to it, and the claim of "recognition" of the fact can almost never be wrong.

The acid added at this point will usually be tartaric; subsequent fine-tuning additions (at the conclusion of the malolactic fermentation and just prior to bottling) may be of any one or more of tartaric, malic or citric acid. The addition of as little as a quarter of a gram per liter before bottling can have a considerably beneficial effect on the taste, and in particular the balance, of the wine.

Deacidification, on the other hand, occurs quite naturally as the wine undergoes malolactic fermentation. Where fine adjustment is necessary, natural tartaric acid is precipitated out of the wine using potassium bicarbonate or calcium carbonate to make it insoluble. Once precipitated, the acid is removed by filtration. This process will eventually start up the natural deacidification chain that leads to malolactic fermentation and is sometimes used specifically for this purpose.

Another measure of acidity is pH: it measures active acidity, where titratable acidity takes account of both free and bound acidity. It simply measures the number of hydrogen ions, and thus tells us the real or active acidity of grape juice or wine. It is this "real" acidity that determines how resistant wine is likely to be to bacterial attack, and is also a very good indicator of how well a dry table wine will age.

What is low pH and what is high pH in wine are questions that have to be placed in a broader perspective. The pH range is from 0 (that of extremely strong acids such as sulfuric or hydrochloric) to 14 (an alkali such as sodium hydroxide). Neutral liquids such as blood or milk have a pH of around 6 to 7. Moreover, the scale of pH is logarithmic, which means that a solution with a pH of 3 has 10 times as much real acid as one with a pH of 4, which is in turn 10 times more acid than a pH of 5. Champagne and sparkling wine have a pH of 3 or less; most white table wine is between 3 and 3.5. Red wines usually range between 3.4 and 3.8, while fortified wines may have a pH as high as 4.

The effect of pH levels on the color of white wine is less marked than in the case of red wines, where the pH has a major influence: young wines with a high pH will have a distinctive slightly dull, blackish purple hue that will rapidly turn brown with only a few years of bottle-age.

Partly because pH does not directly correspond to titratable acidity, some chemists allege that the pH of a wine cannot be determined by taste, but experienced wine tasters strongly disagree. At the one extreme they would point to the soapy, stewed taste of red wines with high pH, and at the other to the hard, almost metallic edge of wines with excessively low pH. And while there is no precise mathematical equation that will convert pH to acidity or vice versa, it is certainly true that the lower the pH, the higher the acidity (and vice versa).

Even the most experienced winemaker cannot tell you in the abstract what the titratable acidity and pH of a wine *should* be. He or she can only give that answer on a case-by-case basis, as so much will depend on the other flavor constituents: alcohol, sugar (if any) and total extract (including most notably tannins).

Cold-stabilization (chilling the wine to below 32°F/0°C) is the only wholly natural method of pH adjustment, and may not have any effect in some circumstances. Adding tartaric acid is the principal legal method in countries that permit it; a technique called ion exchange (banned by the European Union) is another; while the addition of sulfuric acid (almost universally banned) is technically the most effective of all. The longer-term answer is to improve viticultural techniques so as to provide grapes that will have the appropriate chemical balance and bypass the need for adjustment.

Volatile acid is initially formed during fermentation through the action of acetic-acid bacteria that convert alcohol to acetic acid and ethyl acetate. Contrary to commonly held belief, all commercial table wines have a certain amount of volatile acidity; it is simply that, below a certain level, volatile acidity is not perceptible. In most countries there are upper limits of volatile acidity imposed by regulation, ranging between 1.2 and 1.5 grams per liter (expressed as acetic acid).

The threshold at which a taster can detect volatile acidity will vary according to the volume of other aromatic and flavoring compounds in a wine: it will be easiest to detect (at around 0.4 grams per liter) in a light-bodied dry white wine, hardest to detect (with a threshold of around 0.6 grams per liter) in a full-bodied red wine or in intensely sweet table wines (which usually have very high levels of volatile acidity – above 1 gram per liter – and need those high levels to prevent the wine from cloying by giving it a certain degree of "cut").

The effect of volatile acidity is to lift both the aroma and flavor of wine; at low levels it is beneficial, at high levels destructive. Once it has formed, there is little that can be done to reduce it; any chemical reduction will also reduce the fixed acids in the wine.

pH

Effect on color and flavor

Adjustment of pH

Volatile acidity

Tasting VA

The Changes of Age

A major caveat at the outset: this chapter does not take into account the screwcap revolution, which is discussed at length on pages 227–34. The vast majority of aged wines employ corks; it will be another 20 years before some collectors' cellars have a significant proportion of screwcap or other "New Age" closures, and even then such cellars are far more likely to be located in the New World than the Old.

From the moment a technically sound still table wine, white or red, is corked in its bottle, two things will happen: it will progressively lose primary fruit and secondary fermentation flavors and oak aromas and tastes, and (up to a certain point) its aromas and flavors will become more complex. Complexity comes through the formation of tertiary compounds brought about by the largely unseen chemical changes that take place as the wine ages.

The chemistry of bottle development

The chemistry behind the reductive and oxidative changes that take place in the bottle as the wine ages is very complex, and not fully understood. The problem is that it is not easy to relate the theoretical science of the chemical changes that occur as wine ages to the changes in wine color and in other sensory characteristics that we recognize as wine development. Many hundreds of compounds have been identified in wine, and the chemical changes that occur to many of them are interlinked or are dependent on each other such that an almost infinite number of chemical reactions are possible. To complicate the matter further, the manner and rate at which the chemical changes occur will be strongly influenced by the storage conditions of the wine, particularly the temperature.

What is clear is that any oxygen stored in the headspace, the cork or in solution (dissolved oxygen) when a wine is bottled will be rapidly consumed by chemical reactions in the wine. The rate is temperature-dependent: at 68°F (20°C) it will take 14 days, at 37°F (3°C) three months; it would be expected to be faster in red wines containing high concentrations of color and tannins compared to light white wines with low phenolic content. While the oxidative impact of this consumption may not be immediately apparent in wines bottled with the low concentrations of oxygen achievable with modern bottling equipment, a cascade of reactions will have been triggered that will be critical in determining the sensory characteristics of the wine for many years to come – indeed, for the remainder of the wine's life. However, in cases where a large amount of oxygen is introduced at bottling, oxidation may rapidly become apparent, and in such cases that wine's longevity will have been compromised.

In red wines

The tannins and anthocyanins interact with each other, leading to the color change of a red wine from the vivid purple-red of youth to the dark red of full maturity, thence to the brick red or tawny red of old age. This is brought about by the progressive aggregation into ever-larger molecular structures of the anthocyanins and tannins, which gradually form a fine sediment and ultimately a heavy crust or deposit, which falls to the bottom of the bottle. Obviously enough, the greater the starting level of such phenols, the greater the potential for change, reaching its highest expression with vintage port, its lowest with a carefully made Riesling or fine Champagne. A concurrent but less visible change is the softening of the flavor of the tannins as they, too, polymerize.

The second most important change is that of esterification, which is unseen because it has no effect on the color of the wine. It, too, involves the interaction of oxygen, this time with acids and alcohol to form esters and aldehydes. Recent research confirms the previously held view of the majority of scientists that esters are of prime importance in shaping the bouquet of wine. The process of esterification has only a minimal effect on the acidity, pH and alcohol of the wine. Contrary to widely held belief, acid does not diminish; certainly it initially appears to soften, but this is principally due to changes in the other components of the wine (which gain in complexity) and only to a minor degree due to chemical change per se. Indeed, at the very end of the life of a wine, the acidity tends to become more obvious as the other flavor components degrade.

In white wines

Because white wines have almost no anthocyanins, and are very much lower than red wines in phenols (including tannins), the opportunity for change is much more limited, and much less well understood. Indeed, the whole subject of color in white wine is something of a mystery. While it is relatively easy to account for the full yellow color of a Chardonnay that has been given extended skin contact (24 to 36 hours) before pressing, and has then been barrel-fermented, it is much less easy to explain why a dry Riesling, made in a fashion that reduces the phenolic content to an absolute minimum, has any color at all.

Changes in color

The explanation, such as it is, is the presence of a yellow pigment found in the skin of a white grape: a form of glycoside called a flavone. The difficulty is that flavones are present only in trace quantities in the juice and in the finished wine. There is no dispute, though, about the inhibiting effect on color development of high concentrations of carbon dioxide (usually short-lived) and of sulfur dioxide (the higher the starting level, the longer lasting the effect). Both will cause the wine to retain its pale, green-gold or yellow-green color of youth for far longer than wines with smaller concentrations. As they develop in bottle, wines that started with low phenolic levels will gradually become more golden-hued, exceptionally fine wines often shot with green and seeming to glow from within. Those with higher phenolic levels (particularly wines made with skin contact) will rapidly assume a deep yellow color, moving toward an almost orange-yellow (like a dark egg yolk) at four or five years of age. In both instances white wines are intriguingly different from their red counterparts: the latter become progressively lighter with age, the former progressively darker.

A third possible development is the browning that occurs in wines that in due course become oxidized or maderized, often due to insufficient sulfur dioxide. A substance called catechin is the major component of flavones in white wines and is highly susceptible to oxidative browning. It hardly needs saying that color development of this kind is not desirable, and is always associated with a loss of flavor intensity.

Variety and type will also play a role: Gewürztraminers, Pinot Gris and Muscats often have a faintly pink or bronze tinge, while wines affected by botrytis are usually deeper in color at all stages of their development.

Changes in aroma

Both white and red wines undergo progressive changes from the time the grapes are crushed. Smelling unfermented grape juice may or may not be a rewarding task: some juices (for example, Muscat à Petits Grains, Gewürztraminer and Sauvignon Blanc) proclaim their variety, others (notably Chardonnay) do not. Chardonnay juice gives off little more than a smell vaguely reminiscent of hay.

The next stage is the secondary aroma evolved during fermentation. This is usually extraordinarily intense (once one clears the masking effect of the volumes of carbon dioxide continuously liberated from fermenting wine), but is frequently strongly influenced by the yeast. Cold-fermenting Chardonnay using an inoculated yeast, such as Prise de Mousse, is a wonderfully exotic cocktail of grapefruit and sundry other tropical fruits, the taste (with 4 or 5 degrees of unfermented sugar, enlivened by as much gas as one will ever find in Champagne) no less seductive. In Beaujolais they have a word for this indulgence – the drinking of sweet and fizzy half-fermented wine. They call it *Paradis*, until, that is, its potent laxative qualities take effect.

How quickly a white wine loses these fermentation aromas depends to a large degree on what the winemaker does next. A Riesling that is kept under a protective blanket of carbon dioxide after a long, slow fermentation and bottled early will often have a closed, almost sweaty aroma which can only be described as "armpit". It is a New World characteristic much disliked by German Riesling-makers who aver that such wines should be deliberately slightly oxidized to eliminate this character. Such wines may also have a touch of *pétillance* from the ample supplies of dissolved carbon dioxide.

Chardonnay kept on yeast lees and subjected to regular stirring or *bâtonnage* will also retain fermentation-yeast aromas unless and until the reductive (oxygen-absorbing) effect of the lees is terminated by racking. So indeed will Muscadet bottled *sur lie*, in other words bottled direct off its lees, with the concomitant generous dose of carbon dioxide.

"Bottle-shock"   If a wine is bottled with these characteristics it will retain them for some years, and quite possibly never entirely lose the better components of them. If, on the other hand, it is either deliberately or accidentally partially oxidized before it is bottled (or very often as it *is* bottled), these complex secondary aromas will be severely diminished. Certainly the fermentation and yeast aromas will disappear, and the underlying fruit aroma will be much diminished. The latter may partially return with age; "bottle-shock" is a well-known phenomenon which occurs no matter how skilfully a wine is bottled. But it is a fact of life that more white wines are spoiled at bottling than at any other stage of their making, simply through inadvertent oxidation.

The other variable is sulphur dioxide. This is perceptible only as such in its free form, and gives that distinctive prickle or sharp sting in the nose and throat when present in excessive amounts. It gradually diminishes with age as it becomes chemically bound; it is largely responsible for the hint of cabbage in many white Burgundies, or for the flinty, gravelly aroma of Chablis. A small degree of sulphur can and often does merge into the wine as part of the complexity of its flavour, as a positive addition to its character. All too often, though, it dominates the wine, severely detracting from the fruit aromas which one can almost see struggling to escape. Only age can cure the defect, and then no more than partially, for a stale, slightly sickly aftertaste is always there as a giveaway.

Bouquet   Ignoring the special effects of sulphur dioxide (and heavy new-oak influence), bottle-age brings the development of tertiary aroma or bouquet. In fact, the basic distinction used throughout this book is between the primary and secondary aromas (often lumped together under the simple classification of primary) on the one hand, and bouquet on the other. This second stage is often referred to as "vinous", in contrast to "fruity"; it reflects the chemical changes that occur in maturing wine discussed earlier.

In broad terms, the aroma softens and gradually becomes either more honeyed, nutty, smoky, or toasty, according to the variety. Riesling may or may not develop a kerosene character; sometimes it simply becomes toasty. Semillon may take on a strong honeyed/nutty bouquet which gives all the appearance of being derived from oak, even though the wine has never been in oak of any description. Chardonnay gains in complexity on a scale more or less reflecting its quality; it can become intensely honeyed while still retaining some of its primary fruit, which may have been anywhere in the grapefruit/melon/peach/fig spectrum.

Changes in taste   Changes in flavour echo and reflect those of the bouquet, but are as much tactile as they are simply to do with taste. From the exuberant, lively, crisp, tingling acidity of youth, the wine takes on a progressively more languorous cast, becoming more honeyed (in feel and flavour) and soft, before commencing the downhill slide as the fruit sweetness starts to break up and the wine slowly dries out.

These changes reflect underlying polymerization and esterification. If there is any weakness in the cork, the intermediate stage is often referred to as maderization, reflecting the gradual seepage of oxygen into the bottle as the space between cork and wine (known as the ullage) increases. Sometimes a partial vacuum forms; sometimes maderization (or oxidation) simply doesn't occur: it is one of the lotteries of opening an old, partially ullaged bottle. It may be great; it may be quite undrinkable.

How quickly white wines age in bottle depends upon a host of variables: pH, sulfur dioxide levels, storage conditions, quality of cork, grape variety and winemaking methods. The effect of higher or lower yield is by no means to be ruled out either. One of the great misconceptions is that white wines do not repay cellaring. Some do not, but many are just as long-lived as red wines. The German Rieslings of earlier centuries (when yields were much lower) were the longest-lived of all wines; good 1971s (conspicuously), 1983s and 1990s are latter-day examples of fine wines still at their peak. The Chenin Blanc wines of the Loire Valley (particularly the sweet and *liquoreux*) have taken over the mantel from Germany, comfortably living for 50 years. Australian Semillon is frequently majestic at 20 years of age, many Rieslings likewise. Quite simply, white wines can age superbly. Many, just like closed-in mature reds, need decanting to allow them to catch their breath.

There is an immense range of color in young red wine. The grape variety is decisive, but pH and winemaking practices (not least sulfur dioxide additions) also significantly affect both the new wine color and its subsequent changes.

Pinot Noir has the lightest and most unstable color of the great varieties, while Cabernet Sauvignon and Nebbiolo are among the strongest-colored. Some cross-bred *Vitis vinifera* varieties such as Ruby Cabernet, Chambourcin and Alicante Bouschet have particularly striking colors, either in hue or in density. In between there are over 20 recognized shades of red. But it is not simply a question of color as one finds it on an artist's or house-painter's color sheet; clarity (or brilliance) and density are equally important, and tell you almost as much about the wine as does hue.

Wines low in pH have a much more brilliant aspect than do high-pH wines, which become progressively duller as the pH rises. This dullness has nothing at all to do with sediment or suspended particulate matter. Nor does it reflect the fact that low-pH wines require less sulfur dioxide to preserve them from bacterial attack; sulfur dioxide can strip or reduce color in young wine (usually temporarily), but it does not affect the clarity or brilliance of a wine.

Red wine color derives not from the pulp of the grape (the rare exceptions are so-called *teinturiers*) but from the skins, and the effectiveness of the winemaker in leaching the color from the skins will determine (primarily) the density and (secondarily) the hue. There is much debate about the best method of extracting color: should it be sought before the start of fermentation, during fermentation or after? There are proponents of all three. Should it be extracted by fermentation temperatures under 68°F (20°C), between between 68°F and 82°F (20°C to 28°C) or between 82°F and 90°F (28°C to 32°C)? Once again, there are three schools of thought. Is sulfur dioxide the friend or the foe of color? It can be both.

Many drinkers, particularly Americans, believe that the color should be dense and deep purple-red. Any wine that is light in color, and in particular one that has brick or tawny tints, is considered either inferior or "over-the-hill." It is the Achilles' heel of Pinot Noir, and no doubt the genesis of the pointed comment by the late André Noblet (of the Domaine de la Romanée-Conti) about the irrelevance of its color.

It is a simplistic view, one with a sufficient grain of truth to make it plausible, but no more than that. What is important is that the color should be brilliant, that it should have neither black nor blue tinges, that the development of brick or tawny tints should be consistent with the age of the wine, and the depth consistent with the grape variety and source. For it is perfectly possible to overextract color and flavor, producing a coarse, unbalanced and bitter wine that age will not cure; by the time the wine softens, the fruit has dried out, leaving a mere shell.

There is a progressive shift from purple to brown, from dark to light, during the lifetime of any red wine; again the changes are caused by the polymerization of the anthocyanins and colored tannins into progressively larger agglomerates, which finally fall out of solution as a deposit. Anthocyanins have very little flavor; it is the tannins (both in colored and noncolored forms) that primarily affect flavor.

The spectrum of reds

Unlike white wine, a red lightens with age. This immature red Bordeaux is still a rich, dark color.

This mature red Bordeaux has turned a lighter, brick red color.

Changes in color

Nonetheless, the progressive change in hue and lightening of color are a strong indication of the likely changes in aroma and flavor, and it is here that a knowledge of the comparative performance of the same or similar wine is all-important. If there are two bottles of the same old wine, and one is much paler in color than the other, it is highly probable it will be of much lesser quality – even if the ullage (or fill-level) is the same or better than the deeper-colored wine.

Changes in aroma　　It is truly remarkable that so much of each year's production of Bordeaux should pass through six or seven rapid-fire sales steps and reach the consumer as "future," or *primeur*, offerings a little over six months after the grapes were harvested, and a full year before the wine is finally fined, filtered and bottled. Or that the reputation (and price) of each year's Burgundy is so much influenced by the annual auction at the Hospices de Beaune, held on the third Sunday of November, less than two months after the end of harvest.

When the Bordeaux reds are first tasted and traded, they are very probably finishing their malolactic fermentation, with all the off-aromas and flavors this brings in its wake. The Burgundies will have barely finished their primary fermentation, and only a few will have initiated the malolactic. If one is a very experienced taster, one can form a good idea of the overall quality and style of the vintage, and make a pretty shrewd guess about the future of each individual wine. But a final decision on the part of the consumer to buy, based upon hearsay opinion formed thousands of miles away?

The futures market has become steadily more sophisticated over the past 25 years; more and more experts have their say, all connected via the Internet, allowing comparison opinion shopping. If you buy the best wines from the best vintages, the future risk to wallet or palate is minimal, provided you can afford the purchase in the first place. Bargain hunting from "newly discovered" gems in lesser vintages has a high risk that extends to better-known producers in years of mixed success such as 1999, 2002 and 2004.

This digression is prompted by the fact that the aroma of a very young red wine is profoundly influenced by its malolactic fermentation, and seldom pleasantly so – the opposite of a young white wine. Not until the wine nears the end of its allotted period in oak does its raw power start to soften, allowing the taster to form a reliable and accurate view of its future. It is different for the winemaker and the very experienced professional consultant or wholesale wine buyer: they can draw not only on their knowledge of what they are smelling and tasting that day, but what they have tasted in the same château over the previous 20 or more years, and how those earlier wines (and even older wines) have evolved in bottle. The buyer of a yearling racehorse pays as much attention, if not more, to each horse in the family tree as he does to the youngster nervously skittering about the ring. So it is with a young red wine.

The aroma may show the effects of one or more of hydrogen sulfide, ethyl acetate and aldehyde, surrounded by the sheer raw power of the young wine. If new oak has been used, it will often be "splintery" and unintegrated. While raw tannins do not have an odor of their own, experienced tasters can accurately guess how tannic or astringent the wine is simply by smelling it. All this adds up to a harsh and angular smell (more so for Cabernet Sauvignon, Nebbiolo and Syrah-based wines, less so for Pinot Noir) which still exhibits a mixture of primary and secondary aromas.

The formation of the bouquet is in part triggered by the quite rapid dissipation of the carbon dioxide dissolved in new wine in its barrel. This happens both during racking (quickly) and through maturation in oak (slowly). The other triggers leading to the bouquet are the chemical changes of polymerization and esterification (principally in bottle) and of the associated gentle oxidation (in cask and to a lesser degree in bottle). What was once harsh and angular becomes progressively rounder, softer and more harmonious. After the wine is bottled (and assuming the cork is sound), it is limited to the small amount of oxygen stored in solution, which it rapidly (*see* pages 232–3) depletes in the reductive process of aging. Once again, it should be noted the remainder of this chapter ignores the entirely different consequences of the use of screwcaps (*see* pages 230–4).

The bouquet of a young wine will be powerful, still dominated by the smell of its fruit. It reacts positively to air, and hence to decanting. Normally its bouquet will increase in the decanter for three to four hours in a short burst of polymerization and esterification. An older wine, fully mature and at the height of its power, will have developed an intense bouquet that is a balanced amalgam of fruit and that wonderfully complex matrix of cedary, spirity, earthy esters that proclaim a great wine. Exposure to air for some hours in a decanter may improve it, but it may not. In the absence of recent knowledge of the particular wine, it may be prudent to pull the cork, carefully clean all mold and debris from round the mouth, and sniff the wine in bottle before decanting it. If the smell is sweet, leave well alone and decant it shortly before serving. If the smell is musty, decant it in the hope (and expectation) that the "bottle-stink" will dissipate over the next few hours.

A very old wine is necessarily extremely fragile, and reacts rapidly to exposure to air: here the rule is that you can wait for the wine, but it will not wait for you. In other words, decant and serve it immediately; if there is bottle-stink, wait the 10 or 15 minutes it usually takes for it to diminish, and then capture the wine in the short window during which its ethereal fragrance will be at its greatest. Remember that its storehouse of aroma- and flavor-inducing polyphenols will have been all but exhausted during its long life in bottle.

The eternal fascination of wine lies in its infinite capacity to surprise (or disappoint), in the fact that no two bottles of mature wine will ever be precisely the same. This is the basis of the old French saying, "There are no great old wines; only great old bottles of wine." A few very old wines will be extraordinarily robust; one château proprietor in Bordeaux insisted on opening a particular century-old pre-phylloxera vintage 24 hours before serving it. The dregs in century-old bottles, and even the glasses they were drunk in, have been known to smell sweeter the following morning than in the evening when they were drunk.

Given the correlation between bouquet and taste, it is not surprising that the same chemical changes are responsible for the development (and eventual decline) of taste as for bouquet. The more expert the taster, the more attention he or she will pay to the bouquet in assessing a wine. Some Australian wine judges (who regularly judge up to 200 wines a day in Australia's hard-fought state and national competitions) say that 90 percent of their total knowledge of 90 percent of the wines they judge will come from the bouquet: only for 1 in 10 wines will the taste do more than "top up" the knowledge gained through smelling the wine (without decrying the importance of that last 10 percent). For the 1-in-10 wine, the palate will reveal entirely unsuspected qualities, good or bad; in that circumstance the judge, on reexamining the bouquet, may well find the same character there after all.

American wine journalists frequently use the expression "tannin to lose" in discussing California Cabernet Sauvignons. The same expression arose with 1975 Bordeaux wines; the question with such wines is whether the tannins will soften before the fruit fades – will the process of polymerization take out more fruit than tannin? The majority of the 1975 Bordeaux remain austere and tough. A young red wine may be raw and aggressive – the components may be unintegrated and taste as though they are in separate compartments – but it must be fundamentally in balance at the outset if it is ever to be completely satisfying. If it is, the mouth-puckering, tannic astringency of youth, balanced by the intensity of the primary berry-fruit flavors, will slowly soften. A series of flavors that have an affinity with oak (cedary, cigar box, briary, tobacco) will start to emerge as the exuberant sweet fruit subsides. In fact, these flavors derive just as much, if not more, from the grape as from the oak. At the same time, the finish and aftertaste will become finer yet more intense.

Ultimately these drier flavors will entirely dominate the wine as it starts to decline;

"Bottle-stink"

Changes in taste

Bottles of great Bordeaux stored in their own château's cellars not only survive but continue to improve for up to a century, and then only very gradually fade away. The ideal cellar for indefinite storage (here at Château Margaux in the Médoc) has very high humidity (which soon destroys labels).

all the balancing sweetness will disappear, and the acid (as it did at the very start of the wine's life) will become sharp and aggressive, perhaps "lifted" by the insidious accumulation of acetic acid, especially if the bottle has ullaged. In such a case, chances are that the wine will have begun to oxidize, too. While a sound cork is an effective barrier against oxygen, as it loses its elasticity (after 20 to 25 years in the case of a high-quality cork), the passage of air (and indeed wine) past and through the cork becomes a reality, the destruction of the wine only a matter of time.

External influences on aging

Anyone who has assembled even the most modest collection of wine will have had to grapple with the question of establishing a cellar. It is an acute problem in modern houses in temperate climates, although much less difficult in colder countries with old houses (or better still, castles). One of the most celebrated collections of pre-phylloxera claret was auctioned by Christie's of London in 1971. The wine had been stored undisturbed in the cellars of Glamis Castle in Scotland since its acquisition 100 or so years earlier. The temperature hovered around 46°F (8°C) through most of the year, the humidity near-perfect at around 75 percent. The vast collection of magnums and bottles of Château Lafite and Château Mouton-Rothschild were in extraordinary condition, yet there was no suggestion that they had ever been recorked. Their development had simply been retarded, their condition more like that of a 40- or 50-year-old wine cellared under normal (good) conditions. (In November 2001, James Halliday was one of a group that drank a double-magnum of 1865 Château Lafite from the Earl of Rosebery's cellar at Dalmeny House, where it had remained for 99 years before being sold at Christie's in 1967. The top of the neck had been rewaxed by Berry Brothers in 1932, but the original cork was left in the bottle. The ullage was negligible, and the wine was utterly magnificent, still at the peak of its power.)

Most of us, of course, wish to drink the wine we buy within our lifetimes, and conditions leading to a state of suspended animation are no more desirable than practicable. The ideal cellar will have a year-round temperature of 59°F (15°C) and a humidity around 75 to 80 percent, the two really critical features being the constancy of temperature and the humidity. In other words, a cellar that fluctuates in temperature from 50°F to 64°F (10°C to 18°C) will not be as good as one with a constant 64°F (18°C); if the temperature fluctuation is diurnal, it will indeed be extremely destructive, but even a seasonal variation of this magnitude is highly undesirable.

The reason why temperature fluctuation is so harmful is the expansion and contraction of the fluid contents. While the cork is young and retains full elasticity, it will stoutly resist the buildup of pressure caused by increased temperature. If it is of poor quality, or has a flaw, it will be an ineffective seal from the outset. But even the best of corks gradually lose their resilience and elasticity, finally shrinking to the point where they barely maintain contact with the bottle neck.

Long before the cork has reached this stage, minute quantities of wine will have made their way alongside the cork and (usually) evaporated without trace. In extreme cases a sticky deposit will exude, sometimes corroding the capsule, sometimes being trapped within it. It does not always follow that oxygen will immediately enter the bottle to replace the lost wine: modern bottling machines usually bottle wine under vacuum, withdrawing all the oxygen from the space between the bottom of the cork and the top of the wine. This vacuum may be maintained for some considerable time, and even be enhanced with age. It is where the vacuum is at least partially maintained that old wines with significant ullage (as the air-space is called) can show no ill effects; where fresh air has entirely filled the space (the amount of ullage being the same), it is highly probable there will have been some deterioration. A second complicating factor is the period of time over which the ullage develops: the quicker it deepens, the less the chances for the wine. Hence Christie's of London publishes a cautionary diagram at the front of each of its wine-auction catalogs, showing what it regards as normal ullage for a wine of a given age.

The technique of recorking

Even First Growth châteaus have become reluctant to officially recork old wines from outside their own cellars. The propensity of Americans to litigate at the drop of a hat has forced the châteaus to realize there may be an implied warranty that the wine is of prime quality consistent with the high fill-level that follows topping up and recorking. So do-it-yourself may be the only option.

The bottles to be topped up and recorked should be stood vertically for at least a week. The capsule should be cut and the neck of the bottle and top of the cork carefully cleaned, using a fine blade to scrape away hard debris, a damp cloth for less obstinate refuse. One bottle, which is to provide the topping-up wine, should be opened, and a pipette-full (approximately 5 mL) withdrawn (but without moving the bottle from the vertical) and tasted. If it is sound, the air-space should be filled with nitrogen from a small cylinder and tube.

One by one the remaining bottles should be carefully uncorked; have a long, narrow spoon or similar device to retrieve any cork fragments that break off into the bottles about to be recorked. If the wine is more than 20 years old, add 10 parts per million of sulfur dioxide (with another pipette), fill the air-space with nitrogen, fill the bottle via a pipette, and then immediately recork it before moving on to the next wine. Leave all the recorked bottles standing up for at least 24 hours to allow the cork to fully expand, and thereby prevent weeping along the tiny creases that all hand-operated corkers make in the sides of the cork. The key to the procedure has been the minimal movement of any of the bottles during the process, thereby reducing the amount of oxidation. It follows that it should be carried out in a cool place free from drafts; most probably the cellar itself.

The rationale for recorking

The aim of recorking is to minimize the oxygen that comes in contact with the wine. As fresh oxygen becomes available, the normal chemical aging processes are unduly accelerated, and other far less desirable ones may be triggered. These include the buildup of acetic acid and simple oxidation. What is more, off-flavors (typically mushroom- and mold-accented) from the cork itself and from the cellar (particularly if it is moist and harbors mold growth) are likely to taint the wine.

It is to prevent undue ullage occurring that many Bordeaux château proprietors recork their cellar reserves every 25 to 30 years; and that Château Lafite occasionally sends senior cellar staff on odysseys around the world recorking old Lafites with branded corks. Penfolds, too, regularly stages recorking clinics for older bottles of Grange. The process will only be certified if the wine is sound. If the wine has been recorked regularly by skilled tradesmen, and if it has been topped up with identical wine, recorking should guarantee a wine in excellent condition. But what if abnormal ullage had developed before the wine was topped up? It might already be acetic or oxidized, and topping up and recorking it will achieve nothing.

What, on the other hand, if the bottle used to top up is itself out of condition? Or, as is rumored to happen, what if a much younger wine is used to top up? This practice is known as "refreshing," and is said to have once been common in Burgundy. It may indeed improve the old wine. Whether it is acceptable depends on whether authenticity is your first priority.

Wine Faults

Wine fascinates us simply because it is so complex and ever-changing. The interaction between more than 500 substances affecting the flavor and structure of wine makes it very difficult to assess the importance of any of them taken in isolation. Champagne blenders know the magic they can create by blending 40 or 50 different base wines, and will never presume to predict the result of the inclusion or rejection of even one of those wines. Nor will they exclude from consideration a wine that, on its own, may appear to have shortcomings or a minor fault. They know from long experience that it may blend symbiotically with the other wines and add something unique and desirable. Consider, then, the underlying web of differing chemical and biochemical influences at work in each of the individual wines in the blend, and one has a science of such complexity that it can be of practical use only if it is treated as an art.

There are a considerable number of wine faults. Here, many of the more obscure faults described in textbooks are ignored, as they are (mercifully) seldom found in the mainstream of today's commercial wines. Visit an Italian or French farmhouse where the patron makes a little wine for his family and friends, and sooner or later you will find the full array of faults – most probably sooner.

Varietal character or fault?

One of the siren songs of wine is the appeal of the new taste, the new aroma. There is something strangely powerful and exciting about a wine from a region or a grape variety encountered by an experienced taster for the first time. Old-vine Malbec from Argentina; Saperavi, Tannat and Tempranillo blended in Australia's King Valley; Viognier from Greece, or cofermented with Syrah (Shiraz) almost anywhere (outside Côte Rôtie); Zweigelt from Austria – the list goes on and on, some ancient, some new, but all different.

Strangely, so it is with at least some wine faults. In bygone decades, Australian makers of red wine had to contend with hydrogen sulfide formation in their wines that, if left untreated, often forms mercaptans. These give rise to a range of flavors ranging from rotten eggs to burned rubber – none in the least attractive. The occurrence of hydrogen sulfide was once common in the Hunter Valley's red wines, and the winemakers (and the consumers) had, in the past, gradually come to accept it as no more nor less than part of Hunter Valley style, a hallmark of its *typicité*. It gave rise to descriptions of Hunter reds such as "sweaty saddle" (or the smell of a horse saddle after a hard day's ride), earthy, tarry, farmyardy – none intended to be so much pejorative as simply descriptive.

Little wonder, then, that English and American professional tasters were wont to accept the unusual smell and taste of a young Hunter red as simply a strange and exciting manifestation of regional and (if the wine was made from Shiraz, then known locally as "Hermitage") varietal character.

Things are very different these days, with pure fruit aromas and flavors, and regionality in the form of *sotto voce* earthiness as the wines age.

Volatile acidity

No better example can be given of the fine and ever-shifting line between fault and virtue, hate and love, than volatile acidity (or volatility). It is present in all wine to a lesser or greater degree; the threshold of its sensory identification varies greatly from inexperienced to experienced tasters; and its interpretation, or evaluation, by tasters of similar experience varies no less. At the crudest, give two wines to the man or woman in the street, wines that are identical except that one has a normal level of volatility (accepting for the moment that there is such a level), the other a slightly elevated level. It is quite certain the latter wine will be preferred, even though the highly trained taster would (first) recognize the volatility and (second) probably reject or criticize it. The late Professor Peynaud, in his masterly work *The Taste of Wine* (Macdonald & Co., 1987), unequivocally took the latter approach:

> *Some people would have it that a slightly high level of volatile acidity is necessary, that it accentuates the bouquet of some wines or even takes its place. Such people are bad tasters who are talking nonsense. Either they lack sensitivity or they do not know how to tell good from bad.*

Volatility (or the presence of acetic acid and ethyl acetate) is caused in three ways at different times and to different degrees. The initial level (present in all commercial wines) stems from their inevitable formation as byproducts of yeast activity during the primary fermentation. The next cause is the malolactic fermentation, and the last, and most destructive, is bacterial activity: either lactic bacteria (which operate anerobically) or acetic bacteria that, in the presence of air, readily oxidize alcohol to acetic acid and ethyl acetate. The action of these bacteria can easily lift acetic acid levels to the legal limits of 0.92 to 0.98 grams per liter prescribed by the European Union.

Causes of volatility

Acetic acid and ethyl acetate are usually produced concurrently; the legal limits are expressed in terms of acetic acid because it is much easier to measure. Simply because ethyl acetate is much more volatile (and thus more easily smelled), it is often only transiently present, sometimes grossly disfiguring a fermenting wine, but disappearing shortly after fermentation comes to an end.

The aroma and taste of volatility

The level at which volatility becomes apparent varies with the wine (0.4 grams per liter in a light-bodied wine to 0.8 grams per liter in a full-bodied red) and, of course, with the taster. At low levels it manifests itself as an ever-so-slight piquancy. As the level increases, the piquancy becomes sharpness, the slight prickle in the bouquet intensifies and starts to muffle the other aromas; finally, the wine has a vinegary, fiery, sourly acidic finish to the palate, and a solvent-like aroma that many will readily identify as model airplane plane glue or nail-polish remover.

Professor Peynaud was in no doubt that, if volatility can be detected, it is by definition at an unacceptable level. One suspects that, in putting the proposition so trenchantly, he was wearing his schoolteacher's hat, endeavoring to instill certain basic rules and disciplines into raw acolytes, and that his message to an honors class of postgraduate students might have been a little softer.

The late Max Schubert, the celebrated maker and creator of Australia's greatest red wine, Penfolds Grange, deliberately induced higher levels of volatility in Grange by leaving the bungs loose in the casks in the first year of the life of the wine. He argued that the very high levels of extract, the strength of the fruit flavor from the low-yielding vines, the strong new American oak influence and the high tannin levels needed to be cut by a certain degree of volatility to prevent the flavor from cloying. One of his three most celebrated vintages, the 1971 (the others being 1953 and 1955), trembled on the brink: its level was at the legal limit, and – according to the taster and the occasion – it either lifted the wine to the very heights or plunged it into an abyss.

Again, except in old wines, volatility seldom plagues the reds of Bordeaux, but is often seen as a problem in Burgundy. In analytical terms the levels are likely to be similar: it is just that the background structure in Bordeaux is so much more substantial. In Piedmont, traditionally made wines manage to carry off high levels with style; so do such idiosyncratic wines as Château Musar from the Lebanon or Vega Sicilia from Castile. At the end of the day, two questions have to be asked. First, can you detect volatility? Second, does it detract from the balance of (and your enjoyment of) the wine? If both answers are yes, the wine is faulty.

Below: *However good the quality of corks, their useful life is probably over after 20 to 25 years. To avoid the risk of air getting in and spoiling the wine, recorking is necessary, done by hand to keep disturbance of the wine to an absolute minimum.*

The prevention and cure of volatility

The development of reverse-osmosis technology, which is also used to remove water from must or juice, allows the reduction of acetic acid to whatever level the winemaker stipulates. Maintenance of adequate levels of sulfur dioxide, the exclusion of oxygen, cool to cold storage in cask and an appropriate pH level will help prevent the development of unwanted levels of volatility. Once a wine is bottled, prevention of undue ullage (allied with storage under stable, cool conditions) will protect it.

Oxidation

Louis Pasteur was the first scientist to demonstrate the harmful effects of oxygen on table wine, to characterize it as public enemy number one. It is accordingly a fault that most wine-lovers have heard of and most probably think they understand. But there is one confusion that traps the unwary: there is a world of difference between the oxidation of juice or must (before fermentation) and of wine (after fermentation). Here we are concerned only with oxidation after fermentation (and to a minor degree with certain specialized forms of oxidation that occur during fermentation).

The causes of oxidation

There are two principal types of oxidation: chemical and microbiological. Chemical oxidation is a two-stage process. First, oxygen is taken into and dissolved in the wine. Depending on a number of factors, it will then slowly or quickly react with phenols in the wine, causing chemical changes principally seen as a loss in aroma and flavor, color change, and degradation.

Microbiological oxidation is caused by bacteria also being present during the process of chemical oxidation, and results in additional chemical or biochemical changes. One example is the action of acetic bacteria oxidizing ethyl alcohol to acetic acid and ethyl acetate; another is the conversion of ethyl alcohol to acetaldehyde, which in the case of sherry (*see* pages 188–9) is an altogether desirable reaction: the *flor* yeast film responsible for the change is but a special form of mycoderma, a surface growth that, if unchecked, causes a distinctive stale taste in red wine. (Happily, it is easily controlled, and only prolonged neglect will lead to permanent damage.)

Oxygen can be absorbed by wine in almost any circumstance in which it is brought into contact with it, but under certain conditions the rate (and amount) of absorption is increased. Any handling involving movement or agitation will have this effect: racking, filtration (if misused) and transport are three examples. Regular visitors to the cellars of France who taste wine from the barrel will have steeled themselves to the apology from the *maître de chai*: "This wine needs racking" or "This wine has just been racked."

Oxidases

Finally, there are specialized forms of oxidation that are triggered by specialized forms of enzymes known as oxidases that are found in the grapes. The first is tyrosinase, common in all kinds of fruits and invariably present in grapes to a lesser or greater degree. Commonly called polyphenoloxidase, it is responsible (for example) for the browning of a freshly cut apple, and no less for the rapid browning of grape juice that has not been protected by sulfur dioxide. It is relatively easily controlled, and creates significant problems only with certain varieties; indeed, as we have seen, most Italian and some Californian winemakers allow it to carry out its work on white juice musts (in California particularly with Chardonnay). One rarely hears of it in red winemaking, even though its largely unseen occurrence is quite widespread. Polyphenoloxidase acts only on grape juice; it ceases to exist by the time the wine has finished its fermentation.

The other group of oxidases is laccase, which derives from *Botrytis cinerea* and which is altogether more serious. It is difficult to control, and leads to dramatic and irreversible changes in red wine color, the most obvious being premature fading and browning. Some Burgundies from the troubled 1983 vintage were prime examples, although traditional winemakers know what to do in such years: close up the vats at the end of fermentation and go hunting for a month. Chemists now understand why this apparent neglect was precisely the right response. Laccase survives fermentation, but slowly loses its potency in the presence of alcohol (and sulfur dioxide). It needs oxygen to do its harmful work, and a wine at the end of fermentation is saturated with carbon dioxide. If the wine is not moved, pumped or handled, it will remain largely immune to the action of laccase, which, over a period of four weeks or so, will gradually be denatured and disappear.

Oxidation is usually more serious for white than red wine, simply because its consequences are less easily reversible and because the effect (while lasting) may initially be less obvious. If a white wine is highly protected by sulfur dioxide and ascorbic acid while it is still unfermented juice, but is subsequently oxidized as wine, its color will darken dramatically; even if it is protected as wine, its color will deepen in the course of maturation. If, on the other hand, the juice was either deliberately oxidized or incompletely protected, its subsequent color development (given equal exposure to oxygen as a wine made from protected juice) will be much less. What interpretation or value one places on these color changes is another matter. Not so long ago, New Zealand Chardonnays were made with reasonably long skin contact and often had a degree of botrytis present; these were typically deep yellow at two years of age. The learning curve was rapid, and the better New Zealand Chardonnays of today develop far more slowly, especially given the fact that they will almost certainly be screwcapped.

The aroma and flavor of a white wine will be stripped, modified or hardened by oxidation. Oxidation of the juice before fermentation will reduce the range and intensity of flavor in finished wine; in some cases this effect may be intentional and desirable. Oxidation after fermentation is in a different category: if not reversed by the use of ascorbic acid and sulfur dioxide, it will lead to a dull, hard, stale character in the wine. It may happen at any stage up to and including bottling; if it does, the consequence will be largely irreversible, although obviously the degree of oxygen absorption (and of consequent chemical change) will be critical in determining the end result. All wines suffer a degree of bottle-shock when bottled, even where state-of-the-art bottling procedures give them maximum protection from oxidation. Properly bottled wines do recover in due course, producing the bouquet and flavor one is entitled to expect.

Red wines (other than those affected by laccase) are much more resistant, if only due to their much higher phenol levels. Nonetheless, careless winemaking can entirely destroy a potentially fine wine through this one fault. Oxidation will manifest itself in a browning or dulling of the color, the development of an aroma of aldehyde and a progressive dulling of the fruit flavor. Aldehydes in dry table wines are far removed (from the taster's viewpoint) from those in wood-aged fortified wines such as sherry and tawny port. Once recognized, the smell of aldehyde in a red wine is never forgotten: it is a stale, bitter aroma, sometimes likened to stale oil.

Sulfur dioxide both inhibits and can (in certain circumstances) partially cure oxidation. If its use in white wine is supplemented by the use of ascorbic acid, it becomes even more effective. Restoration of sulfur dioxide levels in red wines that have been chemically or microbiologically oxidized, and have developed aldehyde aromas in cask, usually promotes recovery once the source of oxygen has been removed.

Red wine can in fact be positively improved by deliberate exposure to oxygen, an approach most obviously taken during racking. If a wine has become stale in cask, and in particular if it has developed sulfides or other off-aromas, the typical French reaction is to splash the wine through the air into a vat or other holding vessel before returning it to cask. If successful, this technique will rid the wine of the offending odor, but will initially mute the aroma and dull the flavor; in the longer term (if it is not overdone) it will add to the complexity and subtly round the texture.

The effect comes into sharp relief when compared with reductively (or protectively) handled New World red wines. The less exalted of these may spend the first six months in a stainless-steel vat, during which time they undergo their malolactic fermentation, and are then racked, fined and filtered star-bright. They are then put into barrels for six or nine months, with the bungs turned to two o'clock (so they are under the level of the wine), and are left until they are returned to vat for final adjustments: cold-stabilization, another filtration and bottling.

The consequences of oxidation

Modern high-speed automated bottling lines are expensive, but are essential tools in an increasingly cost-competitive wine world.

The prevention and cure of oxidation

These wines are extremely pure in flavor and aroma, but have an unmade, callow and rather hard edge to their character that bottle-age may or may not cure.

The point with both white and red wines is that the die is cast once the wine is in bottle; much can be done to prevent or cure oxidation (and its consequences) up to this stage, but the potential for recovery in bottle is extremely limited. An oxidized wine may partially, briefly recover, but its ultimate demise will be hastened significantly, and it will never approach its true potential. It is certainly one of the least forgivable faults in red wines, simply because (laccase excepted) it is so easily prevented.

Sulfides and mercaptans

One of the prime sources of hydrogen sulfide (and the more complex sulfur compounds that follow in its wake) is elemental sulfur. In many parts of the world, elemental sulfur is used extensively in vineyards to control powdery mildew or oidium. Sulfur, lime and copper, the three traditional sprays of France, are sanctioned by organic growers, and are once again increasingly widely used throughout the New World as grape-growers seek to pull back from the systemic and more sophisticated chemical and biochemical sprays whose long-term side-effects are uncertain. In the New World, winemakers will normally cease using sulfur at least one month before harvest, but there is no withholding period prescribed by regulation, and less well-informed growers do not always follow prudent practice.

Another source of elemental sulfur is the use of sulfur matches, wicks or discs ignited and suspended in casks to disinfect them and prevent the multiplication of acetic acid bacteria. These devices are still commonly used in Europe and to a lesser degree in the New World; they lead to minute fragments of sulfur exploding off the side of the wick or disc and dropping to the bottom of the cask, vat or barrel.

The cause of hydrogen sulfide and mercaptans

Hydrogen sulfide is produced to a degree in almost every fermentation. Even if no elemental sulfur is present, the yeast breaks down certain amino acids and in the course of doing so triggers the formation of hydrogen sulfide.

Any sulfur present is similarly reduced to hydrogen sulfide by the yeasts during fermentation, although any practicing winemaker will tell you that not only does the amount of hydrogen sulfide vary greatly according to the type of yeast used (or the range of wild yeasts naturally present), but that the amount produced by a given yeast or yeasts is unpredictable, and finally that even during the course of fermentation hydrogen sulfide may appear and disappear with equal rapidity. If left untreated, though, it readily reacts with other chemicals in the wine to form more complex sulfur compounds usually called mercaptans, some of which are extremely difficult to remove.

The aroma and taste of mercaptans

The aroma of hydrogen sulfide needs no comment: every child's nose has wrinkled at the smell of rotten egg gas, however or wherever produced. Mercaptans are far more varied, but can be smelled in even tinier concentrations: they are some of the most potent substances known to man, and may be detected in the most minute concentrations. They assume an ungodly range of totally unpleasant personalities: burned rubber, tar, rotten game, fowl manure, rancid garlic, leather and gravel are some of the aromas, while the taste always has a bitter, astringent finish to add to whatever particular flavor it may have.

Of the three deadly wine sins, mercaptan is the least forgivable fault. A little volatility or a little oxidation may make a positive contribution to the flavor and complexity of wine. But despite the famous dictum, "Great Burgundy smells of shit," most believe that mercaptan at any level of perception detracts from a wine. It toughens and obscures the taste; in a recently bottled red wine it may be confused with tannin (particularly on the finish of the taste).

Cure or prevention of hydrogen sulfide and mercaptans

It is remarkable how little discussion there is about mercaptans, either in popular or technical books dealing with European wines. And in truth – although accidents have been known – the occurrence is not great. The likely reason would appear to be the fact that the most effective prophylactic (and cure) for hydrogen sulfide is copper. The most commonly used spray to control both mildew and oidium is Bordeaux mixture, composed of copper sulfate and lime. It is applied with such enthusiasm that some vineyards actually turn blue toward the end of summer, and of course it provides ample copper to combat the sulfur that is also used. A second and possibly equally important source of copper is the widespread use of brass fittings in taps, pumps and machinery; one of the unsuspected consequences of the gradual replacement of brass by stainless-steel fittings may well prove to be an increase in sulfides and mercaptans.

Hydrogen sulfide is also quite readily oxidized by contact with air; if the wine is a robust red, an aerated racking may quickly dispose of the problem. If it persists, the addition of a carefully controlled quantity of copper is the answer. This is usually added as copper sulfate, which combines with the hydrogen sulfide to produce copper sulfide as a solid precipitate; this is then removed by racking.

Once the hydrogen sulfide has become fixed as a mercaptan, its removal is much more difficult. Silver nitrate works, but it is not a permitted additive in winemaking in many countries. All heavy metals are toxic, and trace residues have to be avoided.

Brettanomyces

The issue of *Brettanomyces* (often shortened to "brett") was recognized and briefly examined in the first edition of this book, but has become far more important in the intervening years, now ranking at the top of preventable wine faults. Brett is a genus of yeast, closely related to but different from *Dekkera*. There are in turn five species of *Brettanomyces*, the most commonly encountered species on grapes and in wine being *Brettanomyces bruxellensis*. In turn, Australian researchers have detected six tribes (or strains) of *Brettanomyces bruxellensis*. In the last two decades of the 20th century and the early years of the 21st, a number of seemingly unconnected developments occurred that have made brett the most common spoilage factor in wine.

Higher alcohol

First, there was a move toward higher natural alcohol in the wines of Old and New Worlds alike, although the specific causes were different and, in some instances, not understood. It would be unfair to simply lay the blame at the feet of American critics such as Robert Parker, but there is no denying that the American taste for dense, fat, rich, alcoholic red wines – particularly Cabernets – influenced many makers in California, Australia and Bordeaux alike to delay picking, and to enthusiastically use reverse-osmosis or vacuum concentration techniques. (Much the same can be said of Syrah and the Rhône Valley family.)

Deliberate or accidental?

Not every winemaker or consumer enjoys such wines, but there are other factors at work that can take discretion out of the equation. Climate change is one; "better" vine canopy manipulation to minimize disease and enhance berry maturation is another; and highly efficient cultured yeast a third. The interrelationship of some or all of these factors varies from place to place; the bottom line is that, for example, elevated levels of alcohol in high-quality Australian Chardonnay are a matter of grave concern. The main response has been to pick the grapes much earlier, and to accept there may be some loss of otherwise desirable flavors.

Less SO$_2$ use

The second trend was a move to lower levels of sulfur dioxide (SO$_2$) additions. Old World use of SO$_2$ was more profligate than that of the New World, but in each case levels came tumbling down. The background was a general move to use fewer chemicals in all phases of grape-growing and winemaking; recognition that the powerful antioxidant and bactericide qualities of SO$_2$ could (at high levels) have downsides for both wine flavor and the sensitivity of some consumers; and a belief that modern analysis methods coupled with strict hygiene and, where needed, sterile filtration could reduce or altogether bypass the need for SO$_2$ additions.

Cork permeability

The third factor is the extreme variability in the oxygen permeability of one-piece natural corks, and thence their inability to retain near-constant levels of bottling SO$_2$. (This issue is discussed in greater detail on page 233.)

Riper, higher-alcohol wines have higher pH levels, and "natural" winemaking philosophies militate against acidification, even where legal, to lower the pH.

Higher pH makes SO$_2$ at any given level less effective; add in the effect of lower starting levels and variable depletion, and you have the perfect scenario for the development of *Brettanomyces*. The sinister and unpredictable rate of SO$_2$ depletion from one bottle to the next (using corks) can result in sporadic (commonly called "random" oxidation) and markedly different levels of brett every bit as devastating as sporadic oxidation, the *coup de grâce* being the development of both.

Brettanomyces: a New World disease?

Partly because some of the early research into the biochemistry of *Brettanomyces* activity in wine was carried out in Australia, and partly because both California and Australia unwittingly exposed themselves to infections for the first time, thus clearly able to see the before and after differences in wine odor and taste, there was a perception that it was much more a problem for the New World than the Old. But in 1992, 1993 and 1995, French researcher Dr. Pascal Chatont published groundbreaking papers. His 1992 paper analyzed 100 well-regarded French wines and found that one-third had levels of brett above the organoleptic threshold. With a certain degree of retrospectivity, it became obvious that characters regarded as giving (desirable or acceptable) *typicité* had altogether more sinister origins.

The biochemistry of Brettanomyces

Brettanomyces creates volatile phenols and fatty acids with strong, unpleasant olfactory characters. The principal culprit is 4-ethyl-phenol (colloquially called 4EP), the presence of which can be readily analyzed and which is accepted as the prime marker for brett activity. A second phenol is 4-ethyl-guaiacol, typically present in concentrations one-tenth of that of 4-ethyl-phenol. The third is isovaleric acid; all three interreact. To complicate matters, individual sensitivity of winemakers to brett varies significantly, and 4-ethyl-guaiacol can increase the sensory impact of 4EP. Nonetheless, the commonly accepted sensory detection level is 420 micrograms per liter, and much lower for experts trained to detect its occurrence. The descriptors most commonly used for 4EP are wet band-aid, game and/or horse-stable aromas, typically coupled with a metallic, sour finish to the taste. None are the least bit pleasant. However, 4-ethyl guiacol confuses the issue with a smoky, spicy aroma that can be quite appealing and confused with high-toast oak. Unfortunately, it is always coupled with the negative impact of 4EP.

Is a little bit of brett a good thing?

Given that *Brettanomyces* has been present as part of the red wine scenery for a very long time in various parts of the world, and accepted by consumers unaware of its nature or causes, there are those who suggest low levels of brett can give desirable complexity to wine. There are two problems with this proposition. First, as we have seen, as sulfur levels deplete, brett growth accelerates. With bottles using corks or cork equivalents (not screwcaps), the level of brett in different bottles of the same wine can, and does, vary significantly. It was a lesson Robert Mondavi learned in the 1980s when it embarked on a no-filtration regime, knowing that brett was present in what seemed at bottling to be acceptable levels, and subsequently grew disastrously in some bottles.

Natural wine vs. industrial wine

The second problem can be described as putting art and science on a collision course. Traditional French (and other) winemakers say it is perfectly possible to kill all yeast activity on the grapes with high doses of SO$_2$; use cultured yeasts with known properties; and sterile-filter the wine prior to bottling. They are convinced this removes taste and *typicité*, and is industrial winemaking devoid of art. Better by far, they say, to accept brett as a part of life.

The opposite view

Australian researchers and winemakers take the opposite view. They have demonstrated it is possible to control *Brettanomyces* within acceptable bounds (indeed, eliminate it entirely) with lower levels of SO$_2$ used at the right time and in the right amount. But it is left to Dr. Chatont to put it most elegantly when he agrees that brett causes loss of fruit and *typicité*. He is reported as saying, "If *Brettanomyces* is able to grow in all the red wines of the planet – and this is the case – then all the wines will have the same odor, which is a pity."

The Australian response to the recognition of the problems posed by brett was typically vigorous, and led by the Australian Wine Research Institute. Part of a whole-of-winemaking approach was to add fewer but larger doses (50 to 60 ppm) of SO_2, *The Australian response* with the post-malolactic addition the most important. From a high point in 1997 of mean concentrations of 4EP of over 1,200 micrograms per liter in all red wines tested by the institute, the concentration had fallen to under 400 micrograms per liter (under sensory threshold levels) by 2002, and has fallen further since. The average level of volatile acidity has also decreased over the same period, reflecting lower bacterial activity. It has also been suggested that the optimum outcome of SO_2 use should be measured by the ratio of free to total SO_2, and achieve a 0.4 target or better. (That target would mean 40 ppm free and a total of 100 ppm, i.e., 60 ppm bound.)

The Achilles' heel of the cork and of some oak casks is trichloroanisole (TCA), which imparts a musty, moldy aroma and flavor. The great problem with TCA is that its level of contamination varies greatly. Even an amateur can recognize a grossly corked bottle of wine, but as the level of contamination reduces, so does the effect. Winemakers are resigned to the fact that a significant number of their wines will be found wanting by consumers who do not realize that the faint bitterness they taste in the wine is in fact a cork mold. If it is a cask mold, the winemakers only have themselves to blame, for the contamination should have been recognized long before the wine went into bottle, and the wine disposed of – down the drain, if need be, for there is no way of removing the TCA taint once it has taken hold.

Mousiness

An alternative taint is mousiness formed by certain types of lactic acid bacteria, which may work symbiotically with *Brettanomyces*, and which produce a nearly identical mousy (or mouselike) smell. The preventive is proper levels of sulfur dioxide; once a wine has been infected, the taste cannot readily be removed.

Cork and cask molds

The nonfaults

The story about the diner rejecting his wine because it is corked, pointing to a fragment of cork in his glass as conclusive evidence, may be sad, but it happens. The adverse reaction that some diners (and all too many restaurateurs and sommeliers) have to sediment in wine is discussed on page 225, and is another common nonfault. But there are others, two of the more common being wine diamonds and wine sparkles.

Wine diamonds

Wine diamonds is the name given by harassed German winemakers to the heavy deposits of potassium bitartrate crystals that frequently form at the bottom of bottles of their precious Beerenauslesen and Trockenbeerenauslesen. Commercial white wines made in significant quantities are almost invariably cold-stabilized to remove these harmless, tasteless and odorless deposits before the wine is bottled, and not a few red and fortified wines are similarly treated. The belief that the crystals are sand, glass or other lethal signs of incompetent winemaking is nonetheless widespread. Knowledge and education are the proper antidotes.

Wine sparkles

Wine sparkles, or spritz or *pétillance*, is de rigueur for Muscadet and many Swiss wines, tolerated in most aromatic or light-bodied wines, frowned upon in full-bodied whites, and rejected in red wines. It may be carbon dioxide, but sometimes it is not, and here a little knowledge is a dangerous thing – particularly in the case of red wines. A sign of gas (in the form of a slight rim) may mean excess carbon dioxide from overzealous protection (a minor fault that should correct itself with a few years' bottle-age). It may mean the presence of a mysterious substance that possibly comes from new oak and acts as a foam stabilizer, in the same way as products added to soap powder prevent the bubbles from immediately breaking. Minute quantities of gas in the wine (normally invisible) fill the bubbles caused by agitation; the difference between this type of foam and that caused by carbon dioxide is that there is no detectable prickle or sensation on the tongue when the wine is tasted. Finally, it may mean a secondary (probably malolactic) fermentation is underway, which is totally undesirable. A little knowledge is dangerous, because not a few New World "experts" are prone instantaneously to diagnose the last cause without considering the other possibilities.

The Manipulation of Wine

Wine is arguably the most natural of all of the long-life food substances available. Compared to most packaged foods, the number of added substances not naturally present in wines is tiny. What is more, the legislation of most wine-producing countries proceeds on an extraordinarily restrictive basis: a list of permitted additives exists, and everything not on that list is banned, however harmless (or indeed beneficial) it may be. This chapter looks at the principal additions legal in some or all of the major wine-producing countries, and at the controversial procedure of filtration, reverse osmosis or vacuum concentration and microoxidation. Finally, we briefly look at the most controversial issue of all: genetic modification.

Yeast and fermentation

We start with a one-celled organism without which wine would not exist: yeast. It is ironic that the New World's current fascination with natural, or wild, fermentation (the rule rather than the exception in the Old World) should come at a time when the scientific understanding of and research into yeasts is expanding exponentially.

Louis Pasteur: father of microbiology

Pride of place must still go to Louis Pasteur, who demonstrated that this organism was the trigger for the conversion of grape juice to wine. Pasteur was the father of the science of microbiology, and it is fitting that yeast was the first eukaryotic organism whose genome was sequenced in 1997. Yeast has become the model organism for studying human diseases such as cancer; yeast scientists Paul Nurse and Lee Hartwell received the Nobel Prize for Physiology in Medicine in 2001.

The yeast family

The yeast population has served humankind since the dawn of civilization. The member of overwhelming importance to winemaking is *Saccharomyces cerevisiae*. It best meets all of the requirements for fermentation: ability to tolerate a low pH medium, significant amounts of sulfur dioxide (SO_2), steadily rising levels of alcohol and relatively high fermentation temperatures. Unless stressed, it does not produce undesirable side-effects, and its use extends (via lees) well after its death.

Yeast strains and genetics

There is a vast number of different strains or types of *S. cerevisiae* sold around the world under different commercial names: one of the best-known is EC1118, or Prise de Mousse, sold by Lalvin. In the last 20 years, 5,538 genes have been identified in yeasts, and, in a significant number of instances, the effect of a given gene identified. Some genes are thoroughly undesirable if overexpressed; thus the ATFI gene results in a wine with an overpowering ethyl acetate (nail-polish) aroma. Others are highly desirable.

The fermentation path

The conversion of grape juice to wine is a complex, multistage process, resulting in a liquid that is around 83 to 89 percent water, 10 to 15 percent alcohol, 0.4 to 1 percent glycerol and 0.5 to 1.5 percent acid. Only a fraction of the remaining 1 percent (or thereabouts) constitutes the volatile flavor compounds that give wine its aroma and flavor. It is here that the specific action of different strains of yeast becomes critical, particularly given that grape juice (of any given variety) has much less fruit aroma than the wine it makes.

It is also necessary to distinguish first between grape flavor compounds that are present in both grapes and wines and are not altered and liberated by yeasts; second, grape-derived flavor precursors that are altered by yeast; and third, yeast-derived flavor compounds probably produced as general side-reactions of primary yeast metabolism.

Esters are biosynthesized by the yeast, and confer a range of distinctive fruity aromas, including strawberry, apple, banana, peach, berry and pineapple. Quite why these esters should be produced is not understood, as they do not appear to have any metabolic function. But they most certainly explain why wine writers use such terms. The precursors for some esters, called higher alcohols, are themselves potent aroma compounds, ranging from fresh-cut grass to roses to nail polish. Then there are the volatile acids, mainly acetic acid, also biosynthesized by yeasts. These acids are always present – at low levels beneficial to wine quality, at high levels destructive.

The role of esters

Here choice and consequence become particularly stark. Some yeast strains release volatile thiols, whereas others do not. Jan H. Swiegers of the Australian Wine Research Institute, who has published a lengthy paper on yeast modulation of wine flavor with Professor Isak Pretorius (*Advances in Applied Microbiology*, Volume 57), puts the thiol impact into perspective thus: "One milligram of a certain volatile thiol is enough to flavor almost a million liters of wine." Thiols originate from the grape as aroma-bound, nonvolatile, amino acid–bound precursors. Through the process of fermentation, yeast enzymes split the volatile thiols away from the amino acid, releasing them into the wine. Here they create box tree, passion fruit, guava, gooseberry and (at higher concentrations) sweaty aromas. Once again, wine writers can take comfort.

Volatile thiols

At present, the most effective thiol-release yeast strain can unbind only about 5 percent of the volatile thiols from their precursors. Writes Swiegers (in a separate unpublished paper): "There is a huge, untapped aroma potential remaining in the grape (and ultimately in the wine that we drink!)." Together, Pretorius and Swiegers become even more poetic when they conclude their yeast modulation paper thus:

How far can one go?

> *The infinite number of flavor profiles of bottled wines results from the synergy between grapes and yeast … The blending of the precise amounts of different flavor compounds to produce the distinct flavors of different wines is akin to the blending of the sounds of many instruments [in an orchestra] … When in perfect balance, all the flavor compounds … result in a satisfying sensory experience that the wine connoisseur will declare to be a symphony in a bottle.*

Expressed thus, science becomes art. The artist, however, will have to be careful not to make the painting too colorful. If this technology comes to full flower, it will be most useful with cheap wines made from high-yielding, warm-region vines. These often lack varietal character; enhancement of this would be beneficial *prima facie*. It is an altogether different question with, say, the great wines of Burgundy.

Given the present and future ability to dial up flavor numbers by the use of highly specific yeast strains, where does this leave wild-yeast fermentations (however called), and where do they fit in the choice-and-consequence scheme of things? Well, for a start, most of these yeasts are not found on grape skins, common belief to the contrary notwithstanding. Rather, they are airborne and are carried around vineyards and wineries by the wind and by such vectors as fruit flies.

The health-conscious might be surprised, even alarmed, if grapes were labeled "contains tartaric, malic and citric acid," but these are naturally present in the fruit.

The yeasts responsible for initiating spontaneous fermentations usually belong to four genera different from *S. cerevisiae*: *Hansenula*, *Klöckera*, *Pichia* and *Torulopsis*. These four share a number of things in common. They are intolerant of SO_2, they are intolerant of alcohol, and most will start to expire once 3 degrees of alcohol have been formed by fermentation. They will not populate in sufficient numbers prior to this time to prevent other yeasts (most notably *S. cerevisiae*) from growing.

An ever-increasing number of New World winemakers are working with and studying indigenous yeasts, particularly with white wines. Yalumba (in the Barossa Valley) is led by senior winemaker Louisa Rose, who enumerates the advantages thus:

> *Slower and cooler fermentations; increased flavor complexity; increased textures (not just glycerol); increased longevity; better color in whites (more greens); better oak integration; and less apparent alcohol hotness.*

On the other side, possible disadvantages are higher alcohol conversion from the same sugar level, and less acidity at the end of the ferment. But all ferments complete their course, and there is no greater sulfide production, nor "off-barrels."

An intolerant lot

Research carried on with the assistance of the Australian Wine Research Institute since 2000 has confirmed that for the first week of ferment four to five different groups of non-*S. cerevisiae* yeasts were identified each day, with around 17 groups in total. After the *S. cerevisiae* yeasts took over, there was one group of non-*S. cerevisiae* yeasts that continued through to the end of fermentation, accounting for the 25 percent of non-*S. cerevisiae* yeasts.

Yalumba has also studied the effect of using eight inoculated yeasts outside *S. cerevisiae* that gave rise to different flavors, textures, and chemical analyses. In many cases, these fermentations were preferred to that of the *S. cerevisiae* control fermentation, but in no case were they better (in sensory terms) than the indigenous/wild-yeast control fermentation.

It seems highly probable that over a period of time the winery-resident population of yeasts will stabilize, particularly where the pomace is returned to vineyards near to the winery. The idea that a more distant vineyard may bring a particular character attribute to a specific wild yeast(s) has little scientific support, but the possibility cannot be ignored. As at 2005, Yalumba had done no work to ascertain whether indigenous yeasts played a role past the early stages of fermentation of red wines; the feeling, however, is that winery yeasts (led by strains of *S. cerevisiae*) will prove to be the dominant force.

Sulfur dioxide

While the use of sulfur as a fumigant has been known since Roman times (chiefly by burning sulfur in wine casks), its deliberate use through all stages of vinification and conservation has been very much a creature of the 20th century. Whether this use is a transient aberration remains to be seen: certainly preoccupation with food additives of every kind is part of the nosophobia that has been sweeping the Western world since the last decade of the 20th century, and in this context sulfur dioxide has been cast as public enemy number one.

The nature of sulfur dioxide

Sulfur dioxide is widely used throughout the food and beverage industries because of its remarkable properties. It is both a germicide and an antioxidant at levels that are nontoxic to all but a tiny fraction of 1 percent of the population, and when used to excess it quickly betrays its presence by smell.

It is found in wine in both free (uncombined) and bound (combined) forms. The free SO_2 (often simply referred to as sulfur) is by far the most important portion, both from the viewpoint of the wine and the wine-drinker: it is the free sulfur that inhibits bacterial growth and prevents oxidation, the free sulfur that we smell and most readily taste, and it is the free sulfur that poses a threat to the acutely sensitive asthmatic or other allergy sufferer who must avoid SO_2. Free sulfur in turn exists in two forms, the most effective of which is molecular or un-ionized SO_2.

Levels of sulfur dioxide in wine and other substances

Depending on a wine's pH, between 13 and 60 milligrams per liter of total free sulfur are required to control oxidation and microbial growth. In fact, relatively few premium-quality dry table wines have total SO_2 levels (free and bound) in excess of 100 milligrams per liter. These levels are quite low by overall food standards. Fresh fruit salad and vegetable salad in health-food stores frequently contain 200 milligrams per liter of free SO_2, while other semi-processed foods and beverages often contain significantly higher levels.

The need for sulfur dioxide

Toward the end of the 20th century it became fashionable to reduce levels of SO_2 additions. As we have seen, levels of sporadic bottle oxidation (particularly in white wines) and *Brettanomyces* (in red wines) rose in direct consequence. There has been a reversal in practice, with a single addition of 50 parts per million needed to stifle the development of brett, and a target of 30 parts per million of free SO_2 at bottling for both white and red wines. The advent of screwcaps has not significantly changed the practice or targets, but does guarantee that neither oxidation nor brett growth will occur postbottling. It remains feasible to entirely bypass the use of SO$_2$ in organic winemaking (as opposed to organic grape growing), and the screwcap will extend the otherwise short lifespan of such wines.

Skillfully and rationally used, the effect of SO$_2$ is beneficial, particularly in the case of wines intended for medium- to long-term cellaring. It should not be detectable in the aroma, and certainly not in the taste. The fact that certain types of European wines (in particular) have in the past been heavily influenced by SO$_2$ (and that a few continue to be influenced) is no more nor less than a reflection of ignorance, and cannot be seen as a legitimate part of regional tradition. (Sauternes, Chablis and white Bordeaux are examples of wines that were often heavily and adversely influenced by excessive additions.)

U.S. labeling law currently requires the words "contains sulfites" to appear on (effectively) all wine labels. In Australia, the requirement is to specify either "preservative (220) added" or "sulfur dioxide added." No such requirement exists in the European Union. Indeed, such statements are actively discouraged.

One cannot help but wonder what these warnings achieve. The irony is that from the winemakers' viewpoint they may help in the defense of the hypothetical claim for damages by the consumer who alleges he or she has been harmed by the presence of SO$_2$ in wine. The reality is that persons who are so sensitive to low levels of SO$_2$ will surely be under strict medical supervision of their dietary intake, or will have long since encountered SO$_2$ in far higher and presumably lethal levels in other foodstuffs.

Acidity adjustment

Ascorbic acid is frequently added to white wine in conjunction with sulfur dioxide as an antioxidant, but never to red wine. Its disclosure is required on Australian wine labels in similar terminology to that required for SO$_2$ (either "antioxidant (300) added" or "ascorbic acid added"). The temptation has been to amend the warning to "vitamin C–enriched", for that is what ascorbic acid essentially is, but the bureaucrats in Australia, like their U.S. counterparts are not known for their sense of humor.

The addition of acid is permitted by European Union regulations only in certain zones (or in certain vintages, such as 2003), and only if chaptalization has not been used. Those who have worked in Bordeaux and Burgundy will know the shrug that takes care of such regulations. The average French winemaker is nothing if not pragmatic, and by and large contemptuous of officialdom. (The same comment applies to the ritual of the "official" and the supplementary – or unofficial – addition of sugar in poor years.)

Because these acids are naturally present in grapes, the addition cannot sensibly be regarded as introducing something foreign, or attacking the status of wine as an essentially natural product. What is more, they are added (if they are added at all) for one reason alone: to make the wine a better product, both in terms of its taste and its chemical and bacterial stability. That does not prevent the average European winemaker from criticizing wines that have had acid added, and it does not help New World winemakers to know the criticism is essentially an unscientific one.

Chaptalization

At this level of discussion New World winemakers can and do immediately turn the tables on Old World winemakers, and with about the same level of scientific justification, which is none at all. They also play tit-for-tat in claiming they can taste the aftereffects. Chaptalization has been discussed elsewhere (see page 199); suffice it to say it is used with the sole purpose of improving the quality of the wine, and in the vast majority of instances it does just that.

Watering back

The addition of ice to cool overhot ferments in ripe, hot vintages was an ancient and honorable practice, however illegal it was (and is). Climate change and the insidious rise in natural alcohol levels past desired targets may put the issue of adding water back onto the official agenda. It will be very difficult to counter knee-jerk reactions against the idea, but if it is done simply to make a better wine, why should it be illegal? There are no health issues, only bureaucratic obstacles.

Additives in perspective

Wine-growers from the Old and New Worlds are in total agreement on one thing: the best grapes will require neither acidification nor chaptalization; they will have a low pH and will produce a wine that will retain an acceptable pH after malolactic fermentation; and they will, of course, be free of mold, rot and other defects. The whole thrust of viticulture is directed to growing grapes with these characteristics. However, we do not live in a perfect world, and the perfect grape is a very rare commodity.

Moreover, even if it is produced, the perfect grape cannot produce perfect wine unaided. So additives of various kinds simply have to be used, however transient their presence. In almost all instances they do no more than bolster substances naturally present in fermenting grapes or wine (even sulfur dioxide technically falls into this category), and are simply intended to provide the balance nature has temporarily or permanently neglected to provide.

The bottom line is that wine is a natural product that, given that the basic process of fermentation is a naturally occurring one, is subject to far less manipulation than any other long-life food substance. Fewer unnatural additives are either used in its making or left in the wine when it is bottled (and thereby when it is drunk).

Filtration

The winemaker's and wine-lover's belief that wine is a natural substance can be a double-edged sword; for some, any interference with its natural state is anathema. An eloquent, indeed passionate, believer in natural wines is San Francisco wine-importer Kermit Lynch, whose philosophy permeates every page of his book *Adventures on the Wine Route*. It is a wonderful book to read and there can be no doubting the sincerity of Mr. Lynch's oft-repeated view that filtration absolutely destroys all wine. Speaking of a filtered version of a wine he normally liked, he wrote:

> *Wine is incredibly impressionable. It is influenced by the most subtle details, from the soil in which the vines grow to a neighbor's blackcurrant patch. Squeezed through the sterile pads, the poor wine expressed sterility and cardboard … Three or four times I have seen an unfiltered wine go bad … It may be unrealistic, but I believe customers who have such a wine should accept the loss and shut up about it. Complaining scares your wine merchant, who in turn scares the winemaker, who then for reasons of security begins to sterilize his wines. And who gains from all that? If one loves natural wines, one accepts an occasional calamity. We would not castrate all men because some of them go haywire and commit rape. At least I wouldn't.*

Professor Peynaud took the diametrically opposed view:

> *The phrase "as clear as spring water" reflects the appeal of purity. Besides, a cloudy wine never tastes well, for several reasons. If there is a haze and a deposit in a wine that has been in bottle for only a few weeks, or even for two or three years, there is something wrong. Whatever has caused the cloudiness will also have altered the wine's constitution and impaired its quality. Particles in suspension in a cloudy wine affect one's taste-buds directly and adversely: the organoleptic qualities are masked by the screen of impurities in suspension, and the flavor is distorted … Conversely, the more a wine is clarified, the finer the filtration, the smoother and more supple the wine will taste. Filtration properly carried out does not strip or attenuate a wine; it clears it of internal impurities and improves it. To deny this is to say that a wine's quality is due above all to foreign substances in suspension.*

Bottling straight from the cask here on the Loire means that the wines are unfiltered. They may have a certain "spritz" – a slight prickle on the tongue – indicative of the minute yeast particles suspended in the wine, and taste very fresh and fruity.

Kermit Lynch provides numerous real-life examples of what he perceives to be other filtration catastrophes, including the filtration of some 1983 Burgundies that turned wines that were "almost black" in the cask into "pale orange" in bottle. He recounts his advice to the winemaker:

> *I advised him to bottle his beautiful 1985s himself; why not ask one of the old-timers in the village how the bottling used to be done before the oenologist-entrepreneurs arrived, selling security from the back of a van?*

The qualified winemaker will notice the reference to cardboard in the first disaster, and the remarkable color-change in the second example (coupled with the 1983 vintage). He will know that in the first instance the filtration was incorrectly carried out (removing the cardboard taste from filter pads requires a little care, patience and a sensitive palate, but is an essential part of proper filtration procedure) and that in the second case, laccase (the botrytis oxidase) was hard at work, perhaps aided by careless handling of the filtration equipment: oxidation is an ever-present risk.

The winemaker is not a fool

All intelligent winemakers think hard about both the cost and quality implications of anything they do with their wine. They are acutely aware how easily a great wine can be spoiled or diminished; most are forever seeking ways to minimize pumping, bruising and, above all, the risk of oxidizing fine wine. Large-scale commercial wine, however, is made with different aims in mind: it must be able to withstand all sorts of maltreatment (being left in the sun for a day or two, being left in the freezer, being served immediately after a 24-hour trip in the back of a car, or by a wine waiter trained in a fast-food chain dispensary) and must never show a hair out of place.

The commercial winery has no effective option when it comes to filtration, maintenance of standard levels of sulfur dioxide and so forth: they are disciplines that logically have to be followed. But the criteria for the small producer may be different, and there is a tendency among some New World wineries to eliminate (or reduce as far as possible) filtration of red wines.

Filtration is simply the removal of suspended particles by very fine screening.

Ironically, one finds this in some of the most technically sophisticated wineries, such as Robert Mondavi in the Napa Valley and Petaluma in Australia. They eliminate filtration by using extreme care in racking and fining their wines, by ensuring that the chemical balance between sulfur dioxide and pH is exactly correct, and by ensuring absolute sterility of the bottling equipment and bottling procedure. Through sophisticated microbiological plating procedures and the use of microscopes, they will know precisely what the bacterial and yeast status of the wine is, and be in a position to determine with scientific certainty the likelihood of future problems.

Depending on the type of wine and the amount of fining or racking, the only problem such winemakers are likely to foresee and accept is the probability of a crust or deposit forming in the bottle. In certain wine-drinking circles on the American West Coast, this became a badge of honor, and the whole process is fraught with danger. Bottling and selling Pinot Noir that is distinctly cloudy right from the outset seems to some winemakers to be perfectly normal.

A straw poll of makers of fine Burgundy would probably reveal that they are split down the middle on filtration; those who oppose it tend to do so vocally, while those who practice it do so quietly and unostentatiously. Yet outside of the largest *négociant* houses (and ignoring the quaint habit of the house of Louis Latour in physically removing the sediment from its Burgundies prior to shipment), the knowledge of the nonfiltering producer about the bacterial status of his wine (and very possibly the pH and SO_2 level) is nonexistent. The producer does not filter the wine because he or he does not wish to, not because there is no need to.

In other words, the basis for eliminating filtration can be carefully established by New World winemakers, and the obvious question is why, if filtration does not adversely affect wine, they go to so much trouble to do so. The answer is somewhat nebulous, but there are two things that can be said with certainty. First, filtration is an added expense; second, particularly for delicate red wines such as Pinot Noir, filtration adds to the shock of bottling. If one tastes any wine on its way through the bottling process (that is, from the vat from which it is being drawn before it enters the bottling line and from a bottle taken off the line at the end of the process), there will be a marked difference. Even a wine as exalted as 1982 Château Pétrus showed the effect quite vividly at the time. If one adds an inline membrane filter, and the wine is Pinot Noir, the effect is further magnified. But leave the wine for one, two or three months (one cannot tell how long the recovery process will take), and it is usually impossible to tell the filtered from the nonfiltered wine, provided the filtration and bottling were skillfully carried out.

So in a sense the third reason is the most important, and is really without any scientific base. It seemingly puts the technocrat right into the Kermit Lynch camp: the less a wine is (needlessly) tampered with, the better, and it may just be that an acceleration of the sedimentation and crusting process is a good thing.

The art ... There is, in fact, a difference between the Lynch and technocrat camps, which might simplistically be likened to the difference between the art and science of wine. Kermit Lynch likes to see wine made in old oak vats; he does not like SO_2; he does not like any of the soulless trappings, trimmings and equipment of the new winery. Great wine made this way is a truly magical thing, a spontaneous gift of nature in which the role of the winemaker is an ancient custodial one directed to preserving the traditions of the past. The technocrat arrives at the same destination having used an entirely different philosophy and entirely different tools of trade.

Nor does it stop there. Ask the nonfiltering Burgundian why he does not filter his wine, and he will point to the old vintages in his cellar (which are absolute nectar) and to the fact that the numerous Michelin-starred restaurants of France that buy his wine have never once complained about any problems. The answer, of course, is that the wines have never been subjected to heat, and have only had one short journey in their lives. It is why Kermit Lynch found early on that refrigerated containers were essential if his artisan wines were to be guaranteed safe passage to the United States.

... and the science The truth is that a good 50 percent of those artisan Burgundies and Rhônes are bacterial time bombs. In the best vintages and from the best winemakers, the pH levels may be sufficiently low and the SO_2 levels sufficiently high to withstand the stress of transportation and heat (remembering that sooner or later the wines come out of refrigerated containers and that the United States is a very big country). In other years, even the greatest names may be no protection: it is one reason why domaine-bottled Burgundies have such a checkered reputation outside Europe.

The other problem lies with the sediment. Of course it is harmless; of course careful pouring and decanting will eliminate the problem; and of course any old wine, filtered or not, will throw a crust. The hard reality is that many restaurants and many consumers simply will not accept sediment in the relatively young wines they are used to handling and drinking, a problem of particular significance in emerging markets such as Japan.

In a world in which product-liability litigation is a grim reality, in which health concerns grow in direct proportion to our ever-increasing life span, and in which the bureaucratic imposition of unasked-for food standards has become an art form, the romantic ideals of people such as Kermit Lynch are becoming increasingly impractical. A high degree of technical knowledge and control is a prerequisite, even if it is directed to a hands-off rather than a hands-on approach to winemaking.

Microoxygenation

The technology and methodology of microoxygenation were developed in France in the 1990s by two research scientists, Patrick Ducournau and Thierry Lemaire. In essence, it involves the deliberate use of oxygen in red wine in tank or barrel (i.e., before it is bottled) to soften the tannins and increase complexity. Properly utilized, the technique improves the mouth-feel, enhances the color stability and intensity, increases the oxidative stability and decreases reductive characters and vegetative aromas.

A precisely measured and controlled stream of microsized bubbles is fed into wine in tank through a ceramic diffuser at the bottom. By the time one might have expected bubbles to appear on the surface, there are in fact none, because all the oxygen has been absorbed by the wine. The chemistry involved is extremely complex, but the changes induced by microoxygenation are easily observed. In the first phase (microoxygenation is carried out progressively over a period of between one and six months), the tannins increase in aggressiveness and intensity on the palate, and the varietal aromatics' intensity and complexity decrease. This is called the structuring phase.

The process

The harmonization phase then follows, the optimum end point reached when the wine exhibits the maximum complexity, tannin, softness and suppleness, and with its aromatic qualities returned and enhanced. Excessive oxygenation leads to irreversible loss of freshness and varietal character and to bitter, dry tannins. Skilled use of the equipment, and careful sensory evaluation, are prerequisites if this is to be avoided.

Since the commercial release of the Oenodev (the patent holder) equipment in 1996, many thousands of installations have been made in France (the leader), the United States, Spain, Italy, Germany, Australia, New Zealand, South Africa and Chile. Its use in France extends across the entire spectrum of wine quality from great to ordinary. Michel Rolland is an unabashed supporter of its use.

Used in many countries

The oldest and simplest method of concentrating red wine must is to drain off a percentage (10 percent would be an average) of juice immediately after the grapes are crushed; the French term is *saignée*. Its downsides are an increase in pH, and (for some wines) an impaired mouth-feel. The next techniques to be developed relied on either partial or total vacuum extraction, the latter more expensive, but with less loss of aroma and flavor.

Concentration of wine

The most modern technique is reverse osmosis. A fine membrane that will allow the passage of water but not of alcohol (water has a smaller molecular size) is placed between the must and water. Normal osmosis would see the water pass through the membrane and into the must, but because the must has already been placed under elevated atmospheric pressure, the flow is reversed: hence, reverse osmosis. The great advantage of the process is that water, and only water, is taken from the must. It should be emphasized, however, that if the must is of unripe grapes or is moldy, osmosis will only accentuate the problem.

Reverse osmosis

Also called cryoextraction, this involves partial freezing of white wine juice. Water has a higher freezing point than alcohol, so ice blocks of water form that are removed from the juice (or the juice is run off from the ice). While typically used in the making of sweet white wine, it can also be used to strip out unripe flavors from dry white wine.

Freeze concentration

So long as the debate on genetically modified organisms (GMO) continues, the wine industry in developed economies will not use any GMOs. This is intensely frustrating for scientists and for those who stand to benefit from their use, simply because the opposition comes from a highly vocal minority, some of whom have no scientific training, and can explain their opposition only in vague and emotional language. It is similar to the hysterical opposition to the radical idea of pasteurizing milk proposed by Louis Pasteur over a century ago. It took several decades before it was accepted across the world. On the positive side are the spinoffs that come from molecular biochemistry, including genetic modification. New insights into grapevines, grapes, yeasts and wines allow choices (and desirable consequences) previously undreamed of.

Genetic modification

The U.S. regulations flow from the approach that there is no *a priori* reason to assume the use of GM plants and microbes is more risky than conventional methods of introgressing new genes into organisms and products. Accordingly, the regulations

Different governmental attitudes: the U.S.

require each GMO to be considered on its own merit, albeit with lengthy trials to establish it poses no threat to human health or the environment.

The European approach

The European Union takes the view that GM products have an intrinsic level of risk above that of non-GM products, with a consequent moratorium on all GMOs. In 2003, the United States, Canada and Argentina instigated dispute proceedings with the European Union; whether this will result in a breakthrough is hard to predict.

Globalization issues

GMOs are inextricably linked with globalization issues; it is certain that those who oppose one will also oppose the other. We consider the potential benefits of GM technology next, but first must emphasize that natural diversity in the characteristics of wine is augmented by the appropriate use of technology, and not through its withdrawal. As the team at the Australian Wine Research Institute, headed by its director, Professor Isak Pretorius, says, the concerns that wine will become "standardized and McDonaldized" are without foundation; indeed, the reverse is the case.

Why pursue the GM path?

Research has expanded exponentially in the wake of the sequencing of the genome of yeast in 1997, resulting from the preexisting base of biotechnology following the discovery of the DNA double helix in 1953. The opportunities that now exist are breathtaking in their scope, offering a win–win result for all stakeholders, including the environment, human health and the wine industry.

The opportunities to improve grapevines fall under three headings. First, the improvement of disease and pest resistance: specifically, to make vines immune to downy and powdery mildew; to eliminate botrytis (where desired); and to increase resistance to viral attack. Second, the improvement of vine stress tolerance: specifically resistance to water stress, to oxidative damage and to osmotic stress. Third, the improvement of quality factors through improved color development and improved sugar accumulation and transport.

The one major caveat is that (quite apart from other GM issues) there is no change in the varietal characteristics of the grapes, resulting in a development timeline of not less than 11 and up to 22 years.

Winemaking: yeast and primary fermentation

Here there is an Aladdin's cave of opportunities, with four general areas and 25 specific objectives for the primary fermentation. Here the headings are improving fermentation performance, wine processing, wine wholesomeness and wine sensory attributes.

Selecting a couple of the specific objectives, the aims are to increase levels of resveratrol in red wine (highly cardiovascular-protective); to decrease levels of alcohol (especially for New World Chardonnays and warm-grown Syrah); to reduce sulphite and sulfide production; and to make biological-based adjustments to acidity levels (previously "plastering" was used involving high-pH calcium materials).

Here there are the same four general objectives, and 17 specific objectives. The latter include greater tolerance of low pH and low temperatures (especially relevant to cool-climate winemaking); improved protein clarification; the production of antimicrobial enzymes and peptides; and optimized production of glycerol and enhanced liberation of monoterpenes (potent aroma compounds).

The ideal outcome

The ultimate goal would be the incorporation of all relevant antimicrobial agents into selected strains of wine yeast and malolactic bacteria, thus eliminating all contaminating spoilage bacteria (notably *Acetobacter*), yeasts (notably *Brettanomyces* and *Dekkera*) and molds (including *Aspergillus* and *Trichoderma*) in winemaking.

And so...

It must be emphasized that the underlying thrust of this view of the future is to increase choice for the winemaker. It will in no way standardize or industrialize winemaking or wines. It will be every bit as useful – arguably more so – for the smallest, low-tech wineries as for the biggest high-tech producers. In many instances, there will probably be unarguable benefits for the ecosystems of vineyards and wineries alike.

The Great Closure Debate

Choices and Consequences

In the opening decade of the 21st century, a storm, the origins of which dated back to the 1960s, finally unleashed its energy on the wine world. It challenged a technology that had ruled without question for 400 years: the cork in the bottle. The immediate cause of the challenge was a mold called trichloroanisole (TCA for short), which can be detected by the human nose in minute concentrations; indeed, scientific analysis techniques lagged well behind those of the nose until the late 1980s, but once Pandora's box was open, there was no turning back.

Cork

Why is it that, after 400-plus years of acceptance, cork is under sustained attack and in imminent danger of losing its role as the most common – indeed the only – method of securing the contents of a bottle of wine?

A skeptic might rephrase the question and ask what other technology has lasted four centuries and neither been challenged nor improved. The same person might also observe that until 50 years ago there was little dissatisfaction with cork, nor any credible alternative. Well, almost none.

Early rumblings of discontent

In 1932, Charles Walter Berry, the famous wine-merchant founder of Berry Brothers & Rudd, published *A Miscellany of Wine*. In it he reproduces a letter from a wine collector discussing the shortcomings of cork and his response, both originally published in the September 1932 issue of *The Wine Trade Review*. The correspondent, with the soubriquet "Appreciative but envious," took C.W. Berry to task for not mentioning defective bottles of old wines: in this instance wines from the 1860s and 1870s. "I do not mean unsatisfactory as far as inherent qualities of the wine, but of defects from crushed or decayed corks … there was a bin of Château Lafite 1870 where two of four bottles opened were doomed owing to cork trouble," wrote the correspondent, citing many such examples.

Berry replied: "In these cellars containing old wines of fine quality there is always a large proportion of unusable bottles." He goes on to discuss an attack by weevils that destroyed 92 bottles and 24 magnums of 1874 Château Lafite (among others) in a particular cellar, and other problems of bad casks. More tellingly, he went on to say: "The 'corked' bottle we all know, and none of us understand. Happy will be the man who can find out the cause and the remedy."

Before coming to the alternatives, and to the specific causes of dissatisfaction, it is worth briefly considering the historical role of cork, and the reasons why many of Europe's greatest winemakers will fight tooth and nail to retain it.

Cork in history

While global wine trade prospered over the millennia, as Hugh Johnson's *The Story of Wine* chronicles, it had in fact shrunk to a pan-European business by the time the cork established its supremacy. Heavy but irregular bottles were the weak link, but one that cork was able to overcome, thanks to its pliability and compression capacity.

Cork was in turn harvested from natural forests with no background use of agrochemicals or pesticides. Hand-sorted, generously sized corks (both in circumference and length) were standard. Shipment times were short, and fine wine, whether in the wineries or the purchasers' homes, was kept in very cool cellars. Even then, recorking bottles held in winery museums every 30 to 40 years was common practice. Customers, too, could elect to send bottles back to the winery whence they came for recorking.

Virgin cork forests

The new globalization

Fast-forward to the end of the 20th century, and globalization of the fine wine trade has attained levels never previously reached. Wine travels between northern and southern hemispheres, between New World and Old World, from Europe to Asia and every combination thereof, every day of the year. Ships are the primary mode between continents, and European producers who insist on shipping in winter forget the equator and the opposite time of the year in southern hemisphere destinations.

The perils of shipment

Containers may or may not be refrigerated; they may or may not be stored below deck; they may or may not be transshipped; they may or may not spend days in the blazing sun on a wharf somewhere along their journey. Transport to a designated warehouse may be quick or slow, the warehouse may be air-conditioned, insulated or neither. As the wine wends its way through the distribution chain to retailer, to customer, to the divorce court, to the auctioneer and to its proud new owner, the odds against the cork being able to withstand such mistreatments progressively lengthen.

Lighter bottles, smaller corks

But even this is only half the story. In the New World, the major producers have specified ever-lighter-weight bottles, which are cheaper to make and cheaper to transport, whether full or empty. Smaller-diameter neck-bores mean smaller, cheaper corks. A traditional château-length cork has a circumference of about an inch (24 to 26 mm), and a length of 2¼ inches (54 mm). A standard cork, albeit of high quality, in the New World is 1 x 1¾ inches (24 x 44 mm), with lesser corks as short as 1½ inches (39 mm).

Small wonder, then, that sporadic (commonly but technically incorrectly called random) bottle oxidation (which we explain in more detail on pages 231–33) can and does strike with deadly speed, and that outright failure of the cork to hold the wine in the bottle can easily occur years before the wine has had a chance to reach the full flower of its maturity, be that 5, 10 or 20 or more years from bottling.

It is true there has been resistance by small, quality-oriented wineries that have sourced super-heavy, dark glass bottles from Europe, and paid the maximum amount for the largest, best-quality corks suitable for those bottles. Unfortunately, this does not mean the end of cork taint, nor sporadic bottle oxidation; it simply reduces the incidence at best.

Natural cork: an amazing substance

The next of many observations about the challenge is that natural cork is a quite extraordinary substance, with around about one billion gas-filled hexagonal cells per cubic inch. Its longevity is reflected by fishermen's floats for nets still bobbing in the Dead Sea several thousand years after their initial immersion. Its resilience and toughness are exemplified by industrial uses from cork floor tiles to women's shoes to car-engine gaskets.

Cork bark is stripped, then seasoned for six months before being boiled, thereafter hand-sorted and cut into strips (near right) *before the corks are punched out, and electronically sorted into uniform grades* (right).

Synthetic corks

While increasingly used in Europe (around three billion sold in 2005), the synthetic corks presently available are warranted to keep oxygen at bay for only two years, and are thus suitable only for short-shelf-life wines. The reasons for this limited ability are threefold. First, they cannot adapt to the irregularities of the internal bore of a bottle neck (simply insert your little finger into the neck and those little ripples in the neck will be all too obvious). Second, they progressively lose elasticity, gradually releasing their outward pressure against the glass. Third, some allow the passage of air through (rather than around) the closure.

A fourth fault of synthetics, primarily alleged by the cork-producer lobby, is that they impart a plastic taint to the wine. Most winemakers and researchers dismiss this; the newest polymers are inert. But just as synthetic diamonds have proved more expensive to make than natural diamonds, the properties of natural cork cannot (so far) be reproduced, and for the time being the future for synthetic corks would appear to be limited to low-cost, short-life wines.

Treated agglomerate corks

The first response of the Portuguese cork industry to the problems of TCA was the development of a cork made from agglomerated particles glued together, mimicking the body of a Champagne cork. It rapidly became apparent that the glue tainted the wine (*goût de glue* was the jest) in a very short space of time. The answer was, it seemed, to laminate one or two cylindrical wafers of cork at the end of the cork. Both the first and second versions relied on steam distillation and vacuum extraction processes designed to remove TCA both from the particles and the wafers.

Twin Tops

The Amorim-patented version is Twin Top, and ongoing trials by the Australian Wine Research Institute suggest it has good oxygen-barrier capacity, but there are lingering questions on its long-term performance, on both glue and oxygen-barrier-capacity issues.

ProCork

An interesting hybrid has been developed in Australia, patented as ProCork. It involves the application of a five-layer membrane over each end of the cork, and extending partway down the sides. The primary purpose of the membrane is to trap any TCA, or other cork taints, of which there are several. The outer layer of the membrane has an abrasive texture designed to grip the glass and thereby inhibit the passage of oxygen. The membrane can be applied to synthetic, Twin Top or natural cork closures, and is an interesting development.

Altec and Diam corks

Other membranes exist that progressively become less porous; the near-science-fiction scenario is for a membrane-covered cork to allow some oxygen in the early years to enhance the rate of development of the wine, but then slow it down by providing a total barrier. The second and more recent response has been the development of the Diam cork by Sabate, the second largest wine-closure manufacturer in the world, which announced in 2005 that it had sold its conventional cork business. Diam is a direct derivative of the Altec closure, stemming from research carried out since 1997 by the French Atomic Energy Commission on behalf of Sabate.

It involves the use of supercritical carbon dioxide (CO_2) used to treat finely ground cork "flour." At a temperature of 88°F (31°C) and enormous pressure of 72 bars, the supercritical CO_2 has the penetration power of a gas and the extraction power of a liquid. It acts as a solvent to remove organic compounds with a low molecular weight such as TCA (and any other fungal or bacterial contaminants), leaving no trace in the treated granules.

The first version, Altec, showed major TCA problems, but had excellent oxygen-barrier properties. The taint problem was solved by the CO_2-extraction process, and Sabate (now part of the Oneo Winery Supply Group) moved into major commercial supply in 2005. Here, too, it is a work in progress, however encouraging the early results may be. One of the options available to Sabate is to offer Diam at various densities, allowing some passage of oxygen with the lighter-density version.

As at 2006, Diam appears to be the best "corklike" alternative to the screwcap. There is no evidence to date of any TCA contamination, and it is not accused of

Corks of all kinds can be used with any bottle neck configuration.

causing reduced characters in the wine. Its mechanical oxygen-barrier effectiveness is good; the one question no one can answer is whether it will remain an effective barrier for 10, 20 or more years.

Screwcaps

In the meantime, and since 2000, there had been a mass migration by Australian and New Zealand winemakers to screwcaps. One often sees "Stelvin" and "screwcap" used interchangeably, in much the same way as "Xerox" and "photocopy," but Stelvin was the patented and trademarked product of French aluminum company Pechiney, with other similar products (including Auscap) made under separate patents or licenses. The dramatic shift was slowed only by the inability of the glass companies to keep supply up to demand, and to a lesser (and equally temporary) lack of choice in glass color and shape.

History of the screwcap

The screwcap concept dates back to 1856 for use in sealing glass jars. The screwcap for bottles was patented in England in 1889, and first used on whisky bottles in 1926. In the 1930s, the University of California at Davis conducted trials on bottled wine; in 1979, a bottle of 1937 Colombard was opened and found to be "impressive ... Well-aged, to be sure, but not dead."

1950s and 1960s

Screwcaps, then and now technically known as roll-on, tamper-evident (ROTE), were manufactured by a number of companies, including Le Bouchage Mécanique (BM), which produced a proprietary closure called Stelcap. Initial trials in Bordeaux in 1961 were inconsistent, but further trials between 1964 and 1966 in Burgundy, Bordeaux and Alsace suggested there was no difference between Stelcaps and premium corks. The research was made public in 1967, and in 1968 the Stelcap was officially approved by France as a wine closure.

1970s: rapid proliferation of trials

Trials of prestige French wines (including 1969 Château Haut-Brion), Swiss trials and Australian trials gathered pace, as Australia's glass manufacturer ACI acquired a license to produce Stelcaps, and Yalumba (in 1970) placed Stelcaps over bottles already closed with a cork. In 1973, the Australian Wine Research Institute commenced a research program with seven companies, and in 1975–76 these companies released red and white wines under screwcap, Montana following suit in New Zealand in 1977.

Switzerland takes the lead

However, it was Switzerland that began full-scale commercial bottling in 1972; by the 1980s Swiss winemakers had universally adopted the screwcap for Chasselas, just as the Clare Valley winemakers were to do for Riesling 20 years later. By 1990, Switzerland was using 10 million screwcaps a year, rising to 60 million in 1995. Sutter Home in California also commenced using screwcaps in 1990.

Two steps forward, one step back

In 1979, Château Haut-Brion discontinued trials due to the failure of the liner material inside the screwcap, and by 1984 Yalumba and all the other Australian users

Several screwcap patents coexist with different manufacturers, but the basic design and function is the same.

had discontinued commercial use, not because of any technical problems, but because of market resistance. Ironically, the Australia Consolidated Industries/Australian Wine Research Institute trials concluded around the same time with an unqualified verdict in favor of screwcaps.

Both the liners and the configuration of the screwcap were radically improved in the 1990s, to the point where the basic design of the screwcap is unlikely to change further. (A smooth exterior sleeve, concealing the telltale rings, was an aesthetic, rather than functional, development at an early stage of commercialization.) By 2000, Australian winemakers were so convinced of the superiority of the closure over cork they decided to confront the market head on, led by the Clare Valley.

Technical advances in the 1990s

By 2005, over 80 percent of all Australian white wines were bottled with screwcaps, and over 30 percent of all red wines, the rate of change slowed only by long lead times in the supply of bottles and screwcaps. New Zealand has gone even further, and virtually every wine region in the world has at least one producer using the closure. In Burgundy in 2004, leading *négociant* Jean-Claude Boisset tasted a bottle of 1966 Mercurey (from the French trials of the time) and was so impressed he promptly ordered the bottling of one *premier cru* and two commune Burgundies under screwcap. In Chablis, Michel Laroche bottled his 2002 Grand Cru Chablis Le Clos with screwcaps.

The primary cause of dissatisfaction with the cork was the increasing incidence of cork taint (primarily, but not exclusively, TCA) from the 1970s on, and the refusal of the Portuguese cork industry to publicly acknowledge that there was a problem or to modify long-outdated manufacturing processes. However, the early trials with screwcaps not only eliminated taints, but also showed that the wine under screwcap remained brighter and fresher than that under cork. In turn, it became obvious that cork-finished bottles of white wine showed ever-greater bottle-to-bottle variation as the wine aged. Eventually, this became known as sporadic (random) bottle oxidation.

The reasons for change

The problem is exemplified by cases of wine bottled on the same day and stored in the same environment, in which any number of bottles from one to six or more will be prematurely aged, albeit to varying degrees. Prior explanations were flimsy at best. Modern bottling lines using corks have vacuum jaws that extract almost all air from the bottle a millisecond before the cork is inserted. There are up to 80 heads (or bottling stations on a never-stopping circular arrangement), with fast lines filling 20,000 bottles per hour. The suspicion was that all or any of the fractional imperfections in the bottle (particularly the top of the neck) and misplacement or wear of the filling head could result in partial or total failure to extract the air in a given bottle. At least this proposition satisfied the random nature of the problem, although it did not explain small bottling systems without vacuum jaws, which rely on gas-sparging of the bottles to replace the oxygen prior to filling.

Search for the causes of sporadic bottle oxidation

The cork was also the subject of suspicion. Did the cork discharge oxygen stored in its cells when first placed in the bottle? Were newer silicone coatings on the cork to blame? Did air penetrate through the cork or only along its sides? The second question has not been definitively answered; AWRI trials using Araldite (an epoxy adhesive) variously applied only in the center of the cork, around its perimeter and all over its surface were inconclusive, but most observers believe the passage is exclusively along the sides of the cork. In a sense, this is of largely academic interest, for what is more important is the fact of oxygen penetration, rather than its pathway.

The cork

Just as is the case with TCA cork taint, the fault may be barely perceptible (even to an expert) or blindingly obvious. For the winemaker, the barely perceptible is every bit as worrying as the blindingly obvious. The latter will make the wine undrinkable; the former will likely leave the consumer wondering why the wine in question has a good reputation (if it's well known) or determined not to buy another bottle (if little known).

Subtle or savage

White wine

Sporadic oxidation becomes progressively more obvious as the wine ages in bottle. AWRI research shows it can be predicted from as early as six months from bottling by a color change invisible to the naked eye, but in most cases it will not become apparent until the wine is at least 12 months old, and quite possibly not until it is two, three or four years old. It all depends on the rate of oxygen permeation and sulfur dioxide depletion. But once it shows itself unambiguously, the bottle (or, rather, the wine) in question will be deeper in color, broader in mouth-feel and have distinctly less fruit flavor than unaffected bottles. Farther down the track, it will become maderized at best, undrinkable at worst.

Red wine

Partly because of the added oxidation protection afforded by its tannins and anthocyanins, red wine is less obviously affected by oxidation. Even where it occurs, it is harder to recognize. Color changes in the early to midstage are less easy to see, and flavor and structure changes may be ambiguous: premature softening of the tannins may simply make the wine more pleasurable to drink. Indeed, it has only been in the wake of recognition of random oxidation of white wines that the existence of the problem in red wines (and its cause) has been exposed. Wine consumers around the globe were resigned to the occasional rather flat bottle of mid-aged red wine, and even more willing to accept the aphorism, "There are no great old wines, only great old bottles."

The AWRI trial
1999–2004

In May 1999, the Australian Wine Research Institute began an ongoing trial (to 2007 and possibly beyond) with an unwooded Semillon being bottled under 14 different closures. These included Reference 2 and Reference 3 natural cork (the two most commonly used grades of cork); various synthetic corks; the Amorim Twin Top agglomerate cork, with a disc at either end; Altec (since renamed Diam); and Auscap. At various intervals, bottles with each closure were opened, subjected to exhaustive analytical trials, and the wines tasted under rigorous scientific conditions. At each point the screwcap wine had retained more free SO_2, had better color and brighter, fresher fruit. Altec came next, then Twin Top, followed in turn by Reference 2 and Reference 3 corks, the various synthetic corks lagging well behind on each score. Moreover, at each point the differences between the wines became more marked, strongly suggesting the trend will continue.

Both this closure trial and parallel research into the role of oxygen in the aging of bottled wine analyzed the oxygen permeability of the closures. Screwcaps allowed between 0.0002 and 0.0008 mL per day of oxygen permeation, with a mean of 0.0005; Altec 0.0007 to 0.0013, with a mean of 0.0010; and Reference 2 cork 0.0001 to 0.1227 with a mean of 0.0179. In other words, the screwcap has a range of four times in terms of permeability, cork over 1,200 times.

This figure is hotly disputed by the cork industry and by respected researchers elsewhere in Australia and in Europe. However, all concede that the oxygen-barrier performance of cork does vary substantially, the variability increasing markedly with age.

Old beliefs die hard

Louis Pasteur was the first scientist to declare oxygen the public enemy of wine. Then, in 1898, a French researcher wrote: "In bottles, so long as the cork is sound … the protection of the wine in relation to oxygen is absolute or near-absolute. New absorptions of oxygen are impossible." In 1947, Jean Ribéreau-Gayon compared bottles with good corks and glass flasks sealed with airtight glass stoppers. There was no difference. In 2000, Pascal Ribéreau-Gayon was emphatic: "Reactions that take place in bottled wine do not require oxygen." Yet the belief persists that, if closed with a screwcap and deprived of oxygen, wine will somehow suffer retarded development, a view we will come back to shortly.

Oxygen present
at bottling

Research shows that, no matter what precautions are taken, there will normally be small quantities of oxygen dissolved in the wine and in the headspace below the closure. It used to be thought by some (the authors included) that this would act as a storehouse to be slowly consumed as the wine aged over the years. In fact, it is probable that all this oxygen is consumed by chemical reactions in the wine within days or weeks of bottling.

However, all existing closures in commercial use do allow the passage of some oxygen into the bottle. As we have seen, if this ingress is regular, and of very small amounts, it will have no adverse effect, simply forming part of the mechanisms of bottle development. If, however, the amounts are more substantial and/or highly variable (that is, from one bottle to the next), the situation is quite different. The immediate consequence is the depletion of free and total SO_2 in the wine, its principal preservative. The secondary consequence is the unpredictable rate of development (from bottle to bottle), but which will be accelerated, quite possibly to an unacceptable degree. This, in short, is sporadic bottle oxidation.

Sporadic bottle oxidation

If for no other reason than the obvious changes in color, it has been generally accepted that the retention of free (and total) SO_2 is essential for white wines, and that even limited amounts of oxygen making their way into the bottle will cause premature aging and oxidation. There is a world of difference between an aged white wine with an orange-brown tinge to its color, and one with a greenish yellow tinge that seems as if there is an internal form of luminescence.

White wine development in bottle

In Australia, Penfolds, in conjunction with others, compared the development of a high-quality red wine (1996 Bin 389 Cabernet/Shiraz) from the time of bottling in 1998 through to July 2004. Four closures were used: screwcap, Reference 2 cork 1 x 1¾ inches (24 x 44 mm) and two commercially available synthetic closures. Three bottles of each wine were analyzed and tasted (using rigorous tasting procedures) in 1997, 2000, 2002 and 2004.

Red wine development in bottle

The wine sealed with synthetic closures lost its SO_2 at a consistent rate (as between bottles) far in excess of that sealed with screwcap (which was likewise at a consistent rate). The bottles sealed with cork had lost SO_2 at variable rates: on each occasion between 2000 and 2004, the amount retained varied by 50 percent, the highest retention similar to that of the screwcap, the lowest similar to that of the synthetics. Color development followed a similar pattern.

The sensory analysis rated the screwcap and cork-closed wines as having significantly higher levels of fruit intensity than the wines under synthetic closures. Conversely, the wines sealed with synthetic closures were rated as significantly more developed than those with screwcap or cork closures. Overall, there was relatively little difference between the screwcap bottle development and that of the bottles with the best corks.

The Vino-Lok glass stopper (and attendant capsule) has aesthetic appeal, but has not been in use for sufficient time to prove its long-term seal capacity.

Research conclusions   The researchers (Allen Hart and Andrew Kleinig) summarized their findings thus:

> *From this, we have been able to demonstrate that red wine will continue to mature and develop both with and without additional oxygen being available to the wine. However, increased availability of oxygen greatly increases the rate at which a red wine will mature, and hence shortens the drinking life of the wine. In an anaerobic environment such as a bottle of red wine sealed with a screwcap or crown seal, some wines may develop reductive characteristics. In contrast, bottled red wine stored in a more aerobic environment such as with a synthetic closure, will prematurely develop oxidized characters.*

Other research scientists are at pains to point out the screwcap does not cause reduction, which (if it occurs) is due to a preexisting condition of the wine.

That said, as with all aspects of this debate, yet other researchers assert that the screwcap can cause reduced aroma and flavors to appear that will not occur with the same wine sealed with a natural cork. Here one strays into the territory of the redox potential of a wine, a subject so complicated that most scientists say to winemakers, "Don't even think about it." The reduction-oxidation (hence "redox") potential is a summation of all the oxidative and reductive reactions existing in a wine at a particular time. While work at the University of Bordeaux has established means of measurement, and the ultimate equilibrium reached, the values (measured in millivolts) are no guide to the sensory quality of a wine.

The future   The development of screwcap technology has several immensely important implications for winemakers. First, it will allow a long-term prediction of the rate of development of any particular wine, largely regardless of transport and cellaring conditions. Second, partly in consequence of that ability, the winemaker has a series of choices in determining the amount of free SO_2 and dissolved oxygen in the wine as it goes into bottle, which will have consequences for the rate and type of development. Third, the choice of the thickness and nature of the metal layer in the liner and/or the precise composition of the polymer layers will allow lesser or greater amounts of oxygen permeation and, in consequence, also affect the rate and type of development. Fourth, there is the possibility of incorporating a small amount of the synthetic material used in synthetic corks, which has the ability to remove negative (reductive) aromas.

Winemaking after the event   Up to the advent of the screwcap, the winemaker's role finished the moment the cork was put in the bottle. The consequences thereafter were in the lap of the gods: the only certainty was that no two bottles would be precisely the same, the difference increasing with age. Moreover, there was a distressingly high probability that either through cork taint, oxidation (random or otherwise), scalping (fruit-aroma stripping) or the development of excessive ullage (for whatever reason), the cork would have an adverse impact on the wine. Now, by contrast, the winemaker can choose the future development of the wine.

Life after screwcaps   Given that the dam has been breached, given the immense amount of ongoing research and the importance of the issue for winemakers large and small, there is no question that other forms of closure with a performance similar to (or possibly better than) screwcap will emerge. Glass stoppers with silicone O-rings (Vino-Lok is the first commercial version; trials began in Germany in 2000), membrane corks and improved synthetic corks are all possibilities. The one note of caution is that the internal bore of a bottle neck will always have imperfections; it is the exterior that can be fashioned to very fine tolerances. This gives an outer seal a long head start over inserted closures.

There is still much research into the incompletely understood (and hotly contested by some researchers) mechanisms of change as the wine matures in bottle. As the secrets of the highly complex chemistry are teased out, and as other technical closures become available, the choices will become more numerous, the benefits likewise. And so we bring this book to a close.

Glossary

Acetic acid Present in small amounts in all wines. In excess, causes a sharp, vinegary aroma and taste.

Aguardente Neutral grape spirit used to fortify port.

Amontillado Means "in the style of Montilla." Loosely, any medium sherry; specifically, a fino that has been further aged after the elimination of *flor* (*q.v.*) so that it develops a dry, nutty flavor. Alcohol content of 16.5 to 18 degrees.

Añada Term used in sherry production for young wine of a single year that has yet to be added to a *criadera* (*q.v.*).

Anthocyanins Colored forms of tannins present in the skin of black grapes, responsible for color of all red wines.

Anthracnose Fungal disease that stains grapes and shoots, especially in warm, humid climates.

Assemblage French for "blending." Putting together the components of, e.g., Champagne, Bordeaux.

Auslese German for selected, i.e., quality wine from selected grapes, hence extra-ripe and usually sweet.

Autofermenter Vat in which natural pressure is used to mix juice and skins to extract color. Especially in Australia. Also called autovinifier.

Autolysis Progressive breakdown of walls of dead yeast cells in sparkling wine before disgorgement. Liberates nitrogenous compounds and amino acids that positively affect taste and structure of wine.

Back-blending *Süssreserve* (*q.v.*) in German. Addition of a blend component designed to give finished wine appropriate flavor and chemical balance, e.g., adding unfermented grape juice to sweeten finished wine. Also refers to back-blending unoaked wine with an overoaked one.

Barrique Nearly 60-gallon (225 L) oak barrel, originally from Bordeaux. Holds 24 cases. Increasingly used outside France.

Baumé French system for gauging potential alcohol of a wine by measuring must weight. Determines the timing of harvest. One degree Baumé corresponds to 17 to 18 grams of sugar in a liter of water. *See* comparative chart at end of glossary.

Beerenauslese Very sweet category of German quality wine made from nobly rotten (see Botrytis cinerea) grapes. Can only be made in certain years. Develops with long bottle-age (*q.v.*).

Black rot Fungal disease causing black staining of leaves and shriveling of the fruit, especially in hot, humid conditions.

Bodega Spanish for "wine cellar." May also apply to the winery, the company producing the wine or a shop selling wine.

Bordeaux mixture *Bouillie bordelaise* in French. Bright blue mixture of copper sulfate, lime and water. Treatment for fungal diseases. Approved by organic growers.

Botrytis cinerea Latin name of the fungus that causes noble rot (*pourriture noble*). Attacks ripening grapes in autumn when morning mist and warmth provide humid conditions for its development.

Bottle-age Characteristic of maturity that develops in bottle. Mark of quality.

Brine A liquid used in refrigeration systems.

Brix American/Australian system for gauging potential alcohol of a wine by measuring must weight (*q.v.*). *See* comparative chart at end of glossary. One degree Baumé (*q.v.*) equals 1.8° Brix.

Bunch-thinning Selective removal of a portion of the crop, usually at or around *véraison* (*q.v.*). Designed to concentrate flavor and color of remaining crop.

Cap The mass of grape skins that accumulates on the fermenting must in the vat.

Carbonic maceration French: *macération carbonique*. Fermentation method using whole bunches of grapes that begin to ferment inside their skins in a CO_2-saturated atmosphere. Juice at the bottom of the vat, squeezed out under the weight of the fruit, takes the color and fruit, but not tannin, from the grapes. Results in fresh, fruity red wines, not for aging.

Chaptalization The addition of sugar to fermenting must to increase its alcoholic content. All sugar converts to alcohol: it is not used to sweeten. Not necessary (indeed, not allowed) in the New World. Important in the northern hemisphere, where grapes are naturally more acidic. Permitted in France (Monsieur Chaptal was Napoleon's minister of agriculture) and most of Germany; not in Italy, where concentrated must is used instead.

Charmat process Also called *cuve close*. Process for making sparkling wine in bulk. The second fermentation takes place in the vat, not the bottle. Consistent, cheap, labor-saving method of making sparkling wine. No substitute for the *méthode champenoise*.

Classed growth *Cru classé* in French. Usually refers to the 1855 Bordeaux classification of top 60 or so châteaus in Haut-Médoc, Sauternes and one in Graves. Also used of similar rankings in St-Emilion.

Cold-settle Natural clarification of white grape juice after pressing and before the commencement of fermentation.

Cold-stabilization Chilling wine to about 23°F (−5°C) to precipitate out tartrate crystals that may otherwise be deposited in bottle.

Crémant French term for fully sparkling wine from Alsace, Burgundy and the Loire, but a softer sparkle than Champagne. For distinction, the term is being phased out in Champagne.

Criadera First stage in a sherry *solera* (*q.v.*) where the youngest wine is beginning to age. Translates literally as "nursery."

Crusher-destemmer English term for *fouloir égrappoir*. Device that first crushes grapes between rollers, then removes stems by beaters revolving in a cage.

Cultured yeasts Laboratory-bred strains of natural yeast. Usually subtle in flavor and resistant to higher levels of alcohol or sulfur dioxide in wine. *See also* wild yeasts.

Destemmer-crusher Destems the grapes before the crushing cycle begins.

DOC, DOCG *Denominazione di origine controllata e garantita*. Highest categories of Italian wine. New laws from 1992 modified their status.

Downy mildew Fungus especially prevalent in warm, humid conditions that attacks the leaves. Selective chemicals are now used in conjunction with dosing with copper sulfate or Bordeaux mixture (*q.v*).

Esterification The chemical process by which esters are formed, involving interaction of oxygen with acids and alcohol.

Esters Formed by the reaction between acids in a wine and its alcohol. Flavorful and usually volatile. Over 100 different esters occur in most wines. Can contribute sweet, fruity aromas.

Estufagem Portuguese term describing the process of heating Madeira in an *estufa*, or stove, a specially heated tank in which the wine is "cooked."

Ethyl acetate Formed by acetic-acid bacteria. Present in conjunction with acetic acid. Difficult to measure scientifically; easy to detect with your nose. Causes acetic or vinegary smells or tastes.

Fan leaf *Court noué* in French. A virus spread in the soil. Causes degeneration in the vine, seen in yellowed leaves, dramatic reduction of yield and shortening the life of the vine.

Filtration Sieving process to remove suspended particles. Less gentle clarification than fining (*q.v*). Arouses strong feelings among those who believe filtering strips character, as well as less desirable elements. Very fine filters to remove yeasts and bacteria make the wine "star-bright."

Fining Removal of particles by adding a substance that coalesces fine particles, such as bentonite clay or egg white.

Flash pasteurization Rapid sterilization of sweet or semisweet table wine by heating to about 194°F (90°C) for one minute, then quickly cooling. Prevents undesirable bacterial activity or further fermentation.

Flor Surface yeast developing on fino and manzanilla sherry during its aging period in barrel. Gives a distinctive taste and prevents the wine from oxidizing. Occurs naturally in the Jerez region.

Free-run Juice that runs out of the vat under the natural weight of the fruit. Widely considered to be of better quality than press wine (*q.v.*).

Goût de terroir Describes a smell or flavor in wine, believed by the French to derive from the soil of the particular vineyard from which the wine came.

Governo Sometimes used in making Chianti. Concentrated must from a small percentage of semi-dried grapes is added to vats of normally fermented wine. Induces slight refermentation and softens the wine.

Gray rot Unwelcome form of noble rot (*see Botrytis cinerea*), especially in humid conditions without sufficient warmth to dry and concentrate the grapes. Spoils the taste of the wine as well as leaves of the vine.

Header boards Also known as heading-down boards. Means of keeping the cap of grape skins submerged in the vat.

Heat exchanger A device designed for rapidly cooling or warming wine, grape juice or must, often employing a tube-within-a-tube configuration.

Hyperoxidation Forced oxidation of juice by blowing oxygen through it.

Juice runoff Known as *saignée* in Burgundy; typically involves removal of 100 liters of juice from each 1,000 liters of must to concentrate the remaining wine.

Laccase Enzyme that can occur in grapes (especially in wet conditions). Causes rapid and damaging oxidation of juice and wine.

Lagar Old-fashioned wine press in the form of a stone trough used for treading grapes.

Late-harvest *See Vendange Tardive.*

Leaf roll Airborne virus causing curling of leaves and reduction in yield and vigor.

Lees Sediment comprising dead yeast cells and other particles remaining in wine after fermentation. Red wine is racked off this sediment. Some whites (e.g. Muscadet, Champagne and some Chardonnay) are left on their lees (*sur lie*) to add flavor and complexity.

Liqueur de tirage Solution of wine, yeast and sugar added to Champagne to induce a second fermentation.

Liqueur d'expédition Blend of wine, sugar, and (perhaps) grape spirit that is added to Champagne after disgorgement to balance sweetness.

Maceration Refers to the period during which the must or wine remains in contact with the grape skins. Alcohol acts as a solvent, extracting color, tannin and aroma from the skins.

Macération carbonique See carbonic maceration.

Maderized Critical term for overmature white wine that has darkened in color and become flat. *Maderisé* in French.

Malic acid Component of wine. Accounts for green and sour taste of wine made from unripe grapes. *See malolactic fermentation.*

Malolactic fermentation The conversion by bacteria (not yeast) of malic acid into lactic acid. Softens wine and reduces overall acidity. Now applied to all red but not all white wines.

Marc French word for the residue of stalks, skins and pips left after pressing. Pomace in English. Also a term for the spirit made from distilled pomace.

Mercaptan Derives from hydrogen sulfide and manifests itself in range of unpleasant odors (rotten eggs, burned rubber, gamey meat, garlic, stale cabbage).

Méthode rurale Similar to *méthode champenoise* but without benefit of *remuage* (*q.v.*), which produces more sophisticated sparkling wine.

Mousseux French for "fully sparkling." Usually implies the *cuve close* or Charmat (*q.v.*) method of production.

Must Freshly crushed grape juice (with or without skins), prefermentation. *Moût* in French.

Must weight A measure of the amount of sugar the grapes contain, itself an indication of ripeness. Regularly measured to determine optimum picking date.

Noble rot *See Botrytis cinerea.*

Nouveau French term for new wine, especially Beaujolais, which by tradition is released on the third Thursday in November, just weeks after the harvest. *Primeur* means the same: to be drunk very young.

Oechsle German system for gauging potential alcohol of a wine by measuring must weight (*q.v.*). *See* comparative chart at the end of the glossary.

Oidium *See* powdery mildew.

Oloroso The opposite of fino: sherry that is naturally full-bodied and pungent. Completely dry unblended, but often the base for cream sherry, blended with sweet wines.

Osmosis Concentration of wine or grape juice by removal of water molecules through a special filter. With reverse osmosis the wine or juice to be concentrated passes through the filter, leaving the water behind.

Oxidases Naturally occurring enzymes causing oxidative changes including browning, astringency and coarseness.

Oxidation Chemical reaction of wine to oxygen in the air. Indispensable in aging of wines. Occurring involuntarily, it can damage color, aroma and taste.

Oxidized Of wine that has gone stale and flat from excessive contact with the air.

Passito Italian wine made from grapes semi-dried, traditionally on straw mats, before pressing. Concentrated juice makes strong, sweet wine.

Pasteurization Heating wine to 149 to 158°F (65 to 70°C) for a few minutes to kill any bacteria, prevent further fermentation and stabilize the wine.

Pétillant French for "slightly sparkling." German: *spritzig*. Describes wines that undergo secondary fermentation in bottle and produce a small amount of carbon dioxide that dissolves in the wine. *See also crémant, mousseux.*

pH Measure of hydrogen ions or acidity in a wine. The lower the pH, the higher the acidity.

Phenols Group of closely related substances called anthocyanins (*q.v.*), flavones and leucoanthocyanins that congregate in the skins and pips of the grape. "Phenolic" is used mainly to describe coarse or heavy white wines that, while having much lower levels of phenols than do red wines, are more susceptible to being flawed by excessive phenolic content.

Pierce's disease Spread by insects ("sharpshooters"), especially in California. Causes leaves to yellow, fruit to wilt. Ultimately the vine may die.

Pigeage French term for treading grapes and mixing the skins with the fermenting must. Traditionally done with bare feet.

Pipe A large cask with tapered ends – the traditional measure for buying, storing and selling port. Contains about 56 dozen bottles.

Polymerization Aggregation of anthocyanins and tannins into larger particles, leading to color changes of red wine as it ages and ultimately to deposit of crust or sediment in bottle.

Pomace *See marc.*

Powdery mildew Also known as oidium. Vine disease that attacks leaves and berries, eventually killing the vine. Detectable in the taste of wine if made with affected grapes.

Press Equipment used to separate juice or wine from skins and pips. The most traditional is the basket press, used for five centuries or more. The most common modern alternative is the membrane or airbag press (also known as bladder or pneumatic press). Other innovations are the continuous press (highly efficient but rough) and the impulse press.

Press wine Red wine pressed from the grapes after the free-run (*q.v.*) has been drained off. Often extremely tannic.

Prise de mousse Champagne-making term for second fermentation when the *liqueur de tirage* (*q.v.*) is converted to alcohol and release of carbon dioxide creates the sparkle in the wine.

Protective winemaking New World approach designed to rigorously exclude the effects of oxidation on both juice and wine by use of inert gases, chemicals (sulfur dioxide and, with white wines, ascorbic acid) and extensive refrigeration.

Pumping over Refers to fermenting must being drawn over the cap of skins in vat. Known in France as *remontage*. Essential in the production of red wine.

Quinta Wine or port (or agricultural) estate in Portugal, large or small.

Racking The transfer of wine off its lees (*q.v.*) from one barrel to another.

Rancio The taste of old, often fortified wine, maderized (*q.v.*) on purpose.

Reduction Indicates smells in wine resulting from sulfur combined with hydrogen, not oxygen.

Reductive environment One in which there are decreasing amounts of oxygen available for chemical changes of maturation (e.g., in a bottle).

Refermentation Fermentation initiated by the addition of yeast and nutrients (probably sugar) to a wine that has previously completed its fermentation.

Remontage See pumping over.

Remuage Ridding Champagne of sediment in the bottle after second fermentation. Turning and gradually tilting bottles, from horizontal to perpendicular, coaxes the sediment down the neck for removal.

Residual sugar Natural grape sugar left after fermentation that is usually stopped artificially to retain sweetness in a wine.

Reverse osmosis See osmosis.

Rotary drum vacuum filter Equipment that recovers grape juice from the creamy mud gathered after cold-settling (*q.v.*); also used for filtration of wines, especially sweet wines.

Saignée See juice runoff. Used particularly of rosé so made.

Seasoning Aging of oak in air after it has been cut but before it is made into barrels.

Sélection des Grains Nobles Alsace term for wines made from grapes especially rich in sugar, perhaps nobly rotted. Chaptalization is not permitted. Wines may be sweet or fermented completely dry.

Solera Fractional blending system used particularly in Jerez. Old wine drawn off a barrel is replaced by younger wine.

Spätlese Normally picked one week after commencement of harvest; may be fermented to dryness or made with very distinct sweetness.

Sterile filtration Filtration through an ultrafine medium (often a membrane) that removes all bacteria.

Sur lie "On the lees." The best Muscadet is bottled straight from the vat to maintain contact with some of the sediment (lees) from fermentation. Usually detectable as a slight spritz and gives flavor and freshness.

Süssreserve "Sweet reserve." Unfermented grape juice added to wine to bring it to the required level of sweetness. Used in German winemaking up to and including Auslese level. *See also* back-blending.

Tartaric acid The most important grape (and wine) acid. Cold-stabilization (*q.v.*) causes the acid to be precipitated out in crystal form. May be added to wine that is lacking in acidity.

Teinturiers Black grapes that have red, not white, pulp and juice, e.g., Alicante Bouschet. Used to supplement color of varieties with fewer pigments.

Titratable acidity Usually abbreviated to TA. Expression of level of acid present in a wine. In Europe expressed as sulfuric acid; in New World as tartaric acid.

Tris French term for passes made through vineyards to pick individual grapes for wines affected by botrytis for making sweet wines.

Trockenbeerenauslese The sweetest and most expensive German wine made from selected very sweet grapes, often infected with noble rot.

Ullage The space between cork and level of the wine in the bottle. In young wine indicates a faulty cork.

Vendange Tardive "Late harvest." Term used in Alsace for wines from late-picked grapes. Must be from a single vintage. Same as a Spätlese but a bigger, richer style of wine.

Véraison Point at which grapes change color from green to yellow-green or reddish purple. Marks the commencement of the final ripening stage.

Vin de garde Wine for aging in bottle.

Vino da tavola Italian for table wine. No precise provenance, or grape varieties, may be stated on the label.

Volatile acidity Derives from acetic acid, caused by bacteria spoiling a wine exposed to air. A small amount enhances bouquet and flavor.

Wild yeasts Naturally occurring yeast that can spontaneously initiate fermentation in the Old World, increasingly in the New World. *See also* cultured yeasts.

Alcohol production: from original grape Brix

White wine production

Brix	Baumé	g/L solids	g/L sugar	alcohol
18	10	193	170	10.1
19.8	11	213	190	11.3
21.6	12	234	211	12.6
23.4	13	256	233	13.9
25.2	14	278	255	15.2
27	15	300	277	16.5

Assumes 23 g/L apparent sugar, 16.8 g/L produces 1% alcohol

Each country has its own system for measuring the sugar content or ripeness of grapes, known in English as the must weight. Here the starting point is Brix, which is used in the United States. Baumé is used in much of Europe, including France, and in Australia.

Red wine production

Brix	Baumé	g/L solids	g/L sugar	alcohol
18	10	193	161	8.9
19.8	11	213	181	10.1
21.6	12	234	202	11.2
23.4	13	256	224	12.4
25.2	14	278	246	13.7
27	15	300	268	14.9

Assumes 32 g/L apparent sugar, 18 g/L produces 1% alcohol

Index

Acknowledgments

The publishers wish to thank the following organizations and individuals for their kind permission to reproduce the photographs in this book:

Bridgeman Art Library/Eaton Gallery, Prince's Arcade, London: 8
Michael Busselle: 44, 66 left, 91, 100, 119 left and top right, 155 center, 163 top
Cephas: Nigel Blythe 27, 217 right/Andy Christodolo 60 left, 86, 153/R & K Muschenetz 122/Mick Rock 25 left and right, 29, 31, 37 right, 40, 45 left, 48, 51 left, 52–3, 57, 60 right, 62, 63, 64 left, 68, 70, 72 right, 74 right, 79, 92, 93 left and right, 96–7, 103, 105 right, 108 left and right, 111, 119 bottom, 120, 123, 125, 143, 146 bottom, 147, 148 top and bottom, 155 bottom, 162 top, 167, 169, 170–1, 171, 172, 173, 178, 183 top, 189, 190, 191, 193, 194 left and right, 196, 199, 213, 215, 217 left, 221, 223, 225/Ted Stefan 36, 47, 65/Mike Taylor 16 left/WINE Magazine 135
Corbis/Zefa: 66 right, 127 bottom, 200
Sally Cushing: 64 right
Patrick Eager: 16 right, 46, 72 left, 85, 95 top, 106, 129 right, 208
Gaja Wines: 171 right
Luzio Grossi: 2
E. Guigal S. A.: 160, 163
Claus Hansmann: 43
Hugel & Fils – Riquewihr: 92
Getty Images: 105 left
Krug: 73 left, 119 bottom right
Claes Löfgren: 2, 57, 64, 74, 82–83, 96–97, 105 right, 198, 215;

Kevin Phillips: 184, 185, 187
Miguel Potes: 19
Oeneo Bouchage/R Kutzki: 230
Kim Sayer: 205 top and bottom
Scala: 124
Scope: Jean Luc Barde 39 right, 42 right, 137, 145, 146 top, 149, 152, 155 top, 157, 162 bottom, 163 bottom/Jacques Guillard 20, 23, 30, 37 left, 39 left, 42 left, 45 right, 52, 76, 77, 94 left, 113, 139, 158, 159, 160, 174, 179, 180, 182, 183 bottom/Michel Guillard 17, 19, 28, 51 right, 58, 73 right, 78, 127 top left and top right, 129 left, 130, 132, 133 left and right, 165, 195, 210, 211, 224/Jacques Sierpinski 32/Jean Daniel Sudres 69, 104 left, 142 left and right, 150–1, 158–9, 168 bottom, 192, 207
Supreme Corq: 299
Vaslin Bucher – France: 73 right
Alan Williams: 14, 74 left, 82–3, 104 right
Jon Wyand: 94 right, 95 bottom, 109, 168 top

Picture Researchers: Christine Rista, Jenny Faithfull

Illustrators:
Jane Cradock-Watson: 88–9, 114–17, 140–1, 176–7
Eugene Fleury: 21
Mick Saunders: 59